PORTRAIT OF A PHILOSOPHER:

MORRIS R. COHEN IN LIFE AND LETTERS

Also by LEONORA COHEN ROSENFIELD

FROM BEAST-MACHINE TO MAN-MACHINE

DISCOVERING PLATO
translated from the French of Alexandre Koyré

Contributor to D. Cabeen
A CRITICAL BIBLIOGRAPHY
OF FRENCH LITERATURE, VOL. III

LEONORA COHEN ROSENFIELD

PORTRAIT OF A
PHILOSOPHER:

MORRIS R. COHEN IN LIFE
AND LETTERS

HARCOURT, BRACE & WORLD, INC. NEW YORK

First edition

Library of Congress Catalog Card Number: 62-19591
Printed in the United States of America

To Harry N. Rosenfield in deepest gratitude

ACKNOWLEDGMENTS

MORRIS RAPHAEL COHEN is the first person whom his daughter must thank, if for nothing else than for the array of letters, diaries, and other documents he saved throughout his life. After his death in 1947, I suggested to my brothers, Dr. Felix S. Cohen and Dr. Victor William Cohen, that as a follow-up to his autobiography something be done with the correspondence. They replied that the task was mine.

The second person to whom grateful acknowledgment is made is my mother, who saved Morris Cohen's letters to her going back to their earliest acquaintance, as he in turn saved hers. No matter how cramped for space the Cohen apartments were, Mother saw to it that letters were preserved.

A good start on the massive project of sorting Cohen's papers was made by Felix. He edited the only sizable portion of the correspondence that has been published to date. "The Holmes-Cohen Correspondence," which appeared in 1948 in *The Journal of the History of Ideas,* is reproduced here by kind consent of its editors. May I express appreciation also to Mark De-Wolfe Howe for his original permission. Since Felix's death in 1953, his writings on our father have stood as guideposts to me.

This study could never have been accomplished without the heart-warming response that greeted my appeals for letters by, to, or concerning Cohen, appraisals, and information about him and related matters. The testimony of hundreds of persons whom I have interviewed personally or by correspondence has supplemented the published and unpublished documents available to me. Classmates, students, friends, relatives, fellow philosophers, professional associates, those who knew Cohen from the lecture hall or from his writings talked or wrote to me even when they were critical of him. Before I was through, I had a biographer's treasure-trove at my disposal. The abundance of material has been helpful even where limitations of space prohibited inclusion. I ought really to thank for one thing or another almost everyone with whom I came in contact in recent years, when I carried my book in my mind day and night. To list all the names would take pages. May I merely thank the people whose names appear elsewhere in this book and, among the countless others, express a particular debt toward David Baumgardt, Rabbi Abraham Burstein, Judge Charles E. Clark, Mario E. Cosenza, Robert D. Calkins, I. E. Drabkin, C. J. Ducasse, James Gutmann, Judge Philip Halpern, Granville Hicks, Mark Hirsch, Harold A. Larrabee, Agnes de Lima, J. Loewenberg, The MacDowell Association, Mrs.

Arthur S. Meyer, John Mothershead, Jr., Otto Nathan, Marjorie Hope Nicolson, Max Otto, Sheldon R. Roen, Wilmon Sheldon, Aaron Starr, Marcus G. Singer, Norman L. Torrey, R. A. Tsanoff, Jacob Viner, the late Gregory D. Walcott.

Particular gratitude is due those who granted me the use of previously unpublished correspondence. Without regular secretarial assistance for most of his life and never master of the typewriter, Cohen customarily handwrote his letters, only occasionally keeping a copy in his files. Hence, to retrieve a good portion of them I was dependent on his correspondents. Mr. Justice Frankfurter, the Estate of Albert Einstein, Dean Richard P. McKeon, Professor Ernest Nagel, the Conference on Jewish Social Studies (formerly the Conference on Jewish Relations), and the American Jewish Committee have graciously furnished important segments of Cohen correspondence as well as rights to reproduce their letters here. My published appeals for Cohen letters brought in a few of which I had been quite unaware. In most cases, the letters and permissions have come in kind response to my personal requests. Let me here thank the people, heirs, or executors who have granted me the use of previously unpublished letters.

Unpublished material used here includes, besides Cohen's diaries, manuscript notes, and *realia,* over five hundred contemporary letters by, to, or about him, selected from among many times more in my possession. None have been consulted in libraries. Except for the Holmes-Cohen correspondence and a few other letters included in two of my articles on Cohen, all are previously unpublished.

I appreciate aid from Frederick Reustle, Helen Dukas, Elsie Douglas, Eugene Sklar, and the translators of the Einstein letters (see p. 442).

Thanks to the Cohen papers, to the resources of the Library of Congress, and to individuals, I have been able to explore Cohen's contacts with institutions and organizations with which he was in some way connected. Outstanding among those to whom I am indebted are the following: at City College, Dr. Charles K. Angrist, Dean Morton Gottschall, Professor Sidney Ditzion, the philosophy department, and Harry A. Overstreet, its chairman in Cohen's day. From the University of Chicago, Dean McKeon sent me duplicates of departmental correspondence with Cohen and other documents. I found my father's class lists, the Alumni Association furnished addresses, the old catalogues at the Library of the United States Department of Health, Education, and Welfare gave me names of Cohen's Chicago colleagues. For Harvard, I had the good fortune to know an old classmate of my father's, Dr. Leo Mayer, and to find a former student of Cohen's, Professor Charles Leslie, who remembered some classmates, who in turn led me to others. One, Professor Roderick Chisholm, lent me his student notes of Cohen's classes. Dr. Victor Lowe, Cohen's assistant at Harvard, also lent me notes, class lists, exams, etc. At the Law School of Yale

University, Associate Dean Jack B. Tate was very helpful, as was former Dean Charles E. Clark. Members of the Thomas Davidson Society were most co-operative. May I thank Mrs. Paul Abelson for the loan of source material. The *Journal of Philosophy* kindly put its files of correspondence at my disposal.

I am indebted to the American Council of Learned Societies for a Faculty Study Fellowship in 1951–52 in preparation for my project, to the Library of Congress for study-room privileges, and to the General Research Board of the University of Maryland's Graduate School for a grant-in-aid to assist me in the preparation of "Morris R. Cohen the Teacher," published in the *Journal of the History of Ideas,* October 1957. I thank its editors for their permission to reproduce those portions of that article inserted in the present book. I wish to thank similarly the editors who have permitted me to crib from my other publications on Cohen, "Morris R. Cohen's Philosophy of History," *Proceedings of the Xth International Congress of Philosophy* (1949), "The Philosopher and the Poet, Edwin Arlington Robinson and Morris R. Cohen at the MacDowell Colony," *Palinurus* (April 1959), "Mysticism and Rationalism in Morris R. Cohen," *The Personalist* (Summer 1961), and my Preface to the second edition of Cohen's *The Meaning of Human History* (The Open Court Publishing Co., 1961).

Martin A. Kuhn's *Morris Raphael Cohen: A Bibliography,* published in 1957 by The City College of New York Library as a special supplement to the *Journal of the History of Ideas,* has been of inestimable aid to me, as has *A Tribute to Professor Morris Raphael Cohen, Teacher and Philosopher,* published by "The Youth Who Sat at His Feet" (1928).

My husband's secretaries, especially the late Mrs. Mary Jane Saunders and Mrs. Katherine Johnson, have earned my gratitude for their typing of my manuscript.

Our maid, Mrs. Marie Duncan, is entitled to a special vote of thanks for never having thrown out a single scrap of paper during the years I lived immersed in papers. Without her, this book could never have been written.

Harcourt, Brace & World, Inc., who first published Cohen almost forty years ago and who are now publishing the first book in English devoted to him, have been extremely helpful in the preparation of the manuscript.

It is a pleasure to thank those who have critically read portions of the manuscript—my father's brother, Samuel Cohen, my mother's sisters, Dr. Sara Hirsdansky and the late Bertha Ritchie (née Ryshpan), Dr. Victor William Cohen, Dr. Charles K. Angrist, H. E. Bornstein, Dr. Louis I. Dublin, Professors Cornelius Krusé, R. P. McKeon, Charles Leslie, and Alexander M. Bickel.

Our daughter was most helpful when her mother was tripped by an awkward phrase. Marianne Joan would say sweetly, "Mommy, wouldn't it be simpler this way?" and there it would be, easy.

My husband, Harry N. Rosenfield, married his professor's daughter, and in the last four or five years, found himself wed also to her book. Every chapter was subjected to rigorous criticism. Beset by staggering problems of compilation, condensation, and presentation, I was unfailingly aided by his judgment and heartened by his faith. My debt and the reader's are greater than I can express.

—L. C. R.

University of Maryland

Morris R. Cohen 1880–1947

THE MORRIS RAPHAEL COHEN LIBRARY, erected by The City College of New York in memory of its former professor of philosophy, is a fitting memorial to the immigrant boy who as a child in the Old World ghetto went without bread to rent books and who as a teen-ager on the East Side, working in a poolroom, read Gibbon's *Decline and Fall of the Roman Empire* while he waited for customers. The three-and-a-half-million-dollar library was one of the returns on the investment in a boy's education.

"Why Morris Cohen?" asked Supreme Court Justice Frankfurter, his former Harvard roommate, at the May 3, 1958, dedication ceremony. "Who was he? Why is this building named after him?"

Cohen had many different reputations. A would-be pupil once called him "a whetstone to sharpen brains." It must have been more mentally salubrious than comfortable for students to be ground against that whetstone. His sarcasm was proverbial. To a student who once ventured a hapless remark, the professor shot back, "In the first place you're wrong. And even if you were right, so what?"

Nevertheless, the late Justice Holmes said that in the company of Morris Raphael Cohen he felt the presence of a holy man. What was he? Sage, scholar, cynic, Socratic gadfly, destroyer of myths, or *animateur?* It is time now to examine the man, the teacher, his thought, and his relations with his times.

"You cannot characterize men or periods without caricaturing them, for no formula can express the fullness of life." The reflection is Cohen's, jotted down in one of the private journals of his early manhood. And how can his own image be captured in a formula without caricature? That is the problem.

The present attempt to solve it and to make the man come alive is based on three premises. First, this book aims at presenting his different facets—

the student, the teacher, and the philosopher; the rationalist, the skeptic, and the Jew; the liberal crusader and the builder of intellectual bridges; the erudite contributor to logic and law, metaphysics and social science, the philosophy of history, science, and literature; and, above all, the *animateur* of our intellectual scene. He had a face of many moods. There was his mischievous twinkle or full Voltairian grin; in controversy, the determined set of the jaw bespoke the hunter; at times he seemed a thundering Isaiah; the face in repose had depths of tragic resignation; but there was also the good smile that transfused his hazel blue eyes with unexpected warmth. Only a wide canvas will do.

In the second place, the correspondence* opens a window through which to view Morris Cohen as others saw him. But letters are a two-way medium. The man had a world of friends, and corresponded with many of them, Albert Einstein, Justices Holmes and Frankfurter for example. The exchanges of letters serve as a kind of aperture through which to catch glimpses of them, and of Cohen through their eyes.

And third, the aim of these pages is to allow the man, whenever possible, to sketch his self-portrait through his own words. Thanks to his previously unpublished letters and youthful diaries, his manuscript notes and speeches, as well as copious published writings that include an autobiography, it is possible to reconstitute his own views about his nature, his fundamental drives, aims, and interests, the forces that shaped him and those he helped to fashion. "Even when all the facts are known, psychological interpretation is at best an abitrary game." Again, the adage is Cohen's own, from a letter to Avrahm Yarmolinsky complimenting him on his *Turgenev.* The array of source material as well as eyewitness accounts in this volume allows the reader to make up his own mind as to Cohen's interpretation of himself, or his daughter's judgment of her father.

Harvard's professor of law, Thomas Reed Powell, once wrote to his friend Morris: "You're doubtless more of a Puritan than I am." There was a decided streak of asceticism in Morris Cohen. He was the least acquisitive of mortals. His indifference to clothes, to money, and other possessions was characteristic. One day he asked his brother Sam to help him pick out a new suit, sorely needed. As a young professor, he had been invited to deliver an important address before the Twentieth Century Club in Boston. The two brothers, who looked very much alike except that one was well dressed and one wasn't, went into Gimbel's where Morris tried on a suit. "That one doesn't fit you," said Sam. "Oh," replied Morris, "it doesn't matter. I don't want to waste any more time. My train leaves in half an hour." The salesman suggested, to no avail, that the customer try on some other suits. Morris insisted that he wanted to buy *that* suit. Finally the

---

* The letters have been printed as accurately as possible from the originals; therefore, the actual spelling and grammar have been retained.

salesman protested: "We're not that kind of a store. Gimbel's won't sell you a suit that doesn't fit. The manager will fire me if he sees you walking out the door in that suit."

"Isn't there a side door?" asked Morris. He sneaked out with his suit in time to catch his train.

In *A Dreamer's Journey* Morris Cohen recalls that it was painful to him and Mary in the years after World War I, when living costs soared but not teachers' salaries, not to be able to afford to give each of the three children a whole orange. I must confess that not until I read that passage did I realize the significance of an ingenious game we played with oranges when I was little. Deftly, Papa would peel an orange and then divide it into sections among the children. Never has an orange, whole, tasted so delicious to me as the pieces did in those days when parental ingenuity assured to the three of us a golden childhood, rich in love and imagination and appreciation if not in money.

Cohen never carried much cash. One day he found himself on the commuters' special with none. (For the sake of their small children the Cohens had moved to the Yonkers suburbs.) Down the aisle he located his friend, the businessman Henry Auerbach, and asked for the loan of twenty cents. Auerbach was shocked. "Professor!" he exclaimed. "Here, take two dollars." Cohen was even more shocked: "Two dollars! Do you want me to lead a double life?"

He was indifferent to most possessions but not to books. They spilled out all over the house. At an age when little Americans are immersed in comic strips, the three Cohen kids were turning the pages of Aristotle's *Natural History,* laughing at the strange creatures depicted there. At times we were permitted, after instruction, the honor of cutting the pages of Daddy's uncut volumes. I remember that almost as soon as I could read I helped my father read proof *à deux.* On summer vacations he and Mother would read to us after dinner from among the world classics they had brought along. Sometimes, though not often, all those books had to be dusted.

But it was forbidden to dust or disarrange Father's big old roll-top desk. He had his own touch system. One inch down, ninety degrees to the right, there! He would come up with anything he wanted, most of the time. His memory was better than any filing system. But why did he save so many papers, such quantities of old letters? The mystery was unraveled by the man himself in a letter he addressed to my older brother, Felix. The father on his fifty-seventh birthday confessed to his eldest child how the dream of writing his memoirs had held his heart since he was sixteen.

My childhood was an unusually lonely one and largely given to day-dreaming. . . . I always had a great craving to write something appealing more to the hearts of men than my philosophical disquisitions. . . . I have, however, for over forty years nourished the hope of writing the story of my life as an illustration of the various forces which have met or found expression in my life, especially of currents which have molded Jewish history and which are vividly illustrated in the heroic struggles of my father and mother, under diverse conditions, to earn their daily bread and to bring up their children in decency. . . . I thus have a burning desire to do what so few people that I know can do, namely, outline the basic facts of the great epic— the odyssey, if you like—of the generation which cut its roots in the old home and crossed the ocean into a strange land without any resources other than their own unconquerable fortitude.

Three years later, Morris Cohen came down from New York to Felix's home in Washington to present the first installment of his autobiography as his gift for the first birthday anniversary of his first grandchild, the firstborn of his first-born. Gene Maura Cohen could not yet read, but received a letter that nine years later served as Foreword to "her" and her grandfather's book.

Morris Cohen had been dead two years when *A Dreamer's Journey* appeared, but he knew before he went that his dream was coming true. The early part of the book had already been translated into Yiddish in the Jewish newspaper, *The Day. A Dreamer's Journey* starts by tracing a poignant picture of Morris Cohen's childhood that spanned the Old and the New World. Small, malnourished, and in ill-health, he was called "Kalyeleh," local Yiddish for a poor half-wit. When chided for responding, he answered, "I know they mean me, so I come." "Someday," said his mother in prophetic words, "they will be proud to have known my 'Meisheleh' " (the Yiddish diminutive of his name).

No official record marked the birth date of the youngest son of Abraham Mordecai Cohen and his wife, née Bessie Farfel. It was later set down as July 25, 1880, the ninth day of Ab in the Jewish calendar, which according to certain traditions is the appointed day on which the Messiah is to be born. As a Cohen, the boy was born into the oldest priestly family known to history, a kind of hereditary, spiritual aristocracy of the Jewish people. But in the ghetto of Minsk his parents could not earn a decent living. His father left Russia for the United States in search of opportunity and freedom, hoping to be able to send for the rest of his family.

Meanwhile Morris was often hungry, and sickly; it seemed sometimes that he would not survive. But his inner life was intense. His recollections as an adult went back to the time before he was two years old. His mother was forced to become a peddler, and when Morris was seven, he was sent away to be raised by his maternal grandparents in the little town of Nesh-wies. For three years there (1887–90), he developed intellectually under the stern tutelage of his grandfather and his teachers of Hebrew at "cheder." But emotionally he was bereft. One day he was discovered at a neighbor's well contemplating suicide. After one of his father's visits home, a new baby brother was born—at last he would have someone to love, and he dreamed of the days when the baby would grow up and "we two would be com-panions." But the baby died.

In 1892 the mother took Morris and his younger sister, Florence, to New York City to join their father and the two older brothers, Tom and Sam, who had been working for some years. One of Morris' early impres-sions of the big city was told to his own children: "All over, I see wagons and carts marked 'Ice Cream.' And I think to myself what a rich man he must be, that 'Iche Cream'!"

Morris Cohen entered public school in 1892, and the family moved to Brooklyn during the panic of 1893. Sometimes they had neither money nor food in the house, and Morris would walk across Brooklyn Bridge to the shoe store in New York where his brother Tom worked, to get money to buy bread. Florence went without the pretty clothes girls long for (how wistfully she recalls it!); Sam, an insatiable reader, missed formal educa-tional training for the mind that Morris used to say was keener than his own. In 1894 Morris peddled newspapers after school between Park Row and the Bowery. I remember my father telling me of those days. "Ameri-cans have such fine cakes," he said once to his mother. "Why don't we ever have one?" His mother's answer was immediate. "The recipes say to take a dozen of eggs, a pound of butter, and so on. But they don't say where to take them."

Three years after he came to this country, Morris took the entrance exami-nations for The College of the City of New York, as the municipal institution for free higher education was then called. To his surprise he passed, in fact he came out first, and signed up for the bachelor of science degree. The gold medal that he received was to come in handy upon occasion at the pawnshops.

CONTENTS

Part One

THE MAN AND THE TEACHER

I. *The Youth in Search of Himself*

IN MY HUNT FOR LETTERS by and to my father, a treasure turned up—the old diaries and journals of his youth, mostly in little notebooks but also on scraps of paper, scribbled in his distinctive handwriting, covered with the dust of half a century or more. They had guarded the secrets of a soul in travail. To make public now excerpts from so private a source is pardonable, I think, because without the contents we cannot fully understand Morris Cohen.

He had confided to Mary Ryshpan not long before they were married, "I venture to think that no one ever will know the true Morris R. Cohen except the person who will examine everyone of those scraps with a truly psychologic microscope."

The diary starts on New Year's Day, 1897. Morris Cohen is an undergraduate at The City College. A photograph taken a year earlier shows him as he was, not yet fully grown, and thin. The forehead is imposing, the wide-set eyes hold a level, searching gaze. The lips are set, the squarish chin firm.

It is four and a half years since he had been brought to the United States, ignorant even of the alphabet of his country of adoption. Yiddish is spoken in the home; the language of its learned books is the sacred tongue, Hebrew. Morris has to learn not only to read and write English, but to pronounce it, which explains his references to his tireless study of phonology and the dictations that his sister Florence sometimes gives him. Occasional misspellings betray the newness of the medium, but as time goes on, we note the progressive mastery.

At least three stories are revealed to us by the document as excerpted. The first is an American saga, its setting New York's Lower East Side, where the immigrant child grew up in the grimness of the slums. For a while, in his spare time, he helped his father run a soda-water stand in a

3

poolroom. Only an occasional patch of blue sky above the tenement houses reminded him of beauty in the world of nature. Yet there were opportunities—first, free education, and then public libraries, where he educated himself almost more than the College educated him. He haunted New York's secondhand bookstores, from whose bargain counters he started the lifetime collection of books that in later years he was to bequeath to his alma mater. For fifteen cents he bought the precious volume that most influenced him during this period, Franklin's *Autobiography*. Again, for a few pennies, he could get the newspapers. The Yiddish press was particularly stimulating for its analytical acuity in world affairs and its serialization of literary works. *Die Arbeiter Zeitung* helped initiate him into socialism. The Jews carried with them from the old country their tradition of emphasis on the intellectual and spiritual life, heavier in their baggage than their worldly goods.

Non-Jews mingled with Jews in idealistic movements of uplift that stirred New York at the turn of the century into a veritable ferment, and heroic personalities came to the fore to lead the good fight—Charles Stover, Edward King, Lillian Wald, as well as the beloved Thomas Davidson—crossed Cohen's path. The settlement houses provided a focus for the community life of the underprivileged. It was at the Educational Alliance that the clubs met of which Morris speaks in his journals. He acknowledged the debt in a message he sent for the Alliance's anniversary in 1943: "A window of my life opening up on the soul-strengthening vista of humanity will always be dedicated to the Educational Alliance." It is as American as the melting pot. It could only have happened here.

This is a teen-ager's story permeated with daydreams that came true. Powers of introspection worthy of a Stendhal or a Proust (for whose works Cohen was to feel such admiration) are reflected in these pages in a kind of stream of consciousness startling in one so young. Adolescence is recorded, unblemished by professional touch-ups for publication. One moment Morris sounds as young as a child; the next, his reflections are worthy of his philosophic grandfather. The adolescent alternation of soaring aspirations and black despair à la Werther, the conviction of loneliness and the longing for one true understanding friend, the manifestations of revolt, the crying drive for self-expression in the quest of one's self, find vivid expression here. The undergraduate is naïve at first, but then his mind develops bold vigor, scope, and clarity, above all the habit of rigorous critique, often self-applied. He gropes his way toward greater balance and mental poise in a human document of compelling sincerity.

The third story told by Morris' diaries is the one most distinctively his. Its lines bear witness to the spirit struggling to be born. Here is ambition, intellectual ambition, will, never self-satisfied, an almost frightening absorption with the ego. Selflessness was to catch up with Morris only later, when under the inspiration of Thomas Davidson and Mary Ryshpan he learned love and enlisted in the larger cause of humanity. But for the present, the intensity of self was part of the search for purpose in life, like the intensity of resoluteness.

The diary begins when Morris was sixteen and a half. Years later he confided to a friend, "I wouldn't be sixteen again. I suffered too much."

FROM THE DIARY OF AN UNDERGRADUATE*

Jan. 1, 1897. [First notebook]

I am now going to "turn over a new leaf." I have been doing this all along, every day during the last year. . . . The great trouble in keeping a diary has been that being unable to express my thoughts properly, they look strangers to me after I write them down, and what I really want to say seems to me unsaid. In the beginning of this collegiate year, I kept a diary for a fortnight but gave it up. . . . Certain topics such that I would not like others to read, I wrote in the backwards method. . . . I am now going to have another little book where I can jot down anything and everything that comes into my mind and which I think should be written down in my diary, and at every convenient time write them in this book, always, if possible, writing them the same day, so that it will give a better idea of the state of my mind. . . .

A diary I take to be a history of the mind, and I am now trying to keep one for the following reasons: first, writing, as I will do, the events of every day—a kind of report to myself of what I have done —cannot fail to infuse new moral vigor and help me to govern myself; secondly, whenever I will read it, I hope to be benefitted by the mistakes, and inspired by my own goodness, in the past; thirdly, for the practice it will give me in expressing my own thoughts in writing. I am going to write a history of my past some other time, when I will have more time for reflection, but am now going to attempt to write down what I am now. My principal characteristic is a love for books. Not only for what they contain but also to a degree for themselves. . . . Every cent I can lay my hands on goes to buy some book. . . . The next principal characteristic is my great desire to be good, in the full sense of the word, and my impotency to comply with this desire. . . . I am not only a reformer but a revolutionist. I detest customs that are shams. . . . How I obtained this revolting nature, I don't know. I suppose I brought it from Russia. . . . I like to think that I

* NOTE: Except for my bracketed explanations, the text of the journals is presented "as is." It represents a fraction of the material found in five small notebooks and many "scraps of paper," covering the years from January 1, 1897, through 1899.

am tolerant. . . . I am by nature averse to taking anything for granted—as a law—unless I convince myself that it is right. This is another symptom of my rebellious nature. I do not know to what extent I am either selfish or conceited. I always suspect that I am. . . . If I have any conceit it is due from my brilliant career in the "old country" and in the public schools here. This was perhaps increased by my winning the medal and success as editor of the journal of the B.L.S. [Bryant Literary Society] . . .

I am exceedingly anxious to get good marks though I think it does not show the knowledge of the studies. The reasons being that I am anxious to leave a good record behind me when I graduate so that I may get a position as teacher; partly to gratify my vanity which I excuse by supposing that it will encourage me morally and perhaps financially by having more opportunity . . . to acquire a few more scholars [tutoring pupils]. Up to date I have had no ambition for life but recently have formed an ambition to become a socialistic agitator. For this purpose I have resolved to try my hardest to graduate from college, then acquire a position as a teacher or on a newspaper and from there work my way up. To sustain myself partially while in college is at present the great obstacle, but as I have two scholars now which brings me in $2 per week, I hope to do it with more or less trouble. My abilities as a teacher I sometimes appreciate very highly but sometimes very little. . . . I like to think I am bold saying the truth without regard for anybody's feeling. . . . I also like to be considered cold-hearted and cool-tempered. I don't care much about common pleasure such as theatre, entertainment, etc. I resolved not to eat any candy partly because it may be unhealthy, partly to strengthen my will-power, as the temptation is very great. Though I had great trouble in keeping it, I am now in position to keep it.

I have a habit of putting things off till the last moment and then hurrying to finish them. . . . As I stated before, I am rather indolent. This is at present all I can think of my character, which I yet have opportunity to remould according to future conduct. My opportunities at present when taken advantage of are very considerable. College, Astor Library, my own serviceable collection of books, Aguilar and Bond St. libraries, small but good company of associates are among the best advantages. I do not like to stay in the pool-room, which I have to, in order to let father go home for 3 or 4 hours daily and 5–6 on Friday, Saturday or holiday, because I think it produces a bad effect on my mind and health, though I learn something of the lower state of society. If I tried hard I could spend all the time there in studying or reading, but being interrupted every now and then I lose all interest.

Jan. 3, 1897.

Resolved to have a system of reading. Not to read much in newspapers but to read "The Public Opinion" and "The Review of Reviews" and articles in the magazines when there is a purpose in reading them. To keep resolutions before me whenever possible. To keep a program of what is to be done and what is done. Avoid everything which is not necessary. Keep a book where I can write down any interesting or useful fact which I learn by reading or otherwise. Also to write down any of my own sentiments or those suggested or digested from the books I read, as soon as they come to my mind. Thus not letting any good sentiments or resolutions escape. To search for the truth in everything. To improve my knowledge of Everything and Something. Whenever mention is made of any interesting topic write it down so that you may read about it. Consult Poole's Index. Write extemporaneous compositions every day and "prepared" one every week on topics suggested by reading or otherwise.

Read Charles A. Dana's book on "Newspaper Making" hurriedly in Aguilar Library hoping to read it again as soon as possible and more deliberately, liking the style and thoughts. Increased my desire to become a newspaper man. To renew my knowledge of Hebrew and especially of the Bible. Also that of natural history and other sciences and ancient and modern foreign tongues. The principal thing to be performed is to improve my expression both Oral and Written, Handwriting and Personal force, for I have some ambition of becoming an orator.

Fr. Jan. 8 [1897]

. . . Discussed "philosophy" with J. W. and B. R. I am now known as a "philosopher" around D[ivision] St. Seeing a carriage with two horses, one of them remarked that if you are rich, you enjoy yourself and are happy. I claimed that a man must not necessarily be rich to [be] happy . . . that a man must have his necessities but could do without riches. That the rich has greater desires than the poor, so that both wish something they can't get. . . . I said that we can control our desires by habit. . . .

The trouble is that we don't think of the things we can enjoy at present but of the things we can not, not of the things we have, but of the things we have not. . . . It is better to reduce our desires and to increase whatever means we have to their gratification.

Jan. 12 [1897]

That "candy" habit is getting ahead of me. . . .

Jan. 13 [1897; at the poolroom]

. . . A man claiming to be an officer asked me if I knew a certain

fellow. I told him that I did not, whereupon he asked me not to tell
that to anybody. I said I would not. But as soon as he walked away
I told someone that the officer was looking for such and such a fellow.
I felt sorry soon but could not help it. . . . We can not take back a
broken promise. . . .

Jan. 14 [1897]

. . . Went around looking for books about one hour, at Lovering's,
John Wannamaker's and B. Ketcham 2 Cooper Union where I bought
Franklin's Autobiography, a cover a little soiled, for 15¢. Did not feel
glad afterwards because it is not edited by J. Bigelow and because I
think I can get a better edition at Siegel and Cooper for the same
price.

Monday 18 [January 1897]

. . . Had I had 1¢ more I certainly would have bought Plutarch's
"Lives" complete in 1 volume for 25¢.

Wed. 20 [January 1897]

While walking to college I passed a poor family (?) that was
thrown out of its rooms with all the furniture (?) piled up on the
sidewalk. This set me thinking of Socialism. In my enthusiasm I pictured myself as an orator addressing an assembly of business men at
14th St. (I hardly see how can I become one but enthusiasm knows
no reasons) . . . I pictured to myself how I would show them the
socialist[s] do not want to take away all the property and money from
every capitalist and give it to the workingmen. That at present there
exists no justice the stronger swallow the weaker. . . . I would tell
them that had Franklin and Jefferson lived today they would be socialist. I would break down their prejudice that socialism is non-ameri-
can. I would also appeal to them to study this question. In other
words I would try to bring socialism to the real American through
the newspaper, and platform. I would not follow as "disciple" of the
socialistic leaders but would have ideas of my own. . . .

Through reading it ["Thrift" by Smiles] for some time, I came to
think that necessity *is* the mother of invention and progress, that
much that is good is the result of toil by those who felt poverty. I am
not yet convinced of the good of socialism and ought not be so far as
I have not yet convinced myself by studying the matter. But I have a
socialistic feeling in me probably through seeing the misery of the
east side.

But it is a law that we must wish for something and strive to obtain
it. . . . The world would be a dreary waste if everyone did not wish
to obtain something, strive for some purpose. Without work, life
would be a plague, for indolence is the worst of all maladies. We must

have desires, something to work for, and yet our desires are our principle cause of all that is evil and plagues us. . . .

Also thought of the weakness of some great men and of my own. I sometimes think I have the "stuf" of which a great man can be made, and that by steady industry I may yet become famous. . . . But I can not help thinking that I am "a little off," "undermined," of an indolent nature and unable to impress anyone but myself of my own greatness, at least at first sight, which I must confess never makes a good impression. . . . Still, once we are determined we can accomplish anything and have the courage of our convictions—we are likely to perform some good work. Thus I have increased my estimate of my abilities as a writer since I have obtained a good mark for *it,* my essay on Franklin (8+ in spite of lateness). *Self-respect is a great encouragement.* . . .

. . . Though I am yet a "youth" I am often moody, melancholy, and have strange forebodings. I think too much of *death.* This is perhaps because I don't believe in a hereafter. . . .

Thursday 21 [January 1897]

. . . Compose a letter to the Board of Education for opening the schools at night for boys clubs. Also one for opening a gymnasium in Central Park . . .

Saturday 23 [January 1897]

. . . Resolved to practice Jewish writing and learn all things which may become useful so that I may have recourse to them whenever necessary in the future . . .

Monday 25 [January 1897]

Tender feeling for m[other]. (after giving me 9¢ an apple and a good coat) kissed her . . .

Jan. 26 Tuesday [1897; second notebook]

. . . One of the greatest things I intend to do is to use my time well. I understand that I am about 16 years 6 months old and that I am "in the prime of my youth" and if I want to succeed in life I must use my time well. My ambition is to be able to provide for my parents. This has only lately developed. I am also resolved to appear more active and not so sluggish. To go more among people and gain all the practical knowledge desirable. To be able to do many little things that come into household affaires and to be generally useful. I don't know "what good I am" in this world. . . .

Saturday 13 [February 1897]

I feel that instead of being a burden to my parents I ought to be a help to my whole family who are all in need of it. I think that I may be able to do it yet but I have strange forebodings perhaps due to the repeated discouragement from Sam, papa, and sometimes mamma that I will never be able to work myself up to some degree of affluence. Though I, at present, do not think to become rich in money, I am exceedingly ambitious since lately to help my family.

. . . I have kept my resolution not to eat a piece of candy for a fortnight.

Friday 19 [February 1897]

I remarked to Berk. several days ago that any man with sufficient control of himself, that is, with a strong determination could by continual industry raise himself to the level of authors. . . . But thinking of Scott pouring out book after book without any effort, I am fairly struck with a feeling of awe and admiration. . . .

Thursday 25 [February 1897; after he thought he lost his diary]

. . . If anyone reads it, he will be apt to consider me as partly "off" but the worst will be that my real character will be shown to be different from what I have always pretended it to be. . . .

March 4 [1897; scrap of paper]

. . . I took a look at the night. . . . There seem to be various laws in nature, all operate and all have exceptions. These exceptions are so numerous that some give up the rules. But there *is* order, there are rules! The exceptions are only the interferences of various laws. The stronger force overcomes the weaker. This is the same in action. There *are* rules of action. . . . I was thinking of "Evolution and Degeneration," suggested by Gibbons description of the misfortune or rather unhappiness of the barbarian life. Civilized life is after all happier than that of a barbarian. Progress *is* beneficial.

March 17 [1897]

. . . Having all kinds of reveries when walking up to college, (not so strongly when I run though) a result of enthusiasm of some kind.

Thursday 18 [March 1897]

Talked to myself when walking to C[ollege] about success and its origin in vanity, supposing that I am making an extemporaneous address to some assembly.

Sunday [March 21, 1897]

. . . Wrote a list of my books. About 73 cloth bound and 77 paper volumes.

Saturday 27 [March 1897]

. . . This morning was a very spring morning and walking up to the Ast[or] L[ibrary] I could not help thinking that had I any poetic abilities I would have been able to describe an ideal poetic scene. It was a bright clear morning. The sky was blue, the air cool, and the sun shone softly, alighting as it were, a blaze of poetic glory on the N.Y. tenement houses. The streets were covered with the shadows of the high buildings but this gave a kind of indescribable grandeur to the sunny intervals. The heart feels a strange sensation. Impressions produce thoughts. But these thoughts are vague. We are filled with a peculiar kind of admiration for Nature and it is the only time that I feel there is pleasure in existing. . . .

April 1, Thursday [1897; third notebook]

. . . I began to write the diary for the purpose of improving my writing and handwriting also to make a kind of report to myself of what I have done and in this way keep myself under a restraint, but I have failed in all of them. . . . I wished then to give up this diary business but I am now resolved to begin anew with fresh efforts. This is the beginning of a new month and it is the first time in weeks that I write my "report" the same day that it occurs. I will from now on try to write every day something in it that will interest me if I read it in the future and not make it a dry chronicle of minutes. Also I propose to write essays and index them in this dia which I now will call

THE JOURNAL

OF A

BOY PHILOSOPHER

The thoughts and acts of a *vain fool*
TRYING TO LEARN
HOW TO BE WISE
by Philosophicus

April 2 Friday [1897]

. . . I am always dissatisfied with what I have done perhaps because I expect too much from myself. My ideal of a well-spent day is one of which I am conscious of having accomplished as much as I intended to, which is sometimes more than possible. . . .

. . . In S. [Store, i.e. in the poolroom] I read, as usual, Gibbon 225–248. Wrote out a few of my own sentiments justifying Gibbon against the assaults of Guizot and Millman. . . .

Tried to read parts of Voltaire and Munson's Phonography, but too sleepy. I wished papa would come earlier. . . .

Saturday April 3 [1897]

. . . On my way home I read in the "Bulletin of the Educational Alliance" an account of Hiawatha. I was struck with its beauty which resulted from its simplicity, and also with the simplicity of Longfellow. . . .

Sunday April 4 [1897]

Finished the Journal of the 2d and 3d and practiced phon[ology] till about 11. Had several dictations from Florence. Today is my brother Tom's wedding. Of course there is a commotion. I have no proper clothes to go in. . . .

. . . Pleased with being alone. Thought of writing an essay on "What would I feel if alone in the Astor Lib.," the rest of the world being destroyed. Before going to bed I read the Arabian Nights—the story of Aladdin. I remember having been told it in "Chayder" [Hebrew school]

Tuesday April 6th [1897]

. . . After C[ollege] I heard an address by Dr. Gottheil of Temple Ema-nu-el on "Success in one's calling." . . . So the doctor told us, "first master yourselves and *then* your profession." I thought it was a grave error, since it is harder for a boy to learn his own abilities than the properties of his profession. He can learn about the profession and a great deal by the experience of others, and by books. But he cannot learn himself, that is, his abilities before he has tried them. . . .

In the Ast. Lib. . . . I then took out Graetz, History of the Jews 5 vols. where I read in the 2d volume the whole account of the Rebellion under Hadrian. I was very much pleased with his style and form of narration, and thought of reading it all through at my earliest convenience. Thought about miracles. If I saw one I would not believe it. But why? Because my senses do not conceive something which I believe was never seen before. This doesn't seem strong logic but my prejudices against miracles are too strong. . . . I cannot conceive anything supernatural because I cannot conceive any supernatural power. All results can be accomplished through the workings of the natural laws. There is no use for supernatural laws. . . .

Wednesday April 7 [1897]

"Why *do* so many believe in *God?*"

A. Why *did* so many believe in "Mythology." In general the masses are always deceived, and are ignorant. . . .

There is not much philosophy in here up to the present. There *may* be afterwards.

Monday April 12 [1897; scrap of paper]

Am too conceited in arguing, I do not argue the careful way of Franklin. My natural tendency to conquer my opponent is stronger than reason.

[Scrap of paper, undated, probably April 1897]

. . . pract. pool. Turned the tables on one who wanted to do a trick on me, but got punched in the eye. . . . Went home after 12. Bothered because I did want to go to sleep with a full belly.

Tuesday, June 6, 1897 [Scrap of paper]

. . . I am looking for an opportunity to develop my physical constitution. . . . I would like to go out and play ball with the gang but M[amma] would not allow me to go away on Sunday. . . .

I think that if I had prepared my lessons I could always have come out first in the class, but what is more I feel confident that *If* I treat myself in the right way I could develop myself into a genius. To my opinion the mind is the most (pliable should I call it) easily worked on by everyday influences and if I proceed in the right way, something easy to learn if one is determined I could make anything I feel out of myself. The chief fault I find with myself is that I have not the great will power that is essential for every great undertaking. . . . What I would like now is a freind, one single freind that could understand me and guide me by giving me some encouragement. This is my great stumbling block. I have always succeeded when I had a task, no matter how hard, before me and set out to do it. . . . I am lonely though I have many good acquaintences. There is no one to whom I could speak directly from the heart and all I can do is to talk to myself. This renders me very egoistic. I sometimes think I will never succeed in anything in my life so much have I been discouraged. I never have had anyone point out to me my good points, my abilities. Though it is for me to find it out nevertheless some slight encouragement would envigorate me, being so used to be continually discouraged. . . .

Now I am in a maze what to do. I feel the remorse of being a load on my parents, and feel it so strongly that I sometimes seriously consider the advisibility of suicide. I am not cowardly enough to give up the struggle of life at so early a period, but what bothers me more is a deeper question. "What is this fight for? what am I to gain even if I win it?" In reality, I see nothing to win. Life is a struggle in vain, endless, because we have no real definite aim, and as soon as we attain what we imagined to be our aim we start for something else, so that we never enjoy the fruit of our victory, since we [are] continually engaged [in] fighting. I once thought of arranging these idea[s] in the form of a dialogue between the good and evil spirits of a young man, who thinks over this subject.

June 11, 1897 Sunday

. . . I don't know whether I should continue to delight in books and theories or try and turn practical. That is the great question. Can I spend my life to better advantage by continuing in the paths of philosophy or try to enter the thoroughfares of real practical life. The latter is certainly the more useful but can I be of great use there. If I should try I would have to change the entire nature of my character.

Monday June 12 [1897]

I used to consider my mind to be in a condition wherein it could be easily changed, but now I am convinced that it is not at all an easy task. I doubt my abilities to succeed in the effort. This may be because my heart is already hardened, or perhaps (something that I would not have dared to utter sometime ago), our minds are the work of the nature of circumstances, in other words, chance. . . .

. . . One passage from an article by Wm. D. Howells struck me very forcibly. Its meaning was that by work alone can we achieve happiness, since in working for something or someone else we lose conscious[ness] of self, which is the greatest obstacle of happiness. . . .

June 21, 1897 [Scrap of paper]

Five years ago today I landed in this shore. . . . Barring the last three years, I would like to live my life over again. It was up to that time plain easy sailing, or rather drifting. But in 1894 *I gained consciousness*. . . .

What shall be the purpose of my life

The paying of my debt towards my parents As to myself I shall be content with a moderate income a modest life.

. . . These three years have been revolutionary. Old ideas, hopes, gradually changed and a somewhat new character ensued. I can hardly think to describe my present condition. In fact it is not very clear to myself. I do not know whether to be satisfied with it or not.

I can however improve it. This is my aim.

Wednesday July 14 [1897; scrap of paper]

What qualities do I possess which if cultivated would make me successful in life. And now I question myself what do I mean by "successful in life." Certainly I would like to be in a state of financial independence where I could be a help toward those that are dearest to me, in a state in which I could afford to look calmly "far from the maddening crowd," not so poor as to be looked down by the rich, nor so rich to be looked up by the poor. But I feel that this is not all. It is not enough to look on, I must join in. And now comes the question in what capacity. To become isolated from mankind is not to be happy. Selfishness is the mother of morbidness. We must labor, to be able to drive away melancholy. And since I must chose some occupation, it must be the one for which I am best adopted. To know that I must know two things. My own abilities and the requirements of the occupation I am going to choose. [Morris then considers and eliminates the professions of medicine, engineering, law.] There are two professions which I sometimes consider that I am adopted for, writing, and teaching. Though I see clearly that I cannot write and sometimes apprehend that I am not a good a teacher, I yet feel certain that if I tried I could succeed, a moral conviction which opens the road to success. So I now consider that the only thing for me to do is to become teacher than [then] a writer and perhaps lawyer. . . .

I have not a bit of genuine confidence in me, yet reviewing my past I have a vague hope that I may succeed in everything as I have done at school. And now I think success has left me since I entered college. . . . Yet I have *hope,* my only support. . . . I am going to make a special effort to gain mastery of the English language by translations from other languages. Also to renew knowledge of Jewish, Hebrew, and perhaps Russian. Today while at the stand [in the poolroom] I translated from Roemer [in French], Franklin's account of how he learned the modern languages. After comparing with the original I will try to reproduce the French translation.

Monday August 2, 1897 [Scrap of paper]

After many unsuccessful attempts I now again try to begin to keep a diary or journal. . . . The most important aim of this journal should be to provide a kind of moral government over myself—so that I could spend my time to better advantage. Then it is providing me with a freind to whom I can relate frankly everything that passes within me. Lastly the keeping of this journal provides me practice in extemporaneous composition and penmanship. I think a great deal of that saying, by Berne I believe, that if a man were to write out every evening all that passed within him during the day he would soon become a great writer. The main difficulty comes in the fact that I cannot write out *all* that passed since my pen is not quick enough to follow up my ideas; thoughts pass quickly and I am at a loss how to express them in language. . . .

I am now sitting at the window. It is evening and I would like to go out around Rivington St. and converse with "the Boys," but have resolved to sit down and arrange some system of self-government. For this reason I have read several pages in Franklin's Autobiography as a kind of inspiration. . . .

With regards to character I can by a system somewhat similar to Franklin's, improve my manners and expose myself under the most helpful influences.

Tuesday Aug. 17 [1897; fourth notebook]

. . . I have found out a great truth! To be successful in anything we must be heart and soul in it. Our sympathies as well as energies are necessary. This is why I have failed in the last journal. I felt I was not writing what I wished to, and therefore became disgusted with it.

It has become a part of my nature to rebell against everything and anything merely for rebellion's sake. This, I am afraid, will cause me great inconvenience in life where people are supposed to abide by laws and customs. But I have not as yet tried to counterbalance this pernicious tendency.

This tendency is shown in the number of plans for stories and sketches which I have formed most of which treat of subjects never tried before in the light I intend to (If I ever write them!) I propose to copy nature exactly and show that the unromantic is perhaps greater than the romantic. . . .

. . . I have also formed a plan of describing hell something very like this world. . . .

Thursday August 19 [1897]

. . . In the evening I walked with S. K. We were telling each other of our respective troubles. I told him that the greatest trouble is to be a burden to someone who makes you conscious of it. I also told him how, being in childhood without the direct influence of a father and mother, and being often knocked around, my character became un-lovable and somewhat hardened. At home I thought over to myself the influences that my early life has on my character. The first thing that strikes me is the bad neighborhood of our house. Then my being at first without any monitor, then under grandparents, then under loose control of parents then under no control at all. This I think made my mind unsteady.

Monday August 23 [1897]

If a man could write down all his thoughts the way they occurred to him, what would the record look like? Would it appear real life? would it shock sensitive feelings? These and similar questions have always bothered me. . . .

Tuesday August 24 [1897]

. . . All my thoughts now-a-days are turned upon myself and jour-nalism and though I have recently read much against it I have a natu-ral craving for that profession. I passed by a news stand on which I saw a small paper called the "Agitator" issued by the Socialist Liter-ary Society. I began to muse on what I would write if I were editor of such a paper. I thought of the glory to write out and even print a paper, distribute it everywhere and write in such a tone to move everyone like in the good old days of the French Revolution. . . .

Saturday [August 28, 1897]

. . . Read up to page 40 of Burton's Anatomy of melancholy.
. . . The sentiments there were very much like my own. . . .

Wednesday Sept. 8 [1897]

. . . I sometimes think what a powerful thing it would be were I
to write out all I feel. But I must keep my peace for myself. Though I
care not if this ever fall into somebody else's hands, I am yet disin-
clined to write openly. I guess I need some more courage. . . .

Sept. 11 [1897; scrap of paper]

. . . About the only positive wish of mine, the only ambition
which I ever had is to become a writer, and this I trace back to the
wish to be a power and perhaps still further to the inordinate desire
to hear myself praised. I think this desire is almost all of my character, at least everything is subservient to it.

More than a year ago I was having a literary fit, i.e. I was in a period of literrary activity (literrary being synonomous with writing in my
vocabulary). Then I wrote several sketches which were admired by
all those to whom I read . . . and so I got the idea of being destined
for literature. . . .

Wednesday Sept. 29 [1897; sophomore year]

. . . Last night I went to night school but did not like the instruction in phonography as I imagined I knew it I think I shall be absent
several days.

Tuesday October 26 [1897]

A revolution has, or at least, ought to have occurred in my life. A
revolution, not in action but in feeling, in the source of action. [Mor-
ris' plan, conceived in June of his freshman year, of skipping the
sophomore year remained only a dream. When he found that another
student had succeeded in executing such a project, he realized he
should have persisted. The experience taught him a lesson.]

. . . I might turn this defeat to advantage, by learning to profit by
it, by learning how to avoid such defeats in the future. . . . Whenever I have a plan on hand, as I have now, which may seem impossible, I shall ever have this example before me. . . . Today I shall
make a red-letter day in the history of my life, by starting the system
I had adopted from Franklin.

I spoke of a plan that I now have. It is to become a contributor to
some newspaper and thus make some money. If I succeed in that I
shall have financial, but a great deal more moral encouragement. I
am not sure it is possible, but I may try, and I WILL.

Sat. 30 [October 1897]

I now begin to feel a real weight upon my mind. . . .

To start with, there is the old problem of the struggle for existence. I always thought it a great blessing to be born in poor circumstances. . . . I was under the impression that to fight adversity had a strengthening influence. . . . But now this opinion has been thoroughly shaken by my feelings, or rather by my weakness in meeting the small insignificant struggle that I have to keep up. . . . The taunts of my parents is secretely piercing my heart, insensible as I may have considered myself. . . .

But the *habit* of failing has taken possession of me. . . .

There is a conflict in my mind between feeling and reason, between inclination and sentiment, between theories and experience. I am all at sea, a man in combat with himself. There is within me the "good man," the creation of the books I have read and the "bad man," the result of my life. The first sets his ideals because he knows what is wright but the second is sceptical and lazy.

Many times I think of leaving college and trying to obtain a position and thus earn my living. . . . I am not determined whether I *think* that I have any natural aptitude towards the study of law.

The ambition I now possess to the greatest degree is for journalism. My vanity was rather fired up by the praise my "Essay in Bluffing" received and I think that I should try to get into some newspaper office. . . . I am going to inquire everywhere *possible,* to find out some newspaper man and become acquainted with him. . . .

Sunday Nov. 14 [1897]

Now I am beginning to see how isolated I was during the last 5 years and how dreamy my thoughts have been. I am now conscious my first duty is to earn my living; all others are secondary to it.

Tuesday Nov. 30 [1897]

At last we have removed from our old dark, noisy prison-like rooms in Norfolk St. We have much lighter rooms and more chance of my studying quietly. In fact I may be said to have a room for myself. The library is not yet fixed up and I have no convenient place for the books and writing materials.

Another important event has taken place in my biography. The Journal [essay for his club] was read before a very good audience (of about 150) and it succeeded admirably well though I could easily have made it much better. The old trouble stuck to me that is I could not write it before the last day. Still the result tended to make me even more vain than ever. So that now I am afraid of myself, so vain do I think I have become. . . .

. . . Yesterday we moved and I had an excuse to idle away the whole evening in making up a constitution for the Students' League.

In a way I don't know but that I am sorry for joining that society. I do not receive any benefit from it, nor do I think will anybody be benefitted by it. . . .

Sometimes I think that if I were to write out all my feelings and thoughts it would make a very instructive account. I often think of the intensity of my thoughts and feelings and wonder whether anyone of my size has such advanced thoughts. . . . What a strange book would be the one that would be a true biography of myself.

New Year's Thoughts, 1898 [*Fifth notebook*]

INTRODUCTION

. . . The most important characteristic about me now is, I think, my rebellious nature, my scepticism and proness to look at all established institutions, and life in general, from the dark side only, though my mind tells me there is another way of looking at these things. In this I have somewhat been carried away by the natural enthusiasm which socialistic ideas and the Students League have imbibed me with. . . . Even my own character, egoistic as I am, appears to me only from the darker side and I can see only faults, very few virtues. Probably I do not think as much of my virtues as I do of my faults.

The fact is that I am somewhat awkward and clumsy in society, perhaps the natural consequence of my sedate habits. . . .

. . . Though I am naturally obstinate and never give in even when I am hopelessly beaten, I have a kind of natural timidity. . . .

Even if there is nothing but evil in life it is much better not to be conscious of it every moment of your life. . . .

Looking at the bad side of life makes you look at the bad side of all your freinds neighbors and acquaintances, and destroys all your chances of ever receiving any benefit from them.

. . . It is better to notice only the good traits and try as much as you can to imitate them. And even if you are conscious of bad traits that your freind or acquaintance may possess, try to excuse them. You can easily do this by imagining yourself to have that trait. Then you will very readily find an excuse or the trait will appear to you not needing any excuse whatever.

I have then enumerated the following general characteristics—awkwardness in society, extreme egoism, and a tendency to look only on the bad side of everything, besides a certain superficiality though I do think I am more profound than most of my acquaintances. . . . I have many other traits some bad, some indifferent and some, I hope, good. . . . My character is continually changing now-a-days. . . . I know that I cannot gain anything by taking up arms against the

world (when it has not yet done *me* any injustice). It would be better
to comply with the ways of the world. But my temper has already
been hardened in that respect, since almost from childhood I was,
owing to circumstances, of an unsociable disposition. . . .

. . . However the excessive praises which I received in both societies for my Journals have been productive of no earthly benefit and
have to a certain extent made me unbearably vain. I now think to improve myself in public speaking, where there is plenty of discouragement in sight for me. This I hope will take a little of the conceit out of
me, besides improving my delivery which is to a certain extent just as
important as the art of composition. . . .

Monday Jan. 17 [1898]

. . . I think I am an adult in mind and feeling, though a big baby
in my actions. . . . I am almost certain that in all but two departments I am altogether unfit for anything. These two things are writing and teaching. The latter is not a brilliant *carreer* but one which I
should prefer to the most brilliant (by brilliant I mean shining before
the public gaze).

There is in fact a struggle in my mind between a desire for peace of
mind, not to mix in the struggle of life (with which I have no sympathy), and the desire to overcome, to carry my way, in other words
to fight with humanity and conquer. . . .

Sunday Feb. 20 [1898]

. . . "It seems as if scorn has become the passion of my soul."
This comes to a great extent from having joined the socialists and
reading Ibsen. It seems to me that my tolerant impartial (because
broad minded) mind has been narrowed down to a bigoted partisan
who refuses to look at the other side of the question.

Feb. 22 [1898]

Again my mind is fluctuating between two aspects of life or rather
I am undecided which of the following views of conduct I should let
predominate, "Be virtuous for virtue sake" or "Be virtuous for else
you will not be happy." . . . Of course the torment in either case
results when my mind is not yet fixed in either opinion. I think I am
more inclined to "fix" my conscience than my "practical" spirit.
This is rather displeasing [to] Morris Cohen the book-worm the
reader of the Imitation, Marcus Aureilleus etc. But lately M. R.
Cohen the iconoclast has grown too strong. He wants to do away
with all that sentiment and regard only that which is of practical
value.

March 2 [1898]

. . . Last Sunday [February 27] I heard a talk by Mr. Edward

King on "A great little Club," the society of Mill, Grote, Macauly, Thirlwall, etc. who from the thorough study of a few book[s] before going to their business came to revolutionize England. At the time of the talk I became very enthusiastic . . . I became aware that hitherto I have directed my efforts in a thousand different directions and thus I have missed a great deal of what I may have accomplished. . . .

It seems to me that I should try to get the bright side of things. What is the use of always looking for the dark side. Look for the sunny side and enjoy it as much as possible. . . .

March 30 [*1898; scrap of paper*]

I think the key to my state is the following extract from "The Autocrat of the Breakfast Table." "I shall die and be forgotten and the world will go on just as if I had never been,—and yet how much I have thought, how I have longed! how I have aspired." The struggle within me is that of *feeling* against the rooted sentiment of *Pure Reason*.

. . . Today I felt very relieved by reading Marvel's Reveries of a Bachelor. It aroused new strains of feeling I don't know whether I should be ashamed of wishing to cry, but in this revolt of the feeling I may become foolish, and I think I am so in this diary. In fact my diary is far from representing me at my best.

May 4 Wednesday 1898 [*Scrap of paper*]

. . . I am like a ship without a rudder tossed about on an angry ocean—no—sometimes on a calm ocean, but no land in sight. . . .

July 25 1898 [*Monday, Morris' eighteenth birthday; scrap of paper*]

. . . I have already formed a scheme of study, composed of (A) Intellectual Studies, (1° Philosophy 2° Logic 3° Hist. 4° Polit. Econ. 5° Psychology and Education and 6° Foreign Languages) and B. Liberal Education (1° Novels 2° Criticism and Art (including Music) and 3° Belles Lettres (including study of English style). I fear the scheme is somewhat too elaborate, but I hope to do a good deal of work of the most useful kind the next eight weeks. . . .

Aug. 18, 1898 [*Scrap of paper*]

. . . I am like a ship sailing without a definite course and seldom making any prolonged effort to steer in a certain direction. Sometimes I think that this is due to rapid development, that I cannot follow out a continuous line because I grow wiser and begin to see it is not the right direction, and so keep on changing it.

Dec. 26, 1898 [*Scrap of paper*]

. . . My ambition has taken many vague forms, Journalism, Pedagogy, are still living in my fancy though shorn of their first lustre. Then there is the more romantic career of a social agitator of which I am always dreaming. Perhaps it is possible to combine the three.

Jan. 29, 1899 [Scrap of paper]

. . . So far I don't know one professor who takes a special interest in me, and my chances of getting a position in the college after graduating seem imaginary quantities. I can hardly imagine myself a teacher there; How could I look such men as Parmly or Legras in the face? How could I conduct myself to the other teachers? Who would be my freind? Yet I do not give up all hope. . . . This one, however, (that of obtaining a position in CCNY, in philosophy) seems the nearest and most practical. . . . I am not confident I can win, and there is plenty to lose, for I might meanwhile develop my spirit for *writing,* or make a thorough study of my favorite subject—philosophy. Yet there is a great deal to be gained by the effort. I am going for once to settle the question. "In case I have a task to perform (tasks are never congenial), have I sufficient power to stick to it and do it? . . . For this purpose I am going to (1) reduce outside work to a minimum and devote all my time, thoughtfully, to those subjects connected with C.C.N.Y.

[*Musings on Romance and Unromantic Actions*]

Monday August 23 [1897]

. . . I observed the freindship between dog and master and it seemed to me that there is a store of love in all of us which is bound to go out in some form or other. When we take up a dog on our lap and caress him, the animal itself seems to feel that he is liked. Perhaps love is something sublime but I always was of the opinion that it [is] not a matter of the soul but of the "animal" or "other" as De Maistre calls it. . . . But is all the love spoken of by artists, novelists, and many others merely animal? or is it what Taine says of actors, that playing with life loosens our scruples about morality and that love is merely an animal thing deified by men whose special business it is to talk about it. These questions I have not yet answered satisfactorily.

Wednesday Aug. 25 [1897]

. . . Tonight we had the first meeting of our new society. . . . I tried to make a "speech" . . . against the admission of lady members. . . .

Saturday [Aug. 28, 1897]

. . . Tonight we had the second meeting of our society. . . . Could not hide my adversion towards the "ladies."

March 2 [1898]

. . . I always wished that I had someone who could understand me; someone before whom I could unfold my heart and who could thus help to steady it. I am like a ruderless ship amid ocean driven by winds now here now there.

May 4 Wednesday 1898

I feel there is nothing in this world which I love—and there is no one so far as I know—whom I can lead into the depths of my heart. The preceding may have been a little too romantic, but nowadays I have an inclination to turn in that direction. After all, mere reasoning is not the object of living. (So far I see no object at all!) . . .

Since a few months a struggle is raging within me between old tendencies to cold reasoning, and inclinations to enjoy feelings. Looking over my existence in the past, I see a desultory warfare within me. . . .

[Undated, probably fall 1898]

The sun is down and a kind of vague gloom pervades the air, a gloom that has nothing violent about it, nothing to suggest a storm or darkness, but merely a drear inanity as I look out upon the empty world which greets my eyes in the form of uncouth tenement houses and a patch of sky traversed by the wash-lines. As long as I remember (as back as Nieshwiesh when at times I used to think myself lonely) a feeling of sadness and loneliness pervaded me whenever I gave myself up to contemplation in the twilight or rather at the close of day. . . . I am actually at that state when the timid tears come to the eye . . . at this moment were one to tell me that my life is going to end soon, there would be nothing that I would regret leaving, except the sentiment of leaving my parents miserable and not living long enough to become a writer. I am sentimental enough to think that this loneliness in life would be a little softened were there anyone whom I could love—yes, love, or rather one who could sympathize with me and be a spiritual brother (or sister). This I conceive in what I feign a scientific form, viz. that my mental and physical organism needs another half, a magnetic opposite to cooperate with, but this other half I think (from my scanty experience) utterly impossible to exist in the opposite sex, at least my present conception of her. I would like to open my mind to someone who could read into its deepest recesses. . . . But even when this conception of my other half, my magnetic opposite, my poetic supplement is strongest and most attractive, at its highest, I cannot get myself away from the belief that love is a delusion and that my nature, my incessant introspection and weak character renders me incapable of loving and being loved. . . .

Jan. 29, 1899

    . . . Thus have I come to such a state where the idea I was always laughing at, has demonstrated to me its possibility, not without a certain romantic coloring and I might perhaps say agreeableness. Of course I ought to see it is vain for me to lay siege—

[Scrap of paper, probably fall 1899]

With a mind full of Romantic dreams it is difficult to study declensions, etc.

II. *Love and the Philosopher*

MORRIS AND MARY

THIS IS THE STORY of Morris Cohen and Mary Ryshpan, the tale of a philosopher caught in despair, debts, and doubts, and the girl whose love set him free, of how they married and what happened afterwards. They tell of it in their own words through their letters and diary notes. Mary's mission was the *éducation sentimentale* of Morris Cohen. Of all the masters in his life, perhaps he owed her the most.

"If I saw a miracle," Morris Cohen had avowed to his diary when he was seventeen, "I would not believe it." Mary Ryshpan, however, confessed in a later letter to Morris that having explored her inner self, she had uncovered "cosily cuddled up within her somewhere . . . a belief in miracles. This little pretender," she added hopefully, "once recognized, is being driven forth with energy." Miracle or no miracle, she transformed a raw introvert into a man who learned to read the hearts of others. Reading hers was his initiation. He called it "a great moral lesson." Her gentle strength, her patient understanding, dignity, and love made her indomitable. Morris finally won her, but on her terms. His ship had found its rudder.

They met before they were nineteen. It was early in 1899, in the New York of the gaslights, the horsecar, the "bicycle built for two," and the newly constructed Brooklyn Bridge. The Lower East Side was full of immigrants and their children, some, like Mary Ryshpan, born here.

Women wore their own complexions. Also high-necked waists with leg-o'-mutton sleeves. Long skirts, bustled or unbustled, mercifully covered the tops of the high-buttoned shoes with which they walked incredible distances. For young ladies, parental supervision was inviolate, but Mary and Morris were brought together as fellow devotees of Thomas Davidson, the Scottish scholar who uplifted them by the teachings he volunteered to a group of "Breadwinners" at the Educational Alliance.

Their first exchange of words took place as they were leaving a lecture there. Mary Ryshpan summoned up her courage to address that Brain who didn't talk to girls, who carried Schopenhauer in his pocket even on picnics. "What did you think of the talk?" she asked politely. "To answer your question," he replied with severity, "would take volumes that only the learned would read." "Oh," she said, and left him at the next corner.

When Morris found himself smitten, which happened not too long thereafter, he admitted it to Davidson. "But," he added, "I'm trying to fight it." A skeptical twinkle came into the Scotsman's blue eyes. "Let me know what success you'll have," he said.

Others of their circle envied Mary her conquest. Davidson had once suggested another girl for his protégé—"She's very efficient, Morris." But efficiency was not his criterion. Nobody else but Mary would do.

After spending the summer of 1899 at Glenmore, Davidson's summer school of philosophy, the two found themselves classmates in the fall in David Saville Muzzey's Greek course for the Davidsonians. Morris was too busy to prepare his homework; she always did hers. Before class he would sit down next to her and she would go over the lesson. During class, while she sat back quietly, he would shine.

Morris soon made her his confidante. Through his early letters we glimpse him in his twenties, full of moral earnestness, with more sensitivity, even humility, than he exhibited to the rest of the world. Here is an intimate record of his moods and failings, conflicts and scruples, his unvarnished honesty and his aspirations, his realism and his idealism. We see the two of them growing in contact with each other.

His adolescent cravings to be understood and loved had been expressed in his diaries. But how could he as yet have learned to love, to demonstrate tenderness and affection, to want to sacrifice for love? Unwittingly, he would wound her feelings, then apologize and proffer gifts, as we learn from this note of hers.

> Thank you Morris—and if I were capable of feeling any joy—if my feelings were not dulled, deadened, this gift of yours would make me very happy.
>
> I don't know much of Matthew Arnold. I shall learn. And the pictures—how pretty they are.
>
> MARY R.

Their relationship was full of ups and downs. In his diary, July 28, 1902, Morris refers to "my own unfortunate love—now a hallowed memory though I see *her* quite frequently." The following exchange of letters from a year later indicates one more of the downs.

Morris to Mary:

> . . . But after all we ought not let our feelings get complete mastery over us. Man is man and master of his fate. We are both

children of Thomas Davidson and we ought to rise up to the occasion.
You are young yet and the world is yours *for the conquest*. . . . Let
me only assure you that since the summer of 1899, when we both met
at the feet of our spiritual father, I have always entertained the highest
regard for you, and what you were brave enough to say last night certainly has not lowered you in my eyes. I hope I will continue to enjoy
your friendship, which I assure you I value very highly.

    Your sincere, though unworthy, friend,

MORRIS

Mary's answer (June 23, 1903):

    Morris—

    Perhaps it will lessen your suffering somewhat to learn that I am
sure it was not your fault. So do not say "unworthy friend."

    Had you known woman nature better—had you known sensitive
impressionable nature better—had you been a little more sophisticated
in a worldly sense, this would not have been.

    So, Morris, while it means a certain lack of insight on your part, it
also means that you live in a high spiritual plane.

    Don't doubt that I will keep up through this. It is not as it was the
first time the truth dawned on me.

MARY

Morris' reaction shows up in his diary note for July 7, 1903.

    But a far more important discovery have I made recently and that
is that I have deeply wounded a woman's heart. . . . Whether my
own heart is committed or not I will probably not be able fully to tell
so long as my vacillating temper and excessively introspective analysis
hold full sway. . . . I certainly cannot conceive myself knowing a
person without knowing his faults. At any rate I have passed sleepless
nights and restless days on account of this matter.

The friendship grows. Working for one of her good causes, Mary has
been hurt. Morris consoles her. "There's no use harboring any enmities
against any one. Let the small people wallow in their littleness." Elsewhere,
turning his critical eye upon himself, he admits to "the fault which I so
liberally possess, namely of being too self-centered." To a kindred soul,
he speaks of pity:

    . . . with me one emotion has gained complete ascendancy over
all the others—the emotion of pity. As I look out on life and see the

millions of creatures ceaselessly struggling for what they are incapable
of attaining (to stop struggling is to cease to be), then I feel how
much all other sentiments must be subordinated to that of compassion,
and how really fundamental and essential pity is. —But here again
I may be misunderstood. Have you ever reflected, Mary, of how impossible it is ever to *completely* understand someone else? When I reflect how hard it is for me to understand myself, then I am ready to
accept as inevitable my inability *fully* to understand anyone else.

Another letter to Mary deals with will power and friendship.

To my mind that is the supreme quality of any human being—to be
able to stand up and say I will be what I want to be, not only in spite
of external obstacles but in spite of my own unrational feelings or
other defects. . . .

And now that our friendship has undergone a "Baphometic fire
baptism" I hope it will be the better for it. (I am sure it has been a
great moral lesson for me.) After all what the world needs most of
all is true friendship, the companionship of people who are really and
truly interested in each other's welfare, not simply in their outward
success, but in their internal and moral welfare. For this purpose we
need a clearer conception of the *duties* of friendship, and a truer
approach to frankness and sincerity than our past conventional standards have held up for us—I mean for the world. . . .

With best wishes, I am,

Your sincere friend
MORRIS

There comes a time when he can no longer fight back his feelings. He
writes from his desk at the Breadwinners' College where he and Mary were
volunteer teachers in the Davidsonians' little "Band of Disciples."

Mary dear,

Yesterday, six o'clock came and I looked up many times from my
desk, expecting to see that little brown figure stepping in—Many
times I thought I heard the bell and went to the door only to be disappointed—No dear, I had not realized how much you meant to me
and when a quarter of seven came and still no Mary, it was with a
heavy heart that I took my books under my arm and went downtown. Many times as I walked along E. B'way did I imagine I saw
the little brown figure again—but no—and then the class came—and
yes I am surprised at myself that I was able to get through it as I did
—and then I walked out for a long time before the exec. com. meeting
—and looked up to your window but it was dark. Perhaps if it were

lit I would have gone up and told all—all that for months I had tried to stifle, thinking that it would take me from the larger needs of the world—but now at last—I ask you to take me—take me to your self, to your love, your sympathy, your faith—your hope and trust in humanity, to your simple womanly beauty, take me and inspire me further to my life's ideals—ideals that are one with your own—and together we will reach up to God.

MORRIS

Next we find an unstamped post card of the Kissing Bridge at Lakewood, N.J. The reverse side reads:

to Mary Ryshpan
from her old beau
who was accepted (in a manner)
on Dec. 26 [1903]

Like Davidson, who had foreseen his favorite pupil as one of "the men of his generation," Mary Ryshpan recognized the potential in Morris. What better purpose could her life fulfill than to bring it out? After poring over Davidson's letters to the youth of whom he expected so much, she wrote:

[March 8, 1904]

My dear Morris—

Just a word to thank you for sharing this treasure with me. . . . O my dear, beautiful Morris, he saw truly what you are. I am confident the years will prove it, if you are not hindered overmuch by petty cares. . . . It shall ever be my first care, to keep you free from them; please let me do it . . . again, good night. And—still again—good night.

MARY

Morris scribbles on the back of Mary's letter:

Sometimes I get to have a good opinion of myself—not when I read praises like that of Davidson and of this letter—(praises that have a painful effect because they remind me of how little I have done or am even likely to do to deserve it—to actualize the potentiality they see in me) but when I read of something that reminds me that not in victory is heroism but in the continued painful struggle.

If this were a fairy tale they would marry then and there, and the page would be closed. But this was real life. Mary's young philosopher won a fellowship to Harvard. At twenty-four he went off to Cambridge to work for his doctorate in philosophy. Financially he feels in no position to marry.

From his meager checks, whenever possible, he ekes out something to send home. One of his letters to Mary notes: "I have received the check and have sent the major part of it to my parents."

He occasionally asks Mary to send him this or that from his roll-top desk at home. He invites her to read his private journals and papers therein.

> 29 Divinity Hall
> Friday morning
> [fall 1904]

Dear Mary:

. . . I venture to think that no one ever will know the true Morris R. Cohen except the person who will examine everyone of those scraps with a truly psychologic microscope.

My list of courses include seminars in Ethics and Logic, courses in Kant, Metaphysics, Descartes, etc., the Hebrew religion, the Science of Religion and the History of Religions. . . .

> Your own
> MORRIS

Mary reacts to the diaries and other contents of the "little drawer" with mixed emotions.

> Tuesday night

Dear Morris,

. . . New York has risen a peg in Universal Brotherhood! On various corners about the city can be seen now-a-days, attached to a lamppost, a basin of water with the inscription—"For cats and dogs." For two minutes I experienced unconditional joy, on seeing this new institution, but then there was awakened a new desire—the spreading of education to the cats and dogs of Goshen that they may be able to read and so quench their thirst. . . .

I suppose you don't write because you're too busy. All right, don't let it bother you. Conquer worlds where you are and much joy with you. . . .

> Monday, Oct. 24 [1904]

And the rest of my time is a royal reveling among books, such as I've never had before. I am getting to appreciate what you meant by that desire to get up and do some violent exercise on the inception of a new idea. . . .

I think you ask for what is impossible when you say I should not come to *any* conclusion about the things in the little drawer. It would be misleading, I admit, for anybody to pick these things up, without knowing you otherwise, but as it is, as long as I am able to see things in relation to the rest of you, they're pretty clear reading. . . .

Again good-night.

M.

Saturday afternoon

Dear Morris,

. . . Guess what Morris! I've joined the Grand Army of the Red Hat Brigade. That I wear one now when I wouldn't last year means living one of the characteristics of L.S.N.—one of the fictitious folk of your little drawer. . . .

Heart's best wishes from

M. R.

Monday morning

Dear Morris,

. . . I've read the little booklet. For the most part it was not a surprise to me; just what I would expect from a noble, far-reaching soul such as you are. It is beautiful in many parts. Sad very largely, as life is sad—your reach being so much beyond your grasp—beyond all human grasp. Strange how the greatest among us will feel this sorrow more than all others. Mill felt this deeply. And now you do— you who have done so much more than thousands upon thousands of others, even enlightened others ever do in a whole life. Well, I won't try to console you. Though this state of mind is sad, it would be in-finitely sadder to have you feel perfectly satisfied with what you ac-complish actually. You might though have the former thought lurking in your sub-consciousness.

As for the little surprises in your diary—there is much that I would *say?* no *communicate* to you about. . . .

Again yesterday for the third time I read my diary for what pur-pose you know. But I find that as far as I may go is this:—when next the opportunity offers, to let you read extracts. . . . Frequently in the last two years I went to my diary because that was the only vent I could give to the storm within me. Some of these I can't let you see for I should blush to show you the slavish dependence of my spirit on your slightest word or look. In other places I would not have you see the little hopes and dreams that I know now were built on mere illusions—mere illusions.

MARY

On her own undated scrap of paper, which she never sent:

Morris

Is it possible that you doubt whether you can give me enough?

O Morris, do you not know that sharing the little experiences that in other circumstances would be inconveniences, that poverty with you, would be entirely unfelt in the greater holy joy of being with you, looking into your eyes, working with you, learning from you, being able to give you whatever of myself you ask, looking at the world from the height of your spirit—O Morris—no, the small things would not exist for me—Yes, at one time they did—but then I did not truly know you, nor how entirely my peace of mind depends on you—I did not know how much I love you—Yes, I love you, with all that that means. . . .

A stingy little note from Cambridge now to Mary in New York:

Jan. 4, 1905

Dear May:

Although I am getting to be terribly misanthropic and shun all personal intercourse with everyone, I have not lost interest in what goes on, nor any regard for yourself, dear.

MORRIS

P.S. Please write me as often as you like.

For himself, Morris jots down on a scrap of paper: "But I have entertained remorse most loyally so that she has grown so fond of me that I seldom manage to evade her attentions."

To her "misanthrope," Mary pens one of her Sunday-evening letters.

Dear Morris,

. . . To change the subject—what an interesting, vivid picture you give of your room—and yourself sitting cosily by the open log-fire— so pleasant externally—but internally—such a wretched trio to be rankling within—remorse, passion, disappointment—Poor, poor Morris—you know how sorry I am for you. But of course you understand that I understand this to have been only a mood—that on the whole you are enjoying this tussle with M.R.C. for concentration and the mastering of Kant etc.

Listen Morris (If I may suggest a bit of wisdom to your mightiness) (don't forget the smile here). Is it not because you have climbed beyond the first easier steps in your search for wisdom, that you find now you have to creep cautiously whereas (not where) you used to fly?

Another from Cambridge to New York:

Tuesday morning

Dear Mary:

I have just received your good long letter and the spirit moves me to express not only my heartfelt appreciation but also my deep sense of shame when I compare your full letter with my own scrappy notes. But, Mary dear, you are near a fountain of life while I am here threshing straw most of the time.

I extend to you my most hearty congratulations at the discovery of the remnants of supernaturalism and your effort to get rid of it. It will make for healthy life. . . .

Heart's best wishes

MORRIS

Wednesday Jan. 11, –'05

Dear Morris,

. . . I appreciated (as I think) your desire to immerse yourself in study, and also your own wish to flee from the problem. . . .

But now, for this letter of Monday, great, honest, truly dignified and dignifying, thank you from my inmost heart. . . .

I would have answered your letter sooner, but this was literally impossible, owing to the fact that I have been, for the last two days, on the most adventurous expedition of my life. Owing to the concurrence of a series of strange, fortunate co-incidents, I was the means of rescuing an unhappy immigrant from being deported. The tale is little short of a marvel. . . . From the start to finish it was a most thrilling experience for me. . . .

And now one more thing before closing. You should know by this time that not for the world would I consent to be the cause of your giving up some duty. So you should never write me at a time that you feel "ought to be devoted to Royce." If however at a time that might most profitably be spent with Royce, Kant, etc., you somehow feel it your *duty* to *spontaneously* write to the woman who may someday be your wife, then Morris, please have the grace to go ahead and write without mentioning the Royce etc. fact.

And now good-night . . .

MARY

P.S. Of course, Morris (after all this long letter) you understand that I look forward to the "many things to tell (me)" to which you refer in your letter, be they of whatever harsh nature they may; I feel confident that I can face anything you may have to tell me, before the "great irrevocable choice." So come on.

Best wishes to you always,

MARY

Sunday evening

Dear Morris,

. . . I want to explain, Morris, that I meant it for a joke, the underlining of "duty" and "spontaneity," it was just to accentuate the incompatibility of the two that I marked them, of course it meant merely to tell you write only when you feel free to do so; don't mind, even if long intervals occur, that is perfectly natural. But as for your being paid for studying—surely the folks who gave you the fellowship take it for granted that you may still have the privilege of living to some slight degree at least, outside of your books.

What a surprise your gift was [miniature set of Shakespeare, complete in three volumes] especially now when you're so hard up, and then you know there is a Shakespeare in the house here—as for deserving it, I don't see how. But never mind.

So now you have given me lesson No. 1 in Morrisconology. Very well, yes, it is a serious fault, but then what a glorious thing for you to conquer, as I don't doubt you will. It will be great some day when you'll be able to say—"I have mastered this."

I hear that there was a successful meeting last night. Neilson on H[amlet] at his best—A crowd like that of the Royce night. . . .

MARY

Friday evening
[January 1905]

Dear Mary:

. . . If I remember rightly you asked me in a previous letter what I take up with my club in Boston. The answer is simple—We read and discuss Henderson's Social Elements. Now and then I give them a talk—such as I give to the pupils of the T.D. School. (So far, however, I have had a chance to give them only *one* viz. on the mysteries of life).

Among my miscellaneous papers in the basement of my desk—on the higher shelf and towards the left—you'll find a little bundle entitled Immortality. Will you kindly send it to me? I want to look it over before sending it to [Louis] Roth's Club. They requested my views on immortality and I should like to oblige them.

My exams begin on Monday next and will continue for two weeks.

Nothing more just now. I hope you are keeping well and are not taking the previous letters *too* seriously. Life is so rich in its diversity of moods as well as situations. I am having (almost) daily walks with Leo Mayer and we discuss the most serious problems in philosophy. We are both sorry you can't be with us. . . .

Yours
MORRIS

My best regards to your folks.

Sunday evening
[January 29, 1905]

Dear Morris,

. . . "Life is so rich in its diversity of moods." So well put. I've often thought that but never put it into words, and of late, Morris, talk about diversity of moods and *situations,* I'm reveling in going forth to meet them, and especially those that promise to be uncomfortable. It's great fun, Morris. It's following up thy so often insisted upon commandment, "Thou shalt not coddle thyself." Some day I shall be able to write out a Morrisconian Decalogue which will beat the others all hollow, don't you think? . . .

Mayst thou have the gloriousest results in thy exams—may Mr. Mayer's philosophy come out tip top, with adequate reflection on the fountain head thereof. Amen.

M.

Thursday

Dear Morris.

. . . It seems Morris that you don't really take in earnest what I have been saying. Please do, Morris. Don't think any longer that I could not live without this relationship. I tell you honestly that it is no longer so. After the revelations, written black on white, on the papers that I copied from the little drawer—things are different—so much so that in these last few months I could never picture myself saying to you a definite "yes"—saying it with the feeling that my whole self enters into it—my self-respect, my highest conduct, my best judgment, all these, besides my heart. I suppose I don't express myself perfectly, but it is the simplest, honestest way I know, and I trust your larger wisdom to see more clearly than I am able to say it, just what I mean.

When I said in a little walk of ours lately, that I will never say "yes" unless I am positive that this thing is the best under the circumstances, I meant that I would only do so with the consent of my whole self as I explained above. It was not with the assurance of "perfect happiness or some such thing" that I meant. I see too much of married life about me to go into it under the school-girl illusion that it is a romantic path of roses. Of course I see that it means trials, problems, responsibilities, to be attached to so that there will be brooked no shirking, but still, at the same time, a thing gloriously worth while if one certain thing is not lacking. To trust blindly that it will come after marriage or to believe that love is a habit, is something revolting to me. You will call it sentimental, but I am willing to stake my future on this feeling. . . .

Dear Morris,

Now to continue yesterday's letter. It's a difficult question to answer just how far you should bring your philosophy into the details of life. Of course your philosophy is great and good, especially possessing as it does that bald, perfect, honesty, but it seems to me you do sometimes carry it into foreign fields. It is said that in order to feel something very deeply, it is not necessary to feel it all the time. Don't you think it true? As regards your philosophy I mean. . . .

Of course I am happy to hear of the success of your papers. Very fine, Morris. Your strength here is so great that I am sure it outweighs enormously your weaknesses. These it will not be hard to overlook, for the woman you will love and who will love you and I tell you again, there will be heights of joy for her, in spite of what you say so often to the contrary.

. . . I'm perfectly willing to speak as freely to you about Mary R. as you could possibly wish. Don't think there is any pain at all emotionally these days—that's done with for the greatest part—no matter what comes—even the breaking of our engagement—so don't let the bug bear of my possible pain influence you in your approval of what the final decision will be as far as I am concerned. . . .

So good good-night.

M.

Sunday evening
[March 16, 1905]

. . . Next week Dr. Kim, a Chinese woman whom Sadie [Hirsdansky] got to speak on Efforts for Workingmen's Education in China . . .

This afternoon our Women's Trade Union League had a glorious conference (national). Jane Addams, Samuel Gompers and others spoke. Everybody was there. It was great. I tell you we're going to *do* things. . . .

Good night and best wishes for always—

MARY

. . . Yes, of course April 15 is a good time to say the final word. That's what I've been expecting right along, and have had my mind made up pretty certainly for some time past. I will write you definitely in a day or two.

M.

Monday April 3, 1905
65 E. 100 St.

You are right Morris, marriage should not be based on momentary feelings, and isn't that what marriage would be in our case? Our marriage would be so largely based on the brief feelings of about a year ago that it seems to me it would not be right for us to marry. . . .

Morris dear, you do not know me at all if you think I could marry a man unless I would be able to look straight into his eyes and feel sure that he is mine, united to me by a deep-founded regard, and by his unmistakable need of me, and my need of him. This, together with a mysterious, unnameable something else, I call love, and this alone would make up for all the cares of married life, and there are so many cares. I have been watching with special interest the life of the young married folk about me. . . . Oh! it is hard, and if there should not be absolute, loving, confidence between husband and wife then it would be unmistakeably not worth while. . . .

MARY

29 Divinity Hall
Cambridge, Mass.
April 6, 1905

Dear Mary:

This is not the first letter I have penned since receiving your letter which I suppose I ought to interpret as a categorical refusal? I have been breaking my head for the last 36 hours trying to write you a satisfactory answer, while I am not sure that any answer on my part is wanted or expected. My first impulse is to re-open the question, to try to show you how you mistake my nature and my feelings, and how you judge the whole matter by false and impossible standards. But then do you want me to continue arguing with you? The fact is I do not know what I should do, nor have I any idea of what I can do under the circumstances. One thing, however, stands out clear to me. I stand ready to do whatever you ask of me. What do you wish me to do?

One thing I ask you please to remember. When I ask you to become my wife I do so with a full knowledge of its responsibilities on my part, and a determination on my part to fulfil them. . . .

I am very much tempted to remonstrate with you and show you how you misunderstand me when you make me say that I do not care for you etc.,—also how you fail to understand that all people do not necessarily display their affections in the same way—but is there any use in my doing this?

Yours in perplexity
MORRIS

Saturday
[April 8, 1905]

Dear Morris,

. . . We must either have faith in each other or part. . . .

MARY

Monday

Dear Morris—

. . . Another few days and you'll be among us again—and then— what will be? Morris—tell me if it surprises you to know that I look forward to your visit as the great, grave turning point of my life? I am happy to be able to tell you that I am prepared for it and no doubt you too are glad that it is so. These few months have meant for me something in the way of self-reliant strength. . . .

Again—heart's sincerest wishes from

MARY

Tuesday—April 11 –'05
T.C. [Teachers College]

Dear Morris—

Your letter of Sunday was quite a surprise. Morris, how tender you can be sometimes. You are a strange man. I think we will be able to gain ground by seeing each other and talking wretched doubts away. . . . Dont worry about me.

Keep well. Your father is all joyousness against next Sunday.

Sincerely,
MARY

Tuesday morn

My Morris—

Just a little prattle. Listen. Such a wonderful thing happened last night. Went to bed before 9!!!

As a result—singing, singing, singing this morning. I was thinking
that when we take rooms for both—we'll have to manage that our
work rooms are far apart from each other—for when one of these
singing moods takes me I am a nuisance to those about me. So be-
ware! . . .

Another bit of news. Call thy wits together for another topic of
conversation—for alas—no more flying locks to talk about. I've
bought a veil.

Must run off to school.

MAY

Harvard Ethical Society
Cambridge, Mass.
May 29, 1905

My dear Mary:

I will begin this letter with . . . again asking you to visit Mrs. M.
The reason is just the one that you gave yourself, namely that she
never struck a responsive chord in your heart. This may sound to
you paradoxical and yet it is a very good one when you reflect on it.
You know social intercourse would be entirely impossible if we restricted ourselves only to those who strike responsive chords in our
hearts. One of the things which *we especially* must learn to do is how
to get along with a number of people for whom we have no particular
affection. . . . It is a great education to get to know well people
with whom you *at the beginning* have no sympathy. That's the only
way we can grow—I sometimes think. . . .

Things are going my way at Harvard rather fairly. I have turned
out a thesis of some 70 pages on Kant last week and it was pretty
good. In my exams I came out with flying colors. I'm pretty certain
to get a position here next year—in the department of philosophy. . . .

I'm glad to see you hustling—but please be careful of your health.
You'll have no lack of work when we enter the business of married
life. . . .

Your own
MORRIS

Morris sent Mary to a benefactor of his for advice on their marriage
plans. A tense exchange of letters followed.

[May 1905]

Dear Mary:

Your letter is most tantalizing, and I suspect you wrote it to torture me in return for my sending you to ——. Here you write me that

you saw him and keep quiet on the subject in which I am most deeply interested, what happened during your meeting.

Have you told your parents of . . . our decision? It may be that they will be willing to do that which will enable us to get married this coming summer. If not, the year's training ought to be valuable for both of us.

. . . As for money—do not let it bother you too much. When you need it let me know and I will send it to you. It would be a great pity if at this time we sacrificed our growth to merely monetary considerations. . . .

Your own
MORRIS

Wednesday
Dear Morris,

The reason I did not give you the details about my —— visit was that I knew if I had said what I felt about it, I would have certainly said things to tantalize you more than my silence did. . . .

The saliva was leaving my mouth very fast, in the presence of this stoic minister. Then a word or two about College, about how he had come upon your secret, his opinion of you and his advice that we wait till you are settled financially—this notwithstanding that I had answered to one of his previous questions that we would probably be married at the end of next year, i.e. when you return from your final year at Harvard. . . .

. . . When I left his house . . . I longed for the sight of a human animal. In the car I feasted my eyes on a large comfortable looking woman animal with several children. . . .

. . . Father promises to give us a check for $3000 besides the other expenditures. . . . That money matters bother me is only because I despise getting into debt. . . .

Good-night, and may you be at ease, now that you know *the* details. *Dear* Morris, in spite of your impatience.

MARY

Morris did obtain an assistantship in philosophy at Harvard for the following year. The marriage was put off until June 1906, when he was to return home with his doctorate in philosophy in one pocket, his contract for a job at The City College in the other, and more debts than money in both. That final year of waiting was hardest of all.

A few years earlier he had confided to his diary his feeling of superiority toward mundane "baubles"—society's favors and worldly success. One of the marks of such success is money. But what was he to do without a penny to his name, unable to pay his bills, with nobody around from whom to borrow?

> Glenmore,
> Thursday evening,
> 7/31/05

Dear Mary:

. . . But while I am talking about financial matters I might as well confide to you that I am sorely in need of $30 (which I shall be able to return in two or three weeks), for I am stranded here and had to borrow a 2¢ postage stamp to send this letter off. If you can borrow it for me it will be a great help since I have already borrowed of all the friends I can think of who are in a condition to lend me any money. . . .

Several months later, in a letter from Cambridge, Morris mentions his new roommate and wonders whether Mary can interest Felix Frankfurter in the work of their common project—spreading the gospel of their departed leader, Davidson.

> 1707 Cambridge St.
> Oct. 15, 1905

Dear May:

My work here has already begun. . . .

. . . I have succeeded in getting Pres. Eliot to arrange a date on which to speak to the Harvard Ethical Society—which is a great triumph for yours truly. My class at the Civic Service House meets but once a fortnight so far as I am concerned and we are taking up Bacon's essay on Studies. It is a wonderful introduction for a class in literature. You might try it with your class. It is one of those short pieces that you must read and think over word for word. . . .

Felix Frankfurter, my roommate—and a very pleasant one—is going to be in New York on Thursday (Oct. 19) and he will endeavor to see my folks. If you can think of any use we can put him to please let me know. . . .

Hoping that all's well with you,

> Yours as ever
> MORRIS

> Sunday

Dear Morris—

. . . I congratulate you on your new achievement. Is there a branch of the Ethical Culture Society in Boston? Is this an independent organization or part of the E.C. movement? This is a great thing. Just like you to be at it. I wonder will it become a tie to keep you in Boston. That would be sad for the New York work. . . .

Smilez-vous at this, mon cher ami? I've forgotten how you look when you smile, s'il vous plaît remind me? oui? Merci donc.

Au revoir—
Soon Maurice
MARY

1707 Cambridge St.
Oct. 23, 1905

Dear May:

I have been feeling very depressed mentally and spiritually during the last few weeks, and the last week especially so. Not wishing to cause you pain also, I intended to wait until my "dumps" were over, but now I am really ill and confined to my room on account of acute indigestion. Very sorry that I cannot send you any better news, but my life *seems* to be destined to be miserable and to involve all those who enter into personal relations with me in a similar fate. As for me, misery comes without a sting to it, because I have long ago given up the claim to happiness. The world has treated me as well as I deserve, if not very much better. But it is hard for me to think of the suffering that my misery causes in others. . . .

Yours
MORRIS

Oct. 26, 1905

Dear May:

. . . I blame myself for having written the letter at all on Monday evening when I felt unusually depressed.

. . . It is this uncertainty which makes me weary of life with its ceaseless struggles and prize-less victories. I am sorry if this will make you unhappy but my real sickness is a moral one. It is that which makes me nervous and it is nervousness that is the cause of my bad digestion.

Let us hope for better times.

MORRIS

Oct. 30, 1905

Dear May:

I am afraid that my last letter to you was written in rather un-usually irritable mood, and certainly did not express how fully I appreciate your solicitude about me. Still I hope that you realize that the malady from which I am suffering now is one that renders a person frightfully irritable, and you will with the goodness of your heart pardon me for it. . . .

With best wishes

MORRIS

Nov. 3, 1905

Dear May:

This will be short because I want to catch the last mail so that you will get word from me before Monday. I hope my apology in the last letter was acceptable to you. . . .

Your own

MORRIS

[December 1, 1905]

Dear May:

You know I'm a man of moods and so you can't rely on me doing (or not doing) anything regularly. Sometimes I'm very talkative and at other times very incommunicative. So do not worry when you do not hear from me—nor be vexed with me as I am sufficiently vexed with myself—Will be home Thursday evening.

M. R.

In early February, Morris' health breaks down, and he goes to Watkins Glen for the baths' cure.

The Glen Springs
Watkins, N.Y.
Feb. 27, 1906

Dearest:

I have been very anxious all week because of my not receiving any answer to my letter of a week ago, and today I could no longer contain myself and telegraphed. Your answer is partly re-assuring and partly disturbing.

Do you know, dearest, that since I reached this place I have gained over 8 lbs.? I mention this to back up a singular idea which has been hovering in my mind and of which I cannot get rid. It is the following: You know how the old folks love to see their children married, and so if your father's condition is at all serious he may want to see us married near his bed-side. If so just telegraph to me and I will come by the next train.

Poor dear, what a hard time you must have been having these last few weeks. How I wish I could be beside you and relieve you of some of your heavy burdens.

Your own
MORRIS

The Glen Springs
Watkins, New York
[March 8, 1906]

Dear May:

. . . The doctor has allowed me to begin work on my thesis, and hence I have not written to you as much as I should or would have liked to. But we will soon be together and I will have lots to tell you. I have seldom learned so much as I did in the last five weeks.

Good-night, dearest, and may your heart be strengthened.

Your own
MORRIS

Remember me most kindly to your mother and sisters.

Apr. 8/06

My dearest May:

. . . By July 1st, I shall be [in] debt over $600. . . .

For his doctor's thesis in the dark days of 1906, Cohen tackled Kant's theory of happiness. His notebook contains many additional reflections on happiness—and its opposite. One discouraged note seems to strike home.

Why do miserable people refuse to change their condition when they have it in their power to do so?

(1) They have it *not* in their power—too tired or lazy.

(2) They do not desire any change. The so-called happy state and the exertion to bring it about is not desirable by them.

Why had Morris Cohen fought against his love? Why had he in his adolescence resolved to give up candy? To prove that "man is man and master of his fate"? Or because he hadn't grown up enough? Because he was poor but responsible and proud? Or because he felt called to give himself entirely to philosophy and "the larger needs of the world"? After the habit of unhappiness, it was not easy to adjust to the idea of happiness as his lot. In any event it took time for the two of them to work out a solution to their problem of reconciling their aspirations for personal happiness with goals of serving truth and righteousness.

It was Morris' good fortune to encounter someone who understood him better than he understood himself, a great soul capable of a great love.

Life with Mary helped him out of his early immersion in misery, abruptly and dramatically.

Morris' humor is depicted in a letter Mary sends her sister Bertha shortly after the wedding. The couple are in Maine at the Green Acre summer school for comparative religion, where Morris is the lecturer representing the Jewish faith.

[early July, 1906]

And now dearie Bertha you want to know something of Mary and Morris and their life together. I am positively afraid to say to you how much more sweet it is than what I expected. First of all I find myself necessary to him—he can lie down and think deliberately while he dictates his lectures to me. It helps him and you can guess how I enjoy sharing his work with him. Then he likes to have me read to him and you know how I love that—and last but not least he is a revelation of interest all the time. Such a continuous play of brilliancy—so innately cheery—he awakens with a smile and goes to rest with a smile and throughout the day—well, if "wax fat" really results from the admonition to laugh well—Bertha dear—I don't know where I'll end. He has me laughing till my cheeks ache. . . . He's splittingly funny!

Throughout the years, his work came first with Mary. While he was still struggling as a man in his forties to finish his monumental *Reason and Nature,* she encouraged him:

Dear Morris:

I can't tell you how much I am enjoying Whitehead. Reading his book reveals to me the *raison d'être* for your book as I never understood it before, and makes me more than ever anxious to see it published. I am sure that Whitehead will love it and I can picture how some future Whitehead will expound on the fine contribution of a Jew by the name of Morris Cohen to the philosophy of the 20th century. You just wait and see.

Dearest love to you and to the golden boy. Is he happy?

MAY

When he lectured, she sat in the back of the hall. When he was in a mood to dictate, she was ready with her pen to take dictation in her flowing, legible handwriting. Her gentle criticism balanced her approbation. Her humanitarian causes spurred him upon occasion into heightened social action. He admitted to all the world that his achievement in life would have been impossible without her.

After twenty-eight years of marriage she wrote:

The Belmont
Lake Placid, New York
Adirondacks

Dearest Darlingest Daddy:

I sure was glad to get your letter. I was more lonesome for you,
yes, even more than for Felix [Felix Cohen, their son], so you can
imagine how sweet it was to hear from you. I slept with your letter
under my pillow. (It was even better than hitting a goblin over the
head with a syllogism.) . . .

I am happy with Felix's books and the only thing missing to make
me supremely happy is my dear Morris who I hope is enjoying the
quiet of 854 and the opportunity to get at his work. . . .

Marriage mellowed Morris. The fruit of his mature reflections on love,
philosophy, and marriage shows up in this letter of his to a former student,
Dr. Harry Slochower.

854 W. 181 St.
June 28/29

Dear Slochower:

I am sorry that because of the serious illness of my younger son
(now at Mt. Sinai Hospital) I have not been able to set aside a time
for seeing you and your bride. I have followed your career with a
great deal of interest and should have liked to congratulate your wife-
to-be personally. In any case my very best wishes go out to you.

The love of philosophy is a serious or tragic thing—but all love
that is genuine involves self-sacrifice and the endurance of suffering.
That is not the proper thing to say to one about to be married, but
perhaps it *is* the proper thing. It is certainly true that those who expect married life to be a bed of roses are soon disappointed. But
those who are prepared to suffer the arrows of misfortune together
find their love grow stronger with the years. I hope that your love for
philosophy, like your love for your wife will continue of the serious
rather than the flippant kind. In the long run it is the only kind that
is worth while, and I speak out of a life-time of bitter disappointments. In the long run it is courage and devotion that are the saving
virtues that make life worth while.

With assurance of my best wishes to both of you and with high
hopes for your future,

Cordially yours,
MORRIS R. COHEN

The recipe for a happy marriage as handed down to the Cohens by
the rabbi who married them, June 13, 1906, was for husband and wife

never to get sick at the same time. For thirty-five years it worked. When Morris was weak, Mary was strong. Even more telling than her "courage and devotion," more priceless than her zest against "the arrows of misfortune" in their life together, was the gift of happiness that she offered him. Concocted of sunshine and warmth, laughter and song, it dissolved the doubts. Morris had long ago learned a lesson that he set down in his youthful diary: "In my cynic moods I may regard love merely as a pleasurable feeling but nevertheless it has solved the fundamental question of life for me, without philosophy."

There came a time when the discovery of his wife's incurable illness brought on Morris' collapse. Try as Mary would, she could no longer rouse her tortured body to tend to a husband critically afflicted. The doctors had given him up. Could she with her will still save him? From her sickbed she summoned a new doctor, Mack Lipkin, who had been his student. Two weeks later, she lay dying, happy in the realization that the miracle had worked. The last words that we heard her speak were: "I love him so."

The day after his wife's death, Morris Cohen signified to his younger son, Victor William, seated at his bedside, that he would like to dictate a letter—one more letter to Mary:

June 12, [1942]

Dearest,

Though you have passed beyond the gates which divide us, we give our pledge of love by mail. You'll hear from us, we hope, regularly. We are all thriving as you would wish us.

With abiding love,

> HARRY
>
> GENIE
>
> LEONORA
>
> WILLY
>
> FELIX
>
> LUCY
>
> GRACIE
>
> MORRIS

III. *Davidson, Cohen, and the Heroic Tradition*

MORRIS FOUND HIMSELF by losing himself in something bigger. Franklin's *Autobiography* had encouraged him to try to bring out what was latent in him. A more objective interest in the world was aroused by Thomas Davidson, born in poverty in a humble parish of Scotland's Aberdeenshire, a free-lance scholar by predilection who wandered across Cohen's path and pointed its future direction. In the last year and a half of his own life, Davidson met the boy, thawed him out, broadened his cultural horizons, and encouraged him to continue his studies. He led him into a pioneer project in education for the wage earner, gave him a cause to believe in that replaced the religious faith Morris had lost, sharpened his moral purpose, and inspired him all his life with an heroic ideal.

Unlike Santayana, who had also come to the United States as a child, Cohen did take root. Santayana had confessed at the age of twenty-four, "I have always felt an unsatisfied longing to be one [a hero-worshiper]— but I could find no hero."[1] Morris Cohen found his hero.

If Professor Davidson's four lectures of December 1898 had been delivered as originally planned, at Cooper Union, it might have seemed to Morris' circle of hard-working boys and girls too far to walk to on wintry Wednesday evenings. But the course was transferred to the Educational Alliance, on East Broadway and Jefferson Street. Here was the cultural hub of East Side Jewish youth.

At the turn of the century, many immigrants had come full of hope to the Land of Promise. It was one of the great virtues of the People's Institute of Cooper Union and the Educational Alliance that it brought those to be helped into contact with inspiring leaders of reform and social welfare.

Two hundred and fifty people came to listen to Davidson's first talk on "The Problems Which the Nineteenth Century Hands Over, for Solution, to the Twentieth." By the third lecture, on education, more than five hundred heard him pronounce in his ringing voice:

48

There is money enough and talent enough in this city of New York to give a higher education to all the people if they would but demand it. . . .

Let us all hope that ere the twentieth century reaches its majority there will be in every city ward and in every country township a People's University. . . . So only will it be well with us and our country.[2]

From the audience, Julius Fein spoke up valiantly, voicing what must have been on the minds of many:

It is all very well to talk about education for the breadwinners; but how can people like us, who work nine or ten, and sometimes more, hours a day, who come home tired, who have no convenience there for study, few books, and no one to guide or instruct us, obtain any liberal education?

Davidson replied:

That is just the chief educational problem which the nineteenth century hands over to the twentieth. . . . If you will organize a club of people who . . . will work with all their might, I will devote one evening a week to it.[3]

The response was electrifying.[4] The young people crowded up to the lecturer. Dr. Jacob Blaustein, superintendent of the Educational Alliance, promptly offered a room for the future club. It was agreed to meet on Saturday evenings, beginning January 7, 1899, until the end of April, for what Davidson called "A Class in History and Sociology." Henderson's *Social Elements* was the basic text, but much outside study was assigned, including essays all carefully corrected by the instructor.

Morris did not deign to attend. Why bother with an individualistic attack upon socialism? But, eventually, the thought of going to heckle the professor became irresistible, and he came. Instead of pique at the boy's arguments Davidson showed friendly interest. Cohen joined the class. One evening after the lesson, Davidson invited him to drop in to his bachelor quarters on East 17th Street. Morris hesitated, but one spring day, as he walked home from The City College, then at Lexington Avenue and 23rd Street, he met Davidson in Stuyvesant Square. Engrossed in conversation, he accompanied Davidson to his rooms, captivated by his conversation and solicitude. The unaccustomed warmth and affection melted the reserve with which Morris had shielded his vulnerable self. "Encouragement is the stimulant to the most incredible efforts," he had noted in his diary in his earlier days of discouragement. At last someone beside himself, an older person, believed in his potential.

All his life, Davidson had been seeking a way to create heaven on earth —first Rosminianism, then the Fellowship of the New Life, lastly education in a democracy; three different roads, but leading toward the same goal. "If we cannot make Heaven here," he once wrote to Morris Cohen, "I see no guarantee that we shall be able to make it anywhere."[5]

In his last letter to his friend William James, Davidson spoke with pride of what he sometimes referred to as his family. "My class on the 'East Side' is a great success and promises to be a greater. . . . It is my chief joy."[6] During his last year with his class he said, "I feel as if my whole life has been a preparation for this."

Two thousand feet up, on a partially cleared slope at the foot of the trail to Mt. Hurricane, lies Glenmore, swept by the westerly winds and looking out on the high peaks of the Adirondacks of upper New York State. There is an indescribable grandeur about the mountains so viewed, from Gothics, the nearest, scarred by landslides, through the whole jagged range. The air has an almost Alpine tang, but redolent of the spruce and balsam of the American forest wilderness.

Here in 1889 Davidson had bought a farm, and through his last summer, 1900, he maintained his Summer School of the Culture Sciences. Attracted to Glenmore were such figures as William James, William T. Harris, John Dewey, Wilmon Sheldon, Charles M. Bakewell, Percival Chubb, William Allan Neilson, Stephen S. Wise, and Hugo Münsterberg. Even the collie bore an eminent name, Dante.

Morris came to Glenmore with his belongings tied up in an old sheet. During the summers of 1899 and 1900 he was Davidson's guest, doing odd jobs for his keep. Davidson's weekly letters to his class at the Educational Alliance in New York refer to him, first on July 25, 1899, Morris' nineteenth birthday:

> Mr. Cohen seems to be very happy here. The life in the woods is new to him, and I think he enjoys it. He is learning Latin, reading Hume, felling trees and doing other work. He is looking strong and well.
>
> Miss [Mary] Ryshpan is here and seems very happy, and I may say the same of Mr. Cohen. They are both great favorites and I am delighted to have them. I am only sorry that my health does not permit me to do as much for them as I should wish.
>
> It is nearly midnight. . . . The light in Mr. Cohen's tent is out, and he is probably asleep. You see, he is celebrating the "feast of tabernacles" all the time. He is in the "wilderness" but I think the "promised land" is before him. He has done a great deal of solid work here, and Miss Ryshpan is following his example.

Mary Ryshpan used to dateline her letters from Glenmore "Paradise."
Mountain climbing was everybody's *grande passion*. Morris, like the others, took to the woods and mountains. Robert Neilson, genial older brother of the future president of Smith College, William Allan Neilson,

used to carry a small bottle with him on their climb and, pouring a wee drap of Scotch onto moisture squeezed out of a clump of damp moss, offer his companions near the summit sterilized refreshment.

Often in the evening Davidson turned over the pages of his memory and recited poetry. Davidson and William Allan Neilson, in the resonant Scottish tones native to each, recited Scottish poems and ballads before the open fire. Often the ladies blended their voices with Davidson's magnificent baritone to sing songs of Scotland. The "Laird o' Cock Pen" and "Wi' a Hundred Pipers an' A', an' A' " were among the favorites. Mary and her two singing sisters, Bertha and Sara, acquired a rich repertoire of Scottish songs, and Morris stored up poetry he would dip into for the rest of his life.

Morris Cohen had but recently bridged the cultures of the Old World and the New. Davidson, thoroughly at home in both, now showed him humanistic perspectives. At Glenmore in the summer of 1900 Davidson's students found themselves initiated simultaneously into Dante's *Inferno* and the Italian language. One of Morris' old friends, Louis I. Dublin, who became a leading medical statistician and vice president of the Metropolitan Life Insurance Company, says of these sessions:

> . . . Mr. Davidson set aside an hour every morning to read Dante's *Divine Comedy* with us. Each student was assigned a number of lines to translate and to comment upon. Not one of us knew Italian—but we had studied French and some Latin; and with dictionary and commentary, but principally with his guidance, we soon read with considerable ease. Before the summer was out, we had finished the thirty-four cantos of the "Inferno," and had absorbed a good bit of mediaeval history in the bargain.[7]

"Mr. Cohen has got into his tent today," wrote Davidson to his class on July 11, 1900. "I can see his light through the wet woods as he works away at Parmenides." The study of Plato, though the major, was not the sole, activity of that summer. Davidson reported further:

> There are eight members of the class here now, and they all seem to be enjoying themselves. They bathe, fell trees, make roads, climb mountains, and do everything that can contribute to health. They are all looking strong and robust. We shall have a bonfire tomorrow night.

On August 20 came Davidson's last letter to his class: "It seems probable that I shall have to undergo another operation, but then I hope to be well and keep well." And off he went to a Montreal hospital, in the care of one of his "boys." The sole manuscript that he took with him was his history of the class. It was never finished.

In his last letter to William James, dated May 14, 1900, he had written:

> Three operations in five months are no joke. . . . I am getting

well now. I need not tell you, my dear fellow, that I am deeply grieved at your condition. It seems more serious than mine, which is not threatening to life. . . . I don't for a moment think of leaving this blessed life. . . .[8]

On September 14, 1900, he died of cancer. They buried him at Glenmore. Morris went up. The trees had turned, and leaves were beginning to fall.

At Glenmore the presence of Davidson is still pervasive. Morris paid his respects, whenever he could, by an annual pilgrimage. In November 1902 he confided to his diary:

> When I visited the grave of Thomas Davidson at the end of the last summer I did feel very lonely—to think of that hill on which my tent used to be now deserted and the birch grove behind his cottage formerly so full of his spirit, now a grave yard. After all it is the quietness of it all that has the deepest effect on you—where there was life, now—nothing! Oh the power of silence! If only the language of silence were communicable!

On September 1905 he wrote Mary from Glenmore of "the great void that Davidson's death has left in my life. He was the first real friend that I had. . . ."

The last visit Cohen paid to Glenmore was in August 1941. He wrote to Mary from Lake Placid:

> Dearest,
>   . . . Paul and Helen Abelson came here and I went with them to visit Davidson's grave. It was a wonderful day and we saw everything in golden sunlight. . . .

Davidson and Morris, sixty and twenty, had developed an almost father-son relationship. In New York the older man would occasionally visit the younger and his family for the Friday-night Sabbath meal. On his last visit Davidson spoke of adopting Morris and sending him off to Germany for his doctorate in philosophy. He had done that years before for Arthur Amson, a brilliant Jewish boy whom he met in St. Louis and who died in Leipzig at twenty-two. But Davidson died before he could do anything about it. Morris wrote in his diary:

> *November 1, 1900*
>   I had never loved anything before I met my beloved teacher. He opened my heart and thus showed me the answer to the question which I had almost given up as hopeless—why live?

Sunday, December 2, 1900

When I first met my beloved teacher some time in the last half of April 1899, I thought that now surely I would be able to open a new page. . . . I did become inspired from the first time that I spoke with him privately at his home in 17th St.

In his diary, summer 1901, Morris calls 1899–1900 "the great year for opening up new fields, early history of institutions, philosophy of history, Assyriology, Biblical criticism, and Greek philosophy."

The year 1900–01 was not as fruitful, he notes in his journal, but:

> The things that I did were mostly in connection with the Davidson classes [taught by Cohen]. A little study of Greek History and litera-ture opening up to me certain periods and men whom I did not know before, e.g. Ionia, Timoleon, Pindar, Alcaeus, etc., and in connection with this a pretty careful study of the Agam[emnon] of Aeschuylus especially of the first 500 lines on which I prepared a syllabus of questions. In connection with this I got some pretty definite views of the ancient drama in contrast with the modern drama, having read three of Sophocles' plays (Philoctetus, Electra, Oedipus Tyrannus) and Aeschuylus' Trilogy, Prometheus, Seven against Thebes, and glanced through Persians; while on the other hand I read Shakespeare's Lear and parts of Hamlet. This was done in connection with the Greek History class and the Aeschuylus class. . . .
>
> In connection with the Philosophy Class I wrote on the tenth book of the Republic, 2° and 8° book of *Laws,* and a correspondence with Dr. [William T.] Harris on the 10th; also a pretty exhaustive general account of Aristotle's philosophy and a general account of his *Psy-chology,* particularly the first chapter. I read before the class a rather shallow account of how far Plato answers Arist[otle] in the Sophist and Parm[enides]. In connection with this however I reread part of the latter dialogue and rewrote part of it. But these studies have been rather scholarly than really philosophical.

Many years later, Cohen said:

Thomas Davidson had urged me to work in the field of history in order to temper my interest in the direct analysis of political, economic, and other social issues.[9]

Besides introducing Morris to Plato, Hume, Dante, and in the winter of 1899–1900 to Goethe and Faust, Davidson, who was one of the organizers of England's Aristotelian Society, had introduced him to Aristotle, and also to Kant.

On a scrap of paper Morris Cohen scribbled in 1909:

> When I first met Davidson I was a Junior in College, barely over
> 18 years of age. I had done a considerable amount of reading and
> my cocksureness 'about most questions of life was more than is usual
> even at that age. Needless to add I was very critical about other
> peoples views. I at once recognized in Davidson's philosophy and in
> his social and religious teachings—especially in his economics—views
> diametrically opposed to mine and, therefore, necessarily false. Ten
> years of study and life have not, I humbly confess, radically changed
> my views in that respect. Davidson's extreme individualism is still my
> favorite target. Yet my personal debt to Davidson is probably larger
> than that of any other member of our [Thomas Davidson] society.
>
> Davidson got a hold of me when my soul was parched and all its
> zest for life gone. Through his personal friendship he opened the wells
> of life within me, and caused living waters to flow forth. I stopped
> brooding about the injustice in the world, and went in, with all my
> might and main, into Davidson's work.
>
> The little Latin and less Greek which was all he directly taught me
> I have most honorably forgotten, but the remembrance of my personal
> relation with him is enough to bear me up for a lifetime.

The Breadwinners' College wasn't a college at all, in the conventional
sense of the word—no degrees, credits, fees, or teachers' salaries, and a
budget on a shoestring.

It came into existence immediately after Davidson's death, when Morris
and other loyal students resolved to carry on his experiment. Officially the
institution remained Branch B of New York City's Educational Alliance,
which was its sponsor and financial stand-by. Unofficially it was simply the
Davidson School of the T.D.S., the Thomas Davidson Society. The name
Breadwinners' College symbolized a pilot project in adult education that
did not end until New York City in 1917 officially offered wider facilities
of its own for similar cultural ends.

The truth is, wrote Cohen in a long-buried article for *The American Hebrew* of June 27, 1902:

> Our work just began with the death of Thomas Davidson. So long as he
> lived there was a stream of people coming and leaving the class who had noth-
> ing but a momentary interest in his remarkable personality. When Thomas
> Davidson died, the nucleus of those who had a permanent interest in his work
> alone remained. Since then our lists have been augmented by the addition of 40
> active members, and the average weekly attendance at our classes has risen
> from about 200 to about 600. . . .

Distinguished men, many of them friends or associates of Davidson— C. M. Bakewell, Percival Chubb, D. S. Muzzey, W. A. Neilson, W. T. Harris, John Dewey, John Lovejoy Elliot, Edwin R. A. Seligman, John Clark Murray, and John Graham Phelps Stokes—offered special courses or lectures. But, in the main, this was a do-it-yourself project for young people. The principle behind it was very simple: each person who benefits by educational opportunity pays for it by teaching others in turn.

The relationship between free higher education and democracy was clear to Davidson, who had stated:

What the breadwinners need is evening colleges and evening polytechneums. . . .

. . . the higher education of the breadwinners is . . . absolutely necessary not only for the well-being of the breadwinners themselves, but for the safety of our whole nation and its democratic institutions.[10]

The Davidson experiment, said William James, "ought to stand as a model and inspirer to similar attempts the world over."[11] An American form of the French *universités populaires,* the Breadwinners' College proved of value for those who taught as well as those who learned.

The pupil-teacher relationship is illustrated by this letter addressed in an immature hand to Morris Cohen, vacationing at Glenmore:

N.Y. Aug. 12, 1903

Dear Teacher and Advisor:—

I received your letter Monday night and read it before the club. The members were so enthusiastic about it that they put the letter on the chair and called it Mr. Cohen and asked questions about the book of Job.

Our social was held Sunday evening, we all enjoyed ourselves. Miss Rishpan our Geography teacher and Mr. [Robert] Robinson were present.

At our regular meetting we decided to buy the book of Job for the club and we decided to give fifty percent of each members dues every month to the Thomas Davidson Society.

Hoping that you enjoy yourself I stop writing and send you the best wishes from all the members, not forgetting myself.

Your pupil

LOUIS HELFAND

P.S. Don't forget to get strong and fat and write to us again.

Morris, as chairman of the executive committee, acted dictatorially and too much on his own initiative, said his close friend Eugene (John) Schoen, later a distinguished architect. Nevertheless, the experiment itself, according to the 1903 Annual Report of the Educational Alliance, "has proved successful beyond even the most optimistic expectations." In 1902–03, 783 persons registered for instructional work, 612 for communal work—a total of 1395 young people who benefited from Branch B.

By 1903–04, the elementary school was conducting ten courses, the high-school division thirteen—Latin, French, German, algebra, geometry, biology, physiology and hygiene, ancient history, modern history, etc.

The High School Department of Branch B was primarily a culture course intended to make the pupils broad-minded, able and willing to take an intelligent and active interest in the important questions of life. . . . The teachers all gave their services freely for the love of the work itself, and this enabled them to exercise a greater influence than the ordinary paid instructor. . . . No fees were charged, but everything was done to make it understood that the gift of free education was given as a trust which the persons benefited were to transmit to others: just as the teachers and workers themselves were doing in gratitude for what Thomas Davidson did for them. This altruistic spirit seems to pervade the school, and many of the former pupils of Branch B are now doing good work as teachers and in other activities conducted there. The present pupils have of their own accord organized themselves into a Thomas Davidson Students' League for the purpose of aiding the school both with funds and personal service.[12]

As for the college or "culture classes," they varied somewhat from year to year. In 1903–04, the offerings comprised the Book of Job Class, Philosophy Club, Philosophy Class, and Thomas Davidson Class. Cohen, besides teaching his special course—some years called "ancient," some years "universal" history, but always the philosophy of history—was coleader of the class in Job along with David Klein, future professor of English at The City College. Cohen was principal, too, and was paid $500 for the job in 1903–04. He was succeeded the following year by Simon Hirsdansky, later a principal in a New York City public school. Since Morris felt it his responsibility to substitute for all teachers who could not meet their classes, he came to teach almost every course in the curriculum.

All of the Davidsonians were working in the daytime; a few, like Morris, were also doing graduate work. Some managed besides what was called "neighborhood work." Through the tenements of the Lower East Side they circulated as unticketed social workers for the United Hebrew Charities. They interested underprivileged Jews in educational pursuits and helped them obtain employment.

The Davidson School organized numerous clubs for men and boys, women and girls, mixed groups, and children, and during the summer, children's Sunday outings, and a summer camp for weekends and holidays.

Morris had been an avid baseball fan ever since his brother Sam had initiated him into the mysteries of the great American game. On June 29, 1902, this letter came to

Mr. Morris R. Cohen:

You are respectfully requested by the members of the Thomas Davidson Junior Class No. II to act as umpire in a baseball contest between the Jr. No. I's and II's, to take place Saturday July 5 at 2 o'clock.

Kindly inform us of your acceptance and

Oblige

THE THOMAS DAVIDSON

JR. N. II

Society as well as the individuals involved benefited from the school. One immigrant boy, Samuel Shiffman, took his first lessons in English from Mary Ryshpan, a dedicated teacher. Not long afterward, the Educational Alliance put on his plays. Later still, Broadway audiences applauded the plays of Sam Shipman.

Rose Shore Greenstein, an immigrant and student at the Davidson School in the years 1909–13, found herself in a class of Morris Cohen's. After class one day, she shyly told her instructor, in Yiddish, of her longing to read literature in English. "Start with a novel that's familiar to you," replied Cohen. "You know Turgenev's *Smoke?* Good. Now go to the Rivington St. Library and ask the librarian, Sophie Udien, to give you *Smoke* in English translation. And Rösele," he added, "don't forget to come back and tell me what you think of the English version."

The English and the Americanization progressed. Not long after, Rose, a member of the Ladies' Waist Makers' Union, found herself on the picket line. It was bitter winter. When she got to her class, her fingers were too frozen to wield a pen. The professor noticed. The next day, his wife Mary came to the picket line with a bag full of baked potatoes, piping hot. "Here," she said to Rose and her comrades, "put these in your pockets and keep your hands there. When you're through picketing, you might find some other use for them."

Later, in a mood of discouragement, Rose again confided to Cohen, this time in English. "I can't do it. There are too many obstacles. I'd love to organize women in the labor movement. But first I ought to go to college. It's all too hard. I'll never be able to make it."

Morris Cohen answered, "But you are not alone. Who could do it alone? I, for example, I could never accomplish anything without my wife." Rose persisted and went on to Brookwood Labor College. Eventually, she taught labor history at the Barnard Summer School for Women Workers in Industry. "Just another case, one of many," she told me, "of a person who was helped by Morris Cohen, by a leader who at the right moment steered us."

Davidson had started a chain reaction. Many dedicated members of the

Thomas Davidson Society never knew Davidson personally but were students of his original students. Davidson was convinced that there is a divine spark capable of being kindled into a bright flame in every human soul. His faith in Cohen and his fellow Davidsonians brought out the best in them.

Is there a rational basis for morality, Morris inquired in an undated letter to Davidson (probably drafted between February 1900, when Davidson, at Morris' request, started a class in the history of philosophy, and early July, when Morris rejoined his teacher at Glenmore).

My beloved Teacher:

I write you this letter, first because I have had no opportunity to tell you the substance of it orally and secondly because I think I can express myself better on this subject on paper.

The question that has been bothering me very much of late has been the old question. What is the basis of morality? If there be a difference as you claim between socially desirable conduct and morality, then what is the reason for morality? It is all well to say "Noblesse oblige," but what is noblesse, and why should it oblige us to do even socially undesirable conduct? It is all well to speak of a certain thing as right or wrong, but on what is your scale based? These are the questions which through various causes have lately been forced on my consideration, and I must confess I have not yet been able to give myself any cheerful answer. I can well see a basis for socially desired conduct—namely prudence; but as for morality in the sense of "noblesse oblige," I must confess I have not yet been able to give myself a satisfactory reason. I talk a great deal with as many as I can about this and I find that those who have cast aside the idea of morality as the dictate of a god, have no other [illegible line]. I find few think the right is an end in itself. How could it be if it is open to the rational question—why be moral? The explanation that the moral man is the only one who is really happy, is not borne out by many of the facts of ordinary life. You rightly say that the man of low morality has a little narrow world. But he is satisfied and perfectly happy with it, and wants none of the larger world which from his point of view has little attraction. And are you sure. In fact our standard of higher and lower is quite arbitrary. You say *fullness of being*. But the fullness of being to someone else means something different than what it means for you. Then I am not at all satisfied about life being an end in itself. In my own short life, I have felt more than once that if the question of to be or not to be were presented to me, and were it not for the pain it would cause others, I for my own sake would prefer not to be. I don't mean that I ever actually thought of suicide, but that if it weren't for a certain grim determination to get as far as possible into the question of existence, and a certain blind faith more or less wavering that there is some kind of solution, I would see no reason for *being* at all; the less full the being the better. Perhaps such ideas come only with indigestion, but surely morality must be more than function of the circulation of the blood. If it isn't how can we claim to be in possession of any standard of morality. You spoke to the class in Hist. of Phil. of an objective truth. Is there an objective truth outside of man's individual opinions? Where is it?

This is Davidson's undated reply:

> . . . "What is the rational basis of morality?" Like you, I have never found an answer to that question in any book. I have, however, worked out one for myself. . . . I, as I know myself, am a permanent feeling, which, through experience, gradually differentiates itself into a world. . . . Now, my well-being . . . depends upon the extent and harmony of my world. But that extent and that harmony depend upon the satisfaction of the desires of all those other beings . . . which I recognize as entering into and affecting my world. Therefore I must love my neighbor as myself, since his well-being is my well-being. Thus the completest egoism and the completest altruism are identical, and rigorism is reconciled with Hedonism. But to love one's neighbor as oneself, when properly understood, is the substance of all morality. Hence morality rests upon a perfectly rational basis. . . .

> . . . I hope you will long continue to hold your own against all . . . authorities. . . . By being loyal to truth, you can be of infinite service to mankind. . . .[13]

Three months after Davidson's death, Morris wrote in a diary note:

Dec. 21, 1900

> Instead of letting the moral system grow out of myself I have adopted Mr. Davidson's theory and have been measuring myself in it, and yet have been continually revolting against it. . . .

The growth of Morris Cohen's enthusiasm for moral grandeur may be traced in his diary.

May 4 Wednesday 1898

> . . . I don't see any object for which I should live. The only thing approaching to something like it is a desire to become a benefactor of humanity, by preaching socialism and writing true books. But this is general, vague, and marked by an absence of true enthusiasm which make[s] others plunge into it heart and soul. To benefit others seems to

me to be a very creditable sentiment but I don't *feel* it. At least—I don't think I do, and looking over my character I cannot at present show one sign of generosity in all my past life.

Aug. 25, 1901

There is a thrill of bliss when you feel you have sacrificed yourself for others.

[Undated, in notebook with 1904 "Varia"]

Great *moral* deeds (or deeds *felt* as moral) produce in me an elevating effect unlike any other physical feeling—a state of elevation—holiness, freedom from the earthly material.

Thomas Davidson was a deeply religious man in his own unorthodox way. The ideal society he was seeking to establish on earth was a kind of ideal religious order. His letters to his class illustrate his spirit:

> When our little knot of men and women have fully established themselves in one city . . . they will send out bands of apostles to establish settlements in other cities, just as the mediaeval monasteries did. . . .[14]

> If you found a Breadwinners' College now, and make it a success, you may live to see a copy of it in every city ward and in every country village. . . . Think how full of interest and joy your lives would be if you felt that you had taken the first great step in the emancipation of the millions of toilers that now groan in ignorance! A little knot of earnest Jews has turned the world upside down before now. Why may not the same thing––nay, a far better thing—happen in your day, and among you? Have you forgotten the old promise made to Abraham, —"In thee and in thy seed shall all the families of the earth be blessed"? You can bring the promise to fulfillment if you will. A little heroism, a little self-sacrifice, and the thing is done.[15]

Before he was thirteen, Morris had skeptically renounced the devout faith in which he had been reared and remained an agnostic thereafter. Although Morris retained his opposition to supernaturalism of any kind and remained unswayed by Davidson's faith in immortality, he considered himself a member of the "little band of apostles," and was out to make converts.

A scrap of paper dated October 1900 contains the text of the remarks with which he rallied the nucleus of Davidsonians to start the Breadwinners' project:

> Our first duty, then, is to keep the central purpose of our institution definite in the minds of our members. We are to form a Breadwinners' Culture Institute, in other words, we are here to acquire and spread true culture. This does not consist simply in so-called "refined

manners" or mere learning. Inspired by the personality of our beloved Teacher we are here to become and to make apostles in the cause of truth and righteousness.

On October 26, 1901, in the auditorium of the Educational Alliance, he delivered a memorial address on his master in which he said:

The Church does aim to build up a high ideal in the soul of its members but . . . it is based on a supernatural view of the world. Our own little Society aims to combine the advantages of the College and the Church with that of the home. We form a school insofar as we help each other to master the world's wisdom and learning; a Church insofar as we encourage each other to join and to live up to the highest ideals and to stand by one another in the hour of spiritual need; and we form a home insofar as we try to cultivate among ourselves those deeper cordial relations which, unfortunately, are seldom found outside of the home.

And in a draft of a letter in 1904:

. . . Briefly stated [Davidson's aim in founding the class] is as follows: 1° The formation of a group of apostles who will spread love and righteousness, teach the new faith based on science and rational philosophy with the same ardor and enthusiasm and self-sacrifice which distinguished the apostles of Judaism, Christianity, Islam, etc. 2° The formation of a Breadwinners College where the people doing the world's manual work can get the culture which will make life worth living.

It may seem to you that these two are rather distinct but to me these two aims bear the same relation to each other as soul and body.

Five years later, for the tenth anniversary of the Thomas Davidson Society, Morris scribbled notes for his speech.

The first question that suggests itself is what was the aim of our founder and how far have [we] lived up [to] it in the ten years of our activity? . . .

1° First outwardly it was to found a Breadwinners' College or Culture Institute. . . .

2° Back of this however there was the second and more inner aim of founding a new ethical brotherhood, a society which will not only teach the higher life but also endeavor to live it. . . .

The second or intermediate aim which Davidson had in founding the work, viz. the creating of an ethical fellowship, our society professed to be its own. . . . Yet to describe the Davidson Society of today as an ethical fellowship would be more pretentious than truthful. Whatever it may have professed seven or eight years ago, and whatever some of us profess to this day—the fact is that the Davidson Society . . . is an association of teachers, interested in developing a school of a certain type viz. a Breadwinners' College. . . . What has the Society achieved? Helped to transform shirtmakers into teachers, physicians, biologists, [illegible] engineers . . . heads of settlements.

Better for workers

Better *for society* . . .

Yet as I look back upon the work of the past ten years I cannot help feeling that it has heightened the moral tone of its members.

. . . We have kept up our organization longer than most of our older and wiser friends expected, and what is more some of us *have kept the faith,* pure and undefiled. At any rate we have fought a good fight,— and whether you regard it as a victory or a defeat, I for one am inclined to repeat to my timid friends who could but *did* not help us the words of Henry IV [Henri IV] to Crillon: Hang yourself, Brave Crillon, we fought at Arques and you were not there.

Morris Cohen revered his teacher, but nonetheless he reserved his inalienable right to disagree. How passionately he did so is demonstrated in the two letters excerpted here:

New York
June 9, 1900

My beloved Teacher:

. . . And now as to your misunderstandings about the nature of the Student's League or "Marx Circle." . . .

In the fall of 1897, when I was not yet a socialist, but had by my bitter experience been driven to start real, earnest thinking on this difficult but irrepressible question, I helped to form a little society for the purpose of studying the question of socialism. . . .

. . . I owe a good deal of what is best in me to this society, and you know or ought to know that I hold the cause of truth far above that of any particular doctrine in religion, ethics, or sociology.

. . . You cannot neglect any one department of human knowledge and dream of being "cultured." Most of our members I think can be trusted to begin to solve the problem of socialism. . . . We have most of us seen enough of real life to start to think for ourselves. . . . I repeat, therefore, I cannot see any possible ground for anyone to become alarmed over an organization like the *Student's* Circle, and I beg of you most earnestly . . . that you will permit us to continue our meetings in the rooms of the Educational Alliance. Our circle met for some time in the Nurses' Settlement and you can enquire of Miss [Lillian] Wald whether in all the time that we met there, there was any objectionable feature connected with our meetings. . . . I, for one have a very poor opinion of the theoretical part of Marx's *Capital* and my first exercise for the present circle was to have been a refutation or criticism of Marx's theory of value. When we meet again, I will show it to you, so that you can convince yourself that I at least have never taken Marx or any other body as a source of revealed truth. . . .

And now, my most beloved teacher, with eyes full of tears I do most earnest beseech you not to let these sad misunderstandings mar the relations which have up to now existed between us, and, moreover, that you continue to trust that I am, most devotedly yours, for the cause of truth and righteousness,

MORRIS

N.Y. June 17, 1900

My beloved Teacher:

. . . The phrase *my beloved Teacher* occurs so regularly at the head of my letters that it may seem I am using it by dint of habit, but I want to assure you that every time I use the phrase, I do so with an increased meaning put into it. I have always looked upon the relation between teacher and pupil as a most sacred one, but since I have been fortunate enough to enjoy both ends of this relation at the same time, this short phrase has steadily grown in depth of meaning. Your last letter to me and the ovation which I received from the class last night have moved me to the depths of my nature, but they have also given me a profounder insight into that relation than I had ever before possessed.

. . . There is not an opinion, however dear to me, which I would not give up the very moment when any one showed me that it contradicted the truth. Most of my views which I call socialistic, I was forced to adopt after a good deal of painful thinking over books like John Rae's *"Contemporary Socialist,"* and I have never shut my eyes to the truth, even when it came from Marx, and even Hyndman. . . .

. . . The truth is, that the name "Marx circle" is a misnomer. We are not studying Marx as Marx at all. We are taking up present-day political economy, using Marx as a kind of central reading to be supplemented by books like Adam Smith, Roscher, Walker, Stammler, and others. Thus Marx's theory of value is taken up by Roth in connection with the theory as presented by the English school of political economy, and by myself in connection with modern psychological theories of value, and so on with every other topic. By this we do not hope to get at infallible conclusions, but merely to train ourselves to be able to observe modern economic phenomena

for ourselves & see how far they contain within themselves the adapt-
ability to reformed conditions, how far they must be modified and
how far they must be completely revolutionized. . . .

The fact that I call myself a socialist now, will no more influence
my conduct when I am shown that those principles are wrong, than
the fact that I called myself a member of a party [Socialist Labor
Party] influenced my conduct when it was shown to me that that
party was going wrong. It did not take me long to sever all connection with that party, & it could not take longer for me to cease to call
myself a socialist if anyone were to disprove my principles. . . .

I cannot agree with you that the formal sciences contribute little
to social culture. Of course the old formal syllogistic logic was not of
much value, though the study of Jevon's Logic was the first step
which led me to the study of philosophy. But the formal sciences, by
which I understand mathematics and the modern logic which studies
the principles and methods of the sciences, is at the very basis of social
culture, since the formal sciences train people to accurate thinking. . . .

I will let you know the exact date on which I leave the city. With
best regards from my parents I remain yours most devotedly for the
cause of truth and righteousness,

MORRIS

P.S. Give my sincere regards to Mrs. Ruutz-Rees. If she has anything
in the city which she would like me to bring up I would be glad to
do so.

Even after Davidson's death Cohen continued to criticize as well as pay
tribute to him, thereby wounding some devout Davidsonians. The pupil was
being faithful to the truth as he saw it, and to his teacher's own practice
and principles.

Cohen said of Davidson in his review of William Knight's *Memorials of
Thomas Davidson* for *The American Hebrew* (April 3, 1908):

Despite his prodigious erudition, he did not have the temperament that makes
for great creative scholarship. . . . But, after all, the world can spare many
volumes of scholarly research . . . but it cannot afford to lose the inspiration
which comes from contemplating the life of one who can defy its reigning
idols, such as wealth, power, position, etc., and heroically devote himself to living his own life. Davidson had his full share of human failings, but in any community like ours, with its sodden worship of outward success, the example of
his uncompromising readiness ever to speak and live the truth, regardless of all
external consequence, must ever be deemed a priceless possession.[16]

Like his teacher, Cohen not only taught philosophy, but he also tried to
live it. In his memorial address of 1901 on Davidson, he said:

[Davidson] realized that we do not truly know until our so-called knowledge is tested in real life, that life cannot be learned merely in the study without experience in the arena of life itself, that wisdom is not to be obtained from textbooks, but must be coined out of human experience in the flame of life. . .

He was convinced that the way to lift the people above their degrading and vicious lives was to give them an inspiring outlook on life. . . . Only by dispelling ignorance as to the vital questions of life can we hope to make the lives of men possessed of meaning and dignity.[17]

By contemplating the heroic model that Davidson set, Cohen grew to resemble him. In Cohen's words:

The life of Thomas Davidson was essentially a heroic life. . . . He had a generous faith in human nature, believing that there are heroes and heroines . . . to be found in every street and on every corner, and that it is only our own blindness that prevents us from appealing to the heroic in them.[18]

Davidson's use of the heroic method was based on his psychological postulate that every individual tries to live up to what is expected of him, from which he drew the conclusion that heroic achievements take place only when the apparently impossible is expected of one.[19]

He taught that the highest reverence is due to human reason; that the highest duty is to search for the truth with unbiased mind; and that the highest courage is to follow the truth always and everywhere, regardless of where it may lead us.[20]

To my mind the most fundamental characteristic of Thomas Davidson was that he lived philosophically on a truly large scale. He lived for the really great things of life. . . .[21]

In the year Morris Cohen died, 1947, the Davidsonians turned their annual reunion into a memorial meeting for him. Dr. Louis Roth ended his address with these lines by a retired schoolteacher, one of the Society's "younger group," Miss Freda Abramson.

To me, Morris Cohen was the incarnation of the "Thomas Davidson" spirit. He, more than anyone else, lived the life of the "Brotherhood of Man." All races, all creeds, all classes were equal; and he, Morris Cohen, was their friend and brother. No caste system for him. He looked down on no one, and so everybody looked up to him. All were welcome to his circle of listeners. No one too inferior or unimportant. "Come, all ye, who have the power to hear, and I will bring ye the message of brotherhood." That's what he seemed to say, to me, and I admired him for it. A great intellectual, a greater spiritual personality and the greatest of all the "Thomas Davidson" followers, teachers, and comrades.

No one could take the place of Thomas Davidson, when he went. No one can replace Morris Cohen, his disciple, now, that he is gone. May those of us who knew him, even slightly, try to follow in his footsteps, and carry forward, in the time left to us, the spiritual fellowship, he, Morris Cohen, lived so bravely.

This is the tribute, of the least important follower, of the Thomas Davidson spiritual leadership, to the most important incarnation of the same.

Rest in peace, Morris Cohen. We have all been better and happier for having known you or met you.

IV. *The Citadel of Harvard*

IN 1904 COHEN CAME TO CAMBRIDGE at twenty-four to storm the citadel of learning. He won his spurs in philosophy with his doctor's degree in 1906. "I came out with flying colors," he wrote to Mary from Cambridge. Where he had once studied philosophy at the feet of James and Royce, he would later teach it; and where he had sat in on lectures at the law school, he would lecture to its professors. The circle was completed in 1938–39.

Back in the days when Charles W. Eliot was an undergraduate, there were no Jews at Harvard. During his presidency, 1869–1909, their number swelled, according to *The American Hebrew,* from two or three to almost three hundred. President Eliot even expressed a wish to be succeeded by Louis D. Brandeis, Norman Hapgood wrote in *The Changing Years.* The Hebraic and the Puritan traditions seemed to Cohen to strike a chord of pre-established harmony; both were dedicated to intensity in self-improvement through knowledge, to introspective probing of relentless conscience, and to austere concern with otherworldly values. In the bleakness of New England's Age of Duty, which had chilled Santayana's Latin bones, Cohen felt a certain at-homeness. Were not the Puritans, like the Jews, the people of the Book?

In the comparatively cloistered atmosphere conducive to concentration, Cohen found philosophy taken both creatively and critically; here was a first-rate library, here were other bright young men of varied backgrounds and great teachers—William James, Josiah Royce, George Herbert Palmer, Hugo Münsterberg, Ralph Barton Perry, and Crawford Howell Toy, to name only a few.

Cohen did not go along with Royce's views on philosophic idealism and religion. But Josiah Royce, Socratic figure that he was, with his "indecent exposure of forehead," as James put it, his rigorous reasoning, his erudition, and his concentration on the largest issues, became the closest thing to a model Cohen the teacher ever adopted. James, with whom Cohen differed, often sharply, influenced him to view philosophy primarily as a vision with which men's lives could be brightened. Santayana, although on leave and not in residence in Cohen's time, soon exerted a philosophical fascination upon him. And Charles Peirce, not a Harvard teacher, but a Harvard man whose stimulation was felt on the banks of the Charles, left a marked impress on Cohen's philosophy.

Greatness was always to prove a magnet for Cohen, and living in the daily presence of the great constitutes the best school for greatness. The Harvard of Cohen's student days was blessed with masters who were scholars of distinction, men unafraid to air publicly their independent views, no matter how nonconformist. Here was no backward dwelling on past glories.

Harvard's English department was, of course, a stronghold of the literati, with its "Copey" and "Kitty"—Copeland and Kittredge to outsiders—Barrett Wendell, and Dean Briggs. And where but at the Harvard of 1903 would a geologist get out a dramatic romance in heroic verse, eight hundred pages of it? The bookshops of Harvard Square displayed and perhaps even sold the five-volume sets of *Elizabeth of England* by the famed "story taler," N. S. Shaler, professor of geology and dean of the Lawrence Scientific School. The members of the philosophy department, living in the shadow of Emerson, were also addicted to literature. "Philosophy will one day be taught by poets," he had predicted; already there were two of them in the department—Santayana and Münsterberg. Palmer, the Alford Professor of Natural Religion, Moral Philosophy, and Civil Polity, was best known for his translation of the *Odyssey,* and other literary works. Royce had come to philosophy via his earlier literary studies, and had even tried his hand at a novel of California life. He still taught a course in rhetoric for Harvard's English department. As for William James and his brother, Henry, one might say that of the two, the psychologist wrote like a novelist, whether or no the novelist wrote like a psychologist. An impressionable young man like Cohen could not spend two years in such an atmosphere without aspiring to write philosophy like literature.

This was Harvard's golden era in philosophy. A man had had to go to Germany for the most advanced training in the subject until America's "first well-rounded department of philosophy" was set up at Harvard. Vigorous representatives of conflicting viewpoints were initiating students into philosophy, not in the old way—via its history—but through problems in logic, metaphysics, ethics, or philosophy of religion. Under Palmer's guidance, the department had substituted a new system of original lectures for the old textbook-recitation method. So came into being a training ground for America's teachers of philosophy, at last independent of theology.

Philosophy under the elms was philosophy to Cohen's desire. President Eliot had said as early as 1869, in his Inaugural Address:

It is not the function of the teacher to settle philosophical and political controversies for the pupil, or even to recommend to him any one set of opinions as better than another. Exposition, not imposition of opinions is the professor's part.[1]

Cohen had already learned from Davidson this basic tenet of his teaching credo. "Teach, don't preach" was to be his formula. Harvard and Cohen were in tune.

And the Harvard professors practiced what they preached. "In our lectures," said Palmer, "we were accustomed to attack each other by name." The sting of "Copey's" criticism was proverbial. All this was invigorating air for the student iconoclast. If Cohen pushed the critical habit a little further than was customary, even at Harvard, and criticized the very teachers who taught criticalness, he was not merely following his own bent, he was also proving himself an apt pupil. James called Harvard that "nursery for independent and lonely thinkers."[2]

Cohen had been well prepared for Harvard. His bachelor of science degree at The City College in 1900 had given him a sound background, particularly in science, mathematics, logic, French, German, and history. Although his years there had been barren of any personal rapport with his teachers, at least according to his diary as an undergraduate, he had been brought out of his shell by Davidson's encouragement and warmth. The strenuous program of reading initiated by Davidson, followed by two years at the graduate school of Columbia University, 1902–04, had helped to orient him philosophically. Columbia had offered the finest of teachers— philosophy under Frederick J. E. Woodbridge and Wilmon Sheldon, ethics with Felix Adler, psychology with C. A. Strong, economics with Seager, sociology with Giddings. There were even summer courses in education and genetic psychology. But not until Harvard did Cohen find opportunity for singleness of philosophic purpose. At Columbia he had been doubly distracted, by teaching high-school mathematics for a living and by his more absorbing activities as principal and teacher at the Davidsonian Breadwinners' College.

The $750 fellowship that the New York Society for Ethical Culture, at Felix Adler's recommendation, awarded to Cohen to send him to Harvard in 1904–05, proved a momentous investment.

Cambridge fulfilled his need to be alone with his thoughts. "It is good to think of you in that typically New England peacefulness," Mary Ryshpan wrote wistfully. For her, watching the mails at home, love was paramount; for him philosophy came first. How symbolic seemed his new address, 29 Divinity Hall—"your divine home," as Mary put it. He plunged into a strenuous program, all the more strenuous for his not being sure he would be there another year. He took a first-semester course with James Haughton Woods in Descartes, Spinoza, and Leibniz. The real nut to crack, however, was a year's course with Royce in Kantian philosophy. Then there was a course in metaphysics with James and two "seminaries." The logic seminar with Royce was devoted to "The Logical Analysis of Fundamental Concepts and Their General Relations to Philosophical Problems." Cohen got a B in it. The ethics seminar with Palmer dealt with "Ethics of German Idealism." Here Cohen got an A. In addition, under Toy he took Semitic 13, the Hebrew religion and the philosophy and history of religion; under Woods a semester class in the science of religion. At the end of his first year he handed in a thesis on "The Nature of Goodness According to Kant."

In his second year, his sole course was a seminar with Münsterberg on the "Psychology of Truth, Beauty, and Morality." Psychology had been introduced into Harvard's division of philosophy by James, who brought over Germany's brilliant young professor of psychology, Hugo Münsterberg, Kaiser-like mustache and all. Under his direction the Harvard Psychological Laboratory was to become one of the first in the land. Cohen's duties were to assist Münsterberg as well as Royce for the $250 assistantship that he held in the department for 1905–06. But his dissertation on "Kant's Doctrine as to the Relation between Duty and Happiness" was his major enterprise for the year. Though the thesis was never published, his long-term interest in Kant found other expression in his more mature years. No name occurs more frequently in Cohen's works than Kant's.[3] Years later, he wrote to Richard McKeon of the University of Chicago that his interest in legal philosophy amounted to a concern with justice through law, stemming largely from his doctor's thesis on Kant's ethics. The Kantian tradition was in the air. An underlying ethical concern stamped Cohen and his Harvard teachers.

They, like him, were not orthodox believers. But they all had been early exposed to some form of religious faith. The philosophical culture of the time was still, in America, rooted in religion. Philosophy, like religion, sought answers to man's search for spiritual values.

Cohen's interest in religion, as in ethics, was reinforced at Harvard. His scientific study of comparative religion was aided more than has been recognized by C. H. Toy, who came from the Southern Baptist Theological Seminary to take on Harvard's third-oldest chair. Hancock Professor of Hebrew and Other Oriental Languages, Toy was the author of *Judaism and Christianity* among various learned works, and one of the editors of the *Jewish Encyclopedia*. He was famed for his broad, unprejudiced views.

Here was the leading university center for Semitic culture in the country—five professors, 40,000 books, and a Semitic Museum donated by Jacob H. Schiff. For his advanced students Toy originated Harvard's Semitic Conference, in which Cohen was vice president.

Cohen's interest in the messianic concept was aroused by examining comparative religion. He wrote to the great anthropologist Franz Boas, Columbia's first professor of anthropology:

Oct. 20, 1904

Prof. Franz Boas,
Dear Sir:

Could you kindly refer me to some books wherein I can find some material for an essay on the idea of a messiah or redeemer in folk-lore, especially among the American Indians? I am under the impression that the idea of a messiah (or person whose advent is to usher in a new and better age) is not peculiar to the Hebrews only, but I have not been able to get first hand authorities on this point.

Thanking you in advance for your kindness, I am

Very respectfully yours,
MORRIS R. COHEN

Cohen and Boas were to become friends. Five days after receiving his degree, young Dr. Cohen was to deliver a lecture at Green Acre on "The History of the Messianic Kingdom," with special reference to the American Indians among others.

But as of January 12, 1906, Morris is filling out a form for the Harvard Appointments Office. He lists Toy among the instructors with whom he has come into closest contact, along with James, Royce, Palmer, and young Dr. Woods. When it comes to the question of "church membership," Cohen, who has long ago left the synagogue, answers "Ethical Culture Society." Since his contact at Columbia with that movement's leader, Felix Adler, he has been a devotee. He has organized a Harvard Ethical Culture Society, of which he has become president; its aim, as described in a brochure, to promote interest in practical ethics so as to "influence University sentiment in the direction of the highest ideals in personal, political and social life."

Meetings were held at the Phillips Brooks House. The theme for 1904–05 was ethics in the professions, with Dr. Richard C. Cabot, a former student of Davidson's, speaking on medical ethics, Colonel Thomas Wentworth Higginson on ethics in literature, and so on. Royce lectured on race prejudices, and a discussion was scheduled on "The Ethics of Football, in the light of Pres. Eliot's criticism." Louis D. Brandeis, then practicing law in Boston, spoke on legal ethics. His address on "The Opportunity in the Law" (published in 1914 as the final chapter of *Business—A Profes-*

sion) sounded the keynote of his future career as a defender of the people vs. predatory Big Business. "The next generation," he prophesied—this was May 4, 1905—"must witness a continuing and ever-increasing contest between those who have and those who have not. . . . The great opportunity of the American Bar is and will be to stand again as it did in the past, ready to protect also the interests of the people." Morris Cohen listened and remembered. The jurist who was to become his friend was in a sense his teacher of the lesson that law could be used to help the little man partake in the economic blessings of democracy.

At the meetings throughout 1905–06, current affairs were hotly debated: the labor problem, the peace movement, railroad rate regulations, and municipal reform. Speakers included James, Perry, and Frank Taussig, the latter two being members of the Harvard Ethical Society's Advisory Committee, on which Dean Briggs also served. Cohen's grand coup was bringing President Eliot to address the society on December 5, 1905.

Cohen was still full of zeal for the education of the wage earner. With Dr. Frank Parsons of the Bureau of Economic Research he helped organize a Breadwinners' College in Boston. A letter to Cohen dated October 13, 1905, and signed "Respectfully yours, Frank Parsons" refers to the first meeting of the college faculty and its start at formulating "a system of instruction specially adapted to the peculiar circumstances and conditions affecting the work of this school." During both his Harvard years Cohen taught a boys' class at Boston Civic Service House. The unsophisticated letter below shows his relationship with his pupils.

Boston, Jan. 17, 1905

Mr. Cohen
Dear Sir;

I wish to say there are six or seven boys of the Civic Literary Club who want to continue to study with you the Social Elements [by Henderson]. . . .

In conclusion I wish to say that we desire to continue the study very much. We respectfully, request of you that you will not refuse to come. I therefore hope for your sake as well as ours, we shall continue our study in a way that will not only be instructive but enjoyable.

Your dear friend
EPHRAIM ALBERT
In the name of those who wish to continue.

But Cohen's education at the university reached beyond his efforts in philosophy, psychology, ethics, religion, and social welfare. For a born nibbler like him Harvard's intellectual riches proved irresistible. "I can resist anything but temptation," he used to say. The temptations housed in

Austin Hall were too much for him, for those were palmy days at Harvard Law School. He once confessed in a letter to Roscoe Pound, later dean of the Law School, that he had frequently cut lectures by James and Royce to take in a lesson in law by Dean Ames or Judge Jeremiah Smith. "The atmosphere of Austin Hall in those days was charged with vitality," Mr. Justice Frankfurter has reminisced. "Normally it was teaching by combat and a free-for-all. Quarter was neither given nor asked." "Classes are conducted in the Socratic method, at least the best of them are at the Harvard Law School. Anybody would chip in and break in." "Nothing pleased Dean Ames more than to have you disagree with him, or to have you make him re-think his thinking. He didn't want followers. He wanted thinkers, independent ones." ". . . the place was permeated by ethical presuppositions and assumptions and standards. . . . It was the quality of the feeling that dominated the place largely because of the dean, James Barr Ames."[4]

Small wonder that Morris wrote May on October 15, 1905:

> By the way, what would you think if one of these fine days I should begin the study of *law?* I am getting profoundly interested in the theoretical side of jurisprudence.

Cohen's roommate in 1905–06 was a third-year law student, also from The City College. When Felix Frankfurter was a famed professor at the Harvard Law School, he publicly evoked Cohen's early nips at the law during their year of companionship in 1707 Cambridge Street. Frankfurter used to talk law with him, in addition to nursing him through bouts of illness with a tenderness the ex-patient never forgot.

> I took my law [said Frankfurter in a speech] when Morris, as we say, took his philosophy . . . at all events when he disagreed with Royce and James and Palmer. In those days I had in the course of duty to review books on law, and they appeared . . . duly over my initials in the pages of the *Harvard Law Review*. I now rid myself of the incubus of preening with other people's feathers by telling you that Morris wrote those reviews. I didn't ask him to write them. I simply would put a law book in his hands and say "Morris, what do you think of that" and there are those reviews. . . .[5]

Here are Morris' early impressions, confided to his private journal not long after his arrival at Harvard. The strain of adjustment shows up in the form of his old theme, self-dissatisfaction. He had constantly to prove himself through performance.

Eve of Nov. 1, 1904

I have been a month at Harvard now and besides getting some little insight into Kant and just a few ideas on the primitive religious conceptions of Israel I have gained very little that I can see—in spite of the fact that I have been working nearly all the time and often very hard, indeed at the expense of sleep. True I had several outside things—the Annual Report to Alliance, letters (esp. notice of Book for Ginn)[6] and the first week was rather wasted. But what disappoints me is that I do not seem able to bring out any original ideas from myself. Thus in listening to Prof. James I feel that I ought to be able to annihilate his position logically. Yet the ideas do not seem to be forthcoming. Even on Kant my light is not so much from inner fusion as by dint of continual pouring in from Royce, Caird and Paulsen[7]—although of course these ideas *are* assimilated. . . .

One encouraging feature, however, is that when I begin to talk (where I can talk freely and authoritatively) I do not seem to lack the old fire. Last Saturday was my first philosophical argument with a fellow student at Harvard, and I came out with flying colors having scored a real point. So with Dole. I worked myself up to quite a pitch of eloquence on several religious issues. When however I came in presence of James and L. Morgan[8] my tongue lost its cunning. I seem to be drawing out more of myself in presence of equals and subordinates than I can in the presence of superiors.

How complex are the motives of life. I have seldom realized how really profoundly religious motives weigh with me. . . .

I do not get much out of hard dead study but I do out of general reading—yes desultory reading. Should I break myself into the habit of hard continuous study—or work out a method of my own which should suit my own temperament? The former promises great future gain, the latter immediate results.

Fortunately or no, he never achieved self-discipline enough to break himself of his habit of general reading. For the Harvard Appointments Office, in 1906, he was required to underscore the topics he had studied. He underlined twenty-five in all, ten of them twice as subjects he felt competent to teach—anthropology, astronomy, comparative literature, economics, English literature, government, ancient history, pedagogy, psychology, Semitic; and four more thrice underscored as his "specialties"—logic, mathematics, metaphysics, philosophy. This was no youthful boastfulness on the part of a twenty-five-year-old. There were thirty-nine more subjects listed. Of them he had studied geology at college, a year of Spanish, and, under Davidson, Latin and enough Italian to read Dante. But he did not check them.

Another diary note a month and a half later:

Dec. 17, 1904

Taking things easy—for the first time since serious work began here. . . .

Walk with A. M.[9] and exposition of my views of matter. How unreal matter becomes the moment we try to analyze it or state it in
any terms other than *this* brick, that house, etc.

How my thoughts seem to come out more easily and readily in
conversation (with the proper person only of course) than in writing!

. . . Have just read . . . a novel of Russian (Lithuanian) and
American life when I should have continued studying Kant's Critique
of Judgment. This has made me realize as I have realized but little on
previous occasions that after all I am a *Russian Jew*. The idealistic-
revolutionary being ever secondary to the emotional-longing—I know
not what it is—the Jew within me. Three peoples live on the East
Side—the orthodox Jews, the Russified Jews and the young American
Jews. Of these the last are the least attractive, having no high ideals.
The orthodox Jews are the heroes but they are dying. The Russian
Jews have formed the mass of the Socialist movement but it too is
losing its vitality. Zionism is a spark uniting—strangely enough all
the three.

A quarter of a century later, after Cohen's *Reason and Nature* came out,
an old fellow student from Harvard sent its author this letter, which aptly
supplements the diary notes. Ernest Northcroft Merrington, from Sydney,
Australia, later a Presbyterian minister, was a University scholar in the
days when he and Morris knew each other at Cambridge.

16 Dec., 1931

Dear Dr. Cohen,

I have just read the review of your book "Reason and Nature"
which has appeared in the London *Times* Literary Supplement, and
I have a strong impression that you and I were fellow-students at
Harvard in 1904–5. I would like to get in touch with you again. First
of all, let me congratulate you upon the publication of your book. It
appears to be a *magnum opus,* based on the tendencies at work in
your mind 25 years ago (and more), when you used to champion the
logical, mathematical and ethical interests against all forms of "tender
emotion" and idealism in its humanistic senses. I remember with
much delight some of your conversations with Prof. James after his
lecture-hours, and also some of your critical remarks about his views
and other things. I recall how my wife and I had you in for "tea"
one afternoon at Cambridge. . . . it so happened that my wife, not
knowing I was to bring a visitor with me had bacon for our meal!
Let me have a word from you *s'il vous plaît.*

I am the head of a large, in fact the largest University Residential
College in New Zealand or Australia, and am Acting-Professor of
Philosophy in the University of Otago, New Zealand. The only time

I have had word of you since leaving Harvard was when I was dining with the then Governor of Queensland, Sir Matthew Nathan (about 1921) and Dr. Hertz, the Chief Rabbi told me of your progress and welfare. . . .

I wish you a very happy New Year and hope to have a note from you.

Yours very truly,
E. N. MERRINGTON

The Cohen of Harvard days is brought to life in the memories of his old friend Dr. Leo Mayer, who graduated *summa cum laude* in 1905 and won his master's degree in 1906. They first met in the fall of 1904, as classmates in the philosophy course given by James and Royce. One day they were eating together at the Memorial Hall dining room. It was the time of the Russo-Japanese war. Cohen casually remarked that a particular Russian war vessel had been sunk.

"How do you remember a long, crazy name like that?" asked Mayer.

"That's nothing," Cohen replied, "I can name all the vessels of the Russian fleet," which he proceeded to do. "I can tell you the Japanese war vessels, too." This he did.

Mayer asked whether Cohen's feats of memory were confined to Russian and Japanese names.

"Oh, no," said he, "I can tell you the names of all the Senators if you want to hear them." He started with Maine and named all the rest of the senior and junior Senators. He volunteered to give Mayer the names of most of the members of the House of Representatives, but Mayer demurred.

Almost every afternoon after that they would take a long walk, frequently around Fresh Pond. Cohen soon adopted Mayer as his pupil, in fact, "he became the greatest teacher under whom I worked," Mayer says. "Until he got to know a person he was rather shy, but once he had adopted someone as a friend, he was most loyal and affectionate. I think he loved me dearly, as I certainly did him."

Mayer recalls Cohen's mischievous sense of humor: "He briefed me to ask Professor William James some searching questions, questions which I never would have thought out myself. They floored Professor James, whose knowledge of metaphysics was, in my opinion, far inferior to Morris Cohen's. I still remember the look of dismay on James' face when these tough philosophic conundrums were presented to him. He asked me 'Mayer, how do you think up such questions?' Morris was very fond of James and had great respect for his psychological knowledge but very little for his metaphysical views. For Royce, on the other hand, he had immense respect and at his instigation I made a thorough study of Royce's great work 'The World and the Individual.' "

William James had loomed up as an Olympian figure on Morris Cohen's early horizons. He noted in his diary for December 26, 1898, "I think much of the advice of Prof. James to will something unpleasant every day for an exercise." One of Cohen's first publications was a little essay inspired by James—"Gospel of Relaxation."[10] Just a couple of years later this same James became his best friend on the Harvard faculty, as well as a metaphysical wrestling partner. They were fellow Davidsonians, and this constituted a special link between them.

James's name used to crop up in the letters with Mary. "Morris," she wrote on May 3, 1905, "I wonder are you the fifth part of those 2½ big men Mr. James mentions in his article?"

In the following letters to his student, James demonstrates his characteristic considerateness and generosity.

Feb. 28 [1906]

My poor Cohen:—I am terribly sorry to hear that the "doctor" has had to have a finger in the pie of your present arrangements. You will end by making your way towards lighter work and better health—but the apprenticeship is hard. I dare say that the bank account also suffers—if at any time you need a hundred dollars, don't scruple to draw on yours truly. W. J.

Stanford University
Mar. 4/06

Dear Cohen,

I am ashamed to confess that it was only last night, in a vigilant hour in my lone bed, that it suddenly came across me that I had never once thought of those mid-year examinations in Phil 9, since I left home. As I forgot your address, and as a Cambridge check is the most convenient sort, I am enclosing this to my son Henry, both to address to you and to insert a check for $50.00 to your order. I guess at that as a normal remuneration for 50 books or less. But if you think it ought to be more, pray let me know. I don't want to "grind you down."

I hope that your health is much better again. I find this splendid climate disagreeing with me a good deal (wakefulness etc.) but doubt not that I shall worry it down.

Let me know how it goes with you.

I suppose that [Jared Sparks] Moore read the theses of my men—I am writing to Royce to find out.

Very truly yours,
WILLIAM JAMES

One wonders whether Cohen the young assistant was as gentlemanly in grading those bluebooks as James himself, who once noted on a student's exam, "C. It might have been higher had I been able to read it." At any rate, he had given Cohen an A in Phil 9, metaphysics.

James's sprightly charm, along with the personal interest he took in Cohen, meant much to the young man. A photograph of the bearded James hung in my parents' room when I was a little girl. My younger brother, Victor William, was named after him. We children were regaled with James stories, from Mother particularly. One she told was this: Before my father started teaching at Townsend Harris Hall in the fall of 1906, he thought to impress his pupils with his professorial dignity by growing a beard. (Discipline had been a problem in his elementary-school teaching.) By the time Mary and Morris returned from their summer's honeymoon trip to England and Scotland (in search of Davidson materials), he had a full-fledged beard that, although his hair was black, came out flaming red. He looked indeed so much older than his age that on shipboard an artist begged the young bride: "Could you persuade your *father* to pose for me for a head of Jesus Christ?" James's reaction was more pragmatic, as well as radical and empirical. He told Mary, "Do unto Morris what Delilah did unto Samson." She took the proper measures. When her husband met his classes that fall, he was clean-shaven.

As a born New Yorker, James had an intimate feeling for the city, so that when he needed the antidote for an overdose of gentility, he knew where to find it. The Lowell Lectures at Columbia University, delivered by James before over a thousand people, January 29–February 8, 1907, were in his own words "certainly the high tide of my existence, so far as *energizing* and being 'recognized' were concerned."[11] In the aftermath of the academic plaudits, he confided to Mary Cohen, "I must go down to the Bowery for a bath in humanity."

Did Cohen ever "annihilate logically" the philosophic position of his teacher as he had said in his journal he ought to be able to do? He paid tribute to James's "deep sympathy with common experience"[12] and his "gloriously fresh vision and amazingly daring honesty of expression."[13] But Cohen also took care to point out in all his philosophic appraisals that "absorption in the psychologic factor . . . made him obscure the distinction between the causes of belief and the evidence for the truth. . . ."[14]

Still, James exerted a positive philosophic influence on Cohen. James's lectures on pragmatism tell us that an underlying philosophy of life is held by everyone, even if the name of philosophy is unknown, or anathema, to him. Anyone acquainted with Cohen's philosophical views will recognize how often he stressed that all men make value judgments, whether avowed or not. Again, Cohen defined metaphysics as but the obstinate attempt to think clearly. This was James's definition of metaphysics. James's *The*

Will to Believe made a deep impression on Cohen. *The Will to Illusion,* a book he never lived to complete, but a subject on which he lectured, would have constituted Cohen's statement of a problem vividly posed by James.

Josiah Royce was another Harvard figure important to Cohen. As early as 1902 they had corresponded. At Cohen's invitation Royce lectured for the Davidsonians, and was made an honorary member of the Thomas Davidson Society. Here is one of my father's Royce stories that most pleased us Cohen children when we were ourselves *enfants terribles:*

Mrs. Royce one evening greeted her husband thus:

"Oh, Josiah, would you please see what you can do with your son? Christopher embarrassed me terribly this afternoon at Mrs. A's tea."

The father dutifully closeted himself with his eldest son. "What happened, Christopher?"

"Well, Mother took me to Mrs. A's tea, and I stood it as long as I could, really I did, Father, until I couldn't stand it any more, and then I said, 'Mother, take me home. Mrs. A is a fool, and her daughter is a damn fool.' "

"Christopher, did you call Mrs. A a fool and her daughter a damn fool?"

"Yes, Father."

"Well, I think you caught the distinction."[15]

Another Royce story that my father used to tell I appreciated more after I became a teacher. Professor Royce had been invited to speak at an educational conference. He listened patiently to the educators, then rose to his feet saying, "After hearing of your problems, I shall go back to my problems of the Infinite and the Absolute, feeling that here at least I am on solid ground."

Royce's *The World and the Individual,* Cohen said, is "as regards sustained mastery of technical metaphysics the nearest approach to a philosophic classic that America has yet produced." Its main thesis, "the reconciliation of the existence of the Absolute Self with the genuine individuality of our particular selves, is effected by means of . . . the modern mathematical concept of the infinite as a collection of which a part may be equal to the whole." According to Cohen, Royce's logic is presented as neither primarily concerned with the laws of thought nor even with methodology, but "after the manner of Peirce as the most general science of objective order." This proved to be Cohen's own approach to logic. Royce's realistic logic, Cohen concluded, "enables us to tread our way through an ever-changing world, by revealing the threads of identity which run through all changes and form the tracks along which science moves in exploring the abiding nature of things."[16]

Here again it sounds like Cohen. Peirce's influence on Royce's later work is well known. Cohen, however, had a double dose of Peirce, directly through the man's writings, indirectly through Peirce's effect on Cohen's masters—Royce, who frequently spoke of Peirce in class, and James. Dr. Leo Mayer recalls that while Cohen was at Harvard, he first expressed his admiration for Peirce.

The inside story of Cohen's promotion of Peirce has never been told. Cohen's "Charles S. Peirce and a Tentative Bibliography of his Published Writings" appeared in *The Journal of Philosophy* for 1916, two years after Peirce's death. He was the first to edit Peirce's scattered writings—*Chance, Love, and Logic: Essays of C. S. Peirce* was published in 1923 with an Introduction and a bibliography by Cohen, and a supplementary essay by John Dewey. The publishers offered Cohen $150 for it, and his friend Walter Lippmann advised him to accept the offer.

Royce, James, and Peirce were gone by 1923, when Morris Cohen brought out *Chance, Love, and Logic;* but his old Harvard professor George Herbert Palmer, then eighty-one, wrote to him:

> Dear Professor Cohen—
>
> Do not think I am unappreciative of your kindness that I have delayed so long to acknowledge it. The beautiful book reached me at Boxford just as I was closing that Summer retreat and returning to Cambridge. Now I am settled in this long library and can speak with friends.
>
> Peirce has never been a friend of mine. I thought James and Royce exaggerated his intellectual powers and were indulgent to his moral faults. I could never so sharply separate the two. One who made such a vicious mess of life is hardly likely to be a clear-sighted analyzer of it. But reading your excellent introduction I see that you are likely to reveal to me more merits than I had previously seen, and for that I can already thank you.
>
> What a craving James had for the abnormal! Lame ducks were his favorite fowl.
>
> Gratefully yours,
> G. H. PALMER

September 20, 1923

The book was a significant step in spreading knowledge of America's most original scientific philosopher, till then known only to the *cognoscenti*. The next step was for Harvard University, which had acquired the Peirce papers, to get out an eight-volume edition of the collected papers. Cohen's assistance with this difficult project was little known and unacknowledged. He helped the financing of the project. Harvard made plea after plea to him to raise supplementary funds; their fifth letter, which announced, "This will be the end of our begging," was followed by three more. Among those who responded generously to Cohen's solicitations were Dr. Corliss Lamont and Mrs. Thomas Lamont. Cohen recommended the project for financial backing to the American Council of Learned Societies. He collected some Peirce letters for the project, helped a bit in the preliminary selection of papers to be edited, answered occasional inquiries about editorial problems, and, I believe, read the manuscript in proof.

When the introductory volume of the Peirce papers came out, it contained no mention of Cohen. His review of the first two volumes for the 1932 *Nation* (later included in *The Faith of a Liberal*) expressed admiration for the editors' imaginative labor, thorough and patient intelligence.

Today, interest in Peirce is keen, abroad as well as here. *Chance, Love, and Logic,* re-edited not long ago in this country, was translated into Italian in 1956 by N. and M. Abbagnano. The foreign delegations to the 5th Interamerican Congress of Philosophy, held in Washington in 1957, were each presented by the American Philosophical Association with four classics in American philosophy. One of these was *Chance, Love, and Logic.* In the widened recognition of Peirce's importance—and there is a Peirce Society today—some of the credit is due to Cohen's initiative.

But all of this was in the future on June 27, 1906.

The great day had arrived. The leading university in America was awarding its Ph.D. to Morris Raphael Cohen. Mary, his bride of a fortnight, was at last in Cambridge. Between visits to her husband's friends, she found time to dash off a letter to her family at home.

> 1707 Cambridge St.
> Cambridge, Mass.
> [probably June 29, 1906]

Dear Hearts,

Well at last I can sit down calmly and write you. I have been going about here so much that I have had no chance to write you. . . .

Dearest Bertha, please get my "absence excused" money from the City Paymaster. . . . Please, dear. I hope that by this time you have already sent the $100.00 by special delivery which I wrote for, for Morris' degree. . . .

I have met Thomas Wentworth Higginson,[17] an old man in his 80's and I've also had a word with Professor Hugo Munsterberg, and Prof. Palmer. They are all most kindly disposed to and appreciative of Morris' powers. They are all three beautiful men. . . .

> Yours, full of love,
> MAY

A photograph of Cohen, smiling in his newly purchased academic robe, shows his new air of confidence. Abundant curls frame his impressive forehead. A chiseled face. The dimple in the chin stands out. The eyes behind their glasses seem to be looking out on dreams close enough now to capture.

Cohen's dream to teach philosophy at The City College took years to fulfill, despite the warmth of the Harvard recommendations. The first letters came from Professor Palmer:

He only needs to be known to claim attention in his own right, being a man of unusual power, charm, and scholarship who has already done remarkable work in Philosophy and Social Service. I warmly commend him to all persons of my acquaintance.

G. H. PALMER

Harvard University
May 29, 1906.

December 5, 1906

President Finley [John H. Finley of City College]:
Dear Sir:—

Dr. Morris R. Cohen writes me that he is an applicant for a position in Philosophy in your college. I want to recommend him as strongly as I possibly can. He is a man whom I should be glad to add to our Harvard Staff had we the money—a deep and wide scholar, a lucid expositor, one whom others quickly honor and follow, and a man of singularly beautiful, generous, and influential character. It is seldom that the apostolic traits are so combined with the scholarly. No one can be with him an hour without loving and learning. It must be an extraordinary man who could wisely be preferred to him as a teacher of Philosophy.

Very truly yours,

G. H. PALMER[18]

The letter of recommendation from James has not been found, but it was accompanied by this personal letter:

Dec. 14, 1906

Dear Cohen,

Glad to hear from you again. I enclose a bit of a recommendation and hope you'll get the philosophical place. I shall be at Columbia at Christmas time, but I can't address the Davidsonians. I've been having bad thoracic symptoms this fall, and have to spare myself in all possible ways, and talking to strange audiences causes an added amount of strain.

Count me *out,* hereafter. The time is past.

Things here go on without incident. Santayana is back, more amiable than ever, and I have just finisht with effort, a Lowell course on "Pragmatism," which if it ever gets publisht, will, I imagine, scuff some misunderstandings away. Truly yours,

WM. JAMES

Jan. 6, 1907

Morris R. Cohen, Ph.D.,

My dear Cohen:—

You are at liberty to make use of this letter as the expression of my hearty recommendation of you as a candidate for a position in the Department of Philosophy at the College of the City of New York.

I know you as an advanced graduate student, as a member of my Seminaries, as a leader in the organization of the Ethical Society at Harvard, as a writer of your thesis for the Harvard Ph.D. degree, and as a successful candidate for that degree. In all these capacities you have shown yourself a man of real power, of scholarship, of originality, of philosophical promise, and of sound attainments. You are sure to make a good teacher of the subject. You ought to get a good place in philosophy. I expect to see you make a decided success in our common profession.

Yours very truly
JOSIAH ROYCE.
Professor of History of Philosophy, Harvard.

May 10, 1908

Gentlemen:—

I beg to be allowed to recommend Dr. Morris R. Cohen for the philosophical position in the City College for which he is applying. Mr. Cohen was one of the strongest students of philosophy in our Harvard graduate course, and I remember with high satisfaction the excellent papers he wrote for my seminary. It is highly desirable that he returns to philosophical work and brings his unusual philosophical talents to full development. He is clear and suggestive in his teaching and a thorough scholar.

Very truly yours,
HUGO MUNSTERBERG.

May 11, 1908

To Whom it May Concern:

In behalf of the Division of Philosophy of Harvard University, I take great pleasure in testifying to the worth of Morris R. Cohen, who took his Doctor's Degree with us in the year 1906. He impressed all of his instructors here as a man of rare quality. He is a thorough scholar and a man of strong original mind. Furthermore, his strength of character and his public spirit qualify him peculiarly to occupy a position of influence. I think that all of my colleagues have entire confidence in Mr. Cohen's qualifications as a college teacher, and my personal respect for him is very great. I should be very happy to answer any inquiries concerning him.

Very truly yours,

RALPH BARTON PERRY,

Chairman of the Division of Philosophy.

Years later, City College's President John H. Finley wrote to his professor of philosophy, Morris R. Cohen, apropos of these and similar letters that had backed him, unsuccessfully, for an opening in philosophy, "You have fulfilled the promise of these great prophets."[19]

Cohen had been a student when Harvard built and, in 1905, dedicated America's first building exclusively for philosophy. Above the side portal of Emerson Hall was inscribed, "What is man that thou art mindful of him?" Cohen had jested, "Wouldn't those words be more appropriate over at Radcliffe?" In 1938, more than thirty years later, he was deeply proud to be called back to teach at this citadel of his old masters. He had retired from The City College at fifty-seven, and had been appointed visiting lecturer at Harvard for the fall semester. C. I. Lewis, chairman of the department of philosophy, sent him a letter of arrangements to which Cohen answered:

March 23, 1938

Dear Lewis:

You may announce my course on the Philosophy of Science as a middle group course. . . . I should prefer to give the Metaphysics course on Wednesdays from three to five. I should like also to be announced as available, apart from regular office hours, for consultation by appointment to students working in problems of social philosophy. I have found from experience that I can sometimes do more effective work in that way with advanced students.

With kind regards,

Faithfully yours,

MORRIS R. COHEN

The dean of the Law School, James M. Landis, then invited Cohen to lecture for them too.

June 13, 1938

Office of the Dean

Dear Professor Cohen:

I have just generally been talking with Felix [Frankfurter] and some others about your visit up here next year and I want very much for you to participate in the work here at the Law School, either by giving a seminar in Jurisprudence or participating in a seminar, giving some lectures, or in fact anything that suits your fancy. I hope very much that the idea will appeal to you and I know that whatever you decided to do, you would find one student in myself and also many others from the faculty, to say nothing about some of our prize students. I hope the idea appeals to you.

As for the work we conduct in Jurisprudence, Pound still gives his course—a regular third-year course—and Simpson gives a weekly seminar in Jurisprudence. I mention these to you merely to give some indication of what we are doing here and to reiterate my assurance that we would be delighted to have you aid and abet our efforts to try and treat the law in an intellectual manner, in whatever fashion that appeals to you. We will of course be glad to afford you every facility that is at our disposal.

With my best regards,

Sincerely yours,

J. M. LANDIS

Cohen replied:

June 22, 1938

Dear Mr. Landis:

I have been thinking over our conversation in regard to the possibilities of my doing some work at your Law School next semester. On reflection, I do not think it would be well for me to do much in Simpson's seminar. The latter is so closely organized as a parallel to Pound's lectures that I think my stray and heterodox views may be rather disturbing to the students. I think I can be of greater usefulness to you if you have a group of instructors or advanced students who already know enough so as not to be afraid of losing some of it as a result of any suggestion on my part.

As you probably know, my interest in legal thought centers largely on the things which lawyers generally take for granted but which deserve more critical reflection. Specifically, I am concerned with the relation of law to the other social sciences, such as ethics, politics and economics, as well as with the problem of the extent and limitations of what purports to be scientific method in legal studies. If a group of qualified people are interested in this field, we can meet from time to time rather informally and thresh out some of the crucial issues. That would interest me more than any formal course.

In regard to some public lectures for the general students of your Law School, I am hesitating as to the most appropriate subject matter. But as these lectures must necessarily be limited in number (because of my schedule in the Philosophy Department) I wonder whether it is necessary to decide the matter before the fall. I am, however, looking forward with keenly pleasurable anticipation to some work in the Harvard Law School.

With kind regards,

Faithfully yours,

MORRIS R. COHEN

In the fall he found himself at Cambridge. He liked to tell of a simple test to ascertain what class he was lecturing to. Upon entering, if he said "Good morning," and the students answered "Good morning, sir," he knew they were freshmen. If they answered "Good morning," they were sophomores. If they made no answer, they were upperclassmen. When he said "Good morning" and they wrote it down in their notebooks, they were graduate students. But if when he said "Good morning," his statement was challenged, "What's good about it?" they were City College students. He went to Harvard determined to goad even his graduate students into arguing with him. From all accounts, he met with success.

The lectures were a sellout. Early in the term an unofficial delegation from nearby Wellesley College waited on him. A grandniece of the professor's (now Mrs. Fred Whipple) appeared at Emerson with a small retinue. "Please, Uncle Morris, may we sit in?"

"You know how strict the rule is, Babbie," replied Uncle Morris, "no women here. However, I'm not a policeman. I can't be expected to throw you out."

Cohen's fifteen lectures in the philosophy of science I find outlined in his notes. The first was to be on the relation of science to common knowledge, the difference between common sense and science, the positive traits of science—free inquiry and skepticism, accuracy and measurement, universality and necessity, system. The subjects then ranged from the philosophy of mathematics, physics, biology, geology, and psychology to a series on the social sciences. These topics included, among others, scientific method in human history, and ethics—i.e. individual ethics, social ethics, and the possibilities of a science of ethics. The lecture on the theory of politics dealt with international law, war and peace, and "Is civilized warfare possible?" The lesson on philosophy of law was subdivided into the nature of law, law and logic, the fixed and the flux in law, and applications to the legal system in the United States. The final lecture on "The Practical and Intellectual Values of Science" was to analyze the science and knowledge of reality, and the practical versus the contemplative value of science.

Such would have been the course planned ideally by its instructor. But as between a syllabus and a class, Cohen was never one to throw the class out the window. The course turned out simplified, stripped of geology, politics, and law. It is possible to reconstruct, if not the sparkle of Phil 3a[1], at least some of its highlights, from student notes and memories.[20]

The class met in Emerson Hall on Tuesdays and Thursdays at eleven. The visiting professor questioned his class to elicit the points he wished to affirm. He asked how they would define science. Why isn't a telephone directory a scientific document? How is science to be distinguished from common sense, theology, and technology? Cohen emphasized the self-corrective method of science. A short paper was assigned on scientific method.[21]

The students were kept on their toes by what Roderick Firth, now a Harvard professor, calls "sharp and severe criticism of their remarks, all in the spirit of rough and ready, but friendly debate. Cohen liked to pull the props out from under students who were too self-assured."

Bringing in two of his special loves, ancient Greek science and the history of the University of Padua, Cohen says that the mathematical advances of the sixteenth century could not be applied to qualitative Aristotelian physics. The mechanistic theory first broke down when confronted by the second law of thermodynamics, to the effect that although no energy is lost, its availability can be lost. Modern physics attempts to reduce all phenomena to masses in time and space. The nature of mathematics is the subject of a second short paper now due. Cohen argues the absurdity of the view that pure mathematics is merely linguistic, or that it consists only of tautologies.

From his discussion of the mechanistic interpretation of nature, Cohen leads into probability. The word "proof" involves a demonstration that certain things are impossible. A law of nature, but not a statistical law, makes assertions as to impossibility. A statistical fact does not apply to individual facts. The term "probability" has no meaning applied to a single fact. An event is a member of a class, and science deals with classes. A gambler's fallacy is to conclude after a penny has fallen heads five times that on the sixth throw it will fall tails. All reasoning from samples is however subject to the fallacy of selection. The sample must be fair. Firth describes the way Cohen dramatized the point:

In talking about probability, for example, he asked something like this: "Suppose I tossed a penny and it came down heads fifty times in a row. How great is the probability that it will come down tails on the fifty-first throw?" The "experts" almost tumbled over one another in their eagerness to insist that the probability would be exactly one-half. But after listening for a moment or two Cohen said, "You're all wrong. The probability is that the coin will come down heads again, because there's probably something wrong with the coin."

There followed sessions on biology, the psychologic sciences, history as related to physics, scientific method in the social sciences, ethics, psychical and physical causation. Throughout, Cohen hit at various idols of the era— social psychology, the cult of Darwin's evolutionism, Freudian scientific pretensions, and logical positivism. Freud's theory of dreams, stated Cohen, is based on the unproven assumption that all people in the transitional zone between mental activity and inactivity will have the same symbols for the same things. As for the so-called unconscious, thought is an event. There is no reason to suppose that thought has some kind of continuous existence. When we think, we think, when we don't, we don't. At a time when many of the keenest students were swayed by logical positivism, Cohen attacked it. The positivists claim the mind creates laws, then say the mind does not exist; they assume an ontology, but don't like to examine it and so deny it. Carnap's logical syntax is an ambiguity, he uses language for two things, one of which isn't language—when objects cease to be symbols referring to something, they cease to be language, for words without meaning are merely marks.

In the last lecture on "The Philosophical Implications of Science," Cohen calls the modern distinction between philosophic and scientific truth a malicious means whereby each camp avoids the arguments of the other. Münsterberg, he claims, saw eternal verities beyond empirical phenomena. Royce was somewhat more friendly to science as instrumental in building up external truths, but the latter are less clear in his system than the empirical facts. Positivism regards all metaphysics and all laws as fictional. Hume's approach was that we have sensations and the rest is fiction. Comte and Mach restrict the universe to phenomena. But logic and mathematics deal with the subject matter of all possible worlds. Science is concerned not with phenomena but with knowledge about the world. The term paper for the course was on "The Nature of Science and the Conditions of Its Progress."

Philosophy 9c[1], the old metaphysics course that Cohen had once taken with James, required, besides a term paper, three short papers—on transcendental aesthetics, the causal relation, and Kant on God.

In the Wednesday-afternoon metaphysics sessions in Emerson H, F. H. Bradley's metaphysics was treated respectfully. Cohen both recommended and criticized Strong's *Why the Mind Has a Body*. Monism in metaphysics was attacked. If everything is x, nothing is explained. The students heard from their professor a searching discussion of the principle of polarity, which plays so crucial a part in his philosophy. Every line must be in two directions, every point at the intersection of two lines. All processes must have their reverse if the universe is stable. Force has its counterforce. Where there is life and metabolism, there is death. Evolution brings on dissolution. History shows that civilizations prosper and then decay. Cohen's imprecision, in published writings on polarity, as to whether he meant it as a logical principle or an ontological law has been regretted in an article on the subject by his former student Daniel J. Bronstein.[22] To his Harvard graduate students, however, Cohen explained: "The principle of polarity as exhibited in cosmology and epistemology is not merely a logical principle, but an ontological principle."

Here again, Cohen ran the course in a very dictatorial way. Firth says he cut off questions that were badly phrased or otherwise unclear, saying, "That's enough, you've already contradicted yourself once!" Then he would call on someone else—"the challenge resulted in an unusual amount of classroom discussion."

Charles Leslie, now professor at the University of Northern Illinois, has confessed to me that he used to reserve his questions for after class—"then Cohen was gentle. He put in their place only those who thought they knew all the answers." Leslie was attracted by "the natural way that he mentioned, upon occasion, Christ. Cohen seemed in the tradition of James, never narrowly or technically professional."

Roderick Chisholm, professor at Brown, has written me that Cohen made a profound impression on him and on others:

> He gave us at once the impression of being just what a philosopher ought to be. This was partly due, of course, to his appearance and his personality and to the apparent universality of his knowledge (there was the story of the man who got into an argument with your father and referred him to an encyclopedia article on some esoteric topic, only to discover that your father had written the article). But the impression he made on us—most of us were in awe of him—was due primarily to his philosophical competence and good sense. This was a time at which various philosophical schools were trying to convert us—including those who spoke for the newly arrived doctrines of the Vienna Circle, which, unlike some of the other views, carried with them the prestige of science. Your father was taken in by none of this and had no difficulty in dealing with those who were. I think he helped some of us keep philosophically sane at the time; I know that he led me to see that mathematics and the sciences don't entail any easy positivism, and that the alternative to positivism is not necessarily obscurity. . . .

> I remember that, on one evening, your father invited a half dozen of us to his rooms, where we talked philosophy (I recall there was a bottle of red wine on the table). No one else had thought to do this— at least for the first year graduate students—and we appreciated his kindness.

Victor Lowe, Cohen's assistant, now professor at Hopkins, went to Cohen's house one evening at the end of the term to tell him it was time to draft the final examination. To the astonishment of his assistant, he dictated the whole exam in a few minutes.

A number of the graduate students who took or sat in on Cohen's courses at Harvard became well-known professors of philosophy throughout the United States and Canada.[23] They were hardly with him long enough to become "Cohen men." What he gave them was a method of critique, clarity, and intellectual courage.

Another of Cohen's students, Lyne Few, who sat in on everything Cohen taught, including his seminar on legal thought, was amused to see that Cohen treated the law-school professors "just like his undergraduates. When the time was up, I could never believe an hour had gone so fast. There was nobody like Cohen at Harvard in my day."

Cohen was supposed to return to Harvard for further teaching, but never did. On February 12, 1941, Ralph Barton Perry sent his old friend the following letter:

> Dear Morris,
> We were all deeply sorry to hear of your wife's illness. No public announcement has been made regarding any arrangements for you here next year, so that there will be nothing in the way of a formal commitment. I still hope that you may be able to be with us.
> Sincerely yours,
> RALPH BARTON PERRY

Cohen's Harvard ties were enduring. He gave the *Harvard Law Review* eight articles, more than he wrote for any other law journal. Many of his bright students from The City College went on to graduate scholarships at Harvard, in law as well as philosophy. His son Felix distinguished himself at Harvard with a doctorate in philosophy at the age of twenty-two, twenty-three years after his own. Much of Cohen's teaching and writing reflected directly or indirectly his Harvard associations. As a philosopher he was a credit to his old Harvard teachers. As a Harvard teacher himself, even though briefly, he had a hand in forming, in his turn, distinguished teachers of philosophy and jurists. Cohen was a Harvard Man.

V. *City College*

UP ON ST. NICHOLAS HEIGHTS, New York City built from its gray native rock a great array of Tudor Gothic buildings as new housing for its college. In the fall of 1906, Townsend Harris Hall moved uptown from the old red-brick Dutch Gothic building at Lexington Avenue and 23rd Street, and the next year, the rest of The College of the City of New York followed.

From 1906 to 1912, while his Harvard doctorate in philosophy burned a hole in his pocket, Cohen taught mathematics at his old pre-Harvard job at Townsend Harris, City College's preparatory school. He waited, impatient to get into the game he knew was his.

An unexpected opening appeared in 1908 with the accidental death of the College's professor of philosophy, J. L. McNulty. What happened then within the board of trustees may be inferred from this letter, which one of its members, Benno Lewinson, '73, sent Cohen years later.

August 24, 1926

. . . When McNulty died I was so impressed with the recommendation and certificates which you submitted with your application to succeed him, and thoroughly mindful that you were one of our own as a C.C.N.Y. Alumnus, that I undertook to have the Board of Trustees select you. In this effort I was backed by Mulqueen ['80] (now General Sessions Judge) and Byrne (now Regent). We made a very earnest fight for you.[1]

Where and why we were unsuccessful is a most remarkable story of college (shall I call it?) politics. I do not care to write it out, for reasons that you will find obvious when I tell them to you. Also I shall make it clear that the fight which I made for you cost the failure of *my* reappointment *as Trustee*. . . .

91

Cohen kept on trying at other colleges also, but his efforts to get placed in philosophy became a long-drawn-out purgatory. For the fall of 1911, he was sounded out about a provisional appointment to the College's department of philosophy. He turned it down in a proud letter to Harry A. Overstreet, chairman of the department.

August 3rd, 1911

My dear Professor Overstreet:

In accordance with your request of June 21st, I have looked into the question of a suitable textbook for the classes in logic, and I enclose my recommendation. To prevent misunderstandings, however, I am constrained to add that I have not changed my determination to resist any assignment to your department so long as you continue to have any serious doubts as to my fitness for a permanent position in your department. I ought to add, in justice to myself, that I have no reason to fear that my work in philosophy will be less satisfactory than my work in mathematics has been; and I would gladly comply with your suggestion for a trial, except that such a compliance on my part seems to me unjust to my own record as a teacher, unjust to Prof. Sim who has been kind enough to express complete satisfaction with my work, and unjust to the men like Palmer, James and others who took the trouble to recommend me in such generous terms. Moreover my admission that a trial is necessary might be construed as an admission that the treatment I have received in the matter of my application for a transfer has been altogether fair—an admission which you can see from the letter to President Finley herewith enclosed, I am not ready to make.

Some time after our last interview I saw President Finley and he told me that the relative status of Dr. Turner and myself was not definitely settled. As my plans for next year are no longer pressing, I told him that I did not mind waiting till September to have the matter finally determined.

Dr. Turner is, as you know, my junior in the department of mathematics. He received his Ph.D. a few years later than I did, and I believe his application for a transfer was made subsequent to mine. The granting of his application and the rejection of mine would, of course, mean not only that my relative claims had been carefully considered and found wanting, but also that I had been found possessed of such serious defects as to warrant somebody being passed over my head. After such conviction there could, of course, be no use of any further trial. Moreover, apart from my own humiliation there could be no gain to the College in taking me away from a department where my work is satisfactory and putting me in a department the head of which has serious doubts as to my fitness.

I hope you will not construe any of the above remarks as in any way inconsistent with the highest respect for yourself on my part. I have no claims against you except that you take or leave me. Should there, however, be any attempt to force me into your department against my will and under humiliating circumstances, I shall not hesitate to protest against such conduct as a most unfair abuse of power.

My application has now been before you for some eight or nine months. During this period you have had a good deal of opportunity to find out my personal failings as well as any qualifications which I may have. I am not willing to let this application run indefinitely but want to withdraw it in September. You, therefore, will have to decide whether you want to endorse my application or not. Should you adopt the former alternative, I for one cannot see how the College can lose thereby; if you adopt the second alternative I shall always be deeply grateful to you for terminating a situation which has been more painful to me than I can readily indicate.

I trust that you are enjoying a pleasant vacation, and hope that you will return in better health than when you left us.

Sincerely yours,

MORRIS R. COHEN

Mary feared that her husband's letter to Finley would lose him even his humble post at Townsend Harris Hall. "No," said Morris, "I couldn't be dismissed unless the letter were shown to the Board, and it's too scathingly true to be shown." The gamble worked. Overstreet finally prevailed on Finley to agree to Cohen's terms. Overstreet sent me his recollection of the interview he granted to Cohen.

I had just come to take over the Department of Philosophy in the City College and I found among my letters a request from Morris to be transferred from the Department of Mathematics in Townsend Harris to my department. To take on a mathematician did not seem to make much sense to me, but I set an appointment hour and prepared to meet the applicant.

He came; I listened; and was conquered! And then it suddenly flashed on me: *This was Spinoza sitting in front of me! I was to have Spinoza in my department!*

We had a wonderful time in that first talk. The Spinoza impression never left me. He ground no lenses, but he ground out beautifully clear ideas.

Now, in 1912, the College was finally offering Cohen his opportunity, on his own terms. Would he act the good soldier, ready to teach whatever classes might be handed down? Instead, he seized the initiative himself by persuading his future chief to introduce two new courses of his own. The board of trustees, meeting on March 19, 1912, recorded in their minutes the addition of a new legal-philosophy course and, to start immediately in the fall as an elective for upperclassmen, a course in the philosophy of science. In 1916 Cohen introduced a third new course, the philosophy of civilization.

When toward the end of World War I the upperclassmen were drafted, the College, to preserve the jobs of its professors, sent them to teach at Townsend Harris Hall High School. Cohen was assigned to teach elementary algebra. The boys were thirteen, the sections large. At the end of the first week, Cohen announced to Dean Mario E. Cosenza that he would not report on the following Monday. If the president didn't like it, he would resign forthwith.

The president was Dr. Sidney Mezes, himself a philosopher. He did not fire his insubordinate young assistant professor.

These days at the close of World War I were difficult ones for Cohen. To his fright he found himself sinking deeper and deeper into debt. A later communication between two of his devoted friends shows the help he received at this critical juncture. The reminiscence is contained in a letter of Jacob Billikopf to Arthur S. Meyer, "as you are so close to Morris, perhaps his closest friend."

> Labor Standards Association
> 805 Bankers Securities Bldg.
> Philadelphia, Pennsylvania
> April 29, 1942

Dear Arthur,

. . . I wonder, dear Arthur, whether I ever related to you the following incident—which floated thru my mind during the early hours this morning, and which incident I had almost forgotten.

It was in 1917 or 1918 when Louis Dublin came to see me about Morris, of whom I had heard only by reputation; Morris' health was precarious, three small children in the family, and he had a very difficult time to make both ends meet on the salary of an assistant (either $1800 or $2000 per year). Morris was desperately in need of a prolonged rest to build up physically and every other way. Wouldn't I undertake to raise a fund to enable Morris to stay away from the College for at least a year.

Cheerfully I undertook the mission. When the late Justice Holmes heard that the fund was to be raised, he sent word—I forget now thru whom—that he would gladly contribute $500. I recall his reference to Morris as another Spinoza—it was "our duty to restore him to health and enable him to carry on his great intellectual activities." I asked my informant to advise Justice Holmes that I would not accept $500, that $25 would be sufficient for my purposes. I knew I could dramatize a contribution from Justice Holmes, no matter how small. If my memory serves me correctly, I did raise either $5000 or $6000.

A very interesting bi-product connected with my effort was this: When the then President of the College (it may have been Dr. Mezes) heard to what extent men like Holmes and others were interested in Morris and what they thought of him, his prestige went up at least one hundred percent; and when Morris returned to the College, he was made a full Professor at a salary of about $4000 per year. . . .

> As ever,
> Affectionately yours,
> BILLIE
> *Jacob Billikopf*

Cohen became an institution on St. Nicholas Terrace in his quarter of a century as a teacher of philosophy there. To the philosophy of science, of law, and of civilization,[2] he added another specialty, a course entitled "Logic and Scientific Method." He also gave more orthodox courses in logic, advanced logic, metaphysics, ethics, history of philosophy (one term ancient and medieval, the second term modern), and problems of philosophy. The College catalogue for 1920–21 lists, in a fairly small department, eight term courses by Cohen. During his leaves of absence, no one person could be found to take over his work. Two and once three men had to be hired in his place. He resembled a department more than a single man.

To some of his students, Cohen, with his sphinxlike smile, was a riddle. Cohen lectured to the college's political-science club in the depression of the thirties, claiming that "the difference between socialism and capitalism is in its essence largely verbal, symbolic, and a matter of bookkeeping." Arthur F. Smullyan said Cohen was "at his best when he had hostile students to contend with. They brought out that very incisive wit which still terrorizes me when I think back to my undergraduate days."[3]

The myth of Cohen as all brain with no heart sometimes went the rounds. If Cohen did not enjoy his own legend, he at least never bothered to take time out to scotch it. His severity had many causes, but it must be borne in mind that instruction at the College when Morris was an undergraduate had revolved around a rigid system of demerits and fortnightly merit rolls listing class place. The first president, Dr. Horace Webster, had ruled with a rod of iron. He and General Alexander S. Webb, who succeeded him, were both West Pointers, and their discipline was military. When young Cohen started teaching, he emulated in his own way the old strictness, and very different it was from his easy friendliness at the Thomas

Davidson School. Not until 1951 did the College admit women students to the day sessions of the College of Liberal Arts and Science. Had it been coeducational when Cohen taught, he would have mellowed sooner.

Cohen insisted on rigorous punctuality. Tardy students had to present official excuses, under whose necessity Cohen himself had smarted in the days when he was too poor to spend a nickel for carfare to hurry to class in the morning. One day a boy arrived at Cohen's classroom just as the bell finished ringing. "Go to the office and get a late excuse," ordered the professor. The student protested. "But I was already in as the hour struck. My right foot was in the door." "Go to the office and get a late excuse for your left foot," came the answer.

When I was six, the lavender and black track team used to practice long-distance running on Broadway, along the narrow parklike strip that adorned its center. From our apartment windows overlooking Broadway and 161st Street, I remember calling out to my brothers, "Look, look, there go Papa's boys!"

Long after his students left his classroom, Cohen's memory for their names used to astound them. Wherever he went, he was recognized and greeted by former students. But all this only confirmed what we children already realized. Cohen's career at the College becomes explicable solely in the light of that knowledge—these were "Papa's boys."

In his first year of teaching at the College, Cohen had in his one-semester logic course a freshman by the name of Herbert W. Schneider. Generations of Columbia graduate students since knew him as their own professor of philosophy. In his office at Philosophy Hall on Morningside Heights, Schneider told me how, after he transferred to Columbia and studied for a year under Dewey, the question arose whether he had satisfied the requirement in "Introduction to Philosophy." Schneider went to Professor John Coss and explained to him what he had studied. "I'd say you've had an introduction and a half!" Coss retorted.

Characteristically, in 1924, when Schneider was promoted at Columbia to assistant professor, Cohen sent a note of congratulations. "I hope you will take a large share of the credit for starting me off right with your logic course," Schneider said in his reply of April 26.

More than one of Cohen's students must have smarted at the memory of the wounds inflicted by their master's sharp tongue. But Richard B. Morris, chairman of the history department at the graduate school of Columbia, told me that "perhaps two percent of Cohen's students were rankled by his acerbity. For most of us, to be corrected by Socrates seemed neither a surprise nor a disgrace. He cracked down on the fakers. But to the responsive students he was encouraging and generous. He would seek out a talented student and converse with him as an intellectual equal." Cohen sent on to Roscoe Pound an undergraduate paper of Morris' on Pound's interpretation of colonial legal history, and later introduced him to Harold Laski. Cohen showed a draft of Morris' Columbia dissertation, *Studies in the History of American Law,* to Felix Frankfurter, and this began Morris' working relationship with Frankfurter in legal history.

There were further instances of Cohen's consideration for his students. Paul Weiss, now professor of philosophy at Yale and founder and editor of the *Review of Metaphysics,* writes that four or five men, including Henry Cohen, Morris' nephew, found themselves unable to read Spinoza or to know where to begin or how to understand the key terms. They told Cohen of their difficulty. He would help them during his lunch hour, he said, the only time he had free. "In between bites of a sandwich," Weiss related, "he explained, with great patience and sympathy, the crucial passages in the first book of the *Ethics.* . . . When one thinks how frail he was, how many demands there were on his time, one cannot but feel: 'there was a teacher.' As I look back, this incident seems to me to reveal his qualities as a teacher more than do those spectacular incisive sessions he had in class. . . ." Weiss was one of his many ex-students whom Cohen recommended for a Guggenheim or other grant.

Dr. Charles Hodes, head of the foreign-language department at the Bronx High School of Science, won the logic and Latin prizes in 1929. Just before he was graduated from The City College, he told Cohen that he could not take a graduate course because he had to support his mother. Later, Cohen came to him: "Here is $200," he said, "it might come in handy for graduate study." When Hodes brought the money back to repay the loan, Cohen refused it: "You and Helen have just been married. Young couples have all kinds of expenses. Why don't you wait awhile and pay me back later?"

A professor of philosophy recalls Cohen's kindness and helpfulness to him when as a student he was suspended from the College. Cohen talked with the troubled student's mother and helped him get into Washington Square College: "He was a model of what a philosopher should be."

Cohen used to lecture with the door open, while crowds stood in the corridor to catch his words. He often held his listeners spellbound with stories that illustrate what Samuel Schneider, a former student, who is now an educational official in New York, calls "the weight of a logical dilemma." One day, after a student insisted to Cohen that "a thing isn't real unless it can be touched, tasted, and worked with," Cohen told a tale of three business partners who went off on a holiday trip to Ireland. After a continual round of sinful revelry, they took a bracing walking trip as restorative.

At a bend in the road the devil suddenly appeared before them and said, "You three have had too good a time, and you're coming below with me right now." They told him he was a poor sport, the one thing the devil cannot bear to be called. So he made a wager with them. If he could not do what they asked him to, he would let them go. The Frenchman said, "See that lake? Well, turn it into Burgundy wine." The shimmering green of Killarney gleamed red in the sunlight! Suddenly, there was a flash of flame, a smell of brimstone and sulphur, and the Frenchman disappeared before their eyes.

The Irishman said, "See that mountain? Turn it into gold." The green and purple haze over the mountain turned gleaming yellow in the sunlight. Another flash of flame and smoke, and the Irishman disappeared.

The Jew scratched his head and thought and thought. He turned to the devil and whistled *Dixie*. "Sew a button on that," he said.

Schneider reports that Cohen trained students so they could argue and fight for a liberal view of democracy. He trained them to see many sides of a question as far as the facts would let them go, and to know when to suspend judgment and how to state a case honestly in the light of a paucity of facts. They learned that a theory and a fact are not the same and that no collection of facts constitutes a theory.

Cohen chose Santayana's *Life of Reason* as the basic text of the civilization course, and justified the selection in words noted by Schneider:

> Textbook writers usually write as if all truth flows from their pages in all its glory and infallibility. Santayana at least is a gentleman. He acts and writes as if you, his readers, also gentlemen, are as capable of considering, accepting, or rejecting the ideas considered as he. He assumes that if you are in doubt about his extravagant statements, and there will be many of them, you may meditate upon them; so much the better if you have learned to disagree. What more can a gifted writer hope for than to set his readers on paths of seeking truth, beauty, and justice, each in his own way, and in accordance with his own nature?

The journalist, Joseph P. Lash, says of his teacher:

> No one is more bewildered and injured than the overweening student who suddenly finds his glib generalizations, so easily worked off on other instructors, to be self-contradictory and meaningless when subjected here to logical analysis. . . . But though most of his students never perceive the justification of what they consider his tyranny, they glory in it next term when they see newcomers subjected to the same scathing bath of logical objections.[4]

What Cohen expected of his students he made painfully clear in a letter to one who didn't pass.

June 12/30

Dear ——,

Your examination paper in Legal Philosophy contained some beautiful thoughts very aptly expressed; and I appreciated them highly. Unfortunately, however, there was no objective evidence in it of your having taken the course in a way to get anything out of it. I mean that you did not *show* in it any specific knowledge of any of the things we took up. I thought that possibly you would show this in your thesis. But, alas! that is, as you yourself say, purely historical and not germane to the course in legal philosophy. I should therefore advise you to write something else—say an analysis or critique of Pound, or Cardozo, or Holmes, or else take some legal topic and try to treat it in the manner in which I indicated such topics should be treated if we are to arrive at general philosophic insight into the essence of law.

It is, as you know, too late for you to get your degree at this commencement, in any case. I therefore think it better for you to follow up your course in legal philosophy by writing an essay along the line I suggest.

Sincerely yours,
MORRIS R. COHEN

One of the fables about Cohen at the College is that he never gave A's to his students. He once flunked an entire class, in his early days. He later confessed to Victor Lowe, his assistant at Harvard in 1938–39, that he would not do it again under similar circumstances. A good number of his students through the years did, however, receive hard-won A's. I know of a student to whom he gave an A plus, Sam Klaus, who has since achieved distinction in the law, and Klaus's chief recollection of Cohen today is of his "kindliness."

Cohen used to say that he'd never seen a student cheat at an exam. One of his former students, by this time a professor at the College as well as a scholar of high standing, objected: "Come, come, Morris. Many was the classmate I helped through."

A favorite question of the professor's at the end of the term was "What did you learn in this course?" However, the final question, "What further question should have been asked? Answer it," soon became known as the seal of a Cohen exam. An ex-student, Harry N. Rosenfield, revealed to Cohen as his son-in-law years after: "From the first day of the term, I started working up a topic I figured you'd never ask, to outwit the prof at the exam." The professor grinned, that teasing Cheshire-cat grin of his. Rosenfield says, "If you were serious you couldn't come out of a class with Cohen the same man you went into it. The fire of his ideas and of his enthusiasm for the truth branded you for the rest of your life."

For Hirsch L. Silverman, now an educational psychologist at Yeshiva

University, Cohen wrote an Introduction for his book, as he had done for another student, the poet Alvin Bruch.

The general attitude toward Cohen at the College was of admiration not unmixed with awe. Year after year the students voted him the most brilliant professor. At the close of the 1926 commencement, when Cohen strode down the aisle of the Great Hall in academic gown and Harvard hood, his mortarboard slightly askew, the audience burst into spontaneous applause. They applauded no one else.

The greatest honor that the Student Council can confer upon student leaders at The City College is its Major Insignia. On May 6, 1936, it awarded the Major Insignia for extracurricular activities to a professor—Morris R. Cohen.

What went on behind the classroom scenes is another story. With the boys Cohen had fun, but extracurricular activities were not always fun. Teachers' rights in the early years, then student rights, had to be fought for. The welfare of the alumni had to be promoted wherever he could help, the scholarly prestige of the College enhanced, faculty ties strengthened. Throughout, Cohen exerted a leadership of ideas and principles.

He could give it, but he was thin-skinned about taking it. Why did he, a scholar and a philosopher, allow himself to be consumed by fiery issues to the detriment of his philosophic output? It was partly a question of his characteristic combination of conscience and guts, partly a matter of temperament, or temper, and emotions. Like Voltaire, Morris Cohen boiled at injustice. What he called liberalism must be upheld, he knew, at home as well as on paper. *A Dreamer's Journey* tells us:

> As one of the founding members of the American Association of University Professors, as Chairman of its City College section and as a member of the College's first committee "to report on ways and means to stimulate constructive scholarship among members of the staff," I was naturally subject to call whenever the right of teachers to freedom of thought or speech was attacked. . . . But such service was a small price to pay for one's own freedom—even when it involved long and arduous efforts in fields not my own as was the case when Bertrand Russell was kept from occupying my chair after my retirement. . . .
>
> During the twenties and thirties, however, student problems were a more fertile source of distraction. . . . When problems of student life came before our faculty for consideration, the responsibility for developing basic issues and essential facts often fell upon me. It was a responsibility I could not refuse.[5]

In 1917 Cohen reported on teaching hours in philosophy to Dean Carleton L. Brownson after a survey that he, Cohen, conducted among universities and colleges. In 1922, a year after he had been promoted to full professor, he reported on the practice of sabbatical leaves of absence throughout the country. As chairman of the Faculty Honors Committee in

1926, he helped develop and later direct the college honors program, instituted in 1931. He also worked toward improving faculty democracy, particularly within the departments.

But the real firing line was elsewhere. In the fore of the controversial issues that came to a head between the two wars was compulsory military training at the College, with subsequent alumni-faculty censorship of student publications. When, beginning in 1925, the students, led by Felix Cohen as editor of *The Campus,* fought against compulsory "mili sci" at the College, Morris Cohen defended their views against the administration and the majority of the faculty, to whom he circulated a brief in defense of the boys on December 8, 1925.

The Ephebic Oath, taken upon graduation by all C.C.N.Y. men since 1913, pledges "to fight for the ideals and sacred things, alone, and with many." The professor was demonstrating.

By the end of the 1926 spring term, the faculty reversed itself, accepting the recommendation of the faculty committee, on which Cohen himself had served. The course in dispute ceased to be compulsory in the fall of 1926. The Cohens had won their fight. As a youth keeping his diary, Morris already knew that: "Once we are determined we can accomplish anything."

But Felix Cohen, graduating *magna cum laude,* was blackballed from receiving his Phi Beta Kappa key, with the other boys on the academic honor roll likewise held back. The Gamma chapter, the country's eighteenth, dating back to 1867, was nearly torn apart in the struggle that ensued. A revision of the bylaws in 1928 resulted in victory for the campaign led by Morris Cohen.

The regime of President Frederick B. Robinson was the most troubled in the history of the College. As Cohen reported:

Censorship, picketing, demonstrations, interferences with College programs, suspensions of students, of papers, and of clubs, expulsions, and mass demonstrations against expulsions developed in cycles.[6]

In a private memorandum on Robinson that I have come upon among my father's papers, he declared: "No man is fit to be the head of an educational institution who cannot command the respect of the majority of his students." Robinson could not. Here was an administrator without respect for the student body. The professor rose to the challenge of defending "his boys." He incarnated the conscience of the College. At faculty meetings, he could have been called, like his friend Justice Holmes, "the Great Dissenter." His life became one wrangle after the other. One little incident illustrates the relationship. The president came to the registrar to ask him to arrange a schedule for Cohen with more teaching hours. After going through all the papers, the registrar found that it was not possible. "Let me try," proposed the president. The matter was far too complicated, and he had to give up. "Sorry," said the registrar.

Charles Upson Clark, a Fellow of the Royal Historical Society, eminent archeologist and classical and Romance scholar, states in a letter to me that Cohen spoke frequently at faculty meetings, and was always listened to with attention, "though not always with agreement. He was always for the underdog, especially if students were in question." Clark recalls the free-speech controversy that arose on the campus after President Robinson tried to stamp out the Young Communists. As director of the summer session, Clark gave them "complete liberty, to the disgust of the conservatives in the Faculty but I was convinced that they were mostly young idealists, protesting against the conditions surrounding the sons of poor Jewish immigrants . . . being an old-fashioned New England Yankee, accustomed to speak my mind, I did not care a damn. And I think Morris Cohen enjoyed it."

Although subject to despondency, Cohen was not one to give outward vent to such moods. Nevertheless, early in Robinson's presidency, which began in 1926, my father revealed to me one day the true state of his feelings. We were walking toward the College, its towers and turrets outlined against the sky. "Doesn't it look like a castle!" I exclaimed. "More like a prison to me," came the answer. We were both wrong. It was a fort, and he held it, until the danger was past.

Only Mary fully realized how much her husband took the situation to heart. Although there was no other position in the offing, he was wondering whether to resign, when she and her dear friend Mrs. Henry Auerbach put their heads together to think up something that would hearten him. Auerbach was active in the Associate Alumni. The idea spread to arrange a testimonial banquet. The committee, under the leadership of Max Grossman and others, brought off the affair with éclat. An oil portrait of Cohen, painted by Joseph Margulies, was presented to the College at the occasion.

The scene at the Hotel Astor on October 15, 1927, was Morris Cohen's greatest day of triumph. Felix Frankfurter, down from Harvard Law School, was the perfect chairman—deft, urbane, witty, and brief. Up on the dais were Cohen's parents, about to celebrate their sixtieth wedding anniversary. But this was really Mary Cohen's evening, as Frankfurter said. She sat between Frankfurter and Bertrand Russell in a white satin gown (courtesy of Mrs. Auerbach), with a corsage of orchids (from Max Schling, courtesy of Arthur Meyer).

Professor Harry Allen Overstreet, Chairman, Department of Philosophy, The City College, accepting Cohen's portrait, said: "Spinoza, Voltaire, Socrates, Jew and Greek all rolled up in one. And that is the great person you see in that picture."

And so it went. Comments by Bertrand Russell, John Dewey, Mr.

Justice Holmes, Felix Adler, Judah Magnes, first chancellor of the Hebrew University in Jerusalem, by the journalist Walter Lippmann, by Judge (not yet Mr. Justice) Cardozo, a cable from Einstein, and on and on. But with all that he had to preoccupy him, Cohen in his thoughtful manner brought his children a box of candy on his own big day.

His words of acknowledgment climaxed the evening.

> Most gratifying of all . . . is the fact that this tribute comes from students to a teacher who has at all times tried to tell them what he thought they ought to hear, rather than what he thought they would like to hear. This strengthens my faith in human nature and in the effort to teach the truth at a time when such faith needs strengthening. . . . I am profoundly convinced that there is no royal road up the rocky and dangerous steep of philosophy—not even for King Demos. Students must do the climbing themselves and suffer scratches or worse injuries in the process. The only help that a teacher can offer is to follow the Socratic method and convince his students that they must climb the Hill of Vision or else sink in the mire of conventional error. The best he can do to make the journey more easy is to relieve the students of needless traditional baggage. To convince young people of logical error, that the reasons for their opinions are not well founded, is not an easy nor, in the conventional sense, a pleasant occupation. It is much pleasanter to preach one's own convictions. But, if liberal civilization has any value, the logical manner in which we arrive at and hold our belief is of the utmost importance; and the philosophic teacher, as distinct from the preacher, must stress the supreme importance of weighing evidence and admitting our ignorance when we do not know. Without the critical spirit, doctrines readily become restraints rather than aids in the search for truth. The critical and scientific spirit can be trained in philosophy as it is trained in the special sciences. This, at any rate, has been the dominant idea so far as I have ideas as to the teaching of philosophy.[7]

Cohen, encouraged, returned to the fray. When I once asked him how he stood it, he answered in typical fashion, with a story. In the days when he'd been battling compulsory R.O.T.C. he was introduced at a faculty reception to the wife of the head of the unit. He told her he was glad to meet the wife of so gentlemanly an opponent. Her husband was tall, strong, and handsome. "She eyed me up and down," said my father. "Then she smiled. 'If you've been fighting with him, you must have been able to run faster.'

"No, Madame," he answered, "stand faster."

Through the crisis he served for years as impartial chairman of the six-man Faculty-Student Discipline Committee. Both sides respected him.

Sometimes he saved students from expulsion, sometimes there were other battles. His opposition to the president, who once applied the term "gutter-snipes" to a group of his students, was valiant and in the end successful. The spearhead against Robinson was Morris Cohen. At the professor's resignation on February 1, 1938, he knew that the president would soon follow suit. By the following fall, Acting President Nelson P. Mead was at the helm.

Another outlet for Cohen's energetic defense of the College welfare was his activity for the Gamma chapter of Phi Beta Kappa, where he served more than once as president. In the days of the red smear against the College, such endeavors were particularly telling.

The alumni also would turn to Cohen for guidance, for he maintained relations with a great many graduates, including those from before his time. In accordance with the will of Judge Samuel Greenbaum, his children, as executors, requested Cohen to choose $1,000 worth of books on legal philosophy or legal history for the College library, to be used specifically for Cohen's course in the philosophy of law. This was one of the ways in which he helped build up the library that now bears his name.

A few years later Cohen demonstrated his practical wisdom to James Balsam:

February 23, 1934

Dear Mr. Balsam:

It is very gratifying to learn that your class [1909] is raising about $1,000 for a gift to the college. I think the idea of doing something for the teaching staff of the college is an excellent one, for after all the life of a college depends upon the vitality of its teachers. I think, however, that any help should be directed more to the younger men than to the older ones, not only because the younger men need it more but because help in that direction can be more effective. Now one of the great difficulties of younger men on the teaching staff is their inability to get their papers published and so obtain their Doctor's degrees, which are necessary for promotion. I know as a matter of fact that difficulties of this sort have frequently discouraged young teachers, and in this way the college has lost excellent members of the teaching staff.

Obviously the future of the college depends upon its attracting and keeping young men of intellectual attainment and promise. For this reason I would suggest that your contribution take the form of a publication fund to help young teachers to publish scholarly contributions in their fields. I would suggest that you name some member of your class as a member of the board of trustees of such a fund.

I should be glad to consult with you in any further matters which you wish to bring up in this connection.

Cordially,

MORRIS R. COHEN

To enhance the standing of the College in the community of scholars, Cohen bent efforts not only to encourage individual research (he served for years on the faculty research committee), but also to help his institution serve as a center for joint projects of learning. In his first year there, The Conference on Legal and Social Philosophy, of which he was the chief instigator, held its initial meeting, April 25, 1913, at C.C.N.Y. When Einstein during his first visit to this country delivered in April a lecture on his new theories of relativity and quanta, in German, in Doremus Hall at The City College in 1921, Cohen reported the lecture for *The Campus*.

The Journal of the History of Ideas, since its first issue in January 1940, has been published at the College.[8] Cohen was one of its founders and served on the editorial board under Arthur O. Lovejoy, professor of philosophy at Johns Hopkins. From the beginning, the executive editor has been Philip P. Wiener, a gifted former student of Cohen's, now chairman of the philosophy department at the College. It was essential to the functioning of this interdisciplinary periodical that it unite scholars from different institutions as well as from different provinces of intellectual history. The Journal is a feather in the cap of the College, and in Cohen's cap as well.

We Won't Let Him stated the editorial headline in *The Campus* toward the end of 1937, when Cohen's forthcoming resignation was announced. At fifty-seven, he had served thirty-five years. The Student Council passed a resolution against it. Cohen's letter of resignation to his old boss speaks for itself.

December 9, 1937

Dear Professor Overstreet:—

In accordance with the plan of which I have already spoken to you, I intend to retire from the active service of the College at the end of the present academic term.

This, you will readily believe, is not an easy step for me to take; for it involves a wrench in the roots of my being. My connection with the College dates back to my boyhood days in 1895 when I entered its halls as a student straight from the elementary public schools, and realized even then that without its existence as a free institution the benefits of a college education and of all that is based on it would have been denied me. Since 1902 my life-work as a teacher has been centered at The City College, and I am tied to it not only by my devotion to the ideal of a free higher education to all who are prepared to receive it, but also by the bonds of personal affection for my students and colleagues. The responsiveness and the enthusiastic appreciation which my students have accorded me, despite my painfully conscious limitations as a teacher, have been one of the great supports of my life. The generous attitude of my colleagues has helped me to carry on when poor health and other circumstances tempted me to quit teaching and devote myself exclusively to philosophic study and writing. You, especially, have been great-hearted and high-minded in your patience with my frailties of temper. And I can never forget that but for you I might not ever had a chance to teach philosophy in my Alma Mater. You remember that even after I received my doctorate in philosophy at Harvard in 1906 and brought recommendations from James, Royce, Palmer, Perry, Felix Adler and William T. Harris, that President Finley characterized as the finest he ever read in his life, my application for a transfer from the department of mathematics to that of philosophy was ignored for six years and others were appointed instead. Indeed, you had some difficulty in finally effecting that transfer in 1912, and thus ending a period of frustration and painful humiliation to me. These are matters for which any verbal expression of gratitude must necessarily be inadequate.

While I am planning to retire from regular undergraduate teaching and to be away from New York City for a part of every year, I expect to be able to visit the College from time to time and I shall ever be happy to be of any service to you and to the department which enshrines one of the happiest chapters of my life.

With warm regards,

Ever gratefully yours,
MORRIS R. COHEN

Overstreet contributed this profile to *The Faculty Bulletin* of December 22, 1937:

But about the essential Cohen—the man inside! I have been in almost daily contact with him for the entire time of his service in the Department, and yet when I try to reduce him to a formula, to say what I have discovered in him, I find I am at a loss for words that will exactly turn the trick.

And yet it is not that Cohen is an enigma. The difficulty is that he is a phenomenon. If you listen to him expounding an idea—and he is generally doing that—you will be astonished at the ease with which he moves on intimate terms with the worthies and unworthies of all the ages. He brings forth their wisdom or their folly as familiarly as if he had just met them at breakfast. . . .

This, perhaps, is why he has been to us both an inspiration and a despair. We love him for his courage, his passion for the philosophic life, his deep and never faltering interest in his students, his wise counsel, his profound insight into the difficult problems of our time. . . . But when we think of what that one philosophic head can hold!

Cohen's colleague, the philosopher Y. Krikorian, wrote him:

> Something has gone from the life of the college which is irreplaceable. It was a great privilege for me to have associated with you for so many years. I shall never forget your stimulating and golden philosophic discussions. Rationally to disagree with you was a triumph and understandingly to agree was wisdom.

Most gratifying and moving to Cohen may well have been this tribute from his old adversary on the military-science issue. Major Holton handwrote the following note on his official letterhead:

The City College
Department of Military Science and Tactics
Convent Avenue and 139 Street

12/15/37

HERBERT HOLTON
ASSOC. PROF. HYGIENE
MILITARY PROPERTY CUSTODIAN

Dear Morris:

It was with profound regret that I read your determination to leave the college in today's *Campus*. While our philosophies of ultimate peace have been as far apart as the poles, I nevertheless confess that I always felt a truer sympathy from you than from many in my own camp. I shall miss your warm greeting and your keen appreciation of a fellow sufferer's burdens. Again regrets and good luck.

Sincerely,
HERBERT

A revealing communication came to Cohen from the dean under whom he had served. Carleton L. Brownson had himself quit the deanship with Robinson's ascendancy to power in 1926, though he retained his professorship of Greek. He was a gentleman, a scholar, and editor-translator of Xenophon.

Dec. 23, 1937

Dear Professor Cohen,

You told me a number of weeks ago that you intended to ask for retirement from February first, but I have been hoping that some decided improvement in your health or in conditions at the College might lead you to reconsider that intention. Now, however, I learn that you have taken final action in the matter, and I am very, very sorry. Not, of course, as your friend, but as a friend of the College. You have given it standing and distinction, and a great many people, both within and without, whose good will and good opinion have been precious, will lose interest in the place when you are no longer there. I realize fully, as I am sure most of your colleagues and friends do, that it is for the sake of the College and out of your love for it that you have held on for as long as you have held on, and they and I must needs be glad on your account that you are bringing to an end a service which has been hard and disagreeable for you in many ways. You have sacrificed enough already.

I don't know whether the College has been or in the near future will be worth any good man's sacrifices. The students, some of them, yes, but I can't be sure about the institution. A new administration will bring new hopes, but the effect of a decade of lowered standards and debased moral tone can't be done away, it seems to me, within any short period.

I still love the place and cling to the belief that some day or other it will renew itself. But the memories I really prize are of individuals, —fine, earnest students and able, straightforward colleagues. And one of the things I remember most pleasantly is our discussions in 219A, when we were always about three quarters agreed and very serious over the fourth quarter!

Yours sincerely,
CARLETON L. BROWNSON

Official honors were now heaped upon Cohen. He who had once defied an order to teach at Townsend Harris Hall was awarded a Townsend Harris Medal: "In you Alma Mater finds particular reason to rejoice." The Board of Higher Education, which Cohen had so often battled, New York City's Teachers' Retirement Board and the faculty passed resolutions of commendation. The Associate Alumni tendered a banquet.

Here is a student letter to Cohen, the kind a teacher cherishes:

Dec. 14, 1937

Professor Cohen:

I've been a student of yours, and I fear a very stupid one. However, I merely want to add my good wishes to those of greater personalities and keener intellects, for I know I express the thoughts of the thousands who came before me. . . . You gave to each of us that spark of knowledge of our deficiencies. . . . at least we once knew that the search for wisdom was not an axiom or a pipe-dream, but the only "way of life." . . .

Students of City College will never forget your withering cross-examinations—we loved them.

BERTRAM BUSCH ['39]

Cohen's answer stated that "No tribute which I have received means so much to me as the good will of recent students, and I am therefore very grateful indeed to you for writing to me as you did."

The Board of Higher Education, on January 18, 1938, made Cohen Emeritus Professor of Philosophy. He conducted a seminar in legal philosophy after his retirement, in February and March of 1939.

Unofficially, but none the less urgently, the students called on Cohen, as seen in an undated letter:

Morris R. Cohen Society
c/o Dr. P. P. Wiener
Faculty Advisor

Dear Professor Cohen,

We, a group of students at City College, interested in philosophy, have formed a Morris R. Cohen Society under the aegis of the Department of Philosophy. The choice of name arises from our feeling of kinship to the spirit and direction embodied in your work. . . .

We think it appropriate to ask that you open our program . . . with a lecture on some subject related to "the statistical view of nature." . . .

MURRAY HORWITZ, President ['40]

"If ever I were to teach at my Alma Mater," Morris had written as an adolescent, "Who would be my friend?" He had his answer.

At Cohen's retirement he did his best to honor his chair by having it entrusted to Bertrand Russell. This proved to be one fight that Cohen lost. After the Board of Higher Education on February 26, 1940, announced that Russell would teach mathematics and logic at the college for two years beginning in 1941, the New York State courts nullified the appointment. The whole procedure, with its lack of due process of law, constituted an affront to justice and a setback to the cause of public education, academic freedom, and the principle of tolerance. The story has been told by Cohen himself along with the other collaborators of *The Bertrand Russell Case,* edited by Dewey and Kallen in 1941. Cohen was also one of the sixteen educators who sponsored the American Civil Liberties booklet on the case, published the same year.[9] One little incident connected thereto Cohen told privately to his family, not without pride in the common man of his city. Cohen was registering the Russells at one of the big hotels downtown.

The clerk, seeing the name, asked Cohen, "Is that the Russell we've been reading about in the papers?" "Yes," replied Cohen. "Sir," said the clerk to Cohen, "I just want to tell you that I'm ashamed of our city."

Meanwhile, Cohen had been trying to see that other top-notch figures were brought in to teach philosophy at the College. He suggested Fernando de los Rios, former minister of education in the short-lived Spanish Republic, to teach his old course in the philosophy of law, and Alfred Tarski, the great Polish symbolic logician, for logic. Tarski did teach in the spring semester of 1940. Cohen wrote to Daniel J. Bronstein, once a student of his whom he had recommended for a Harvard graduate fellowship, by then chairman of The City College department of philosophy.

South Salem, N.Y.
Oct. 17 '39

Dear Danny:

It would be nothing less than a calamity if any technical reason prevented the College from availing itself of the services of such a pre-eminent scholar as Tarski. But I do not believe that there is any such difficulty. For I remember that on two occasions when I took leave of absence, two men and once three men were appointed to carry on my courses.

You may show this letter to Acting-President Mead, but I expect to see him on Thursday and talk to him about it.

Cordially
MORRIS R. COHEN

Cohen also tried to persuade Brand Blanshard, then at Swarthmore, to replace him. Here is Cohen's second letter to him, as unsuccessful as the first.

December 6, 1940

Dear Brand Blanshard,

I have your high-minded letter and though I am naturally disappointed that the College which has meant so much in my life cannot have your services, I appreciate the force of your second reason. It is always a risky thing to move away from a place where you feel that you have taken root spiritually. The pursuit of philosophy is, when taken seriously, such an arduous enterprise, that one who engages in it is entitled to as much peace as this world can afford.

On the other hand, I must say that your first reason seems to me to overemphasize the argumentative gusto required of a teacher of philosophy at the City College. The City College boys are, of course, (because of their past history) not only open-minded but very eager to get at the truth. But they are willing to listen if anyone has something to say. I do not know anyone less argumentative than Overstreet; but he had no trouble with our students though many of them wished that he took more interest in technical philosophy than in the passing issues of the day. Perhaps but some consider my own gusto for argumentation as only the expression of impatience due to excessive irritability and consequent lack of restraint. In any case, our students are certainly highly appreciative of any effort to meet their needs and as you yourself recognize the field of service for a good man thus open is immense.

With kindest regards,

Cordially yours,

MORRIS R. COHEN

In the days of public charges of "subversive activity" at the College, Cohen, like the entire Associate Alumni, tried to counter ugly exaggerations besmirching its name.

Cohen's letter below delivered a stinging rebuke to a colleague at the College:

July 20, 1941

Dr. Moses J. Aronson
Managing Editor, Journal of Social Philosophy

Sir:

The right of any teacher to resign from an institution with which he does not feel in sympathy is questioned by no one; and that may carry with it the privilege of stating whatever good reason induces such resignation. It surely does not carry with it the right to defame by groundless accusations an entire group of one's fellow-teachers and the young men who form the student body. Least of all does it justify the departure from the decent custom of honorable men to send such letters first to the college authorities rather than first to the public press.

Surely if there were the least scintilla of evidence to justify the wholesale accusations in your letter of resignation you could have brought it before the College Administration which has suspended and is trying all teachers suspected of being Communists; or you might have communicated it to our State Legislative Committee which is now investigating "subversive" activities in our public educational system. Instead you chose the path of notoriety and made your charges through the daily newspapers so that you would not yourself be examined and asked to substantiate your intemperate accusations. . . .

And now you have chosen to bite the hand that fed you and to join the pack of jackals that are attacking the College because it has been a truly liberal educational institution.

Your conduct in this case does not seem to me to conform to the standard prevailing in scholarly and academic circles and I cannot, therefore, be associated with you in any public enterprise. I am therefore asking you and the other editors to discontinue the use of my name on your advisory board.

Sincerely yours,

MORRIS R. COHEN

Another way to enhance the prestige of the College was to bring in lecturers of repute. Cohen brought Bertrand Russell as speaker in 1941. At the height of the commotion subsequent to legislative investigation via the Rapp-Coudert Committee, Cohen sent Judge Jerome Frank this invitation to speak in the College's 1941–42 lecture series:

October 23, 1941

Judge Jerome Frank
United States Circuit Court
New York City

Dear Jerry:

The New York City College (I trust you do not believe all the horrible things that are being said about its being a communist nest) is having a series of lectures by distinguished people in regard to what are the great outstanding problems that the youth of America must face and the Director of this course, Professor George W. Edwards, is under the impression that I have a certain amount of influence with you and that if I write and ask you to be one of the speakers, you will be more likely to accept. The lectures are given in the evening and you can pick the topic and the date. We should prefer some evening the latter part of November or at any time in December. My own idea would be for you to talk about your experience in SEC [Securities and Exchange Commission] and what the problems that that commission deals with mean to our fundamental economy. A purely historic and academic talk would not be out of place in a college, nor inconsistent with the judicial function. But you can judge best. I do hope that you will give this your most favorable attention. Confidentially the college needs the increased prestige which favorable publicity can create and the fact that [a] judge consents to come before it will, I am assured, be very helpful. Please take this into account when you make up your mind.

With kindest remembrances to Florence and Barbara as well as your good self,

Cordially yours,
MORRIS R. COHEN

In November Cohen came home on business for a few days from the University of Chicago, where he was teaching under great strain. Mary had been too ill to accompany him there. He found her much worse. A press of matters awaited his attention. First those pertaining to the Conference on Jewish Relations, the brain child on which he was still lavishing enormous efforts. And on November 8, 1941, George Edwards, chairman of the economics department at the College, wrote Cohen:

I have an uneasy feeling of what the immediate future holds for the College. I was glad to hear that you will be back in New York continuously in the near future. Your help will be badly needed.

Cohen sent a letter to the Conference's secretary, Joshua Starr. Alma mater was uppermost in his thoughts as he excused himself from a Conference engagement for November 15. "The situation at C.C.N.Y. is such that my presence at the Alumni dinner is urgent."

At the 1941 meeting of the American Philosophical Association held during Christmas vacation at Vassar, Cohen suffered a heart attack. It was a minor one, but it was to lead to irreversible and ultimately fatal complications.

On February 18, 1942, Edwards reported to Cohen that

Our lectures are being well attended, and I am sure they have improved the public relations of the College. Judge Jerome N. Frank is the speaker on March 18, and we are looking forward to having you with us as alumnus chairman.

The invitation, forwarded to Cohen at Mt. Sinai Hospital, where he lay fighting for his life, was one last call he could no longer meet.

Many have wondered why Cohen stayed for so long at an undergraduate teaching post. (Not until 1961 did New York's municipal colleges merge into The City University of New York.) His City College students he found second to none in love of learning and keenness of grasp. His *Preface to Logic,* published not many years before his death, was dedicated to "The College of the City of New York and its students who gave zest to my life." Together, they helped mold the form of his teaching and even, to a certain degree, of his thought.

He trained his students in the critical spirit. His cardinal achievement was to inflame them, to make them feel some of his own passion for scientific method and the life of reason. The search for truth became their quest, too.

His City College students' pursuit of a liberal education in the face of generally adverse circumstances Cohen identified with his own early struggles. Teaching at The City College was a challenge, he said:

> Here was the front line of the struggle to liberalize education in a democracy. To make available to the poorest member of society the highest experiences of the human mind had been the driving objective of my early socialist dreams.[10]
>
> In Europe . . . liberal education has been regarded as a privilege of the upper or wealthier classes. . . . With us the democratic tradition assumes the inherent right of every child to receive the best possible education. . . .[11]

At the College, Cohen was in a position to maintain Thomas Davidson's tradition of offering treasures from the world's cultural heritage to youth selected solely by stringent scholastic criteria, without regard to financial and social status, or even "leadership." A distinguished member of the bar is reputed to have said that without his free education at The City College, he would have been a bartender. The City College for Morris Cohen was in a sense an extension of the Breadwinners' College. Davidson's faith in human potentiality was transmitted in Cohen's attitude toward his College students. As Felix Cohen, who after his father's death taught his old course in the philosophy of law, put it:

> No city in the world had ever built a college whose doors would open to all its sons, without distinction of race or class or creed. . . . It was the half-illegal labor unions and Tammany Hall and the immigrant vote and all the other disrespectable forces of democracy that helped elect Jefferson in 1800 . . . that eliminated the last property qualifications from city voting in 1842, and then, as almost the first fruit of universal manhood suffrage, in a popular referendum in 1846, overwhelmingly approved the establishment of the Free Academy, as the College was then called.[12]

The portraits of father and son hang near each other in the Morris Raphael Cohen Library at The City College.

Cohen's was a modern-day immigrant's version of Jeffersonian democracy at work in education. "The vast majority of the New York citizens with a college education," he once wrote to Ordway Tead, a new member of the city's Board of Higher Education, "acquire it at the city colleges, and the moral and intellectual tone prevailing in these institutions is a large factor in the spiritual life of our great city."

Here he could work to put into effect the Jeffersonian ideal of education and its connection with democracy and humanism. Theodore Fred Kuper, former national director of the Thomas Jefferson Memorial Foundation for Monticello, has told me of the talks he used to have with Cohen: "Dr.

Cohen had a deep understanding of his ideas on education. Learned tomes have been written on Jefferson by people who have never 'met' him. Your father had 'met' Thomas Jefferson."

Morris Cohen expressed his consciousness of indebtedness when he wrote on March 9, 1938, to Louis Taylor, secretary of the Teachers' Retirement System:

> . . . If I have been of any service to New York City, it is but a small recompense for the educational privileges which it has accorded an immigrant boy.
>
> In the history of mankind there have been few great cities so wisely generous to all comers, and I hope that the generosity of which the Teachers' Retirement System is representative will continue to characterize the government of New York City, and thus continue to set an example of tolerance and good will to a troubled world.

Cohen was honored after his death at the dedication of The City College's Morris Raphael Cohen Library on May 3, 1958. There was considerable swapping of old Cohen stories in the crowd that day. Here is one that went the rounds:

Morris Cohen, after his demise, knocked on the Pearly Gates. St. Peter stuck his head out the window and asked, "Who goes there?"

"Morris Cohen," came the answer.

"Prove your identity," countered St. Peter, peering over his spectacles. "Otherwise, I can't let you in except provisionally. I have a man over there by the name of Mussolini. He thinks he's God. Prove to him that he isn't."

Upon these words from the Saint, the good professor took Mussolini aside to a quiet corner of Paradise, and by means of logic soon forced him to make a public statement that he was definitely not God.

This time St. Peter took off his spectacles, looked the candidate up and down, and set a more difficult task. "You see that chap over there? He goes by the name of Father Divine. Can you prove to him that he is not God?"

Undaunted, Professor Cohen, armed only with the concepts of the Trinity and the transcendental ethics, accosted Father Divine, who within a few minutes formally disavowed any connection with the Divinity.

St. Peter, scratching his head, now set a third task. "Go over to that old man with the long white beard," he told him. "You'll have to straighten him out. His name is God, but he thinks he's Morris Cohen."

At the formal exercises, the Honorable Charles H. Tuttle spoke. As long-time chairman of the City College Administrative Committee of New York City's Board of Higher Education, he had been on the opposite side from Cohen on many a burning issue through the years. But deep loyalty to and pride in the College united them.

Another alumnus of the College, Mr. Justice Frankfurter, responding to the bidding of President Buell Gallagher, came up from Washington, where Court was still in session, to deliver his tribute to his old roommate. As he hurried into the building from the miserable rain outside, reporters asked him if he had a press release for them. "What I have to say is here," he replied, pointing to his heart.

Frankfurter's words cut through the hush.

> . . . For all of us were students of Morris Cohen, whether we had the great fortune to sit at his feet or outside the class room. . . .
>
> [He gave us] A new sense of curiosity, a new sense of eagerness about existence, a new sense of the zest of life, a new sense of purpose, and all with a new sense of humility. . . .
>
> I say that Morris Cohen was one of the great instigating, inspiring, radiating teachers of our lifetime. He was that rare thing, a person so critical of self . . . that he made the same exacting demands of his students. And the exactions made those students different people, with an awareness that they must . . . examine the meaning of their profession whether it was the law (and he influenced an enormous number of men in my profession, whether as practising lawyers, as law professors, or as judges) or some other calling. He had that magical ability to make life richer and deeper because he had that divine gift of making his students more important than they ever thought themselves to be. . . .
>
> He was a man whom to know was to love. And to have known him either directly or through his life's works, was to have one's life refreshed, enlarged and fortified.[13]

VI. *Chicago*

NOWHERE ELSE had Morris Cohen ever been quite so feted and lionized as in his four years at the University of Chicago, from April 1938 until late December 1941. It was to be his last teaching.

After the turmoil of New York, philosophy more or less unadulterated was a joy. John Pickett Turner, his old colleague from the early years at The City College, wrote to him on June 8, 1938, from Brooklyn College's department of philosophy:

> As to the hemlock, Morris, you have been drinking—there is no doubt about that. But now you seem to be reaching heaven. It is sweet to see this happen after all these years.

The skeleton framework of his teaching at Chicago may be traced through letters Cohen exchanged, occasionally with the acting secretary of Chicago's philosophy department, Professor Charner Perry, and more frequently with Richard P. McKeon, professor of philosophy and Greek and dean of the humanities. The correspondence reveals Cohen in a productive stage of his career, hard at work on his papers and especially his books, which supply the threads to those years.[1]

Cohen made McKeon his intellectual confidant. The friendship was based on mutual respect and common interests. They were both men who combined great learning with critical acuity. "I look forward with keen anticipation," Cohen wrote McKeon, "to the intellectual companionship which you offer."

Back in Chicago in the summer of 1923,[2] at the invitation of Professor James H. Tufts, Cohen had taught graduate courses on "Thought in the 19th Century" and "Foundations of Modern Physical Science." In 1930 he was invited back to Chicago for the spring of 1931. He did not accept. But as Cohen's retirement from The City College approached, McKeon pre-

117

sented an irresistible offer. McKeon prided himself on having once been a
student of Cohen's (as a junior of eighteen at Columbia he had attended a
summer course that Cohen gave in 1918). McKeon proposed that he think
of the appointment primarily as a research appointment with occasional
teaching duties. Cohen was invited to deliver two initial lectures.

March 4, 1937

Dear McKeon,

Even though I know that I am not an historian I am highly gratified (as well as surprized) that you should want to consult me on the
history of science concerning which you probably know much more
than I do. But the fact is that I have had some favorite ideas about
the history of science for more than thirty years and would love to expound them to anyone willing to listen, preferably to those who know
something about the field and can check up on what I have to say. It
would be, also, a pleasure to me to give a lecture on the general history of physical science and one on three periods in the history of
medicine (Hippocrates, Peter of Abano, and Dr. John Brown.) But I
cannot come except the week beginning Easter Sunday, when we have
a vacation. . . .

With kind regards to your wife,

Cordially yours
MORRIS R. COHEN

On April 1 and 2, 1937, Cohen lectured at Chicago on "What Is the
History of Science?" and "Three Periods in the History of Medicine," before an audience composed largely of graduate students and faculty members from different divisions of the university.

By July, arrangements were concluded for Cohen to be in residence at
Chicago during one quarter of the three succeeding years. He was to be not
a visiting professor but a full member of the philosophy department, with
all the responsibilities and ties thereby entailed. The proposal came to him
at Stanford University, where he was teaching philosophy that summer.

Cohen was offered his choice of courses, not quite so simple a matter as
it may appear to the outsider.

Nov. 20/37

Dear Charner Perry:

Let me, first of all, express my profound gratitude for the very kind
tone of your letter. The regard of one's associates is one of the main
rewards and supports in a teacher's life.

Just a day before receiving your letter I wrote to McKeon offering
either a course of ten lectures on American Thought or six lectures
on Recent Trends in Logic, and asking him which would fit in best

with the needs of the University. Of course I should be highly pleased to give a seminar course in the philosophy of law—provided that it does not duplicate or conflict with the work of Prof. Mortimer Adler. If I do this it might be better for me to give some public lectures on Law and Justice. The topics would be: (1) Justice in the Criminal Law (2) Fault and Liability, with special reference to Labor Law (3) Law and Politics, and the Nature of Constitutional Law (4) Justice between Classes (5) Justice between Nations, and (6) Law and Religion.

Let me assure you that I look forward with great pleasure to my association with the men who constitute the department of philosophy at Chicago University.

Cordially yours,

MORRIS R. COHEN

November 26, 1937

Dear Professor Cohen:

. . . I think I prefer your original suggestion to the one which the Philosophy Department put forth. I have called Perry and I think the decision is clear. We shall put you down then . . . for a seminar in Logic, and we shall announce later a series of ten public lectures on Recent Trends in Logic. I have the impression that the center of student interest in philosophy has moved to logic at present, and that the general atmosphere and attitude toward logic would be much improved by what you have to say on the subject.

. . . Can you decide now what you should like to give in the spring of 1939 and send the titles to me? I should imagine one seminar course and one course on the lower divisional level, lecture or discussion as you choose, would be a good division of your energies. . . .

We are looking forward to welcoming you to Chicago. Best wishes to Mrs. Cohen and to your sons and daughter.

Sincerely yours,

DICK

November 29, 1937

Dear Dick:

Your suggestion is O.K. Let it be a seminar in logic next spring [1938] and on philosophy of law the next year [1939] (provided the latter course does not interfere with Mortimer Adler's work) . . .

With warm regards,

MORRIS

On December 11, McKeon replied at length explaining why it would be wiser to let the Law School initiate work in the philosophy of law, for which it had set up a committee. He then added:

> . . . the further feeling that the Philosophy Department has need of your work in specifically philosophical subjects, and I should feel cheated if we lent you, so soon in your residence in the University, to a subject peripheral to philosophy.
>
> Let me know how you feel on this question and whether you would be content to suggest some subject other than the philosophy of law for the second spring.
>
> It occurred to me that you would like to be brought into closer relation to our students than your program, as constituted at present, would permit. Do you think it would be desirable to set down a course to be called a reading course, which would mean that for certain hours of the week you would plan to be in your office to converse with students, advise them about their readings, and listen to their reports?
>
> As the time for your arrival approaches, I am looking forward with increasing enthusiasm to the pleasure of having you here.
>
> Sincerely yours,
DICK

Dec. 13/37

Dear Dick:

In regard to the *Philosophy of Law* I cannot see eye to eye with you. I do *not* regard it as "peripheral" to philosophy but rather as an essential, or as you would put it, "specifically" philosophical subject. It grew largely out of my doctor's dissertation on Kant's ethics, and I do not care what the law school thinks or does—that is, as a philosopher. Of course I do not as a member of the University want to offend the law school and am willing to call the course Applied Ethics or Social Ethics, or Logical Analysis of Social Ethical Concepts. But the substance of what I am interested in has to do with the nature of justice as expressed in legal thought and institutions. If Mortimer or some member of the philosophy department is considering giving such a course, I may want to offer one on the philosophy of history. But my first preference is for a course on the philosophy of law.

Of course I am anxious to meet graduate students and listen to their reports; and any arrangement which produces that result is agreeable to me. I do, however, have a great distrust of formal courses. Students take them for credit and that really interferes with the single-minded pursuit of the subject matter. The less formalism in the arrangement the better I shall be pleased.

I share your enthusiasm as to the agreeable consequences of our reunion in Chicago.

Cordially,
MORRIS R. COHEN

McKeon's answer stressed two factors. First, the philosophy of law is not peripheral to philosophy in terms of subject matter, but it is peripheral in the programs of studies followed by students of philosophy. At Columbia, where McKeon had himself taught legal philosophy with Professor Patterson of the Law School, in four years only three of the students who took the course were from the philosophy department. McKeon's second factor was the complicated situation of teaching in the philosophy of law: Mortimer Adler was professor of the philosophy of law; McKeon had been urged to resume his courses in the philosophy of law; and instead of introducing a third professor into the problem, he thought it wise "to leave the solution of the question to the Law faculty and to Adler." Still, added McKeon, the choice of what he wanted to teach was up to Cohen. "I shall look forward," wrote McKeon in closing, "to seeing you at the meetings of the American Historical Association, and to learning about natural law from you."

Cohen did not press the matter. Instead of "Legal Philosophy," his seminar was called "Social Philosophy."

Cohen found, as well as enhanced, an invigorating atmosphere at Chicago. By 1938 Bertrand Russell became visiting professor of philosophy there. Not long afterward, Eduard Benes arrived on campus from Czechoslovakia, faithfully shadowed by a bodyguard. Mortimer Adler was at the university, very much so. The great classical scholar from Germany, Werner Jaeger, served on the philosophy as well as the classics staff. Richard H. Tawney of the University of London was visiting professor of economic history. The social sciences were also enriched by professors like Jacob Viner, William F. Ogburn, Frank H. Knight, Louis Gottschalk, and Louis Wirth, with all of whom Cohen had contacts. Newton Edwards was making Chicago *the* center for school law. At the Quadrangle Club, Cohen would meet Señor Madariaga among other stimulating luncheon companions, and breakfast on occasion with Paul H. Douglas, who had not yet left the economics department for the United States Senate. There were lively discussions at the Wednesday luncheon meetings of the philosophy department. A little later Enrico Fermi, Harold C. Urey, *et al.,* were to conduct atomic research at Chicago. Vision combined with money was building up a world center of thought in the bustling metropolis of the Middle West;

all this was under way by the time the university celebrated its fiftieth anniversary in 1941.

Chicago's East 58th Street, in the days just prior to World War II, used to resound to heated arguments about philosophy that nearly ended in blows. Shades of Paris' Latin Quarter in the Middle Ages! The battles raged about Aristotle or neo-Thomism, courtesy of Mortimer Adler, versus logical positivism à la Rudolph Carnap. Into this surcharged atmosphere stepped Cohen to take his own stand.

Just after Cohen arrived, a master's oral examination was scheduled in logic. The candidate, without the slightest notion that Cohen would be one of his examiners, had near the end of his thesis casually contrasted Aristotle's view of the principles of contradiction and excluded middle with that taken by Cohen and Nagel in their *Introduction to Logic and Scientific Method*. One may imagine the student's consternation when he was warned by McKeon that not only would Cohen be one of the examiners but that he considered himself much closer to Aristotle than the contrast in the thesis would indicate.

At the exam Cohen got quickly to the point. "Now, as I understand Cohen and Nagel, their view is . . ." The candidate, Manley Thompson, now chairman of the same department, has described the ensuing scene:

He [Cohen] continued throughout to speak of the authors in the third person, and never once identified himself as one of the authors, or indicated that the view in question was his own. This made the going much easier for me, and I was much less inhibited . . . than I might have been otherwise. I was quite grateful to your father for conducting the discussion in this manner. . . . I thought your father's questions eminently fair. . . . I was pleased with the way things had gone.

. . . he was known as one professor who refused to tolerate trifling or contentious argument in his classes. I remember hearing that he once threatened to deny a certain student (who was generally regarded as one of the brightest around) speaking privileges in class unless the student kept his arguments to the point and refrained from trying to reopen issues which the rest of the class was willing to take as settled.

The Daily Maroon for April 1, 1938, carried this interview with Cohen, conducted by Alice Meyer:

"Aristotle is the beginning of wisdom," declared Morris Raphael Cohen, new professor of Philosophy, "but not the end. No man can do effective work in intellectual pursuits without understanding his writings, and then going beyond him."

Formerly a member of the faculty of the College of the City of New York, Dr. Cohen was attracted to the University by integration work in the physical and social sciences attempted in our philosophy department. Interested in the metaphysical aspects of logic, he is a prominent American authority in the field of law and philosophy.

Defines Logic. Defining logic as dealing with the primary question of determining the weight of evidence, Cohen sees a need for the application of more rigorous methods to the social sciences. In his own field of Jurisprudence the necessity is particularly pressing. . . .

History of Science. Interested also in the previously neglected history of science, Cohen lectured on the subject here last spring. Scientists, he says, know their work only in its present state of development: generally historians do not have a sufficient knowledge of science to explain clearly its earlier stages. Philosophers have not lost interest in explaining the growth of science as part of the movement of human thought.

When asked his opinion of recent attempts to compare Marxist theory and Catholic doctrine, Cohen found emphatic similarities. "Both are dogmatic and intolerant of differences," he stated, "so both Catholics and Marxists take similar logical positions." Admitting only the things which support their arguments, "they are opposed to the spirit of free inquiry and necessary skepticism."

The Marxist theory of value, he thinks, is too dogmatic. Making the class struggle too simple, it ignores the diversity of human interests. Fascism, on the other hand, appeals to more powerful emotions. In this country, Cohen believes, Federalism is our protection from Fascism.

For students interested in applying logic to the physical and social sciences, Dr. Cohen will present a series of public lectures in Social Science 122 every Monday at 4:30 from April 11 to May 16. Along with his other work this quarter, he will be engaged in writing a "Prolegomena to Logic."

A sense of intellectual excitement reigned in Cohen's classes on the Quadrangles. Professors, students, and sometimes alumni turned out to see him perform. A friend remonstrated with him after one of his public lectures: "That was brilliant, but aren't you afraid it was over their heads?" "I aim it," replied the professor, "where their heads ought to be."

Cohen's dramatic encounter with Mortimer Adler, the leader of Chicago's neo-Aristotelians, is recalled by Charles Morris, now professor of philosophy at the University of Florida: "the two carried on a debate in Mandel Hall. The place was crowded—an outsider was taking on the local boy who talked so much, so loudly, and so confidently. Adler came out much the worse, and I have often wondered whether his later change of views was not in part due to the encounter with Morris Cohen." Professor Max Rheinstein of Chicago's Law School has written me that he considered Cohen's presence "as a welcome counterpart to the dogmatism of Mortimer Adler."

Against the logical positivists, Cohen found ample opportunity for defending his own views on logic in his lectures on "Recent Trends in Logic."[3] After discussing what logic was not, he expounded his views on what he thought it *was*—the heartblood of philosophy and metaphysics. He had once confided to a fellow philosopher that he found such logical positivists as Carnap inclined to be lacking in a sense as to what have been the vital issues of philosophy. A student of philosophy may well outgrow such a background, Cohen felt, but no philosophic education is complete without it.

During his first quarter at Chicago, Cohen shared an office with Carnap. When Ernest Nagel asked Cohen about his relations with Carnap and the rest of the department, Cohen replied, "My relations with Carnap and other colleagues are most pleasant and I have no reason to differ from any of them since in my presence at least they do not use linguistics as a refutation or substitute for metaphysics or ontology."

In Cohen's public lectures, the audience would overflow the Social Science Assembly Room, with people sitting on the window sills and leaning in from outside.[4] One of the students there, Harold Winkler, later president of the Pacifica Foundation, as an old Harvard classmate of Daniel Meyer knew the professor in the intimacy of the Scarsdale home of Dan's father, Arthur S. Meyer, Cohen's closest friend. Winkler, a strategic witness of the public lectures, writes that bright young men—instructors and sometimes assistant professors—who taught the subject of the particular lecture would attend Cohen's sessions and stay late to ask highly technical questions. Cohen would listen, then say: "You misunderstand this paper, because I would guess by the nature of the question, you haven't read Professor X's earlier paper," to which he then referred. "Never, at least to my knowledge, was he caught," Winkler testifies.

He describes another typical Cohen episode. Professor Harold Lasswell had asked Cohen a question that took about two or three minutes to unfold. Cohen simply responded, "No." "My dear Professor Cohen," replied Lasswell, "I don't think you quite understood my question, may I repeat it?" This time, for perhaps four minutes. Cohen again replied, "No." Upon which Lasswell started once more; Cohen interrupted him and said, "My dear Professor Lasswell, no matter how many times and in how many ways you put the same question to me, my answer will still be 'No.' Now, may we have the next question?"

One member of the audience preferred, perhaps understandably, to put his question by letter. G. Stannius wrote Cohen that he enjoyed the lectures, but that the one on probability raised a question in his mind about causality, arising out of Eddington's view that the proposition of determinacy or causality is meaningless for science, since it is impossible for man to gain enough knowledge to move from probability to scientific certainty. Cohen wrote back:

May 19, 1938

Dear Mr. Stannius:

I have your letter which asks my opinion on Eddington's doctrine that the law of causality is meaningless for science. My reply is that science would have no meaning if facts were not connected by determinate relations, and such determination is what makes science possible.

I shall try to touch upon this matter in my concluding lecture on May 23.

Faithfully yours,

MORRIS R. COHEN

In Cohen's reading course, the graduate students expected a New York radical. At the start he had them nonplused. He would start questioning them on the philosophical classics assigned as reading. Then he would pick up the discussion himself. The first reaction, when the students heard his sympathetically understanding treatment of, for example, Plato, was "Oh, so he's really a Platonist!" But no, the next time he would be something else. One of the students, Ervin Anderson, now an international financial consultant in Washington, said Cohen "made a tremendous dent on us." He took them back to authentic sources on how to conduct a philosophic discourse, and "ventilated" every major problem in ethics, social philosophy, metaphysics, logic, and epistemology. Until then, the students at Chicago had the impression, he reports, that you had to be a neo-Aristotelian or, if a liberal, a semanticist. "Alone, without benefit of trumpets, he blew those walls down."

A formulation of Cohen's disagreement with the semanticists is found in a previously unpublished letter of his to the director of the Institute of General Semantics in Chicago, Alfred Korzybski, who requested his help. General semanticists, claimed Korzybski, find most personal, national, international tragedies, and scientific confusion as well, stemming from the lack of realization of "the over/under defined character of our language. If only scientists and mathematicians would study neuro-psychiatry," urged Korzybski, "they might find a preventive and counteracting solution in the consciousness of neuro-linguistic mechanisms involved." Cohen replied:

July 23, 1940

Count Alfred Korzybski
1234 E. 56th St.
Chicago, Illinois

Dear Count Korzybski:

. . . In regard to the issue which you raise, and concerning which you are kind enough to ask my opinion, I may say that I have embodied most of whatever wisdom I have on this subject in an article called "Concepts and Twilight Zones" published in the Journal of Philosophy in 1927. Briefly I think that words and symbols have various degrees of definiteness and indefiniteness in their denotation. To define a word is after all to give its equivalent by a number of words. The latter has the advantage of indicating the intersection of the common points of a number of classes, or more generally of creating more definiteness by indicating the various dimensions or parts of the thing defined. Instead of saying that a symbol is incomplete (which literally is nonsense) I prefer to say that the definite nucleus of meaning is smaller compared with the penumbra of indefiniteness.

I disagree with the linguistic doctrines of recent positivists who fail to realize that no linguistic system is complete and that it needs non-linguistic experience to give it meaning. Ultimately linguistic revisions must rest upon non-linguistic experience. I do not however think that neuro-psychology is relevant to the analysis of the nature of meaning. That men become incapable of rational conduct is unfortunately true, but I do not believe that the existence of the word psychiatry proves that we have very much knowledge on the subject. In any case, I do not believe in confusing logic with psychology. The former has to do with the nature of the objects considered, the latter with the personal biography of the one who happens to be studying or interested in the subject matter. I may also add that all talk of non-Aristotelian logic seems to me to be based on a confusion and misunderstanding of the essence of Aristotle. I cannot for the life of me see how any kind of logic is possible that denies the laws of identity, contradiction, etc. Doubtless modern mathematics has discovered more serviceable tools than syllogism but the validity of the syllogism is not thereby refuted or overthrown.

Sincerely yours,
MORRIS R. COHEN

Student reaction to Cohen in that first year of his at Chicago is perhaps typified in this vivid impression confided by an auditor of his 1938 logic seminar, Duncan E. Littlefair, now minister of the Fountain Street Baptist Church in Grand Rapids, Michigan. Littlefair was "vividly grateful that I was only sitting in." It was, he recalls, "a frightening illustration of as sharp a mind as I ever saw operate, working on graduate students . . . in his ruthless shattering of inadequately founded notions. . . . I am not a timid soul but I can assure you that I was intimidated by it and would not have exposed myself to it readily." Nevertheless, he says, "in spite of this carnage, one had to admire and respect him for his incisiveness and his wisdom . . . his impression on the whole university was marked . . . that is exactly where he belonged. It seemed strange to me that he had spent so many years in New York."

"At Chicago, I am teaching what is for me an extremely light schedule," wrote Cohen to his friend, the legal philosopher Hermann Kantorowicz. That was in 1938, when he wrote Nagel, "The Chicago situation is a pleasant interlude in my life." By 1939, as we shall see, it didn't seem so easy. By 1941, still less so. With searing memories of his start in academic life lingering in the back of his brain, Cohen never ceased being grateful to Chicago for its treatment of him and, at the risk of overtaxing his limited strength, tried to express his appreciation effectively. In 1939 he wrote to Perry as follows:

March 21, 1939

Dear Charner:

My experience last year indicates that a late afternoon, say between 4:30 and 6:00 is a better time for a course of lectures than a morning. I noticed some older people (presumably former students of the University) in my audience last year and this seems to indicate that they came to the lecture after business hours. Isn't it worth while for the University to provide such opportunities? Of course, regularly enrolled students are entitled to preference. But are they not more likely to be free in the afternoons than in the morning?

Despite these queries in my mind, I am perfectly willing to give my public lectures at such time as you think best. I should prefer it if you could start them in the first week of April. At the end of May students begin to be troubled about examinations.

In regard to my seminar in Social Philosophy, I do not wish to admit any auditors. I want only such students as are ready to work and make reports. The temptation for everyone to talk on social matters without adequate knowledge must be eliminated if a seminar in Social Philosophy is to be effective. I trust, therefore, that I shall have a small group of really active students, rather than a large gallery of auditors as I had last spring.

I accept the assignment to discuss the papers on Ethics at the meeting of the Western Philosophical Association in Columbus, Mo.

With kind regards to Faith and yourself,

Faithfully yours,

MORRIS R. COHEN

The seminar in social philosophy met weekly for two-hour sessions. Each student had to prepare and read a paper, at least to start reading. One student, Martin Gardner, now an author, said it was hard to get very far with the reading. He recalls one student who had written a paper on the philosophy of Ortega y Gasset. After he had read the first sentence, Cohen interrupted and asked for clarification of one of the words. This led to a general class discussion for two hours, after which Cohen thanked the student for having presented a very interesting paper. Gardner also remembers being shocked by Cohen's disparagement of psychoanalysis as largely myth unsupported by sound evidence. "I have since decided that he was quite right."

Cohen gave eight public lectures on "The Development of American Thought," to which he alluded in two letters to Nagel.

April 28, 1939

. . . It is true that I am giving far too many lectures and meeting far too many students in classes here at the University, but this is largely the result of some misunderstandings and misadventures to which I do not think it important to offer resistance at the present. In a few weeks I hope the strain on me will be considerably eased. In any case I am doing some useful reading on the history of American Thought, which will enable me to get my book on the subject into better shape.

July 11, 1939

The response to my lectures on the subject at the University of Chicago last spring strengthens my feeling that the publication of the book will have considerable value.

The book *American Thought* figures incidentally but significantly in another letter to McKeon.

June 13, 1939

Dear Dick:

. . . My work at Chicago and especially the public lectures on the development of American thought proved a great stimulus to me intellectually, and I greatly regretted that an unfortunate physical strain depressed me considerably in the latter part of the spring. I hope that I shall have a pleasanter time next spring.

Mary joins me in cordial regards to Muriel and yourself, as well as our best wishes for Peter's continued prosperity.

Cordially yours,
MORRIS

A sudden chill blowing in off the lake one spring afternoon had proved too much for Cohen, coming as it did after an overcrowded year— Jewish affairs, Harvard in the fall, followed by an active program at Chicago. He felt obliged to cancel the legal-philosophy course that he was scheduled to give in 1940, the course on which he had set his heart.

South Salem, N.Y.
Oct. 7/39

Dear Dick:

Please consider this as a strictly personal letter to you. I retired from the City College partly for reasons of health and partly to have a little more leisure to write a few things that are very close to my heart. When in the spring of 1937 you so generously offered me a position in the University of Chicago I was especially attracted by your remark that I would not have to give any more courses than I was inclined to do. Well, I tried to do my best for the University, to express my appreciation of the very kind attitude that you, Hutchins and others have taken towards me. But last spring I strained myself hurrying one afternoon to get home in the cold (which came on suddenly). . . . I hate to disappoint the Law School, but I think it would be extremely unwise for me to commit myself. . . .

Under the circumstances I am inclined to forego my visit to Chicago next spring, or else ask you for a lighter schedule. In any case, I want you to know the situation as it appears to me at present. Needless to add, I shall be greatly influenced by your judgment.

With warm regards to Muriel and your good self and high hopes for Peter.

Cordially
MORRIS R. COHEN

McKeon suggested that Cohen give only a seminar in metaphysics, "and you can spend the rest of your time admiring Chicago, thinking, and writing a book." Cohen's gratitude was promptly expressed.

South Salem, N.Y.
Oct. 23, 1939

Dear Dick:

I am very grateful to you for your very kind letter. It is perhaps unfair to blame Chicago or my program last spring for the strain which I did suffer. My health has always been precarious, and every once in a while something . . . pulls me *down* though not as yet *out*. . . .

My own inclination is all along the line of your suggestion, to give a seminar in metaphysics, and a reading course in the philosophy of science. I confess, however, that I am somewhat embarrassed about backing out of my engagement with Dean Katz and the Law School. If you will be good enough to explain the matter to Katz, I shall take it as a great favor.

Having in an evil moment agreed to write the paper on Dewey for the next meeting of the Philosophical Association . . . I have had the ordeal of reading Dewey's works for the last six weeks. But I'll soon be through and face the natural world with less *moral* strain. After disposing of two or three more papers that are on my *must* calendar, I am going to write a *textbook* on Metaphysics. One of the reasons for going to Chicago for the spring quarter will be to read what I have written to you. You remember that I read parts of *Reason and Nature* to you before it was published.

Have you come to any decision on the Source Book of Medieval Science? I have among my papers a reference to Droz, *Documents Scientifiques du XVe siècle.* Do you know anything about that book? [It was published by Droz.]

I trust that Muriel and Peter as well as your good self are thriving and as happy as one can be in these days.

With warm regards,

Cordially

MORRIS

Pardon the horrible script. I am writing under difficulties [probably in bed].

October 30, 1939

Dear Morris:

I was so pleased to learn from your letter that the removal of the course in the philosophy of law from your schedule was all that was required to bring you back to Chicago that I went over directly to the office of Dean Katz. He was rather shaken by the news, but is reconciled to the decision and completely sympathetic with the reasons that necessitated it. You are therefore relieved of the course and the breach, I think, is completely healed.

I can understand the state of mind you find yourself in as the result of six weeks of uninterrupted study of Dewey's works. The echoes and reverberations of celebrations and influences of Dewey have been almost enough to affect me similarly without the addition of any first-hand reading. I shall look forward to seeing the paper which you prepare. I am much more anxious, however, to see your textbook on metaphysics, or such portions of it as are finished. I remember vividly the sessions on *Reason and Nature,* and the institution of similar, though smaller, meetings on metaphysics would seem to me an excellent additional reason for urging you to return to Chicago. I spent part of the summer writing some chapters of a book which will be on metaphysics, but I am afraid it will neither be a textbook nor easily intelligible to our colleagues of the American Philosophical Association. I should like to try out some of the ideas on you during the Spring Quarter.

I have not done anything further on the question of a source book of medieval science, largely because at the present moment I am struggling to fulfill my engagement to get out a book of selections of Aristotle for the Modern Library Giants. The selecting part has been easy enough, but I am in the midst of a rather chaotic introduction to the volume in which I have had to fight a tendency to say several things about Aristotelian scholars for every single thing I say about Aristotle. When I get that job out of the way I shall try to make a tentative list of desirable inclusions in a medieval source book on science. By that time you will be here and I can discuss the decisions with you. I have not seen the Droz to which you refer, but I shall try to get hold of it.

This letter is intended, however, to be primarily an expression of pleasure at the news that you will be with us during the spring. The program you suggest is even heavier than the one I had in mind.

I had taken the reading course in the philosophy of science out of your program when the seminar in the philosophy of law was put in, and therefore when the seminar in the philosophy of law is dropped your program will consist only in the seminar in metaphysics. Do you want me to put back the reading course in the philosophy of science? Apart from the pleasure I know that you get in meeting with students, I should be inclined to urge you to keep as much of your time free for writing as you would find efficient toward that end. But I leave the decision concerning whether you give one or two courses, only a seminar or a seminar and a reading course, in your hands.

Cordially yours,

DICK

November 2, 1939

Dear Dick:

Thanks for your very kind letter of October 30th.

I want to give the reading course in the Philosophy of Science because I understand that the course was originally announced to be given in the spring and there may be a few good students to whom next spring may be the only opportunity for doing work in this field. I think that I can take care of myself in a course of this sort by not encouraging students to take it who are really not both interested and qualified. In any case, I feel I ought to be available for students who are interested in the field. Is there a way in which I can exercise the same privilege in selecting students for the Seminar in Metaphysics? Last spring and the spring before I had several students who were entirely unprepared for Seminar work and it was rather embarrassing to all concerned to carry them along.

I am delighted to learn that you are getting out a volume of readings in Aristotle for the Modern Library Giants. When I was a student there was a very thin little volume of extracts in the original edited by Edwin Wallace and I remember that I found it very helpful, Wallace's comments being rather brief and to the point. It was published by the Cambridge University Press. I mention it because some brief comments on obscure passages seem to me necessary if Aristotle is to be read intelligently by the audiences for whom the Modern Library Giants are intended. But you have doubtless thought about these matters more than I have.

With kindest regards to Muriel and yourself and best wishes for Peter too,

Cordially yours
MORRIS

P.S. Jaeger told me that he left the Mss of Readings in Greek Science with you. I should be grateful if you can look them over and make any comments.

11 November 1939

Dear Mr. Cohen:

We are now making up the list of courses to go into the Announcements for 1939–1940. Have you any ideas as to what you would like to teach? I suppose that you will want to give one seminar; but I do not know what your preference is in regard to the public lectures. You might give another series of lectures along with the reading course, as for this year, or you might if you preferred offer a second course, elementary, advanced, or graduate. It certainly is the case that there is a large demand among the undergraduates for a course under you; but the public lectures are valuable as a means of providing some philosophic instruction for members of the faculty and for students in other departments. Please decide what you would prefer and let me know as soon as is convenient. . . .

We have missed you and Mrs. Cohen this autumn. This arrangement for a visit in the spring is excellent on the whole, no doubt, since the winter climate here is bad; but we would much prefer to have you here all the year.

Faith joins me in sending our best regards to you and Mrs. Cohen.

CHARNER PERRY

I received your check for the Western Division dues [American Philosophical Association] but I couldn't read your street address.

When in the fall of 1940 the American Philosophical Association designated Cohen as its sixth Carus Lecturer, he chose as his subject the philosophy of history. He wrote to McKeon about it.

Nov. 10, 1940

Dear Dick:

Possibly you have heard that I have been appointed Carus Lecturer and I suppose that the lectures will be given in 1941. I have chosen as the topic for the lectures, *The Meaning of Human History*. Under the circumstances it would be of some advantage to me if I could change the course that I am to give in the spring from *American Thought* to *The Philosophy of History*. If any students have actually enrolled for the former course I might give it as a reading course. Of course I do not want to do anything irregular and if this involves anything contrary to the policy or *mores* of the University, treat the suggestion as if it had not been made.

I trust that Muriel and Peter are thriving and that you yourself are as cheerful as these days will allow.

Cordially
MORRIS

McKeon of course acceded to the request, and Cohen's last seminars at Chicago, in the spring and fall of 1941, were in the philosophy of history.

Although Cohen had taught closely allied subjects, he had not, to the best of my knowledge, taught the philosophy of history since his youthful start at teaching for the Davidson School in 1899–1900. *The Meaning of Human History* incorporated the reflections that had been maturing in his mind since before he was twenty. The seminars followed the lines of thought traced in the book. The theme of the philosophy of history had been his first teaching performance. It now became his last.

Cohen was sixty. It was a long time since he'd climbed a mountain, yet his step remained agile, his body light. His curls, still thick on the classically shaped head, were sprinkled with gray. The hair receded from the forehead; the lines had deepened on his face. The eyes under dark, bushy brows held one. The thrust of the chin, the habitual pointing gesture of the index finger, and the voice projected authority. But under his frequent witticisms lay an ironic acceptance of fate and the tragic view of life. His face in repose showed an inner sadness. All this is caught in Ann Wolf Graubard's bust done a few years later.

The war profoundly depressed him. In his diary he wrote on May 26, 1940:

Mrs. Carnap yesterday remarked how tired I looked and I had to admit that I felt that way. I have tried hard not to let the horrible progress of the war affect me too severely, but it does depress me. I know that even the triumph of Hitler in the whole war will not upset the whole trend of civilization—that his domination of all Europe cannot last, so long as the nationalist feeling in other countries is fanned by his kind of Germanism. Besides, as a philosopher, why worry about this change in history more than about the fall of Greece, or Judea, or the Roman Empire, or the Saracen civilization? Still Hitler embodies so much of what is hateful to me that his triumph depresses me perhaps more than did the death of my father in 1934. The latter event made life seem peculiarly vain and empty and unreal. But father had lived to a ripe old age and his sufferings the last few months made death a great relief. (Incidentally, the noble life, hard toil, and terrific suffering of my father made the notion that the world order is just seem a bitter mockery.) But the progress of German arms annoys me almost every other minute. Everyone talks about it, the headlines hit me in the face and I cannot induce May to stop buying newspapers or tuning in on the radio reports.

In the fall of 1941 Mary was ill in New York. To those at Chicago who had known him of old in New York, he seemed more rigid, more impatient in disagreement, as if he sensed he had no time to lose.

Still, Cohen was never one to spare himself. Even at Chicago there was still Conference on Jewish Relations' business to attend to, with all its offshoots, including the Research Institute on Peace and Post-War Problems that he had helped set up under the American Jewish Committee. There were editorial responsibilities for *Jewish Social Studies* and the *Journal of the History of Ideas,* both of which he had helped found. His voluminous correspondence continued, especially heavy in Jewish affairs.

In that last lonely session, Cohen was as active as ever. The zoology department's ecology group had him lecture on "The Individual and the Environment." The University's Oriental Institute, under the directorship of John A. Wilson, asked him to lead a discussion of the Near East Club on W. T. Albright's treatment of philosophies of history. The History Club had Cohen as speaker at their banquet. In November he even skipped off to speak at the University of Michigan.

There were students to be helped, too. Cohen's lifetime interest in the history of the Jewish Labor Movement is reflected in this note of his to Paul H. Douglas:

December 12, 1941

Dear Professor Douglas:

A student of yours bearing my family name but no relative of mine has shown me his master's thesis on the History of the Jewish Labor Movement. I think that I am exceptionally well qualified to judge of its accuracy because my father and my brother [Sam] were in the movement as far back as the eighties and I have followed it closely since my arrival in America in 1892. I may say that I was brought up in it.

I find Mr. Cohen's treatment to be unusually competent, wide in its grasp and accurate in sizing up relations of the principal figures. I think the thesis ought to be published and I hope that you will use your good influence to that effect.

Sincerely yours,
MORRIS R. COHEN

Above all, there was the teaching. Unlike The City College of Cohen's day and unlike Harvard, then still a stronghold of masculine exclusivity, Chicago was coeducational. Cohen liked to complain about the intellectual inferiority of women—in theory. In practice, he admired quite a few of these inferior creatures. At Chicago it was more often than not his coeds who received the A's.

Harold Winkler recalls a group of ten or so beautiful coeds who took "a certain amount of fiendish delight in pretending to be typical Big Ten beauty queens rather than very serious-minded girls." One Mary Jane, who had read all his books, stopped him once in the social-science building and twisting on a toe said in a high tremulous voice, "Oh, Professor Cohen, do tell me, tell me all about polarity." And Cohen tried, then and there, to tell her. When Winkler told Cohen this story in front of Arthur and Marion Meyer, Cohen became "a little testy" and spoke with annoyance about her chewing gum and "all that lipstick." But Winkler noticed "a lovely high flush in Morris' cheeks as I told him about the following that he had."

One of Cohen's students, Grace Cairns, now professor of the department of philosophy and religion at the Florida State University in Tallahassee, sent me her memoirs of her teacher. He preferred, she said, a discussion kind of class and therefore kept his classes small; he eliminated all who were not serious enough in their motivation. She took the metaphysics and the philosophy-of-history seminars. Once a student wished to air his knowledge of Wittgenstein, entirely out of context. Professor Cohen cut him off saying, "This is not a course in Wittgenstein's philosophy." Students were kept to the subject.

"Only once did he make an error himself in those two classes I had with him." This was in an argument with a student over a nonbasic point in Kant's *Critique of Pure Reason*. At the next class, Cohen acknowledged his error before the class. "The class admired his integrity," said Dr. Cairns.

Cohen's views were "not popular" with her professors in the Divinity School at the University of Chicago. She pointed out that he had "little sympathy with the superstitions, the dogmatisms, the irrational hatreds and fanaticisms of many so-called religious groups," nevertheless she felt that "he was actually one of the most profoundly religious men I have ever met. I made his views basic in my doctor's thesis."

Dr. Cairns and others there considered that Cohen never resorted to "face-saving devices, the political and ambitious scheming of the 'get-aheaders' in the academic world."

For Cohen's last meeting he invited his seminar in philosophy of history to his apartment because he had been sick. He could not restrain occasional expressions of pain. "This was the last time I ever saw Professor Cohen," said Dr. Cairns.

When Mary's condition proved incurable, her husband's health broke down. In the winter of 1942 Mary lay ill in one New York hospital, her husband in another, where he received word from Chicago that a lecture series on American Philosophy of Democracy was to be given that spring under the sponsorship of the Walgreen Foundation. He was scheduled for two addresses—"Natural Law in American Philosophy" and "America's Conception of Its Role in History." He could not deliver them.

For some years the University of Chicago held Cohen's old position open for him, but he was never well enough to return. This letter from McKeon touched him deeply:

September 26, 1942

Dear Morris—

It is difficult to express the distress I felt on learning of Mrs. Cohen's death. Not only do I think of her as an old friend whom I have known for many years, but I also know how important she was to you in everything you did and the emotion I feel is increased by reflection on your own pain.

I had known that you were ill—friends had written to me from New York and I had made more direct inquiries on my rare visits East. I had hoped that you would be well enough to receive visitors and that I might learn about your recovery and your plans from you. Naturally you will want to rest and take it easy until you are back in health. But eventually you will want to do a little teaching, and I want you to know that you have friends here in Chicago who are anxious to welcome you back. Let me know whenever you want to come out—we can arrange our schedules. Meanwhile take good care of yourself, and keep me informed of your progress. And if there is anything that I can do please let me know.

With affectionate regards

Yours

DICK

309 W. 104 St., N.Y.C.
Oct. 12/42

Dear Dick,

You will be glad to learn that my health is slowly but steadily improving, and I am increasing the extent of my daily walks. The doctor thinks I made a marvelous recovery, but I am still not free from headaches and other sequelae of my illness. I hope I shall soon be able to do some work. Thanks for your kind note and thank Muriel for her lovely note, which touched me profoundly. Your suggestion of my resuming my work at Chicago is very friendly, and adds to my courage, but I must wait till I am able to move more freely.

Please remember me most kindly to Hutchins and explain to him why he hasn't heard from me for so long.

With affectionate regards to you, Muriel and your son,

Cordially yours,

MORRIS R. COHEN per L. C. R.

Chicago recognized that it was the logical place for Cohen. From its very start it had been a graduate university with a college attached. Like Johns Hopkins, Chicago resembles European universities in encouraging leading scholars to develop their own research, with teaching a means to that end, rather than vice versa. Chicago realized also that a university is more than a collection of schools. President Robert M. Hutchins said in *The State of the University, 1929–1949:* "the problem of integrating a university . . . is really that of bringing good men into fruitful contact with one another" [p. 91].

The department of philosophy at Chicago, first chaired in 1894 by John Dewey, furnishes the key to Chicago's interrelation of the disciplines. According to the university catalogue: "Although the Department of Philosophy is located in the Division of Humanities, its work is related to all major fields of study in the University." Cohen actively related philosophy to the social sciences, the physical sciences, law, and medicine.

His graduate students from Chicago went into professional and intellectual life throughout the country and occasionally beyond the continental limits. One of them, Ricardo Pascual, became professor of philosophy at the University of the Philippines; another, Jaime Benítez, with whom he had fiery clashes in seminar, though Benítez greatly admired Cohen, later became chancellor of the University of Puerto Rico.

Above all, what stamped the Chicago phase of Cohen's teaching was the wide and active faculty contact. Following the university's tradition, professors from the various divisions not only attended Cohen's lectures but also participated in his seminars.[5] "A genuine Encyclopedist" he was called. "This is a teacher of teachers."[6] His role at Chicago became that of *animateur* of the whole university. Legal philosophy, for example, was stimulated by Cohen.

Edwin H. Levi, Provost of the University and the Law School's dean; its former dean, Wilbur Katz; as well as Professors Malcolm Sharp, Friedrich Kessler, and Max Rheinstein attended Cohen's seminar on social philosophy. Kessler remembers their discussion of the law of contract: "I am sure that all the participants shared my feeling that the seminar was a most exciting experience . . . he has exercised a very great influence on my way of thinking."

Herbert Lamm, associate professor of philosophy at Chicago, has written me that he owes to Cohen the whole stimulus to philosophy as an activity and a career: "I have never done anything in which his spirit has not had a hand."

President Hutchins reported that Morris Cohen is "one of the bright spots" in his recollections of Chicago:

He was almost the only man I ever met who was wise and witty enough to see through everything and who did not become cynical as a result. As you know, he was enormously popular at Chicago with both faculty and students. I think this was because of the qualities I have mentioned. He could and did tear things apart in the most devastating and entertaining way; but he was "constructive"; he had a real message of his own. His kindness and his real humility tempered the wind to the shorn lamb.

I think he liked Chicago. He could hardly fail to do so, when it liked him so much.

VII. *The Teacher*

I have had an unusually varied experience as a teacher. I have taught at the primary and grammar grades of the New York public schools, even the 1A or the ABC class which men generally are not privileged to do. I have also taught in private schools, in public secondary schools, in college, in graduate schools, in diverse universities and even four law schools. But as I look back on four decades of teaching, I still must confess to myself that I know little about it. . . . Every lesson is still an act of faith, but I cannot for the life of me, see how any book or discussion of education can help me. . . . Every lecture or lesson is an entirely new problem, and the complexity of it shames every attempt to bring it within the so-called science of education. It seems to me like writing on the Science of Managing One's Wife and Children. My sense of humor will not allow it.

The above is a fragment from an unpublished, incomplete manuscript by Cohen on his philosophy of education. It reveals the humility and respect he felt for a calling in which the world considered him a master.

The manuscript goes on to express a second conviction that guided Cohen in his teaching—that there is no substitute for old-fashioned learning.

Every once in a while I hear it said that the old education sinned by conceiving of education in terms of transmission of values, or learning—that the real process of education is not the learning of old ideas, but the acquisition of power to deal with our own problems of today. This seems to me to be a vicious dilemma. There is no way in which men can acquire the power to learn except by first learning what others have learned. That has always been the case and I do not see how it can be different. Learning in Physics, as well as in Economics, the power to think new thoughts in these fields is directly proportional to the amount of knowledge, and no one has ever made an important discovery except on the basis of thorough and sound knowledge of what others had done before him. This does not mean that all who are learned have also acquired that power of originating things. There is no way in which

139

we can train inventors or creative thinkers, any more than great creative poets. But the world's work must be directed by those who have learned the ropes. And a schooling which does not insist from the beginning on docility, on learning fully and accurately what others have achieved can bring nothing but added perils to an already perilous world.

A third principle—emphasis on the arduousness of the necessary toil —follows as a corollary.

We have added all sorts of new devices to make the acquisition of knowledge easy—Encyclopedias, Year Books, Indices to Books, which save us the trouble of reading them, etc. But in the end real knowledge can be acquired only by arduous labor, for which no amount of play can be a substitute.

Cohen's "Education and the Changing Social Order," in *The Faith of a Liberal,* drew a telling analogy to illustrate his point that in education there is no easy way, no royal road:

. . . the overcoming of intellectual difficulties is necessary to the growth of intellectual power, just as the overcoming of physical difficulties is necessary to the development of physical strength [p. 277].

Cohen's students were aware, sometimes painfully so, of this aim of their instructor's, for especially in the undergraduate courses at The City College it was carried out rigorously. One devoted ex-student, now Rabbi Victor E. Reichart, wrote from Cincinnati to express his gratitude for just those "hours at your feet when I first learned the delight and exhilaration of strenuous mental exertion."

One day a City College student raised a thorny question toward the end of the hour. The professor had started to answer, when the bell rang. A day or two later, he met the student in the corridor. Cohen plunged right in: "As I was saying . . ." And he proceeded to complete his reply.

Despite his sharp criticism of education in the United States, Cohen was attached in theory as well as in practice to the American concept of democratic education. His *American Thought* put it this way:

I do not wish to extol the continental classical conception of education above the democratic American ideal. The democratic ideal in education is inherently more difficult to put into practice. But, as Spinoza has remarked: All things excellent are as difficult as they are rare. . . . it is not impossible to combine the classical idea of discipline in education with the democratic ideal that education should provide the best opportunities for all members of society, provided we recognize the inherent diversities of temperaments and native abilities and aptitudes [pp. 40–41].

For the cardinal tenet of Cohen's educational philosophy—never to indoctrinate—he acknowledged indebtedness to Davidson, who in a letter to Morris had expounded the precept that became his pupil's:

You know, of course, that the true teacher is not an apostle, or an advocate. . . . Don't be too anxious to make them [the students] come to conclusions. Allow facts to simmer in their minds, till time and reflection can do their work.[1]

The letter was dated October 24, 1899. Davidson was writing to Cohen, then a nineteen-year-old senior at The City College, to wish him well with his first teaching venture—delivering to his fellow Breadwinners a series of thirty lectures on the history of civilization. At the end of his first year of teaching, Cohen addressed a lengthy letter to Davidson. In it were these words:

N.Y., June 17, 1900

. . . In the letter which you once sent me from Bar Harbor, the only direct instruction which you thought fit to give me on how to carry on my history class, you wrote: "The true teacher . . . keeps his own views in the background and strives merely to help his pupils to insight of their own. . . . Be willing that your pupils should contradict you, and come to conclusions entirely different from yours, even on points that seem essential." I have lived up to these instructions as a teacher. . . .

Generations of Cohen's students were tantalized by their instructor's shying away from revealing his own views and predilections. This letter explains his credo:

June 24, 1936

Prof. Paul H. Linehan:
Director of the Evening Session,
College of the City of New York
New York City

Dear Dr. Linehan:

. . . My own conviction has always been that a teacher of Philosophy should refrain as far as is humanly possible from indicating his own attitude to the questions under discussion in the classroom, since the primary object of Philosophy is to develop the capacity of the student for independent thinking on fundamental issues and there is a tendency on the part of students to accept the teacher's opinion rather than go through the labor of thinking through the problems before them. However, while this is a desirable objective, it is very difficult indeed to attain it.

With best wishes for the summer vacation,

Sincerely yours,
MORRIS R. COHEN

A letter of Cohen's to his former student, the philosopher Lewis Feuer, now at the University of California, brings the point home to Cohen's own teaching practice. The best department of philosophy, Cohen wrote him on October 22, 1940, has all points of view represented:

> . . . for in the clash of divergent opinions the student has the best chance to work out his own views. When the department must be limited to a few men, I should want to select those who have the capacity to represent a variety of points of view so that the student will not be merely following the instructor's own point of view. I believe that preaching is not good teaching. I may add the fact that so many of my pupils differ from me is, I think, some indication that I have myself tried what I regard as the right method.

At the memorial services following Davidson's death on September 14, 1900, Cohen spoke these words of tribute for the man who had been his greatest source of inspiration:

But with all his deep erudition he did not overestimate the value of learning. He was interested in knowledge only as a motive to right living. He insisted on our becoming acquainted with every branch of human knowledge, science, philosophy, art and literature, but only in so far as they help us to lead rational lives.[2]

This was another of Cohen's own educational aims. The last was a later, mature expression, confided to me when I began my own teaching career; in fact, the only direct advice on the subject I ever received from him:

You can't *make* them learn. You can only fire them to want to learn. Enthusiasm is contagious. You can make them sense by your own devotion to the subject that it exists.

Cohen's teaching practice was shaped not only by his theories and formation but also by his own personality. To his diary he confided in an undated entry, circa 1938:

> To draw me out fully, to release most fully the flow of my thoughts, I need the stimulation of conversation with certain kinds of people, people with enough intelligence to appreciate the meaning of what I say even if they do not agree. Indeed, relevant objections are most stimulating provided the objectors are not too bumptious. . . .[3]

We are not surprised then that the Socratic method was used by Cohen in his classroom whenever the size of the class permitted, and even to a lesser extent during the question-and-answer period in the lecture hall. To an extent he was Deweyan in method—you learn by doing, and you learn to think by thinking. Shock your students into thinking. It is hard, painful, but indispensable in the acquisition of education.

Cohen's way of teaching was a combination of erudition and iconoclasm. Harvard's Josiah Royce was, in Cohen's view, the best teacher he ever had. The manner in which Royce brought his great learning to bear on the specific point at issue could not but constitute a model. Cohen's erudition, precociously begun, became prodigious in its range and incisiveness. It was put at the service not only of an unbelievable number of persons, but, for himself, to further understanding of relationships and general ideas. His love of intellectual honesty and truth, plus his skepticism, led to iconoclasm. In an early letter to Mary he said:

> My lecture yesterday on Davidson's youth offended the Old Guard terribly—Professor . . . being very much incensed because I tried to tell the *truth*—but I do not mind it.

Cohen occasionally used shock treatment. One day, at a gathering of the City College Menorah Society for discussion of "The Jewish Problem," he stood up, proclaimed: "Gentlemen, there is no Jewish problem," and then sat down. Consternation reigned among the sponsors. Thereupon, Cohen rose and proceeded to explain why the Jewish problem cannot be considered in isolation.

His recipe was wit and kindness, sprinkled with pepper. "In the handling of mental rapiers I know of no one who is your equal," wrote William H. Walden. At The City College a repertoire of tales has been handed down demonstrating how deftly smarting pricks were administered to adolescent egos. Once the professor pressed a student to explain his assertions. The young man's rhetoric was beginning to run down. Off guard, he fell back on, "But that's obvious."

"Why?" queried the professor.

"Any damn fool knows that."

Cohen administered the fitting *réplique*. "I take your word for it, sir."

Another sophomoric oration was allowed to run its full course, with the professor's eyes fixed dreamily through the window at some far-off vista. When the torrent of words had finally run itself out, amidst dead silence, the professor's gaze returned to the classroom, and he asked mildly, "Did you say something?"

The philosopher William C. Gruen of New York University, who says he got his own start at Cohen's New School courses, describes one discussion period where a member of the audience launched into an interminable speech. Cohen broke in, saying, "I'm the only one paid to waste the time of this class." But the sequel was related to me by Mrs. Henry Auerbach, who used to transport the Cohens in her chauffeur-driven car to and from the New School on Monday evenings. "Morris," admonished

Mary as they relaxed in the automobile after the lecture, "you were a naughty boy. Did you realize who that was? That was Will Durant!" "No, May dear," he replied, "I didn't know. If I had known, I'd have behaved worse."

At the inception of the New School for Social Research in New York City, Cohen was elected its first lecturer. He continued to give lecture courses there for years. Alvin Johnson, the New School's founder and director, wrote him: "there is only one man who can give courses that really get under the philosophic skin of our people, and that's you." Cohen's classes helped make the New School the real force in American intellectual life that it soon became. At the memorial services there for Cohen, Alvin Johnson testified that he "helped us to develop the philosophy for which The New School stands. It will do everything it possibly can for the enlightenment of its friends, but it will do nothing whatsoever for their indoctrination. . . . in this sense Morris Cohen is with us in the philosophy and in the structure of The New School and will forever remain."

In Cohen's first formal course on the philosophy of civilization, 1899–1900, he discussed the themes that he developed a half century later in *The Meaning of Human History*. Among his pupils was Mary's sister, Bertha, who has shown me her class notebook. "Morris' lecture, from eight to nine thirty on Tuesday evenings," she recalled, "was followed by a half-hour question period. The sidewalk forum continued for another hour. We then walked each other home, still hotly discussing till midnight. The world that Morris opened up to us was enough challenge to last us the rest of our lives."

Cohen's teachings were remembered by his students long after they left his classroom. Jim Cork, in *The Call* for February 10, 1947, wrote:

In our student days, we always divided the faculty of City College into two parts—Morris Cohen on one side and the rest of the faculty on the other. No memory of my entire college career other than that of Cohen and his classes remains with me. . . .

Some of us who early had become enthusiastic supporters of the Russian Revolution, won by the idealism and sacrifices engendered in its early, more heroic days, disregarded certain warnings of his. We regarded him then as an old-fashioned liberal who had been left awash by new and heroic events with which he had been unable to keep pace.

But, it must be admitted today, he proved right in certain fundamental questions, and we had to learn the hard way about the terrible logic of ensconced power; about the social and human devastation that can be wrought by a dictatorship responsible to no one; about the necessary harmony between means and ends, and finally that the good society is inseparable from . . . the extent to which it allows freedom of enquiry, guarantees human liberty, creates the conditions for the development of the free, dignified human being.

Morris Cohen taught for more than forty years. Why did he bequeath no school of philosophy? Living up to his credo, he refused to indoctrinate, and there are no disciples to carry on. The great majority of his students, he realized, would pursue paths other than technical philosophy. He trained them to apply philosophy to their problems in whatever their walks of life. Some of them became plain good citizens. Others went on to leadership in American professional, government, and business life. The attorney Max Grossman wrote: "I am very grateful that at the crossroads of chance I came into your life, so that you might make mine so much richer and more beautiful." Solomon Dubow thanked him from Harvard Law School for "showing us the way to a Life of Reason, a life which you lead and which we strive for."

A 1955 book on *American Philosophy,* edited by Ralph B. Winn, calls Cohen "a maker of young philosophers." Some of the outstanding philosophers in the country were Cohen-trained.

Another group of students through whom his teachings continue were the students of the lecture hall, some of whom heard him only once. "I was at Chapel Hill," one such person told me, "when I saw everyone hurrying one evening. 'Where are you going?' 'Come along, you'll see.' And so I chanced to hear Cohen, and my life has never been quite the same. The importance of learning to think has mattered to me ever since."

Cohen's students also included his fellow teachers. In 1940, Joseph C. Turner, of the department of the practice of medicine at the Columbia University College of Physicians and Surgeons, thanked him for having furnished "real help in understanding certain biological problems with which I am immediately concerned and clarified my thinking about them. . . . I can now return to the ideas of Poincaré, Whitehead, etc., with a new insight and sense of their meaning that I never had before." An associate dean of a law school wrote that he had inspired him to try to set down his own values. Sheldon Glueck of the Harvard Law School said of Cohen's article on scientific method in the *Encyclopedia of the Social Sciences,* "If I had the authority I would compel every college student to study this article. . . ." He liked Cohen's insistence that a method dubbed "scientific" in one field is not necessarily adapted to another; specifically, that the techniques of the physical laboratory are not fitted to the criminologists' problems of crime, punishment, and deterrence.

John Herman Randall, Jr., of Columbia's philosophy department, called Cohen's "The Faith of a Logician" the only reasoning he would ever be inclined to take on faith: "There is no man in the world I had rather be than yourself."

Not the least important were the students of the book. Charles E. Ozanne from Cleveland wrote in 1937:

> You see, you teachers who are also writers have a double set of classes; those whom you see before you when you lecture, and an-

other, and perhaps larger, group of pupils who may possibly be thinking of what you say even more keenly and whom perhaps you influence more deeply than the former set. So as a pupil of yours who unfortunately was sitting too far away from the lecturer for you to have noticed me as yet, I should like to stay after class a little while and talk with the professor. May I?

The secret of Morris Cohen's relentless energy in leading as well as teaching the life of reason lies at least in part in his faith as a liberal and as a logician; faith in the educability of students; faith in the superior viability of the truth; and faith in the potentialities of liberal civilization.

"Live heroically," Davidson used to say, and Cohen's spirit drove his far-from-robust body.

Davidson would not have been disappointed in his protégé. Cohen's words on Davidson's life apply to his own: "He lived for eternity and that is why the effects of his life cannot easily die."[4]

VIII. *The Author*

[Diary, 1897] Yet how grand a thing it is to be the Author of a book. Whenever I think of it I am astounded.

[Diary, 1898] Were one to tell me that my life is going to end soon, there would be nothing that I would regret leaving, except the sentiment of leaving my parents miserable and not living long enough to become a writer.

[Diary, August 2, 1902] But why am I anxious to see my feelings made public? Is it the desire for fame to which I am far from being proof? I do not think so. I think it is the natural desire to see our feelings objectified. Feelings are things to be expressed and we do not express them by letting them pass. Nay we do not fully experience them by letting them pass. Every one desires sympathy and you can get very much more sympathy (in your mind) in the reader to whom you reveal your heart than from a most intimate friend.

Morris Cohen did live long enough to become a writer.

On March 19, 1931, his first book, *Reason and Nature, An Essay on the Meaning of Scientific Method*, is out at last. The students at New York's City College circulate a bon mot: *Question:* Why is Cohen greater than God? *Answer:* God is the Author of Nature, Cohen of *Reason and Nature*.

Among the letters of praise that Cohen received was one from Edwin Arlington Robinson. Walter Lippmann congratulated his friend on his "noble" book, "a superb book and a great gift to the world." The French philosopher, Emile Meyerson, wrote from abroad. So did Santayana (see Chapter XVII). From the Institute of Mediaeval Studies in Toronto, Gerald B. Phelan sent word that Cohen was not only an Aristotelian, but, "and this is different, you owe a debt to your study of St. Thomas." H. L. Mencken wrote Cohen that he was writing a book on morals and that "you will find many echoes of your own thinking in it."

Years later, long after *Reason and Nature* was out of print, its author received this letter:

30 Oct. 1943

Dear Mr. Cohen,

Some time ago after much diligent labor I obtained a copy of your book "Reason and Nature." It was part of a library I'd been collecting for some time to hold me while at sea.

Unfortunately my last ship went down and "Reason and Nature" with it. As I had found your book of much value in the development of a personal philosophy another copy is earnestly desired—but the prospect of slow correspondence re: advertising, price etc. is not pleasant.

I have therefore had the temerity to write you and enclose $25, hoping that you would see fit to have someone chase down a copy and mail same to me. It is an imposition, yes—but dammit—otherwise I'll probably be trying to get ahold of a copy for the duration. Was going to ask for any bibliography you might have handy relative to books of equal merit—that are as stimulating and provocative —but will save that request for a subsequent letter.

Please don't return any money—just toss in books until its used up.

The development of a solid, comprehensive understanding of my individual relationship to man and matter is more than a fancy—it is a necessity.

And the back drop of war, oddly enough, seems to provide an excellent basis.

Thanks—and here's hoping I hear from you soon.

Sincerely,

EN. CLYDE DEAL

Address:
Ensign Clyde Deal U.S.C.G.C.(R.)
U.S.S. Sellstrom (DE 255)
Fleet Post Office
New York

The author's reply went out on November 9, 1943.

3708 Oliver St., N.W.
Washington, D.C.

Dear Ensign Deal:

Your letter stirred me deeply, as it also did my children who have the same humane intellectual interests.

I am sorry that I have no extra copy of "Reason and Nature," but

I shall advertise for one and as soon as I can obtain a copy I shall forward it to you.

It is very encouraging to me, as one who has devoted his life to purely intellectual pursuits, to find support from one who has braved the sea with its ever-recurring dangers. During the First World War I read some letters from a German soldier to the effect that the determination of Kant's questions is the most important thing in his life, as well as in the life of humanity at large. But your letter strengthens my faith in the issues which my book attempts to raise in its poor fashion.

Naturally I am deeply grateful to you for this support of my own absorbing interest to which I have devoted my life.

I send herewith two books of my children: one by my son "Ethical Systems and Legal Ideals," and the other by my daughter "From Beast-Machine to Man-Machine." As soon as I can obtain a copy of it, I shall send you my book on "Law and the Social Order"; also the particular copy you want of "Reason and Nature." I shall keep the money you sent me and return to you the unexpended balance.

With high appreciation of your letter, I am

Cordially and gratefully yours,
MORRIS R. COHEN

Cohen privately boasted that he'd had a hand in writing his own reviews by furnishing in his Introduction quotable material suitable for three categories of reviewers—those who wanted to praise, those who wanted to damn, and those who wanted to read no further. Actually, he provided for a fourth category of reviewer, he who never sees the book. One of Cohen's fellow philosophers has made this confession to me. He had to review *Reason and Nature* on board ship where no copy was available. "After all, I knew Cohen. He'd lectured for us. I'd heard and read his papers. When I set foot off the gangplank, the review was ready. I had every intention of explaining things to him. But he wrote me expressing so much gratitude for my understanding review, that I never had the heart to tell him the full story."

John Dewey wrote in *The New Republic* (April 29, 1931):

I know of no recent work, save that of Meyerson, which unites such command of scientific material, ranging from mathematics and physics through biology and psychology to the social sciences, with both insight and the power of lucid exposition.

And Henry Hazlett in *The Nation* (April 15, 1931):

The appearance of *Reason and Nature* . . . seems to me destined to mark an important milestone, perhaps even a turning-point, in the history of American philosophic thought. Even a critic unsympathetic to its temper and typical conclusions can hardly refuse it a place on that modest shelf of American philosophic classics which holds the works of a bare handful of thinkers—Peirce, James, Santayana, Dewey.

Cohen's was a precocious intelligence. Why then did he wait until he was fifty-one before bringing out his first original treatise? Teaching was the first competitor to writing in his life. In a letter to his former student, Dr. Joseph T. Shipley, himself a writer and drama critic, Cohen explained his dilemma.

Nov. 16 [1927]

Dear Shipley,

It was very kind of you to write me the lovely letter on the day after my dinner. But I have refrained from answering it because, frankly, I cannot answer your question as to whether it would be better to abandon teaching for writing. There was once a man who was in love with two ladies and much torn as between them, but being a Mohammedan—Well I am not a monist.

If you have nothing better to do come around and see me some day.

Cordially,
MORRIS R. COHEN

A second deterrent to the rapid production of books was his perfectionism. How it operated in the preparation of *Reason and Nature* shows up in his correspondence with "The Courageous Thinker and Loyal Friend" to whom he dedicated it, Mr. Justice Oliver Wendell Holmes, Jr. (see Chapter XVI). In 1920 Cohen wrote Holmes that for several years he had been planning a work on the foundations of physical science and as a preliminary exercise had undertaken to write a more or less popular book on its major points. The "preliminary exercise" turned out to be the 470-page *Reason and Nature,* published eleven years later.

Cohen's hesitancy to get out anything as final as a book lies behind the lines of this letter to the editor of *The Journal of Philosophy,* his old teacher Frederick J. E. Woodbridge.

Jan. 2/29

Dear Woodbridge:

. . . I wish to add my personal appreciation of what the Journal has meant to me in my own philosophic development. You and [Wendell] Bush encouraged me in my first philosophic efforts. But even with your personal encouragement I could not have ventured to write my earlier pieces if the Journal were not so well adapted for philosophers with limited time and energy who wished to say something and did not care much about elaborate formal development. In that respect, as in others, the Journal has been a civilizing influence in American philosophy and a great encouragement to honest thinking.

Cordially yours,

MORRIS R. COHEN

In 1933 appeared *Law and the Social Order,* dedicated to Mary. Max Lerner likened it to Holmes's *Collected Legal Papers* in terms of inner symmetry and "disinclination to . . . run with the scholarly herd . . . the same acrid and canny capacity to pierce intellectual pretensions, the same final dignity of thought."[1]

The historian Charles A. Beard wrote Cohen that his book was "like old wine, good to taste and exhilarating. . . . I shall draw upon it for wisdom."

Of all Cohen's works, his *Introduction to Logic and Scientific Method,* 1934, written in collaboration with Nagel, his brilliant former student, has sold the most copies. The United States Army, during World War II, ordered 15,000 copies for G.I.'s.

"Life is a conspiracy to prevent the scholar from concentrating on his writing," the great French scholar and academician Paul Hazard said to Morris Cohen in the fall of 1938. It was just after Munich. Both were conscious of the ominous threat of war. They were torn by a double dedication—to their writing, and to something bigger than themselves, whether the cause of France or of Jewry. Each was spared long enough to finish the magnum opus he was writing, but neither lived to see it come from the press.

From time to time the leading American philosopher is chosen by the American Philosophical Association to write a book, three chapters of which are delivered as the Carus Lectures. Cohen was selected in 1940. He chose the philosophy of history as his subject. I used to take out books at his order from the library at Columbia, where I was a graduate student —armloads of books that I thought would keep him busy for a while. But never for very long. His thoroughness in preparing *The Meaning of Human History* was bottomless.

The Carus Lectures were read in May 1945 at The City College. The light filtered through the mullioned windows of the Faculty Room upon a stricken figure. Mary was gone. Morris was broken in health; his words were read by his son Felix.

Cohen's *A Preface to Logic* appeared in 1944, and was soon translated into Italian, Japanese, German, and Spanish. *The Faith of a Liberal* came out in 1946, illuminating further his role as a crusader for liberalism. For Cohen critical reason, wrote Granville Hicks in *The American Mercury,* is "the best guide we have in our efforts to discover the good life."[2]

"His profession of faith was published when Professor Cohen had reached what he called 'post-rheumatic wisdom,' " said an obituary editorial in the New York *Herald Tribune*,[3] for, a year after the book came out, the author was gone.

Nine posthumous works appeared: *The Meaning of Human History,* 1947; *A Source Book in Greek Science,* 1948, by Cohen and I. E. Drabkin; *A Dreamer's Journey: The Autobiography of Morris Raphael Cohen,* 1949; *Studies in Philosophy and Science,* 1949; *Reflections of a Wondering Jew,* 1950; *Reason and Law,* 1950; *Readings in Jurisprudence and Legal Philosophy,* 1951, by M. R. Cohen and F. S. Cohen; *King Saul's Daughter: A Biblical Dialogue,* 1952; *American Thought,* 1954. The last, in Russian translation, has recently been published in Moscow.

So long as Cohen's works are read, he stays alive. Time alone can tell which of his writings will endure. Meanwhile his books, five of them in paperback, continue to sell and to remain in demand in libraries.

The Meaning of Human History Cohen considered his magnum opus. Said Sidney Hook, his former student, in his review for the Sunday *Times* on February 22, 1948:

> Although he preferred to call himself a logician, Morris Cohen was primarily a critic and moralist. The qualities of intellectual penetration and practical wisdom which made him a unique figure in contemporary American Philosophy, are very much in evidence. . . .

But for Perry Miller, *A Dreamer's Journey* was "the book by which Morris Cohen will be longest and most widely remembered."

> It will demand a permanent place among the classics of immigrant narrative, and one not too far behind the greater classics of intellectual biography. And because it reveals in human terms, with humility and yet with a touch of vanity, the sources from which his strength was gathered, it explains why he conspicuously succeeded in writing philosophy that can be read as literature.[4]

Morris Raphael Cohen: A Bibliography, compiled by Martin A. Kuhn and published in 1957 at the Library of The City College of New York, lists sixteen books for which he was responsible, three with a coauthor, nine published posthumously. He contributed to some twenty-six books, including three encyclopedias, and published several hundred articles. *Reflections of a Wondering Jew* was put into braille by the New York Guild for the Jewish Blind. But because prior to 1931 he had acquired a tenacious reputation as a great teacher who published little, even today the legend dies hard.

But his books are read, in unexpected places, as this incident reveals.

Suzanna Lloyd, a teen-age drama student (the daughter of the actor-director Norman Lloyd), stepped into a taxi in New York one day. Her mother's Uncle Morris had been a presence in her home, and she found herself talking about him to the friend who was with her. The cabbie broke in. "Is that Morris Cohen the philosopher, the professor from City College, you're talkin' about? Yeah? He was quite a guy. I never travel without that book of his around. See. Here it is!" And he reached down to pull up a much-thumbed copy of *A Dreamer's Journey*. "Did you know him, miss? You're his grandniece? Say, is this where you girls wanted to go? Oh, no, you don't owe me nothing, miss. Not a niece of Morris Cohen."

Part Two

THE PHILOSOPHER
AND HIS TIMES

IX. *Journey in Philosophy*

TO PHILOSOPHIZE was as natural to Cohen as to breathe, and just about as necessary. His was the Aristotelian view that "philosophy grows out of our native curiosity or wonder about the world at large."[1] "If philosophy is viewed broadly as the love of wisdom or general knowledge," he wrote in "The Faith of a Logician," "I may say that such a love was awakened in me between my seventh and tenth year by my grandfather, a poor tailor in the Russian town of Nesviesh."[2]

Cohen once called philosophy "a science concerned with everything and anything between the two poles of metaphysics and logic,"[3] and metaphysics "a bogeyman only to infantile minds. It is, after all, as James said, but an obstinate effort to think clearly."[4]

Philosophy differs from other specialized disciplines such as history, science, or law, Cohen held, in that philosophy puts greater emphasis upon interpretation, system of assumed principles, and final synthesis.[5]

During the 1920's and, increasingly, during the 1930's, Cohen developed a reputation as the *enfant terrible* of American philosophy. According to this interpretation, to which his Voltairian grin lent credence, he relished the role of mocker, and his favorite part was that of *advocatus diaboli*. The more it was expected of him, the more he performed it—even upon occasion against himself. It is related that at Harvard he once read a paper in philosophy to which no objections were voiced. He thereupon rose to the occasion, proclaimed, "Here is what *I* could say against the position," and proceeded to demolish his own thesis.

After he delivered his presidential address to the American Philosophical Association, "Vision and Technique in Philosophy," the *Journal of Philosophy* reported in its official summary: "A little less brimstone than usual."[6] Nothing was said about less fire. As *Time* put it on January 29, 1938, Cohen was "a modern Socrates with an acid tongue."

He joined so energetically into the trading of blows with which philosophers greet each other's work that he became their "Socratic gad-fly," in Harold A. Larrabee's phrase. But his sting was without venom. Fulton Anderson of the University of Toronto's graduate school of philosophy said to me, "Morris Cohen argued only the issues. He was sweet. We all loved him." Another Canadian professor of philosophy told of his first encounter with Cohen: "As a budding philosopher, I gave a talk that provoked his biting criticism. Afterwards he came up to me and asked, 'Was that your maiden effort? Not a bad start.' Then, slipping his arm through mine, 'Come on, let's go to lunch.' "

"To search for the truth in everything," had been Cohen's ambition, set down in his diary when he was only sixteen. At twenty, he wrote Davidson that "the study of Jevons' Logic was the first step that led me to the study of philosophy." Two years later Bertrand Russell's *Principles of Mathematics* led him to formulate a method of scientific inquiry founded on mathematical logic. Here was the guide for his journey in philosophy.

Logic

The validity of logical reasoning is axiomatic in Cohen's philosophy. Russell's demonstration that pure mathematics asserts only logical implications or relations that "cannot be identified with either psychologic or physical events, but are involved as determinants of both"[7] proved the point of departure for Cohen's "independent journey." His philosophic realism was based on logical realism, i.e. belief in the reality of abstract logical or mathematical relations. It is typical of Cohen the pluralist that in defining his realism he spoke not of *eidos* or essence but of relations.

As a logical realist, he rejected nominalism, "a metaphysic from which the juice of life evaporated in the Middle Ages,"[8] and its variants—empiricism, subjective idealism, positivism, or any denial of the reality of universals. Empiricism he called "myopic and stingy."[9] The subjective idealist spins "the physical world including his own body out of his own mind."[10]

Logic is the lifeblood of philosophy, he held, for it is the formal aspect of all being—objects and events in time and space, as well as nontemporal, nonspatial relations. Logic must not be restricted to the time-honored study of formal syllogisms nor the closed game of symbols that symbolize themselves. Both of these things he did, and did well. In 1938 he wrote to Charles A. Baylis that the Association for Symbolic Logic, which he had himself helped to found, "seems to me to be becoming entirely mathematical and of little interest to one who, like myself, is primarily interested in philosophy." The same year he wrote Ernest Nagel: "I hope you can take the editorship of the Journal [of Symbolic Logic]. It needs a philosopher to rescue it from pure symbolic manipulation."

The foreword of Cohen's *Preface to Logic* calls logic "an indispensable element of liberal civilization and free thought." His applications of logic to all kinds of fields are indicated by the titles of some of his studies—"The Place of Logic in the Law," "The Logic of Critical Judgments on Art," "The Logic of Fictions," "Logic and the World Order."

His gift for spotting connections was matched by his neatness in making distinctions.[11] He insisted on clear differentiation between logic and psychology, logic and semantics, logic and epistemology. Of the latter he observed dryly: "the effect of our current reduction of philosophy to a purely formal discipline, viz., epistemology, cannot be said to have as yet increased vital interest in philosophy."[12] For him, logic appeared not only to philosophy but also to the law, the social sciences, or statistics. "The Statistical View of Nature" discriminated between correlation and causation for the statisticians at whose annual meeting the paper was read. Causation is a necessary connection between events: "Where there are genuine causal connections we should expect statistical correlation, but the converse is not necessarily true."[13]

Scientific Method

"The method," as Cohen expounded it,[14] holds up as its ideal the interconnection of facts into a unitary system: "ultimately all science goes back to the classical conception of nature, according to which the variation of phenomena is to be referred to some unitary law."[15] The method of logical proof is the essence of mathematical and exact science, and scientific method models itself upon mathematics or logic, though adapting itself to the particular science concerned.

"Scientific method pursues the road of systematic doubt."[16] Every scientific investigation begins as a question or problem. Where evidence is inadequate, propositions, even seemingly self-evident propositions, are questioned by science, one at a time. Constant verification or self-correction is sought by approaching the problem with a number of alternative hypotheses in mind. Assumptions are reduced to a minimum and made explicit. Conclusions can be drawn only after rigorously exact observation, evidence, measurement, experimentation, and testing of hypotheses in favor of the simplest and widest in best agreement with the facts. Measurement is the clearest way of making terms definite. Science, however, is not restricted to the numerical or quantitative aspect of nature. It is interested in selected, invariant relations of things. Give and take between facts and principles is required. We cannot begin with pure facts any more than with pure theory, but always operate with both. It is well to bear in mind that there are two types of scientific theory, the physical and the mathematical, both equally valid. Scientific exploration is progressive, from laws to wider laws or theories, so as to reveal relationships between apparently isolated propositions: "Science is above all an organized effort to eliminate as much inconsistency from our view of the world as our knowledge will permit."[17]

Science is distinguishable from common sense "by the rigour with which it subordinates all other considerations to the pursuit of the ideal of certainty, exactness, universality, and system."[18] System involves connectedness, completeness, and logical order.

In explaining completeness, Cohen falls back upon Charles Peirce's view that the meaning of a proposition consists of its possible deductions or consequences.[19] "A logical pragmatist"[20] he called himself in a letter to his friend Justice Holmes in 1920.

The scientific method cultivates doubt in order to stabilize beliefs by founding them on the best available evidence. It not only perfects knowledge; it seeks to extend it—for example, through induction, termed by Russell more or less methodological guesswork.

Cohen relates his scientific method to problems of man and society. Only through logical reflection can man be liberated from regarding the familiar as the only possibility.

In general, the chief social condition of scientific method is a widespread desire for truth strong enough to withstand the powerful forces that make people either cling tenaciously to old views or else embrace every novelty because it is a change.[21]

Polarity

By 1921 his contact with Einstein[22] had strengthened Cohen's conviction that "a philosophical approach based on the reality of relations would be serviceable in the understanding of scientific method generally. . . . Such an approach might eliminate many false alternatives and antitheses, I felt, in the social as well as the natural sciences."[23] *Reason and Nature* illustrates the point:

. . . change and constancy are strictly co-relative terms. The world of experience certainly does not show us anything constant except in reference to that which is changing, nor any change except by reference to something constant [p. 412].

From emphasis upon relations, the transition was made to a concept of polarity, on which Cohen came to rely, both as a logical and ontological principle.

Instead of being stumped by dichotomies or irreconcilable differences, he tried to find a way out by abandoning "monistic prejudice" and analyzing opposing elements or categories. Often he was thereby able to advance, if only obliquely. Nature contains more than reason—mysticism lies beyond. The known and the unknown, law and contingency, order and spontaneity, spiritualism and naturalism, the absolute and the ephemeral, continuity and discreteness—the universe has room for them all. He described his view to Justice Holmes:

> Unity and diversity are the two blades of the shears with which we try to cut out a pattern of the universe, and it is only our human weakness that makes us emphasize one of these blades at a time. [See p. 335 for complete letter.]

Venturing into one technical field after the other, armed with his thesis of polarity, which he combined with logic and scientific method, he became an interdisciplinary pioneer. As early as 1909, in a paper before the American Philosophical Association, he deplored "the present anarchic tendency to overspecialization" and urged a return to the older sense of philosophy as a working view of the universe and of man's place in it. "We need some integrating study," he pleaded, "that shall keep apace with and balance the progress of specialization."[24] It is customary to think of Cohen as no system builder. Yet his flexible but general utilization of an over-all method, and his emphasis on the liberal (i.e. critical) temper throughout, tied together the numerous branches of his philosophy.

The Philosophy of History

In following the path of history Cohen was deviating from those who give themselves wholeheartedly and exclusively to logical analysis. But his students had no cause for surprise. Just as his teaching stressed textual mastery along with ability to reason from the facts, so Cohen could not ignore history in his own pursuit of learning. Since boyhood he had been nourished on history, Hebrew history at first. His grandfather, his Rabbi and teacher Nehemiah, and his early reading of Josephus had awakened in him an interest that never died. Cohen's "Philosophies of Jewish History"[25] was the culmination of a lifetime of reflection. His reading of Gibbon, in between customers at the poolroom where he worked, was a memorable experience of his youth. When he first embarked on the graduate study of philosophy, Adler showed him the limitations of historicity into which Davidson had initiated him. The study of history alone does not provide philosophical analysis or ethical culture, but without its record and perspective man is insular.

The Carus Lectures, *The Meaning of Human History,* present Cohen's critique of one-sided versions of history, along with fresh light on his views of liberal civilization and on historiography. What is distinctive about human history, according to Cohen, is the perspective that makes understanding of individual happenings in time and place central. History is not made by the historian but discovered by him. His goal should be to find out what happened, rather than to find "the spirit of the age." We understand the significance of what did happen only if we contrast it with what might have happened. Without the consideration of alternative possibilities, history would sink to an unilluminating chronicle. Cohen distinguishes between absolute and relative determinism. Contingency cannot be entirely eliminated, but neither can relative necessity.

Great men in history are great at the points of intersection with great social forces. The inadequacies of the cyclical view of history, as typified for example by Spengler, are pointed out by Cohen, who sees the task of the historian as a charting of the high tides and low tides of history, of the oscillations between freedom and fear, progress and inertia, good and evil, among other polar components.

For the philosopher interested in human problems, history represents the indispensable focus.

Linking history and philosophy, Cohen holds up as his model the critical reasoning of scientific method. One cannot remove history "from the application of rigorous tests of truth, which constitutes the essence of scientific method."[26] But the relation of science to each subject matter varies. History and the various sciences have this difference—history uses laws to explain facts, the sciences use facts to discover laws. The historian cannot avoid tracing causal connections. However, the phenomena of civilization are more complex than those in the physical sciences, and the terms of social and historical causation less clearly defined; the search for laws of history is therefore more complex than the search for laws of physics. Insofar as history deals with evidence critically, Cohen defends it as a science. History at its best, tracing ties between facts and issues, is both scientific and artistic reconstruction.

History necessarily involves value judgments and ethical interpretations, witting or unwitting.[27] The philosophy of history must concern itself directly with ethics, which, like any philosophic quest, Cohen sees in the light of critical reason. Speculation as to what might have been, contrasted with what happened, appears to him to afford rich opportunities for further ethical evaluation. Cohen's view of history is an ethical view, the tragic view.

. . . Witnessing the great tragedies of history chastens our spirits and widens our sympathies, making us recognize our common human limitations and our common humanity.[28]

The History of Science

To his interest in history Cohen joined a keen realization of the importance of science. *A Dreamer's Journey* puts it thus:

The Hellenic ideal of science as a rational inquiry into nature seemed to be the foundation of the distinctive intellectual traits of Western civilization . . . no synoptic view of liberal civilization could be adequate which did not include an understanding of science [p. 184].

He went on to reveal one of his lifelong dreams:

I had a driving desire to trace the unending adventures of the human mind from Pythagoras to Einstein which are at the source of all enduring achievements in the history of Western civilization [p. 192].

Cohen never lived to compose a complete history of science, though parts of what he had written were occasionally incorporated into other works. Thus, there is a provocative section on the history and philosophy of medicine in *The Meaning of Human History*. The one historical work on science that he did get out was on the Greek beginnings of science. *A Source Book in Greek Science* was written in collaboration with Cohen's former student, the distinguished classical scholar and historian of science I. E. Drabkin.

The book combines classics, linguistics, and the art of translating with ancient history and the history of science, now proven to be considerably older than had been popularly supposed. Cohen was fond of reminding the positivists that deduction accompanies induction in scientific achievement. It was important likewise to remind the historians of science that science leans on theory as well as facts. *Reason and Nature* tells us that one of the roots of the error that is "the basis of all empiricism, is the assumption that science necessarily deals only with the actual."[29] Just as general history becomes more meaningful against a philosophic background, so, too, the history of science is viewed in wider perspective against the background of the philosophy of science: "The power of significant synthesis seems rarer than the power to dig for individual facts."[30] *A Source Book in Greek Science* is not only a monument of scholarship; it also bears the philosophic mark upon it.

Legal Philosophy

When in 1912 young Morris Cohen first urged "Jurisprudence as a Philosophical Discipline" upon his fellow philosophers of this country, they seemed as loath as the jurists to join their two trails. This native narrowness of outlook was all the more provincial compared with the foreign tradition of legal philosophy as an integral part of humanistic training and endeavor. Nevertheless, little by little at first, then with increasing momentum, the meeting of the minds took place among lawyers and judges, general philosophers and specialists in ethics, economists, sociologists, and anthropologists. Cohen's example was followed by other philosophers. Law schools granted wider place to legal philosophy. Before long, Cohen was launched on what was to be a powerfully influential though secondary career as legal educator.

Legal material pointed up for him old issues in logic, ethics, and metaphysics. "Law, philosophy, and social justice have thus become merged," he wrote in the Introduction to his first book on legal philosophy. To trace those currents, he used polarity and scientific method.

Cohen, the first editor of Charles Peirce's essays on scientific method, seems to me to have been undeniably influenced in his jurisprudence by Peirce's principle of pragmatism: that the meaning of a proposition is found by considering all its possible experimental consequences. In both of Cohen's major works on legal philosophy, he sounds this note. "It is an error," he declared in *Reason and Law,* "to think of the meaning of a *legal proposition* as something completely independent of its consequences."[31] In his earlier *Law and the Social Order* he had stated:

> The theoretical sciences now select their fundamental propositions not because of their immediate self-evidence, but because of the system of consequences that follows from them. A practical science like the law ought not to despise that procedure [p. 175].

Cohen's own writing on the law analyzes the social consequences of legal ideas. For example, he starts with two concepts traditionally considered wide apart, "Property and Sovereignty," the first relegated to private, the second to public law. He traces their interconnections in actual practice, from feudal times to the present. Knowledge of history, economic theory, and law he combines with scientific and philosophic acumen.

He directed deadly ridicule against what he baptised as "the phonograph theory" of an unchanging law, which the judge merely plays back to pronounce his decision. The law is constantly being modified by the very process of judicial decision. The claim that every decision of the Supreme Court follows logically from the Constitution Cohen characterizes as a national delusion.

"It is a superstition to suppose that the judge's opinions on social and economic questions do not influence his decisions." The Supreme Court, he contends, is more than a court of law. The issues before it involve "questions of economics, politics, and social policy which legal training cannot solve unless law includes all social knowledge."[32]

What then is the law? An art as well as a science, "one of the essential arts of civilization"; law is an ever-changing human product, not identical with reason, not a purely logical system like mathematics, yet utilizing, along with social experience, legal reasoning, juristic logic, scientific method. Just as science needs fact as well as logic, so law needs phenomena as well as logic. As "My Philosophy of Law" puts it, logic is a necessary but not a sufficient condition for the human experience we call law. And we must distinguish "the use from the abuse of logic in the law."[33]

The task of the law, for Cohen, is the setting-up of norms to govern the world of actuality. Jurisprudence must avoid both positivism and the opposite formalistic extreme. He warns: "Law without concepts or rational ideas, law that is not logical, is like pre-scientific medicine—a hodge-podge of sense and superstition. . . ."[34] But a purely formal jurisprudence, purged of the existential, sets up a dichotomy between mind and matter, which would make the law a homeless wandering ghost, "a world of function without substance, a grin without a cat."[35] For Cohen, "there can be no normative or critical legal science without a thorough knowledge of the actual facts of human conduct."[36]

On the classical controversy as to whether the law rests on justice or force, Cohen cites Lord Coke, who in an argument with King James urged that law was nothing but reason. The King replied, "Have I not reason too?"[37] Hobbes's comment, that Coke's authority was based on the King's power, points to the element of force necessary to law. But principles of justice are also involved in the law, which is thus related to ethics—"normative jurisprudence thus ultimately depends on ethics and yet is relatively distinguishable from it."[38] Not only ethics and logic, but metaphysics, sociology, anthropology, economics, statistics, politics—all converge on law to follow the royal road to reason that leads to liberal civilization.

Social Philosophy

The spirit of Theodore Roosevelt, conjured up by Morris Cohen, asks: "If philosophy cannot solve our present social problems, of what actual earthly good is it?" In reply, Cohen says that the philosopher serves truth first, rather than reform. The lover of truth sets up "a standard of a developed critical spirit without which all solutions of human problems lack the essence of liberality."[39] "Intellectual liberality" is Cohen's phrase in a letter to Holmes. "Science means progress," says Cohen, "because it is constantly correcting itself,"[40] and so must liberal society. He says in *The Faith of a Liberal:*

This open eye for possible alternatives, each to receive the same logical treatment before we can determine which is the best grounded, is the essence of liberalism in art, morals, and politics [p. 8].

Tolerance and the possibility of human progress are the principles of liberalism. Its credo is faith in the superior vitality of the truth, including ethical truth, and faith in human effort. Humility or consciousness of human limitations, and courageous tenacity, must accompany the liberal in his struggle for freedom. Liberalism results from the application of logic and the scientific method to the problems of society. Cohen's social philosophy was rationalistic. His faith in liberalism was described by Judge Nathan R. Margold, one-time student of the professor's, as an "abiding confidence in the power of reason to give arms to that love of humanity which, without arms, is so pitiful a figure in the world of today."[41]

The poet Edwin Arlington Robinson once said of his friend: "No, Dr. Cohen won't bother you. Not unless you make a statement."[42] Or as Holmes put it to Laski: "He does not lightly yield to popular superstitions."[43]

Cohen's omnipresent scientific method and his awareness of polarity set him eternally on guard, so that he could spot more than one danger at a time, on the extreme left or on the extreme right. He was taken in neither by "dictatorship of the proletariat" nor "unlimited free enterprise," neither by "a government of laws and not of men" (paraphrased as a government of lawyers and not of men), nor by "the mushroom science of psychoanalysis." ("Thank God for my inhibitions," he used to say.) Critical, jealous of the mission of the philosopher, Cohen eschewed the instrumentalists' "too ardent desire to improve the world." Overconcentration on affairs of the market place, he argued, leads to neglect of the cosmic roots of philosophy, hence to its impoverishment and illiberality; for "practical interests corrupt our reasoning power." Cohen, like Peirce, claimed that "Morality is necessary for the good life but it is not the whole of it."[44]

Despite a less down-to-earth, more visionary approach than the pragmatists', Cohen fought with them against many a common foe, for many a common cause, and for many of the same principles. He defended equality of opportunity, the right of the people to be free from exploitation; he argued wherever possible for civil liberties, individual and social rights, and for the advantages of cultural diversity.

The end was a liberal society where the freeman leads the life of reason —free to contemplate, study, and philosophize to his heart's content. Cohen said in his *Preface to Logic:*

Tolerance, the avoidance of fanaticism, and above all a wider and clearer view of the nature of our beliefs and their necessary consequences, is thus a goal or end which the development of logic serves. In this sense logic is a necessary element of any liberal civilization [p. 187].

The theoretic study of the law and of ethics, like the advancement of science and logic, seemed to him direct routes to the good life and good in themselves.

Cohen did not keep long on any one path—there were so many to map —the candle flickered out too soon. Hence the incompleteness (sometimes even the fragmentary quality) in parts of his writing. Unfinished though his work was, he achieved, along with a systematic method, a many-sided but cohesive effort toward his single goal.

Huntington Cairns called Cohen "the chief critical philosopher the United States has known. No other mind in the history of American thought has devoted itself with such acuteness and clarity to the exposition of the necessary assumptions which lie behind the branches of inquiry."[45]

Irwin Edman, professor of philosophy at Columbia, described Cohen the philosopher in the memorial services for him at the New School on February 2, 1947:

To know Morris Cohen at all was to know a philosopher . . . for he had always the classic note of the philosophical temper. He could talk of many things, often unexpected ones . . . like baseball, for example, or the military history of the Civil War, on which he was long a kind of private expert. But whatever he talked about he raised to the plane of resolute and revealing philosophical analysis . . . though critical of orthodox theology . . . he had the deepest piety to the nature of things as reason revealed it to him, and a deep piety to the human wisdom in the ritual and tradition of his people; and, with his scrupulous intellectual detachment, he was, in the best sense, an unworldly man.

. . . conversation with him was a philosophical experience of the first order. Often when the specific subject matter was not philosophy at all . . . one felt one was dealing with genuinely philosophical issues in a way that conversation with technical philosophers does not always make one feel. . . .

But they are mistaken who, because Morris Cohen refused to allow nonsense or confusion to go unrebuked, think that pure methodology or pure controversy was his interest . . . he had . . . a lifelong passionate conviction that vision, intellectual vision, is both the goal and the blessing of philosophy . . . he saw in philosophy itself the greatest liberation.

He sometimes rather sharply rebuked those who wished to make philosophy the uncritical and hasty servant of human welfare or current notions of human welfare, but his sharpness was but the cutting edge of his deep devotion to the contemplative ideal. For like Spinoza . . . he felt that all freedom was lost where the mind is enslaved. And the freedom of the mind and the joy of it for its own sake were the lessons he taught a whole generation of students and of his fellow philosophers.

. . . he stood out as the Socratic personality of our time . . . the philosophy that he admired above all was Spinoza's and, among contemporaries, Santayana in his Spinozistic moments. And Morris Cohen himself exemplified in his point of view at once detachment and a passionate faith in reason. . . . Realizing the human plight and the human tragedy, he looked to philosophy . . . as both a consolation and a spiritual resource . . . philosophy itself was a way of life, a contemplation of things in their true and ultimate worth. . . .

. . . he remains a most eloquent voice in our generation of the hope of life, the joy that lies in reason; the incorruptibility proper to and indispensable to both that joy and that hope.

Other philosophers leave a school based on philosophic dogma. Cohen has left instruments and charts instead. Even more than *a* philosophy, his was a philosophic way to philosophy, and a way of life very much in the ancient tradition of Socrates, Plato, and Aristotle. It was to the compelling and exalted sense of the function of philosophy that he dedicated himself. If, as Cohen says, "the pursuit of truth gives us the divine spark of blessedness,"[46] then he has struck that spark for his age.

X. *Cohen on Dewey and Liberalism*

IN RETROSPECT, the first half of the twentieth century shines out as the Golden Age of American Philosophy. Peirce, James, Royce, Santayana, Whitehead, Dewey, and Cohen, to name some of the giants, all were alive during the first decade of the century. The first three died within six years of each other, 1910–16. The last four survived until mid-century, dying within the five years of 1947 to 1952. Morris Cohen was one link among the seven. The pupil of James and Royce, the first editor of Peirce, and one of the earliest to spread recognition of Santayana, he was also a personal friend of Whitehead and of Dewey.

The relationship between Cohen and Dewey covered half a century. Cohen's vigorous criticism of Dewey's philosophy and Dewey's of Cohen's were public knowledge, for the echoes of their thunderous debates resounded beyond the ivory towers. In 1939, at the American Philosophical Association's meeting in honor of Dewey's eightieth birthday, Dewey and Cohen stepped before us on the stage of Columbia University's MacMillan Theatre. Pale with earnestness, each pleaded his cause, isolated in his own universe of discourse, so intent on his own convictions that he could not perceive its possible kinship with the other's. I doubt if anyone present could avoid the impression of witnessing one of the great philosophic duels of the century.

Although he rejected Dewey's social approach, Cohen established his own brand of liberalism. Besides the fundamental differences, one may point to less recognized resemblances of practice and theory between their social philosophies. Cohen's was itself tinged with a kind of pragmatism.

The Yankee John Dewey, born and reared in Vermont, and the Jew Morris Cohen, born in Tsarist Russia and reared first in a ghetto, then in the ferment of New York's Lower East Side, met at Davidson's Glenmore before the turn of the century. They shared, with a common taste for

169

the Adirondack wilderness, a common devotion to Davidson and his heroic ideals.

This early bond between Cohen and Dewey helps to explain the terms of Cohen's acknowledgment of Dewey's role in his own early development:

I am personally deeply grateful for the illumination and inspiration which I have drawn from his writings and from conversations with him since my boyhood days in 1899. His Textbook on Psychology and his early volume on Leibniz were among the first readings that led me to philosophy.[1]

But beginning in 1916 and not ending till 1954, Cohen's publications disputed with Dewey. Cohen's attack on Dewey's social philosophy, like his attack on Dewey's naturalism, fired at anthropocentrism and instrumentalism. A composite critique may be synthesized from Cohen's numerous pages on Dewey. Cohen's objections to the instrumentalist approach may be ascribed to underlying differences between the philosophers of emphasis, proportion, and attitude.

Cohen decries in Dewey "too much absorption with human problems." On the question of proportion, Cohen finds Dewey slighting a crucial part of the philosopher's task, because of "too great concentration on the problems of practical education and empirical psychology. Concentration upon practical or social applications have, for instance, led Mr. Dewey to belittle, if not to ignore, the interest in physical or cosmic issues." "The too ardent desire to make philosophy a means to improve the world" seems to Cohen "the source of the limitations of Professor Dewey's educational and political philosophy."[2]

I should not wish to deny that social problems can be viewed as offering genuine philosophic issues; I have made some attempts in that direction myself. But I cannot agree that this is the only proper field for philosophic reflection.[3]

Dewey's *Reconstruction in Philosophy* strains the facts, according to Cohen, in contending "that philosophy originated not out of intellectual but out of social and emotional material." The moralist's "distrust of the pursuit of knowledge for its own sake" gives Cohen misgivings. For him, "the theoretic life needs no justification."

His own inclinations in the matter are summed up in his reply to Ernest Nagel:

Aug. 1 [1931]

Dear Ernest:

. . . The question as to my attitude to my contemporaries does not trouble me in the least. You may be perfectly right in saying that I overemphasize my differences from them. But then I would have nothing to say if I agreed that philosophy is concerned only with helping the man in the street to solve his temporal problems. Detachment *is* to me of the essence of philosophy. . . .

. . . At a time when the contemporary aspects of things are over-emphasized by all the ruling forces of our intellectual life, there is no harm in stressing the other phase, especially as it does not prevent me from paying close attention to contemporary thought and even writing a book on it. . . .

MORRIS R. COHEN

Two later letters to Nagel allude to Dewey. The first, on July 11, 1939, said: "He seems to me to be systematically evasive on all the important cosmologic problems." In the second, Cohen confided to Nagel his feelings about writing his paper for the 1939 celebration.

August 18, 1939

. . . I at first refused to undertake it but yielded because I fear that the cannonization of Dewey's empiricistic and moralistic philoso-phy will choke the speculative urge which seems to me to be the life-blood of philosophy. . . .

MORRIS R. COHEN

Martin Gardner, a student of Cohen's seminar in social philosophy con-ducted at the University of Chicago in 1939, recalls, in a letter to me, Cohen's fundamental criticism of Dewey:

One day the topic somehow drifted over into the question of what Dewey meant by truth. Cohen spoke of the fact that Dewey's recently published Logic had only one page reference in the index to the word "truth," and this was merely a quotation from Peirce to the effect that truth was the eventual outcome of the process of inquiry, or some-thing to that effect. The question was whether Dewey believed that there was an actual external world, with some sort of structure, so that there would be a meaning to the correspondence theory of truth. Cohen, of course, like Russell, was a "realist" in his acceptance of a correspondence theory; and this was one of his principal disagree-ments with Dewey. I recall Cohen speaking, with sadness in his voice, of various attempts he had made to find out exactly what Dewey thought about this, and of his inability to pin Dewey down to an answer. He had finally written Dewey a careful letter, explicitly asking him for light on the point, but had received only a polite, but still eva-sive reply.

"I disagree with Dewey, but I respect *him*," Cohen once said in arguing acridly with a fellow philosopher. It would be missing the point to minimize

Cohen's very real philosophic rebellion against Dewey. Yet the pronounced intellectual and moral admiration of the younger man for his senior must also be noted throughout Cohen's published works. Dewey's acumen and learning are extolled, and he is praised even above Cohen's own beloved teacher James. The laurel wreath is placed upon Dewey's head in Cohen's *American Thought:*

> John Dewey is unquestionably the pre-eminent figure in American philosophy; no one has done more to keep alive the fundamental ideals of liberal civilization; and if there could be such an office as that of national philosopher, no one else could be properly mentioned for it [p. 290].

Dewey and Cohen collaborated as philosophers in the Conference on Legal and Social Philosophy. Cohen's edition of the first collection of essays by Peirce, *Chance, Love, and Logic,* appeared in 1923 with an Introduction by Cohen and a "Supplementary Essay on the Pragmatism of Peirce" by John Dewey.

Righteous indignation in these two men was translated into action. Many was the social cause in which the two crusaders found themselves aligned on the same side. Each used his pen in defense of the rights of Sacco-Vanzetti; both contributed in 1934 to *The Meaning of Marx, A Symposium,* for which they were both lambasted in the Communist *New Masses.* They were associated in one way or another with the American Civil Liberties Union. Both backed the League for Industrial Democracy and the Tamiment Economic and Social Institute. Beginning in 1936, the two of them lent their names to the American Friends of Spanish Democracy; and Cohen lectured in 1937 for the American Committee for Anti-Nazi Literature, of which Dewey was a sponsor. In 1938 they were both among the 115 American educators who signed a pro-Loyalist, anti-Franco statement directed against the Spanish rebels' attack on education and intellectuals. Each of them aided Alfred M. Bingham's *Common-Sense.* Cohen contributed a chapter to the *Bertrand Russell Case* (1941), edited by John Dewey and Horace Kallen with an Introduction by Dewey. Dewey and Cohen similarly supported the International Relief Association. And so on.

As James T. Farrell recalls: "Several times John said 'I like Morris.'" Two letters from Dewey are typical of their relationship.

June 5, '31

Dear Cohen,

A committee of 35 or 30 is being formed to consider the public educational system of NY and work out some kind of a constructive plan for bettering teachers morale and securing more effective leadership inside the system. We hope to cooperate with the Graves inquiry, but will have an independent organization and do some investigating on our own account. Dean Russell, Kilpatrick and others of the Teachers

College, Lindeman, Nudd of the P E A, Linville, Mrs. Swan and Mrs. Pollak are already agreed to serve and quite a no. of others. Those who are interested are desirous to have you on the committee too. The membership will be confined to educators with some others who have shown a definite interest in public education; we hope it will become a fairly permanent organization. All who have followed previous investigations are agreed that one reason nothing has been done was because there was no body of organized opinion to pursue the matter.

Sincerely yours,
JOHN DEWEY

June 25 [1931]

Dear Cohen,

Thanks for your acceptance. The only work done during the summer will be in examination and summarizing of previous surveys, examinations of proceedings of the Board etc wh[ich] will be done by persons engaged for the purpose. The Committee won't need to meet till fall.

Evelyn [Dewey's daughter] and I were so sorry not to get to your Silver Wedding Anniversary. We had expected to be there and were prevented at the last moment.

With our regards and congratulations to you both,
Sincerely yours
JOHN DEWEY

In view of Cohen's reputation for philosophic detachment, it is appropriate to look at further instances of Cohen's social action, not too far in principle and practice from Dewey's own. On October 21, 1910, a letter of Cohen's appeared on page eight of *The Evening Post*. It was signed "Unafraid of 1912." Backing Henry L. Stimson for Governor of New York, Cohen attacked the Roosevelt-haters who were campaigning against Stimson as part of their opposition to Teddy Roosevelt's Bull Moose movement.

Mr. Roosevelt is branded as a public enemy because he doubts the wisdom of the majority opinion of the Supreme Court in a decision where that Court was divided five to four. . . .
I have never been an ardent admirer of Mr. Roosevelt, and have always voted against him, but his recent activity in New York State politics has certainly been a comfort to the friends of Governor Hughes and good government.

A prompt thank you from Teddy Roosevelt on the letterhead of *The Outlook* assured Cohen that he was "pleased and touched."

In a letter to the editor of the New York *Times,* June 13, 1933, Cohen wrote apropos of criticism of student disorder:

The right of citizens to criticize public officials for serious shortcomings and especially for acts exceeding their authority is inherent in our constitutional system and in the spirit of our common law. The notion that the mere criticism of any public official is itself illegal has no place in a democracy; and if my old-fashioned view be radicalism, more of it will save us from Czarism, Hitlerism and other forms of irresponsible autocracy.

Cohen, like Dewey, never forsook the cause of labor. With his start in the atmosphere of the Jewish Labor Movement and the Socialist Labor Party, and after his association with the Breadwinners' College, Cohen remained all his life sensitized to working-class rights.

Nov. 19/37

Dear Mr. Hartley:—

I have your letter of Nov. 17th enclosing a copy of your code of Practice for the brewing industry. The code is good so far as it goes, but it omits a vital question, viz. the relation of the industry to the people who do the work involved in it. And this means not only the wage scale but also the extent to which the men are allowed a voice in determining the conditions under which they spend the major part of their day. No code can claim to be scientific, or to recognize the rights of the public, which ignores this aspect. Society has no right to produce beer at the expense of human life or dignity.

Sincerely yours,

MORRIS R. COHEN

Through the years Cohen gave lectures and lecture courses at the Manhattan Trade School, the Cooper Union, the Rand School, the Labor Temple School, Camp Tamiment's Economic and Social Institute, the Debs School and the League for Industrial Democracy. Letters testify to his effectiveness in those forums.

Rand School of Social Science
March 26, 1931

My dear Professor Cohen,

. . . I hope you realized something of the pleasure of the audience as you were speaking. You may be an anti-socialist, but you deliver the sort of lecture that Socialists like. I, personally, got from you some material which is proving useful.

Incidentally you proved to us that man is not always controlled by economic motives. You made a sacrifice to come to us. If you get some theoretic satisfaction out of the demonstration, you are surely entitled to it.

Very sincerely yours,
WILLIAM E. BOHN

On June 3, 1932, G. F. Beck, the director of the Labor Temple School, wrote:

> Maybe the fact that I kept on talking with you long after I had gone to sleep the other night, in my bed, discussing some of the great matters you had opened up so generously and liberatingly in your wonderful lecture at Labor Temple School, will tell you better than conventional compliments could, how greatly your lecture was appreciated. It left me with a sense of being liberated and disentangled from a lot of nonsense and rubbish that was so exhilarating that for hours afterward I still felt, in my dreams, that I was seeing things more clearly than I had seen them for a long time. . . .

Another letter of Bohn's from the Rand School of Social Science, on Sept. 13, 1934:

> . . . I think it would be much worth while for you and the other men of your sort to do something for the education of the working class. I often think of old Huxley and his lectures in the Workingmen's College. Those were lectures, and they still have influence. . . .
>
> Most of our more or less distinguished scholars have little to give. And they would not know how to give it. But you know the working class. You could talk to them. I think you could do as much as anyone to bridge the gulf that yawns between the workers and American scholarship. . . .

Bohn, as secretary of Tamiment's Organization Committee, wrote again on June 30, 1936:

> Thanking you is like thanking God. I don't think you expect it or care a whoop about it. But we all are really grateful to you for what you did to our labor conference. From the moment when you got hold of it the conference was a different thing—more vital, live, human.
>
> I am reporting to the Tamiment office that your expenses were $4.50. . . .

Cohen raised $50.00 for the Passaic Strikers' Relief in 1926, thanks to the generosity of his friend Arthur S. Meyer, and served on the Citizens' Emergency Committee of 1931.

His views on economics were scarcely conservative. On a Sunday afternoon in the thirties, Eli Bernheim, a retired banker, was visiting his favorite nephew, Arthur Meyer, in Scarsdale. Harold Winkler, then a Harvard classmate of Meyer's son Daniel, tells how sad Uncle Eli was about the economic ills that were besetting the free-enterprise system. Cohen was walking around the room, glancing at books on the library shelves. Suddenly he broke into the conversation, saying, "I know the solution, I think, to these various problems."

Bernheim replied, "Why, Professor Cohen, I am delighted. I have been studying and thinking about these things for a long time. Do tell me what the answer might be."

"Socialism," said Cohen.

There was dead silence, and then Mr. Bernheim pulled himself to his feet and was helped out of the room. Winkler overheard him say as he went out, "Arthur, you know that I esteem Professor Cohen very highly. He is a great scholar. But, Arthur, do you think it's wise, when your young son and his friends are home from college, to have this dangerous radical mind around?"

Norman Thomas thanked Cohen right after election day for his support in the 1936 socialist campaign.

November 5, 1936

Dear Professor Cohen:

In a campaign which has been a duty rather than a lark—Time Magazine to the contrary notwithstanding—there have been some very bright spots. One of the brightest was the dinner which the Thomas-Nelson Independent Committee arranged in New York City. Your message meant a lot to me personally and, what is more important, I think, a lot to the cause. May I send you my very deep and hearty thanks.

Sincerely yours,
NORMAN THOMAS

When the short-lived Spanish democracy was threatened by rebels, Cohen sent a letter to Ambassador de los Rios, accompanied by a personal check for a hundred dollars. De los Rios thanked him in a wire:

June 8, 1937

As I am about to leave Washington to sail on the Queen Mary I read with deep emotion and sincere appreciation your kind letter and expression of adherence to the loyal cause My heartfelt thanks for your noble and generous attitude Cordial regards

FERNANDO DE LOS RIOS
Spanish Ambassador

Cohen wrote to Samuel G. Inman, American Friends of Spanish Democracy, on October 31, 1936:

Dear Prof. Inman:

I have your letter of October 29th suggesting that I reconsider my sponsorship of the Friends of the Spanish Republic. Permit me to say frankly that I am surprised at the illiberal tone of it. Why should not two organizations devoted to the same purpose work together, and why should you waste time, energy and postage to try to create difficulties for another organization which works for the same purpose? I know that there is a certain economy in unity of effort. But I am not sure that the advantages of different organizations do not overcome the purely economic one. At any rate, I suggest that at a time when the Spanish people need all the help that we can give them, it will be much wiser for you to cooperate with Amador's organization rather than try to wreck it. I think also that your own organization will profit by a liberal rather than a narrow attitude toward other organizations. I think it has been the ruin of liberal movements that they are more anxious to fight each other than the common enemy.

Please do not take this letter to mean any disapproval of the work of your organization. I have admired Bishop Paddock for almost forty years and there are other members on your Committee for whom I have the highest regard. The work which you have done up to now seems to me to have been admirably conceived; but I think you are making a great mistake in taking a narrow attitude to Mr. Amador's organization unless, indeed, you can show that the latter is dishonest or inimical to the best interests of Spanish democracy.

With all good wishes,

Sincerely yours,
MORRIS R. COHEN

Cohen hotly defended the Spanish Republic's need for arms.

February 23, 1938

Mr. John F. Finerty
120 Broadway
New York, N.Y.

Dear Mr. Finerty:

I have received a copy of your letter of February 10 to Mr. Paul J. Kern in which you object to the petition and memorandum of law on the embargo against Spain on the ground that if we are permitted to send arms to Spain today, we may also have to send arms to

Germany and Italy when they try to suppress rebellion in their own countries. Permit me to say that your argument seems to me too legalistic in the bad sense of the word; that is, it relies too much on the theory of precedents when the facts do not at all fit them. It seems to me that in a rapidly changing world we must be opportunist. Today we are actually helping Japan to suppress China, and indirectly also helping Germany and Italy to suppress not only opposition within their own boundaries but also to suppress democracy in Spain. Under the circumstances, everyone who is genuinely interested in seeing that a democratically elected government is not overthrown by military dictatorship, must do his utmost to see that the Spanish people obtain arms with which to defend themselves. The actual effect of your reasoning is to throttle the Spanish people, and when that is done rebellion against Hitler and Mussolini in Germany and Italy will be made more highly improbable.

Sincerely yours,
MORRIS R. COHEN

The growing strength of Hitler forced Cohen, in the crisis, into even more urgent action. When in *U.S. News* of April 11, 1938, the question of the week was "Should America Offer a Haven to Europe's Political Refugees?" Cohen wrote on behalf of the *Conference on Jewish Relations:*

The founders of our republic cherished the ideal of our country as a haven for the victims of political or religious persecution. The efforts of our State Department to provide some aid to the victims of the present brutal oppression in central Europe should therefore be supported by all those who still share the old American faith. Our immigration laws should be so modified as to allow the entrance into this country of those, who like Carl Schurz and the other refugees of 1848, can in these troubled days reinforce our national loyalty to the ideals of liberty and democracy.[4]

Cohen led two lives, an inner life of philosophizing and introspection, an outer life of strenuous pursuit of intellectual and social goals. Only by interweaving the two could he fulfill himself. There was a time for writing and a time for living. To his youthful diary he had confided on July 14, 1897: "It is not enough to look on, I must join in. . . . To become isolated from mankind is not to be happy." Thirty-nine years later he wrote in his diary, "To be too detached, to walk this life like a ghost would not give us anything at all to see." In the end, he spent himself for Jewry.

Yet, Cohen did criticize Dewey for excessive concern with human troubles, and it is legitimate to ask if he, the critic of Dewey's focus on "affairs of the market place," has left in his own writings a philosophy as well as a practice of liberalism.

Cohen never lived to give us his last word on social philosophy. But in

1946 *The Faith of a Liberal* brought together many of its strands. He tells us that he thinks

> . . . of the liberal temper as, above all a faith in enlightenment, a faith in a process rather than in a set of doctrines, a faith instilled with pride in the achievements of the human mind, and yet colored with a deep humility before the vision of a world so much larger than our human hopes and thoughts. . . .
>
> . . . liberalism means a pride in human achievement, a faith in human effort. . . . The philosophy back of that is summed up in two great faiths or beliefs: the belief in progress, and the belief in toleration. I believe those are the two fundamental ideas of liberalism [pp. 437, 449].

Specific precepts for liberal society emerge from Cohen's writings: support of academic, intellectual, and religious freedom; endorsement of federalism—political, legal, religious, and cultural; opposition to the dangers of militarism. He urged use of the social contract in the broad sense of the term; support of the separation of church and state; and revival of the classical doctrine of natural rights. He opposed Plato's preference for government by philosophers; defended increased governmental participation in economic planning; he was against corporate despotism and economic anarchy; he called for liberalization of immigration; he debunked racism. He believed the jury system superior to trial by judge alone; he considered governmental responsibility a proper accompaniment of governmental power; he believed in the primacy of the electorate.

To cite a few examples of his views, there are these from "Socialism and Capitalism," in *The Faith of a Liberal:*

> From this inherent instability of business there develops that terrible plague of modern life, the uncertainty of employment, an evil which private capitalism cannot possibly remove [p. 99]. . . .

> Another product of the unequal distribution of wealth is the constant temptation to crime which modern wealth offers . . . it is hopeless to find remedies for modern crime so long as we do not or cannot at least mitigate the intensity of the cause [p. 102]. . . .

> . . . some combination of the principles of individualism and collectivism is possible in a well-ordered society [p. 108]. . . .

> Free thought, which must include some right to dissent and to express the ground of the dissent, finds as little toleration under Communism as under Fascism and Czarism [p. 106].

Liberalism, as Cohen saw it, must reach beyond individual rights, to men in relation to society:

> The liberalism that began by glorifying freedom of speech, thought, religion, and association in terms of absolute individual rights is learning at last to speak the language of social welfare.[5]

Together, the elements of Cohen's social philosophy in his diverse writings constitute a program for liberalism. Its symbol is evoked in *The Faith of a Liberal:*

. . . it has always been of the very essence of liberal civilization that the organic or basic motives of man should be regulated and controlled by the light of reason [p. 71].

A leitmotiv running through Cohen's works is his philosophical creed of the foundations of liberal civilization: logic and reason; skepticism and tolerance; detachment and otherworldliness; free inquiry and scientific truth; ethical truth as the fruit of reason; the application of scientific method to social problems; and the subjection of our most fundamental dogma, even of liberalism itself, to the critical spirit.

This critical spirit as a necessary condition to true liberalism guarded Cohen from shibboleths and from the romantic illusions to which liberals may fall heir. His sense of the function of philosophy was an exalted one. The philosopher must remember that he is neither statesman nor social worker, economist nor preacher. His job as a social philosopher is to examine philosophically the bases, methods, and forms of our human conduct in society, even when the concepts, like that of democracy, seem above suspicion.[6]

Just as doubt has meaning only in relation to something fixed, so the method of critical doubt is connected in Cohen's mind with men's eternal search for the light of reason. Tolerance is the child of such systematic critique. Axiomatic also are his beliefs in the usefulness of human effort, the process of enlightenment, and the possibility—not inevitability—of progress. All these beliefs that Cohen professed in his writings and lived up to in his life added up for him to the faith of a liberal.

The Puritan spirit in Dewey had set highest store on activity to achieve the common weal. "The essence of pragmatic instrumentalism," he writes in *The Quest for Certainty,* "is to conceive *both* knowledge and practice as means of making goods—excellencies of all kinds—secure in experienced existence" [p. 37]. Cohen praised effort but claimed that the exercise of the mind is also activity. For him, the Hebraic tradition, akin in this respect to the Aristotelian hierarchy of values, raised up as *summum bonum* the sanctity of study and contemplation. Such "refined sort of enjoyment" was scorned by Dewey, in whose ideal society there would be less sitting still than in Cohen's. Cohen, however, wrote in his diary:

The condemnation of the speculative life as an "escape" . . . need not be taken seriously by an intelligent being who is not afraid of epithets. . . . Escape from suffering is what we all try to effect. In some instances we can escape by changing the external social conditions. But human power or the power of any one individual in this respect, is very limited. The other way is to cultivate within ourselves those adjustments that will enable us to lighten the burden. The two ways are not always compatible but they are not always mutually exclusive. And in any case a wise man will use both ways.

Dewey would probably not have accepted Cohen's "detachment and otherworldliness." And Dewey would doubtless have been less resigned than Cohen to "The Tragic View of History." But certainly Dewey had every right to claim as very much his own Cohen's precept of "the application of scientific method to social problems." In general the axiomatic beliefs of the men were parallel: knowledge and truth, freedom and humanity, the critical spirit, and courage were Dewey's as well as Cohen's desiderata. Dewey's was an empirical search, Cohen's a theoretical search, but each sought truth to guide mankind.

Cohen's was the liberalism of a rationalist; Dewey's the liberalism of a pragmatist. Yet, pragmatically, Dewey's and Cohen's social programs were attuned. Cohen, like Dewey, practiced what he preached—devotion to the cause of liberalism. In theory he did not agree with Dewey's identification of practice and theory. In practice, he often acted on it. When Cohen called the light of civilization "a hard won prize of strenuous effort," he was expressing in his own way a Deweyan exhortation to activity.

Cohen and Dewey were philosophically closer than they or their contemporaries generally realized. In a letter to Justice Holmes (see p. 326 for complete text), Cohen, while protesting his difference from Dewey, avowed that he, Cohen, was a logical pragmatist after the manner of the founder of pragmatism, Charles Peirce.

August 7, 1920

My agreement with pragmatism extends to the main point made by Peirce, viz. that the way to make our ideas clear is to examine their possible consequences, or in technical language, all their possible implications. It is an attempt to extend the experimental method to the handling of ideas, and very fruitful if used logically, for the essence of intellectual liberality consists in the realization that what is familiar to us is only one of a number of possibilities. . . . This aspect, however, has not been developed by James or Dewey because they are not interested in logic and metaphysics but only in psychology.

Cohen's conscious acceptance of Peirce's major tenet of pragmatism seems to me a significant link between Cohen and Dewey. Particularly noteworthy were Cohen's applications of his pragmatism in legal philosophy.

Felix Frankfurter saw the Dewey-Cohen relationship from a wide perspective and wrote from the Law School of Harvard:

May 3, 1923

Dear Morris:

Just as I was on the point of writing you a further word, aroused in me by your fugitive comments the other day on Dewey, comes your letter.

(1) As to Dewey. It occurred to me, during those high moments of thinking when I shave in the morning, that you are unjust to Dewey by emphasizing the defects of his quality instead of his quality. I cannot imagine that in the course of a long walk with you he would whistle tragedy down the wind much more than you do. His emphasis, for the time, is combating what I assume you agree with him in regarding as the most pernicious tendency of our period, namely, anti-intellectualism. Couéism and Fascismo, in all their manifestations, are the dragons he is out to slay. In the process he, of course, indulges in the usual exaggerations of a protagonist.

Nor do I think his other defect one from which we are suffering too much at present, namely, his insistence on the efficacy of effort. The Fates steadily do overtime in showing up the undue limits of Dewey's optimism, and I don't feel too badly about his over-emphasis. You see my eclectic soul thoroughly believes both in Dewey's insistence on the intellect as an instrument and your insistence on its limitations; i.e. "—a wisely cultivated attitude of resignation to inevitable ills." . . .

Yours always,

F F

Sidney Hook, according to Joseph Blau, also indicated that there was a convergence between the two masters of "rival" philosophies:

Professor Sidney Hook of New York University, one of the many naturalists who studied under both Cohen and Dewey, finds that these two varieties of the naturalistic temper are closely akin to each other. The difference between the two complementary emphases was exaggerated in discussion.[7]

The "exaggeration in discussion" prevalent among their followers is evident in this letter:

Labor Temple School
New York

Sept. 17th, 1931

Dear Dr. Morris Cohen:—

My very heartiest thanks for your generous reply. I cannot tell you how happy I am that you have consented to come to the School and address our people, some time in the new year after Febr. 15th. You see, we shall have about double the unemployment in our district this winter and, though it sounds strange to the uninitiated, these people, the vast majority of them, are feeling more than just a material hunger and want. I put a questionnaire to them some time ago, asking for their choice of subjects for this winter's program. Economics was the eleventh subject, in the matter of votes put down for a course, and Philosophy, literature and music were way at the head of the list, receiving an overwhelming majority of votes. In other words, they have a mental or spiritual hunger that is even more urgent than the distress caused by their material wants.

Again, in Woodstock this summer, I found several groups of my students living in tents, with wives, sweethearts and children, studying, arguing, writing and debating, infinitely more concerned with questions of logic and dialectics than with problems of economy. I think we have an amazing phenomenon here, one that is rarely alluded to by our economic and political quacks. . . . But as to pragmatism, these Russian Jews, boys and girls, simply despise it from the bottom of their hearts. One of them, a brilliant fellow, who sat under a tree by a running brook, as hairy as the great god Pan, with his wife and child tumbling about, on the grass, said to me.

"Beck, it comes to this. Cohen believes in Thought without Action. Dewey believes in Action without Thought. Give me Cohen every time. We shall always be poor. Wealth is inside a man, not outside of him."

That is why your generous answer fills me with joy. You will come and talk to these folks. I shall let lots of them come in without paying. But many will pay and pay gladly. And that shall be all yours.

With my very heartiest thanks,
Yours very sincerely
G. F. BECK [Director]

At the Hotel Astor dinner in 1927, Dewey had paid this tribute to Cohen:

Wherever there has been any oppression, there the oppressed have found a friend in Morris Cohen. . . . in writing ourselves down his friend, we are in some measure also identifying ourselves with the friends of truth, the friends of freedom, the friends of that freedom which is both the parent and the progeny of truth, the friends of that truth which alone makes humanity free.

Then with a ghost of a smile lurking under his mustache, Dewey added dryly:

I might almost say that the only thing I have against him is his undue fear lest somebody else agree with him.[8]

Those who knew Cohen acknowledged the neatness of the thrust.

A psychological *aperçu* in Dewey's intellectual autobiography furnishes a possible explanation for the heat of the exchanges between him and Cohen:

. . . a case might be made out for the proposition that the emphasis upon the concrete, empirical, and "practical" in my later writings . . . was a reaction against what was more natural. . . . It is, I suppose, becoming a commonplace that when anyone is unduly concerned with controversy, the remarks that seem to be directed against others are really concerned with a struggle that is going on inside himself.[9]

For Cohen, the more doughty the adversary, the more gaily he entered the philosophic lists. And so, after spreading knowledge of and espousing Peirce's "pragmaticism" himself, he rode hard against Deweyan pragmatism.

The years brought the two philosophers all the closer. When Cohen lost his wife, Dewey, who had also been widowed, came to see him on Riverside Drive. This was the last time I saw the two of them together. During his wife's illness, Cohen had been stricken with an affliction that affected his speech. Dewey at eighty-three had become increasingly hard of hearing. I served as interpreter between them. The subject of conversation? Principally Greek philosophy. The old spark that had seemed extinguished in my father's face came to life again. He seemed to get better from then on.

In Cohen's lonely last years, Dewey was faithful with his letters. Here is one of them:

> 1158 Fifth Avenue
> New York 29
> April 14 '46

Dear Morris

Many thanks for your note; it makes me happy that an expert on Peirce like yourself found something to approve in my article.

This morning I received your volume of The Faith of a Liberal. I hardly need say that I am glad you put together these articles and made them readily available. I want also to thank you [for] remembering me with a copy. With warm regards and best wishes

> Sincerely yours,
> JOHN DEWEY

James T. Farrell, out of his acquaintance with both Dewey and Cohen, showed a novelist's perceptivity in a letter to me on January 28, 1958. He spoke of

. . . liberal civilization as the core around which your father's teaching and writing centers . . . beneath his reason there was great or at least intense passion, controlled, concentrated, released by wit. And the passion centers in a love of liberal ideals. . . . The differences between your father and Dewey were clear ones, but their common faith was one.

John Dewey and Morris Cohen battled hardest against common foes—injustice and inhumanity, irrationalism and illiberalism.

XI. *Cohen and the Law*

MORRIS COHEN never became a lawyer. Yet judges, Supreme Court justices, and deans of law schools were in a sense his students. Holmes envied the youth who sat at his feet. His philosophical treatment of the law in relation to man and the social order may prove in time to be his foremost sphere of influence.

"The subject-matter of the law," he once explained, "is the regulation of the conduct of individuals living in those more or less permanent relations which we call society."[1] "For law is one of the means by which man tries to control his fate."[2] And the theoretic study of the law he saw as "one of the ways in which we can attain a deeper and wider view of human existence, and that is good, if anything is."[3] Cohen's principle of polarity, which he likened to the interaction of the upper and lower jaws, proved especially fruitful in a discipline that by Anglo-Saxon custom weighs opposing sides and considers contradictory possibilities.

He was fascinated by the interplay of law and life. Reading the law, writing and conversing on it, corresponding and constantly adding to his acquaintanceship in the field, lecturing and teaching legal philosophy, he pursued a lifelong inquiry into the meaning of law and its possibilities as an instrument of human justice. Judge Nathan R. Margold saw him as "the first American philosopher to interest himself in the law, as Holmes was the first American lawyer to interest himself in philosophy."[4]

Cohen once said that his interest in the law was rooted in the fact that the substance of his first education was Mosaic and Talmudic legislation.[5] At seventeen he confided to his diary: "I now consider that the only thing for me to do is to become [a] teacher than [then] a writer and perhaps lawyer."

Within three years, he was teaching and before another year was up had seen his first modest literary effort in print, appropriately enough, about his teacher Davidson. But no advance was made toward the law until he got to Harvard, where he sat in on occasional law-school lectures during 1905–06 and talked law with his roommate Felix Frankfurter. Yet the profound interest in theoretical jurisprudence, which tempted him to begin the formal study of the law, sprang largely out of his doctoral dissertation on Kant's ethics, as he wrote many years afterward to his friend McKeon, adding: "The substance of what I am interested in has to do with the notion of justice as expressed in legal thought and institutions."

During that year with Frankfurter, Cohen's interest in legal philosophy was stimulated by what he termed the arbitrary and often unenlightened character of judicial decisions in labor cases. His "Faith of a Logician" tells how he was eventually led to question the adequacy of the principles of the Bill of Rights, which form the justification of such decisions. "Equal protection of the law," admirable in the abstract, turns out to be unsatisfactory when applied to unequal individuals. Cohen sought refuge in the old doctrine of natural law and natural rights. The law, he was convinced, must consider moral demands and humane interests.

After Harvard, when Cohen's hopes of teaching philosophy seemed ill-fated, and when his salary as instructor of mathematics at Townsend Harris Hall High School was insufficient to meet the needs of his growing family, he heeded the advice of his lawyer friend Sam Rosensohn and took evening courses at New York University Law School, 1909–10. He never completed work for the degree, but "the feel of cases and legal method that I gained in this way," he acknowledged in *A Dreamer's Journey*, "helped me overcome the fear that keeps so many philosophers from trespassing on the premises of the law" (p. 137).

In philosophy Morris had been privileged to receive training at the hands of great teachers. In jurisprudence he was largely self-taught. But like the man who wills to be a winner, he chose his sparring partners from among the champions. As a first-year graduate student at Harvard he had defied William James in philosophy; a couple of years after his first and only year at law school, he challenged the wisdom of our overdevotion to "the case system of instruction [that] has tended to unduly emphasize empiricism in the law" (see p. 298). And this to Roscoe Pound, soon to be dean at Harvard Law School, where the case system had been established as the basis of our country's legal education. (Legal education has of late seen the need to supplement the case system.)

As soon as he was seriously considered for the philosophy department of City College, he proposed that a new course in legal philosophy be instituted. Harry A. Overstreet, chairman of the department, was surprised—courses in the philosophy of law were practically unknown among academic philosophers at that time—but could not resist him: "he had a way with him that made one feel that he spoke with authority. The department scheduled the course and came to be mighty proud of it."

The course was scheduled for Cohen to teach in the spring semester of 1913. But he did not rest there. He tried in vain to get his fellow philosophers to see the light. "Jurisprudence as a Philosophical Discipline," the paper Cohen read at the annual meeting of the American Philosophical Association, Eastern, Division, late in December 1912, found no converts —for the moment.

Cohen then began to organize kindred souls who felt as he did about dealing with law in conjunction with philosophy and ethics, social science and anthropology. He initiated a joint venture, the Conference on Legal and Social Philosophy. John Dewey was elected chairman; W. E. Hocking, reporter; he was secretary. The first conference on "Law and Social Values," was held at The City College, and at Columbia in 1913. Pound, the pre-eminent exponent of the approach among jurists, came down from Harvard Law School to open the session with a discourse on "The Philosophy of Law in America."

"The Process of Judicial Legislation," the paper Cohen read on his "phonograph theory," created more stir than anything he had yet written —largely unfavorable at first. Later, Margold called it "an epoch-making paper."

"*Jus Naturale Redivivum*" was Cohen's contribution to the Conference's spring meeting in 1914. A defense of that concern with justice evidenced in the old concept of natural law, it became a block for building his later comprehensive *Reason and Nature*. Giorgio Del Vecchio, Italy's leading legal philosopher, was won over by the essay.

At the fourth and final session of the Conference at Columbia in November 1915, Cohen presented a paper on " 'Real' and 'Ideal' Trends in Civil Law." Its moral was that the life of the law is explained neither by materialism nor idealism alone but depends on a combination of social factors, jurisprudence, and ethics.

Cohen wrote on the law for a wide variety of periodicals. Twenty-nine articles appeared in law reviews from 1912 to 1946. Beginning in 1915, he published eighteen pieces on law in *The New Republic,* eleven more in an assortment of other nonlegal outlets.

On the Continent, legal philosophy was flourishing vigorously. The Association of American Law Schools launched the Modern Legal Philosophy Series to provide English translations of outstanding European studies of the subject. John Wigmore, learned dean of Northwestern University's Law School, was the leading spirit of the enterprise. At his suggestion, Albert Kocourek, then professor, later dean at Northwestern, invited Cohen to join the association's editorial committee. He edited Volume 13 in the series, Tourtoulon's *Philosophy in the Development of Law,* translated from the French. It was Cohen's first book, appearing in 1922.

His first original treatise, *Reason and Nature* (1931), dealt in part with his legal philosophy, and Roscoe Pound found his theory of polarity "exactly what we have been needing in social and legal philosophy." The publication of *Law and the Social Order* (1933), Cohen's first tract on law, was acclaimed by the critics. Cohen's *Reason and Law* came out posthumously in 1950, and in paperback in 1961.

The last law book was *Readings in Jurisprudence and Legal Philosophy* (1951), edited by Felix S. Cohen in collaboration with his father. This anthology constituted a much-enlarged edition of their earlier *Readings in the Philosophy of Law,* privately published in 1930 for Morris Cohen's classes at the St. John's Law School and at The City College. Two other of his books bear in part on the law. The first, *The Faith of a Liberal* (1946), included papers on constitutional and natural rights, the Sacco-Vanzetti and Bertrand Russell cases. The second, *American Thought* (1954), was a posthumous work, which set among its chapters, against a wide canvas, a historical sketch of legal thought in America from Colonial times to the present. He also contributed legal chapters to other books of joint authorship, and helped direct work in jurisprudence for *The Encyclopedia of the Social Sciences.* Cohen is in the curriculum in law schools today.

Cohen was an inveterate letter writer, even though he had no secretarial assistance for most of his life and never mastered the typewriter. He corresponded with many leading figures in the law. From 1905 on, he maintained a lifelong correspondence with his former roommate, Felix Frankfurter; a selection from their correspondence appears in Chapter XIV. His sparkling correspondence with Justice Oliver Wendell Holmes, Jr., reproduced in Chapter XVI, was initiated in the spring of 1915. Judge Learned Hand, another learned correspondent, called on Cohen "to guide my nascent steps as a legal philosopher." Del Vecchio, professor of law, then rector at the University of Rome, started writing to Cohen in 1919. Cohen corresponded with Sir Maurice S. Amos, British specialist in comparative law; the distinguished German legal philosopher Hermann Kantorowicz; Supreme Court Justices Stone, Rutledge, Cardozo, and Brandeis, whom he had known since 1905, when he spoke before Cohen's Harvard Ethical Society. Some of his correspondence with Judge Learned Hand, Roscoe Pound, and Cardozo is reproduced in Chapter XV.

The first law-school course taught by Cohen was at Columbia in the summer of 1927. It was a three-ring seminar, with Sir William Searle Holdsworth in legal history and Robert Lowie in anthropology as the other performers. The Law School of St. John's College (later University) in Brooklyn had Cohen on their staff from 1928 through 1931. At Yale Law School he was visiting professor in 1930 and in 1940. He gave seminars in legal philosophy at the New School for Social Research, lectured at New York University Law School, delivered the Irvine Lecture at Cornell Law School and a lecture series on law for the University of Buffalo and spoke for the New York State Bar Association and the Association of American Law Schools. In Washington, in 1935, Cohen's address on "Philosophy and the Evaluation of Legal Theory" was the last in a distinguished series on "The Scientific Study of Law and Its Administration" run by The Brookings Institution. At Harvard he gave a seminar on legal thought for the Law School in the fall semester of 1938–39. In 1940 he spoke before the 8th American Scientific Congress on "Legal Philosophy in the Americas," a paper published in 1943 by the State Department.

After retiring from The City College, Cohen returned there to deliver a seminar in 1939 in the philosophy of law—his last teaching for his alma mater. The seminar in legal philosophy that he wanted to teach at the University of Chicago turned out to be listed as a seminar in social philosophy, but Cohen told Professor McKeon that he considered the philosophy of law, whether presented in a law school or a department of philosophy, "a specifically philosophical subject."

When Felix Cohen took his doctorate in philosophy at Harvard, he disappointed some who expected him to continue in philosophy by announcing his intention of studying law thereafter. A letter of his from Cambridge to his father in 1927 said: "Paul [Weiss] is dreadfully worried that you too will forsake philosophy for the law." But there was no dichotomy between them in Morris Cohen's mind.

Charles L. Stevenson, professor of philosophy at the University of Michigan, as an assistant professor teaching ethics at Yale audited Cohen's course in legal philosophy. He reports that he was both "surprised and amused" at Cohen's classroom technique. He "tempted unsuspecting students to make unqualified ethical generalizations; and thereupon proceeded to give counter-example after counter-example, showing that the student's generalization was one that the student himself, even, wasn't prepared to accept."

Cohen's classes in logic as well as those in legal philosophy supplied a basic training for future lawyers. Sometimes his best students at The City College went into law instead of philosophy. One who did, Monroe Oppenheimer, now a Washington attorney, describes Cohen's teaching:

His technique, of course, was to pose a question and then tear apart the answers that he evoked. . . .
I will always remember how much encouragement he gave me just before I graduated from college. I was a very shy and timid boy, perhaps because I was

only eighteen years old. . . . Just before commencement I was concerned as to what I could do to make a living. I decided to get your father's opinion as to whether I was too presumptious in teaching high school. He almost snorted his reply. "Look at the teachers you have right here in college," he snapped. "That will give you your answer." He then spoke more warmly and said, "I suggest you suffer from what my enemies, the psychoanalysts, call an inferiority complex. Actually I have just read your examination paper in Logic and you tied for the top paper in the class." Sure enough, I received a certificate of equal merit with the medal winner. . . . (I think he was Ernest Nagel or Sidney Hook). . . ."

Another ex-student, Judge Margold, wrote in the article cited previously that "the impact of the early training we received in Cohen's classes is a constant and dominant force in our daily professional lives."

Cohen's approach to law was that of the confirmed pluralist with a feeling for the complexity of human causation. In social philosophy he warned against embracing a doctrine because of opposition to its rival. Just as in historiography he showed up the inadequacy of single-minded views, so in jurisprudence he laid bare the insufficiency of one-sided schools, whether they stress experience without logic, logic without experience, might without right, right without might, law without sociology, sociology without law. Neither *stare decisis,* principles, nor judicial discretion alone. Each must temper the other.

There is an appropriate story about three umpires discussing their calling:

First Umpire: I calls 'em the way I sees 'em.

Second Umpire: Me, I calls 'em the way they is.

Third Umpire: Man, they ain't until I calls 'em.

Substitute judges for umpires, and the pertinence is obvious. Umpire number three's nominalism is exemplified by Chief Justice Hughes's dictum that the Constitution is what the judges say it is, and in more extreme form by Professor Joseph Bingham's view that rules are "mere subjective ideas in the minds of those who think about the law."[6] Nowhere in his philosophy is Cohen's attack on nominalism more pungent than in his legal papers, such as "Philosophy and Legal Science" and "Justice Holmes and the Nature of Law." Cohen himself believed that the judge fills the gaps in the existing law. "It is surely," he proclaimed, "a most childish fiction to pretend that our judges have had nothing to do with making our constitutional law what it is today."[7] But he affirmed with equal conviction that judicial discretion does not confer license to depart from conformity to the law. As for the relation between decisions and rules, it is "analogous to that between points and a line."[8]

Cohen showed the limitations of legal systems such as legal positivism, the formalistic or Vienna school, the sociologic school, "living law," legal

realism, the behavioristic school, the psychoanalytic school, the functional-
ists, the analytical school, the historical school, the school of "free interpretation," *Begriffsjurisprudenz* or mechanical jurisprudence, *Interessenjuris-
prudenz,* and the "anarchistic error." Coming upon a devastating review such
as his "The Legal Calvinism of Elihu Root," readers might exclaim on
Cohen's "destructiveness." His reputation for negativism dies hard. Yet
even his negative teachings were apt to imply or point to a positive moral,
and others were more thoroughly constructive. Even Harold Laski repeats
the old legend of negativism in a piece on Cohen for the *University of
Chicago Law Review* for 1948, after which he discusses positive themes
that seem to him central in his friend's jurisprudence. His conclusion is that

[Cohen] made it his major function, in the field of legal philosophy, to arrest
the drift to irrationalism by making the symbols clear by the vigorous process of
logical scrutiny. . . . it was a contribution of great value to see as Morris
Cohen saw, that only the logical analysis of experience can make men able
consciously to shape their own destiny [Vol. X, p. 587].

Partly because Cohen was outside the guild, he had philosophical detachment and perspective from which to view legal principles. He identified
unacknowledged assumptions behind the law as value judgments that had
crept in at the back door, and he stressed the importance of disclosing for
rational analysis, the ethical judgments back of conduct and law. His legal
philosophy is rich in what Holmes so much admired—*aperçus* and the
ability "to see so far as one may and to feel the great forces that are behind
every detail."[9] Cohen's forward-looking jurisprudence opened up vistas into
the future that the law has since often pursued.

His treatment is suggestive rather than exhaustive. The range, meatiness,
flexibility, and constructive character of Cohen's jural concepts are illustrated by the following examples on the nature of law, law and society, law
and logic, law and ethics.

1. The law, according to Cohen following Pound, is a means, not an
end. "The end is a just life between living human beings here and now."[10]
Although primarily directed toward certainty, the law is dynamic. It is a
balance between the existential and the normative, force and justice, custom and rule, the contingent and the absolute, the fixed and the flux,
the concrete and the universal. Legal analysts are tempted to separate law
from the context of life, but the law is not a set of rules "hovering over
and above human affairs." It is alive and ever-growing, drawing its nourishment from social facts, legal systems, and ethical ideals.

. . . the stream of judicial decisions has a continuity, and judges in deciding
actual cases are to some extent influenced by the logical demands set by the
prevailing conception of what the law is or ought to be. The law is not in fact
a completed, but a growing and self-correcting, system. It grows not of itself but

by the interaction between social usage and the work of legislatures, courts, and administrative officials, and even legal text writers. . . . We try to extract from past decisions rules to guide the future ones, and we test the appropriateness of these rules by the consequences to which they lead.[11]

2. When in 1915 Cohen reviewed Judge Edward A. Parry's *The Law and the Poor,* labor and social legislation in this country had not yet made their subsequent strides. The poor were really downtrodden. The logical pursuit of abstract legal doctrines easily blinds us to actual living conditions, Cohen states in praising Parry's work. Inequality of wealth may incite men to crime.

Cohen's boyhood in Tsarist Russia, his experiences in a poolroom frequented by dubious characters,[12] his early immersion in the socialist labor movement, his years at The City College—all gave him a firsthand familiarity with the plight of the underprivileged not common among the established class of judges, professors, and jurists. His tone mellowed as he grew older, but success never made him soft or fat in mind or body. The ascetic stamp was there for good. In "The Sanctity of Law" he derides the moral smugness of the rich:

The law may pretend that rich and poor are equal before it but in fact that is not true, and if we go to Sing Sing and find that the overwhelming portion of its inhabitants come from poor people, let us not be deluded by the idea that the rich are not there because of their superior moral courage.[13]

3. Criminal law, "the pathology of civilization," represents for Cohen "a basic phase of the whole legal system." An adequate discussion of justice in the criminal law must therefore deal with the ethical issues of the law generally as well as with social realities.

. . . the criminal law cannot be distinguished from the rest by any difference of moral principle. Some crimes, to be sure, are shocking; but there are many crimes that are felt to be much less reprehensible than many outrageous forms of injustice, cruelty or fraud, which the law does not punish at all, or else makes their perpetrator liable to money damages in a civil suit. . . .

Yet, the legislative question of what acts should be made criminal and which should no longer be so treated cannot be settled by ethical principles alone. To apply the latter we need to have factual knowledge as to what are going to be the various consequences of the enactment or repeal. . . .[14]

4. The law of contract, rooted in questions of intent, effect, and custom, seems to Cohen not only a branch of public law involving questions of public policy, but also somewhat parallel to criminal law in standardizing conduct by penalizing departures from the legal norm. The law of contract provides assurance that agreements will be fulfilled. But over and beyond this, its problem is the distribution of risks, the determination of the rights of the contracting parties in contingencies for which they have

not provided: "Just as the process of interpreting a statute is really a process of subsidiary legislation, so is the interpretation of a contract really a method of supplementing the original agreement by such provisions as are necessary to determine the point at issue."[15]

The institutional approach is suggested for the fruitful study of contract. Contracts, especially collective ones, tend to grow into institutions. In a sense, government rests on contract: "as men become more enlightened, they can treat government as if it were a contractual affair, i.e. judge the services of government rules by the price we pay for them."[16]

5. François Guizot said property and sovereignty, when confused, spell feudalism. Cohen clarifies the picture of the modern relationship between property and sovereignty by focusing on social ethics. Pound has shown, writes Cohen, that the Supreme Court has stretched the term "property" to include freedom of contract. In practical effect, sovereign rights are conferred by our property laws on our captains of industry and even more on our captains of finance. Is it not dangerous to grant too much sovereign power to those concerned only with materialistic considerations? In the era just preceding the New Deal, Cohen urged: "that if the large property owner is viewed, as he ought to be, as a wielder of power over the lives of his fellow citizens, the law should not hesitate to develop a doctrine as to his positive duties in the public interest."[17]

Just as the state through the right of eminent domain may condemn private property, so governmental regulatory action is necessary to control private property in order to meet social or communal obligation. The whole business of the sovereign state Cohen sees as depending upon "its rightful power to take away the property of some (in the form of taxation) and use it to support others."[18] The absolute theory of private property is untenable in any civilized legal system.

6. Cohen questioned the oracular *mystique* of the bench along with the doctrine of judicial omniscience. A judiciary always independent, its decisions invariably following necessarily from the Constitution, is, he holds, a fiction. He notes that no foreign country copies our system of judicial supremacy. His Introduction to *Lawless Judges* (Frankfurter criticized him for so honoring such a book) states: "We are committed to the view that . . . our security consists in realizing that all officials are fallible human beings and therefore open to criticism. . . . Why should judges be beyond the scope of this democratic faith?"[19]

Vis-à-vis the other branches of government: "our courts are less in contact with the actual facts of our complicated economic and social life, have no power to initiate investigations, and by pretending to pass only on the law and not on the facts, leave the door open to most uncritical opinions."[20]

7. The judicial process, as Cohen sees it, impinges on the legislative. Judges through their decisions modify and help to create the law, while claiming to be only, as it were, phonographs that play back the law's words. Here was a bold attack on one of the law's sacred cows. Some law-school deans wrote him, he said,

. . . that while the contention that judges do have a share in making the law is unanswerable, it is still advisable to keep the fiction of the phonograph theory to prevent the law from becoming more fluid than it already is. But I have an abiding conviction that to recognize the truth and adjust oneself to it is in the end the easiest and most advisable course. The phonograph theory has bred the mistaken view that the law is a closed, independent system having nothing to do with economic, political, social, or philosophical science. If however we recognize that courts are constantly remaking the law, then it becomes of the utmost social importance that the law should be made in accordance with the best available information, which it is the object of science to supply.[21]

8. Cohen at times protests against the mortmain of the past that holds the law in its grip. He pleads for a new forward-looking perspective on the law: "When judges and conservative lawyers speak, as they have, of being bound by law rather than economic theory, they assume their antiquated economic theories to be self-evident facts and, as such, part of the fixed legal order."[22]

The notion of the free-labor contract Cohen calls a historical myth. His "The Bill of Rights Theory" first appeared in 1915, but its relevancy to contemporary labor law is clear. "There never was a time when the relation between master and servant was not the subject of governmental regulations, except that formerly they were almost invariably and openly in the interests of the employers."[23]

Legalism Cohen considers our American form of clericalism. He quotes Emerson's words: "Why should we grope among the dead bones of the past . . . ? Let us demand our own works and laws and worship."[24]

9. Administrative law, Cohen claims, is no more arbitrary than law in the courts. When Cohen uttered the words, before the establishment of the system of administrative law that developed with the New Deal, administrative law was still in its infancy. Not until World War II was it smuggled into most of the nation's law-school curricula, via the back door.

10. In legal education the student must be trained to look for the influence of reason on the law:

. . . neither legal history nor contemporary social information can eliminate the necessity of a juristic analysis of the fundamental aims at the basis of the different legal institutions. . . . there is need also of a source-book which should give the different views as to the rationale of legal institutions in the words of their original or most powerful proponents. . . .[25]

"But if law is a fit subject for university study," Cohen adds, "it deserves to be studied not merely for its practical consequences, but also for the insight it offers as to human life."[26]

The source book by Cohen and Cohen was an attempt to fill the bill.

11. The relations of logic and scientific method to law are analyzed by Cohen. But "law is a specific type of existence, and its specific nature cannot be deduced from something else,"[27] not even logic. "The attempt to derive concrete or particular consequences from metaphysical assumptions alone is an impractical one, since modern logic has shown that from universal premises alone no particular conclusion can be drawn."[28]

Just as in building, materials are needed along with the rules of architecture, so in law empirical elements are necessary to concretize theory. No set of rules can be adequate for all time. The judge must be inventive. Still, judges, jurists, and advocates should develop a trained sense of scientific method. Science for Cohen does not mean positivism, the glorification of fact at the expense of principle. Rather, it demands a combination of deductive and inductive processes.

12. Cohen explores the "twilight zone"[29] between law and ethics and elaborates on the concept of legal fictions, notably with respect to the "communal ghost."[30] Is the soul of the community (*Volksgeist*) real, or a legal fiction? Laski, who first held for its reality, was later won over by Cohen's insistence that back of the communal ghost and the corporative fiction are simply men of flesh and blood: "There linger in my mind vivid memories of long arguments with Professor Cohen. . . . I was myself converted by Professor Cohen's power of logical analysis to see the error of my ways."[31]

13. Natural law is "the appeal from positive law to justice, from the law which is to the law which ought to be."[32] Ultimately, its essence is "the view that any established or proposed social order or institution must defend itself before the bar of human welfare."[33] The way to defend the principles of natural law, Cohen maintains, is to show: "that like other scientific principles, e.g. the Copernican hypothesis in astronomy, they yield a body or system of propositions which is preferable to that which can possibly be established on the basis of their denial."[34]

14. Pragmatism, not James's or Dewey's version but his own brand strongly influenced by Charles Peirce, lies at the base of Cohen's legal reasoning and is just as applicable to his ethics. Rationalist philosopher, he nonetheless recognized the limitations of theory in law and saw its reliance on empirical as well as rational factors. For "principles alone (i.e. without knowledge or assumption as to the facts) cannot logically decide cases," he tells us.[35] Cohen's two-way pragmatic test, useful in law and ethics as in science, is described thus:

Law and morality can coincide only in the fundamental assumptions as to the proper procedure to enable us to correct our mistakes. Their common ideal is thus like that of science, to wit, a system that corrects itself by the process of testing principles by their consequences, and conversely, judging actual consequences in the light of principles.[36]

15. The principle of polarity is Cohen's key to the problem of reconciling positive law with the basic ethical principles that must underlie it, whether held "anonymously" or expressly. "Natural Rights and Positive Law" exemplifies the principle: "justice and the law, the ideal and the actual, are inseparable, yet never completely identifiable."[37] And man must wear out his life in the pursuit of the imperfectly attainable ideal. His craving for the absolute is necessary for human dignity.

16. Normative jurisprudence, for Cohen, can be approached scientifically. The science of rational ethics determines his outlook on law, which "draws its sap from feelings of justice and social need."[38] "It is only when law is thus seen as part of the life of reason that the ideal of just law can become a real force for genuine beneficence."[39]

17. Just as Cohen warns us against an overdose of logic in the law, so in ethics he bids us guard against the fanaticism of righteousness. "The supreme virtue of the law, justice, must frequently yield to the more humane virtue of charity."[40] "The lawyer . . . sees the shadows as well as the lights of human life. . . . Such a sense of imperfection together with a spirit of tolerance is one of the best safeguards against the spirit of fanaticism that uses vigorous principles to shut the gates of mercy on mankind."[41]

Pound, then dean of Harvard Law School and, in another sense, dean of legal philosophy in this country's law schools, wrote of Cohen:

The pioneer in the revival of philosophy of law in America has been doing a service to our social order which I venture to think some day will be reckoned quite comparable to the work of those who laid the foundations of the polity which served us so well in the simpler conditions of the last century.[42]

Cardozo, while chief judge of the New York Court of Appeals, said:

If insight into the essence of the judicial process, if profound appreciation of the fundamental principles and concepts and methods of the law can make a man a lawyer, then Professor Cohen is a lawyer and a great one. . . .

We shall never separate the law from the study of philosophy unless we are ready to condemn it to barrenness and decay. In maintaining the relation between the two spheres of human thought scholars like Professor Cohen are keeping open the road to the steady progress of society along the paths of peace and order.[43]

While Frankfurter was still professor at Harvard Law School and not yet Justice of the Supreme Court, he said—and before Cohen's books had appeared: "There isn't a thinking lawyer in this country, there isn't a judge who reflects on his task, who hasn't been . . . impregnated with the contributions of Morris Cohen to jurisprudence."[44]

The philosophy of law, with its balance between the rational and the empirical, like classical drama, appealed to Cohen's power of rational thought and his underlying moral passion. Where better than in the legal arena could one watch the living play of the social order in the light of logical method and ethical purpose?

Felix Cohen, Morris Cohen's legal collaborator, paid this tribute to the accomplishment his father helped effectuate: "It is no longer possible, as it was forty years ago, to write or discourse at length on American philosophy without referring to the philosophy of law. Nor is it possible today, as it was then, for any jurist or philosopher anywhere in the world to deal comprehensively with the problems of jurisprudence and legal philosophy without referring to American writers."[45]

XII. *Mysticism and Rationalism*

COHEN WAS AS GLEEFUL a pricker of ideological bubbles as ever wielded a logician's pen. He delighted on occasion to dip the point in acid. He is known as the great philosophical exponent of scientific method, an agnostic and a skeptic. It will therefore come as a surprise to some to hear him called a mystic; yet it was he who applied the term to himself, at least as he defined it, and he did not intend it as a clever paradox designed to shock. Cohen's definition was different from most people's conception of mysticism, but he was dead serious in his statements on mysticism. It is hardly possible to follow his philosophy, with its rationalism and polarity, without noting his mysticism.

Of his friend, the poet Edwin Arlington Robinson, Morris Cohen once said, "A mystic is a man who recognizes that there is something beyond . . . and doesn't try to describe it. Robinson, in that regard, was a true mystic."[1] And so was Cohen himself.

In the Preface to the work that most fully presents his over-all philosophy, *Reason and Nature,* Cohen offers this guide to "readers who have a predilection for conventional labels":

I am a rationalist in believing that reason is a genuine and significant phase of nature; but I am an irrationalist in insisting that nature contains more than reason. I am a mystic in holding that all words point to a realm of being deeper and wider than the words themselves. But I reject as vicious obscurantism all efforts to describe the indescribable. . . . I am willing to be called a materialist if that means one who disbelieves in disembodied spirits; and I should refer to spiritists who localize disembodied spirits in space as crypto-materialists. However, I should also call myself an idealist . . . in the Platonic sense according to which ideas, ideals, or abstract universals are the conditions of real existence, and not mere fictions of the human mind [pp. xii–xiii].

As a consistent opponent of supernaturalism, Cohen was a naturalist, in that sense a materialist. But between his materialism and the materialism

199

of one who admits only matter in the universe, there lies the long shadow of Plato. Cohen's idealism or antinominalism, his belief in the reality to which words point, was based on something like Platonic *eidos*. He liked to call it "logical realism," basing it on the reality of logical or mathematical relations.

Reason and Nature deals with mysticism in three passages.

[Genuine mysticism] asserts that all intellection and language move in the mist of appearances and cannot reach the ineffable reality. Genuine mysticism always holds fast to the idea that the substance of reality is altogether beyond the power of language [p. 452].

Mysticism is vicious or obscurantist if it denies the definite or determinate character of things in the interest of beliefs which cannot stand the light of reason [p. 154].

Cohen's kind of mysticism is distinguished from obscurantist mysticism:

Rationality does not exhaust existence. The relational form or pattern points to a non-rational or alogical element without which the former has no genuine meaning. . . . If this doctrine that our universe thus contains something fundamental to which we may point but which we cannot fully describe be called mysticism, then mysticism is essential to all intellectual sanity. . . . if we use the word *mysticism* to denote this faith in a universe that has ineffable and alogical elements, we cannot too sharply distinguish it from obscurantism. For the former denies our power to know the whole of reality, while the latter holds reality to be definitely revealed to us by non-rational processes. . . . the essential difference between rationalism and obscurantism depends upon whether our guesses or obscure visions do or do not submit to the processes of critical examination and logical clarification. Our reason may be a pitiful candle light in the dark and boundless seas of being. But we have nothing better and woe to those who wilfully try to put it out [pp. 164–65].

Among the reviewers of Cohen's *Reason and Nature,* Henry Hazlett in *The Nation* emphasized the centrality of its author's concept that there are necessary limitations of reason in nature. Here, he said, lies the very core of the book. "Nature is more than reason; always there remains the beyond . . . the unexplained, the contingent."[2]

In "Concepts and Twilight Zones" (which first appeared in 1927, later in *A Preface to Logic*), Cohen wrote:

The rationalists are those who love sharp distinctions, clear subdivisions of structure, and hate blurred outlines and overlapping areas. They regard themselves as the clear-minded, opposed to the muddy-minded mystics. But the mystic is conscious of the wealth of being and possible experience, not yet made definite, which perhaps never can be made definite [p. 78].

He did not share the rationalist's derision of the "muddy-minded mystics." One of his letters to his friend Justice Holmes (see p. 327) makes clear that his scorn, if any, is pointed the other way.

Holmes shared with Cohen "the spirit of resolute adventure" that impelled each of them to seek for light to pierce the shadows of ignorance.

Cohen admired Holmes's "combination of scepticism and mysticism," according to which "we do not and cannot know the ultimate nature of things but we are controlled by forces bigger than ourselves. . . ."[3]

Indeed, the last words of *Reason and Nature* evoke "the abysmal mystery of existence."

In January 1939 Cohen told his metaphysics class at Harvard that he was a mystic in not believing that words include all of reality. Thought and language refer to something more than thought and language. Roderick Chisholm's old student notebook quotes Cohen in a definition reminiscent of the one in *Reason and Nature:* "True mysticism is the realization of the fact that there is something more than what is described."

Cohen considered the biologic phenomenon of life as a mystery. After he spoke once to The City College Biology Club on "Philosophic Phases of Biology," especially the mechanistic and vitalistic conceptions of life, *The Campus* (April 6, 1925) reported his words:

The more additional information we get, the more is life a mystery to us. . . . The idea of reducing all biology to mechanics has not succeeded. Science is not satisfied with the mechanistic tendency.

The roots of Cohen's recognition of mysticism's attractions can be traced in his journals. He was twenty-one when he confided to his diary:

July 26, 1901: While I was always (at least since meeting T. D. [Thomas Davidson]) opposed to sentimentality and mysticism my readings on the subject of mysticism and the reflecting on it, together with Mr. [Percival] Chubb's defense of Tennyson's sentimental mysticism have made me, in spite of myself, realize the great truths behind this conception of life. In this my few meetings with Mr. [David S.] Muzzey have been of great service. My "conversion"—if it may be called one—(for it is not a complete change of view) has not come about suddenly nor by any arguments that the "other side" brought up. It came about simply because in trying to refute it, I began to see the truths on the other side. I am not yet a sentimentalist nor a mystic, but I have come to realize on cool rational grounds that there is an experimental basis for this view of the world. . . . My studies in *mysticism* from Récéjac, Inge, Royce and Vaughan have been more fruitful in the main. . . .

Jan. 14, 1902: Refreshing to read Emerson. Possessing more experience than formerly especially of the "mystic" type I find that I understand him now (knowing why I did not understand him before).

On June 12, 1902, Cohen's diary note refers to his recent article on "The Gospel of Relaxation for the East Side" published in the *Alliance Review:*

> Of course [William] James' article had a good deal to do with it —suggesting many expressions, etc.—but the thought of it was the outcome of my mystic experiences and my reading of Emerson.

Unfortunately, Cohen tells us nothing about the nature of his "mystic experiences," more likely literary than religious. Before he was thirteen he had lost belief in the God whom he had been brought up to venerate. Later he defined his God as an ideal of holiness,[4] all the while rejecting monotheism. Nevertheless, he perceived "The mystic sees God in a swoon . . . in the sense of vividness, the phenomenon may have the greatest possible reality." The impression was jotted down in an undated notebook of Cohen's, evidently used when he was twenty-four to twenty-six.

He was no more a monist than he was a monotheist. "There can be no monism in my heart," he once wrote. His was no all-inclusive rationalism; in the same notebook he wrote:

> My thoughts, and observations (influenced by experiences, moods and perhaps *liver*) lead me more and more to a systematic view of the universe—viz., that the universe is not an actual harmony but only a potential one—i.e., that there are many independent sources working in different directions. . . . The foolishness in ascribing all that happens to one *personal* force or one constant impersonal force. *One* force could not produce a world of strife, and real movement, and progress. The multiplicity of experiences refuses to be codified into one law. Beyond the world of law and order there is always a fringe of *chaos.* Progress would be a delusion if there were no real chaos.

"Chaos" sounds like Peirce's "chance," but it also applies to the mystical in Cohen's Nature.

Nevertheless, as "The Faith of a Logician," Cohen's intellectual autobiographical essay, made clear, mysticism in his view could never supersede rationalism.

Though I am singularly sensitive to the literary charm of certain types of mysticism such as that of St. Bernard, or Tauler, it seems to me amazing that anyone should argue as James did that the mystic's ecstasy can prove any of the dogmas of religion. I can see no proof that the object of the mystic's experience has any more objective validity than the similar visions of one under the influence of drugs.[5]

Looking back over the passages examined, we may distinguish two elements in Cohen's mysticism: the chaotic or nonrational, and the Platonic realm of being, deeper and wider than the words themselves, to which the words point—both beyond our grasp. In either case, Cohen refused to relinquish faith in man's best guides—"critical examination," "logical clarification," or the scientific method.

Just as Russell spoke in *Mysticism and Logic* of logical mysticism originating in Parmenides and Plato, so Cohen could speak in terms of the mysticism of a rationalist—a mysticism without swoon or ecstasy, prophecy, religious conviction, or sense of the ineffable. His mysticism was not tinged with the supernatural; it was impregnated with humility and a sense of human limitations. It formed part of his nonanthropocentric view of the cosmos. Less optimistic than that of a Descartes or a *philosophe* of the Enlightenment, Cohen's was a "rationalism rational enough to envisage the limitations of mere reasoning."[6] Truths can be discovered today that yesterday seemed unknowable. But "endowed as we are at birth with infinite ignorance," we must acknowledge the unknowable as limitless. Subtracting from infinity leaves infinity. Cohen knew that men can never circumnavigate "the dark and boundless seas of being," or become gods.

Mysticism and rationalism cohabit Cohen's universe like the north and south poles, opposite and complementary. There can be no fixed without reference to the unfixed, no truth without reference to nontruth. His principle of polarity he called "the leading idea in all my own philosophic synthesis."[7] Without reference to it, Cohen's simultaneous belief in mysticism and rationalism may seem puzzling. Conversely, to grasp the completeness of his polarity one must bear in mind that it applied to his fundamental vision of mysticism and rationalism. Mysticism is thus a necessary doctrine in his philosophy, not only because of our inherent inability to know the whole of reality, but also as the point of differentiation with rationalism.

It would be misleading to end this sketch without stressing again the difference between Cohen's mysticism and more common connotations of the word, and without reiterating the basic soundness, albeit incompleteness, of the popular view that recognizes Cohen's great contribution as rationalistic. Unflinchingly, he defended rationalism, even when it hurt—this in an age that has witnessed attacks upon or substitutes for reason from all sides, respectable or otherwise.

Morris Cohen dedicated himself to the life of reason. At the twenty-fifth anniversary of his teaching at The City College of New York, he expressed something of what rationalism meant to him:

I know that this faith in reason is not popular today. . . . Though science is a word to conjure with, the terms rational and intellectual are means of opprobrium. . . . How indeed does the life of man differ from that of the beast except by the possession of a few great ideas which open a window on the great seas of eternal being? Logic may not fathom the depths, but it may train us to look fearlessly into the abyss which surrounds us.[8]

XIII. *The Jew*

UP ON THE LECTURE PLATFORM, Morris Cohen is delivering a lecture on a Jewish subject. He accents his words by rocking slightly to and fro. Any orthodox Jew in the audience would have known why, for pupils in the cheder and the Yeshiva are trained to sway rhythmically as they read and intone the books of the Mishnah and the Gemara. The habit, early engrained, cropped up throughout Cohen's life, a remnant of his Old World Jewishness.

For the Judaic stamp had been laid on Cohen from his earliest days. Orthodoxy was his first way of life. His grandfather, Hirsh Farfel, stimulated his philosophic curiosity, the cheder taught him how to study hard, and his early reading of the Law imbued him with the old Hebraic concern with justice and morality. As a boy he almost never played, but his diary note of June 12, 1902, reveals:

> I have been leading a very intense subjective life ever since my twelfth year when I got the ambition to be a redeemer to my people like Bar Cochba or Jacob Tiradie—and carried a wooden sword with me and ran over the streets with enthusiasm dreaming of charges against heathens etc. . . . .

Morris' religious fervor came to an abrupt end shortly after he arrived in America. The twelve-year-old overheard a double theological challenge to his father. "Prove," said a Jewish friend, free-thinking Mr. Tunick, "that the Jewish religion has more evidence in its favor than any other and prove, if you can, the existence of a God who listens to our prayers." Abraham Cohen replied simply, "I am a believer." On reflection, the son ceased believing. He wrote in *A Dreamer's Journey:*

> My abandonment of Judaism as a religion was later reinforced in my mind by my scientific, historical and philosophical studies [p. 70].

205

Here was a man who broke with his faith. A child of the Enlightenment, Cohen became steeped in the Hellenic as well as the Hebraic tradition. An antireligious current engulfed much of his youthful generation and cut it off from parental roots. But can a nonbeliever, a nonpracticing Jew, even a non-Zionist, be a good Jew? Cohen's struggle between his rejection of orthodox religion and his adherence to Jewish learning and to the Jewish cause was his way of being a Jew, honest to his mind and loyal to his heart.

The Bible, which had been Cohen's first storybook, never ceased to fascinate him. One of his earliest publications—he was twenty-two—was entitled "Amos and his Disciples." "Even in the years when I was most consciously rejecting the supernaturalism of Orthodoxy," he wrote, "I was devoting a large part of my thinking to Biblical history, Biblical criticism, and comparative religion."[1] Beginning in 1899 and for many years thereafter as a volunteer teacher of the Thomas Davidson School, he gave courses in the Book of Job, the Hebrew prophets, and other religious subjects. In his diary for 1902 he noted that he was studying biblical criticism and Hebrew history and making a special study of the Book of Job in the form of an essay. His first paid lecture was on the legend of Hagar.

Groping throughout his adolescence for something to keep him from drifting, he found in Thomas Davidson a spiritual anchor to windward. During and after his short time with Davidson, Cohen sought a rational basis for morality in lieu of a religion. After Davidson's death, he responded to Felix Adler's answer to that search—ethical culture. While promoting ethical culture at Harvard, he did not, however, forsake his heritage. He was vice president of the Semitic Conference there, and advanced his study of comparative religion in general and Hebrew religion in particular. His diary jottings in his first year at Cambridge reflect his awakening to the fact that despite his revolt from the religious faith and practice of his people, he remained essentially a Jew, a Russian Jew, with interests profoundly religious.

Meanwhile, the question of his marriage to the daughter of devout Jewish parents had come to a head. His unorthodoxy and his scorn for material goods (not to mention the very material debts he had already acquired) were hardly calculated to reassure prospective parents-in-law. But through the centuries the Jews have looked up to the "Talmid Chocham," the searcher after wisdom, as a leader in the community. Solomon and Sheba Pearl Ryshpan recognized in Cohen consuming love of learning, deep ethical concern, and a concentration on the eternal rather than on the here and now. They gave their blessing to the match.

Cohen had been married a little over a year when he delivered a lecture at Glenmore on agnosticism. To his wife, occupied at home with Felix, aged one month, he wrote:

The Inn [Hurricane, N.Y.]
Monday night
[August 5, 1907]

Dearest,

I lectured this morning on Agnosticism in this beehive of religiosity —and what do you suppose happened? A few squirmed during the lecture but nearly all of them afterwards fell all over themselves praising the lecture. I really believe these people here will swallow anything at all.

My points were as follows:

Agnosticism (like a red rag to a bull) provokes some people to a passion, but passion is not the mood in which to discuss any view of life. We ought to give it at least as open a mind as the Catholics do to the devil's advocate. —Most people don't like negatives; they would rather live in an unsafe tottering house than camp out in the open. But negatives are necessary as preparations for the good, e.g. Moses destroying the golden calf. Besides, negative and positive are relative terms, what is positive from one point of view is negative from another. —All great religious teachers more or less agnostic—some like Confucius entirely so. Intellectual *belief* played a very small part in hist. of religion before St. Paul. As an attitude to life agnosticism summed up in saying of Micah—to do justice, to love mercy & *walk humbly with the Lord.* Agnosticism makes much of intellectual honesty & courage. According to it, the cardinal sin is spiritual pride —the assumption of knowledge where knowledge is impossible. Huxley's characterization of science as Cinderella. Agnosticism regards both pessimism & optimism as futile and presumptious. With regard to the nature of the world as a whole we must remain ignorant in large measure. But though we cannot know God we can *be* godly, at any rate strive to act the godly. Everybody admits certain things are good & others bad. Let us join our forces & work for the good & against the evil. —As to immortality as a religious doctrine its value consists in making life valuable, but life cannot get its value simply from its continuance. (Hence the recognition that certain parts of life *are* valuable is for the agnostic as good as immortality.) Finally agnosticism has its consolations which are in many respects more effective than those of the orthodox religion. Orthodox religion warms you by external support—agnosticism by compelling you to exert yourself & develop your own heart, e.g. the mother in Tennyson's Home They Brought Her Warrior Dead (i.e. the bereaved person should be shown that there is something to live for.)

Tuesday morning

I am feeling fairly well and am thinking now of beginning a little work. —The Inn here is not as well managed as it was last year. If I don't hear from [Felix] Adler soon I guess I'll come home. Goodby for the present. Take care of your diet and don't forget to write me how Baby is doing.

With love

MORRIS

Cohen adhered to agnosticism all of his life. I never knew him to attend religious services. He definitely did not belong to that brand of philosophers who, in the words of his friend Professor C. J. Ducasse, act like public-relations officers for God, handing out press releases from cosmic head-quarters. Nor did he consider himself on such intimate relations with the Almighty as did his old Harvard masters. The story is told that Cohen's younger son as a small boy asked his father one day: "Daddy, what has God been doing since He created the world?" To which the father replied, "Of late, Willie, He's been busy sitting for His portrait by James and Royce."

Atheism, however, was not to Cohen's liking. "Those who called themselves atheists," he once wrote, "seemed to be singularly blind, as a rule, to the limitations of our knowledge and to the infinite possibilities beyond us."[2]

In two instances worthy of recall, Cohen used the word "God" with positive effect, the first in his letter to Mary Ryshpan, when he implored her to "Take me and inspire me further to my life's ideals—ideals that are at one with your own—and together we will reach up to God." Later, he defined God as "not only an existent power but an ideal of holiness, which enables us to distinguish between the good and the evil in men."[3]

When the Judaeans, a cultural society in New York, invited Cohen to membership back in 1911, and he pointed out his status as a nonprofessing Jew, the society notified him that he was nonetheless specially "fit." Benno Lewinsohn, onetime trustee of The City College, who did the inviting, assured Cohen that "you are too great a philosopher to make the fact of want of religiosity aggressively obvious; on the other hand I believe that you are only too glad to acknowledge the racial kin."

Lewinsohn was right. Cohen was glad to identify himself as a Jew, the more eagerly when there was something to be fought for. "Interest in Jewish affairs," he once said, "has never been for me a purely intellectual matter."[4] How could it have been otherwise with Mary by his side? All his life he was quick to spring to the defense of Jewish rights, whether the victims were sufferers from pogroms in Eastern Europe, or City College boys. He supported Jewish causes and scholarship, and lectured widely on Jewish subjects.[5]

His early concern for problems of the Jews is illustrated in his response to a letter from Frankfurter, in which Frankfurter requests his views on a memorandum marked "Confidential" concerning the possibility of abrogation of our treaty of 1832 with Russia. The issue had come up apropos of Russia's proposed expatriation of Russian-born American citizens of the Jewish faith.

The College of the City of New York

Nov. 21, 1911

Dear Felix,

I know next to nothing about the treaty of 1832 nor about the subsequent diplomatic relations between the U.S. and Russia. I am not sure even that Russia has fully admitted the right of expatriation, so that many whom the U.S. would regard as citizens of this country would be regarded as Russians and so treated as soon as they crossed the border of that country. Under the circumstances I am not in condition to make any suggestion. Nevertheless, there are a number of points which seem to me clear and definite.

1) *If* the treaty of 1832 secures the right of entry into Russia to American citizens, then, of course, it is the plain duty of the U.S. government to use all the means at its disposal to bring about the equal enforcement of this right to all classes of our citizens. I suppose no one doubts that the treaties of the U.S. with foreign countries are *laws* of the U.S., and the duty of extending the equal protection of the laws of the U.S. to all classes of citizens is not to be lightly set aside by figures of speech such as Pandora's Box or other metaphors. [The phrase "Pandora's box" was evidently used in this connection by President William Howard Taft.]

2) The fear that the abrogation of our treaty with Russia may result in harm to the Jews of Russia seems to me entirely unfounded. The Russian government presses the Jews down as much as it can at all times. It is not, however, omnipotent (though autocratic) and can do no more than it does. Thus at present the government finds that *"pogroms"* will not fit in with its policy and hence they do not take place, though the assassination of Stolypin has offered a good excuse or pretext.

I must likewise characterize as groundless the fear that any vigorous defense by our gov't of the equal rights of all our citizens abroad may cause the spread of anti-Semitism in this country.

3) I am inclined to think that when Russia realizes that the U.S. is determined to have the treaty of 1832 enforced or else abrogated,

she will be inclined to yield. You know that the laws of Russia against the Jews are full of exceptions. Thus merchants, graduates of the Universities and others are exempt from the limitations of residence etc. Russia can, therefore, without much inconvenience to her internal policy allow Jews of foreign countries to come in. The present premier Kokovtsev like all of Russia's financiers realizes that the persecution of the Jews is a great hindrance to the economic development of Russia.

4) If vigorous diplomatic representations to Russia on the subject fail she cannot very well—in view of her interest in the Hague tribunal—reject the offer of arbitration. Arbitration is certainly preferable to abrogation.

It is rather late now and I am rather sleepy anyway so that I will close my opinions on international affairs. I hope you will be able to come around and make the acquaintance of Wm. J. Cohen very soon.

With best regards,

MORRIS

David Savan, a graduate student of Cohen's at Harvard, once asked him whether being Jewish would be a serious handicap to an academic career in philosophy. Cohen reminisced a little about the difficulties he had had in his early days. He said he had taught mathematics at first because it was more open to a Jew. "But now-a-days," he concluded, "being Jewish is a relatively minor handicap."

Many American Jews, like Savan, now professor of philosophy at Toronto, have made their mark in philosophy. To the old fantasy that a Jew could not be a professor of philosophy in the United States, which had traditionally reserved such posts for Protestant clergyman, Cohen dealt the *coup de grâce*. He made the way brighter for those who followed him.

Cohen was responsible for demonstrating the importance of non-Christian medieval philosophy by proposing the inclusion of Jewish philosophy in a session on medieval philosophy held at Harvard in 1926 by the 6th International Congress of Philosophy. As a member of the executive committee he contacted two authorities, Professors Isaac Husik and Harry A. Wolfson, who were favorably disposed. Wolfson himself read a paper.

The Talmud had been a pillar of Cohen's early education. In 1928–29 with the learned Chaim Tchernowitz, as chairman of the Talmudic Library he did his best to bring into being a Talmudic Encyclopedia. It was one of the disappointments of his life that he did not see this dream come true. He was made a fellow of the Jewish Academy of Arts and Sciences in 1935 and from 1936–42 served as its president.

One day, while preparing a learned article on biblical exegesis for *Jewish Social Studies,* he found himself so swept away by the tragedy of Michal in her relations with David that at one sitting he sketched out the framework of a five-act tragedy. For the rest of that summer of 1938, he developed *King Saul's Daughter,*[6] scene by scene. It was characteristic that his philosopher's holiday should have been in the shadow of the Bible.

"Philosophies of Jewish History" reflected his lifetime interest in the philosophy of history and religion. He later wrote an essay on Maimonides, and shared in commemorating the nine-hundredth anniversary of the birth of Rashi, the medieval French commentator of the Bible and the Talmud.[7]

Cohen's "What I Believe as an American Jew" and "Roads for American Jewry" represent a working philosophy for twentieth-century American Jewry. When *Reflections of a Wondering Jew,* which brought together these and other pieces, appeared posthumously in 1950, reviewers pointed out that it provided thoughtful reading for Jew and Gentile alike.

Despite his Judaic erudition, Cohen played devil's advocate in portraying "The Dark Side of Religion," in an essay first published in 1933; it points a reproving finger at religious fanaticism and recalls how deeds of violence and cruelty committed in the name of religion stain the pages of history. The religious spirit, by nature dogmatic and intolerant, is contrasted with the scientific spirit, to the detriment of the former. "There may be more wisdom and courage," we read in the conclusion, "as well as more faith in honest doubt than in most of the creeds."[8]

A year later, Cohen expressed his scorn for nonbelievers who associate themselves with a church affiliated with supernaturalism. An exchange of letters with the Reverend Frederick Reustle follows.

St. George's Church
Stuyvesant Square
New York

December 10, 1934

My dear Professor Cohen,

In your lecture at Cooper Union last night I was sorry that you did not present the secular view of life in greater fullness with its implications for art, religion, ethics, and society. You spent far too much time in a tirade against supernaturalism to an audience that has not an iota of interest nor belief in the priestly view of life. It can only have the unfortunate effect of arousing an indiscriminate prejudice against all religion. If you knew the work carried on in this neighborhood by St. George's with its free clinics, clubs, personal guidance, family assistance and naturalistic view of life you would see that the matter is infinitely more difficult than a change from a priestly to a secular view of life. I once thought it was only necessary to scrap supernaturalism and life would blossom as the rose, but the greed, sluggishness, brutality, insensitiveness which makes life so harsh has its roots in human nature.

I thought you were rather unfair in listing Christian atrocities and explaining that they were the product of a priestly view of life when actually the sins were those of a brutal age, when even a Marcus Aurelius could justify the feeding of slaves to fish on the ground that "men-fed fish taste better." As to Galileo being persecuted by the Church, if we can believe Randall (Making of the Modern Mind pp. 233–5) it was fellow-scientists who opposed Galileo, who enlisted the Catholic Church on their side, and maliciously persuaded Pope Urban to banish him. You were also guilty of an elementary abuse of logic when you reasoned that altruism could not be an attribute of Christianity because Calvin and others like him were Christians but not altruists. There is a St. Francis yesterday and an Albert Schweitzer today.

The above are small matters. My contention is that the approach is a wrong one. Instead of waging a futile war against supernaturalism, present the philosophy of a secular view of life so persuasively, with such honesty, and positive beauty that its superiority will be immediately apparent. Your approach can only arouse resistance or ill-will to religion while the peaceful penetration of naturalism which is now going on will be halted. There are enlightened men who go into the church purely out of a social motive to enrich the mental lives of people and to help them in their daily struggle to get more of this world's goods. To my mind a united front is needed of all men who honestly seek the good and beautiful and are determined to fight for the truth. I have no more use than you for the priestly view of life, but I know men who share that view and are patterns of human excellence and whole-heartedly devoted to their fellowmen.

There were two questions that I wished to ask you Sunday night and if you are minded to answer them I would appreciate it.

1. You said that laws in physics and biology are more complicated than we supposed. Is it your view that law and order is an ultimate characteristic of nature and because of this intelligibility, what is known by reason is rational? (not, of course, reasonable) If so, is this not making a religion out of knowing?

2. While you are pious toward nature as a knower are you not morally rebellious, so that your science and morality supplement each other without being mixed, and only your science is religious?

It was my privilege to hear you for the first time last Sunday and it has given a new significance to your book.

Faithfully,
FREDERICK REUSTLE

December 16, 1934

Dear Mr. Reustle:

I have your letter of December 10th and find myself in cordial dis-agreement with every one of your statements, except that in regard to the good work carried on by St. George's church and as regards to greed, etc. having its roots in human nature. Possibly you will un-derstand my point of view better if you read my article on the dark side of religion in the volume on Religion Today edited by Prof. Arthur Swift. Let me briefly indicate why I cannot share any of the views which underly your letter.

In the first place, I cannot subscribe to your view, now fashionable, which associates religion with something vaguely philanthropic di-vorced from supernatural dogmas. That seems to me a woeful confu-sion which honest men should reject with all their might. The great historic religions cannot be divorced from their supernatural teach-ings. No one, it seems to me, can rightfully say that he is a member of the Christian Church but that he does not believe in the divinity of Christ or in the efficacy of prayer, baptism, and other historic rituals. To say that, it seems to me, involves a method of interpretation of historic documents which would make anything mean anything else. I see no earthly advantage in pursuing such a method. Let those who are philanthropic or believe in efforts for the amelioration of human conditions devote themselves to that effort and cut themselves loose from entangling alliances with historic superstitions. The notion that belief in the supernatural is necessary in order to promote humane conditions seems to me entirely unwarranted. On the contrary, for people who do not believe in the supernatural to associate themselves with Churches that do and to pussyfoot the distinction between natu-ralism and its denial seems to me to be as morally corrupting as it is intellectually confusing. I was not guilty of any logical fallacy (as you wrongly suppose) when I insisted that there is no necessary con-nection between religion and benevolence. For if Torquemada and Calvin are religious people and if the preachers of crusades, of the extermination of heretics, witches, and the like are inspired by reli-gion (and there is no good reason to doubt that) then one must admit that religion does often lead to cruelty (for which Christians often accuse Mohammedans) or else confess that religion is powerless to assuage the natural cruelty of some of its most distinguished repre-sentatives, such as St. Augustine. If St. Francis's philanthropy was due to his religion the Christianity of his time was certainly not benevolent, else there would have been no need for his preachment, which in fact, was not very effective in promoting brotherly love, not even in his own order, as subsequent history clearly showed.

The example of Albert Schweitzer today only serves to heighten the callousness of Christian Churches and Jewish Synogogues to the dreadful exploitation of negroes in Africa and in our own land. Did not the Churches of our South defend slavery as a divine institution approved in the Bible? Historically, their interpretation of the Bible was certainly sound.

As to Galileo, you ignore the fact that the Church opposed the spread of the Copernican astronomy and that in this country it has fought the spread of the doctrine of evolution on grounds which are antagonistic to the interests of science.

Your two questions addressed to me involve an assumption as to the nature of religion which I do not share and therefore I cannot answer them in your terms. I do believe that there is a certain amount of order in this world but it does not mean anything to me to assert that this is making a religion out of knowing. The desire for knowledge is a purely natural phenomenon to which religion has not always been friendly. Nor do I know what you mean by saying that only my science is religious. Religions existed long before science came into this world and they have not done much to advance it. As to being morally rebellious, I think that is largely a matter of sensitivity to the evils existing in the world. If there were a personal God responsible for that evil, I should certainly be in rebellion against him and say, Though he slay me, I cannot deny his cruelty in creating man to endure so much unnecessary suffering.

These views of mine, I know, are not fashionable, nor in good taste. It is popularly supposed that we have outgrown them. But they seem to me to be elementary truths and those who argue against them seem to me devoid of an adequate sense of logical cogency or regard for the distinction between what is pleasant and what is true. I think the fight between naturalism and supernaturalism is still very important and I am glad to have had an opportunity to impress that fact on my audience at Cooper Union. I was only sorry that my weak voice and the absence of amplifiers made it difficult for a large part of the audience to hear me. On issues of this sort perfect unanimity is not to be expected.

With assurance of my high regard for the naturalistic and temporal works of St. George's Church,

Sincerely yours,

MORRIS R. COHEN

Van Wyck Avenue Congregational Church
102–40 Van Wyck Expressway
Richmond Hill 19, N.Y.

January 8, 1958

Dear Mrs. Rosenfield,

. . . The occasion was a lecture on religion at Cooper Union when some of us expected that Prof. Cohen would follow the lead of Dewey and indicate what religion would be like stripped of supernaturalism. We were disappointed when the entire lecture did not get beyond a criticism of supernaturalism.

Events have proved Prof. Cohen to be correct, at least in part. The revival of orthodoxies of all kinds are more blatant than ever they dared to be in the thirties. Perhaps a broad attack upon supernaturalism might have made revival more difficult. In any case the compromise course of trying to broaden religion so as to sluff off the antiquated and elevate the rational and ethical has not been very successful. The most any of us can do is to hang on, endure events rather than influence them, and wait for a change of intellectual climate that a decline of communism and a certainty of peace would bring.

From the enclosed letter you will see that Prof. Cohen's attitude on religion is consistent with his philosophical position. His sentence, "Our reason may be a pitiful candle light in the dark and boundless seas of being. But we have nothing better . . ." should be shouted from every house top.

Sincerely,

F. REUSTLE

On May 16, 1935, Cohen wrote to Henry Levy, a young representative of the Jewish press:

Dear Mr. Levy:

My niece, Miss Sylvia Cohen, sent me your Metropolitan Comment of January 25 relating to my address at the Welfare Conference; and I wish to thank you for your very kind words about me personally. . . .

. . . While I admit and cannot help admitting that I am a Jew, I do not see that that in any way prevents me from being an agnostic, an atheist, or if [I] should care to be one, a Buddhist. That this should seem strange to anyone I cannot understand. Do you not find among your acquaintances many Jews who reject not only the Jewish but all other religions.

You are also mistaken in thinking that Hitlerism had any effect or influence on my views as to the Jews. I have been interested in the

Jews all my life and have always believed that the position of the Jews
(and indeed the position of all people) is essentially precarious so
that a study of the actual situation in which we find ourselves is necessary for self-respecting people. I do not know what on earth you
mean by saying that I am more of a Jew than I think I am. Nor do I
understand what you mean by "Jewishness." You are also incorrect
in referring to my "ill concealed" scorn for the professional Jews.
My views that they are worse than useless are expressed without any
concealment. I do not mean that those who are interested in Zionism,
in Jewish communal affairs, and the like, are not doing a useful work.
But those who preach Judaism either without knowing what on earth
it means or in no way practice what they profess, are a terrible handicap to the advancement of our people.

Sincerely yours,

MORRIS R. COHEN

To David M. Hausdorff, editor of the *Jewish Educator,* published at the
Institute of Jewish Culture and Learning, Cohen wrote:

July 23, 1938

Dear Mr. Hausdorff:

I wish to thank you for your courtesy in sending me a copy of the
Jewish Educator. I wish I could say that I think very highly of it, but
I regret that I cannot do so. The information which you offer is
scrappy and inadequate for any practical purpose that I can see.
Moreover, you are positively wrong in thinking that the account in
Genesis can possibly be removed from scientific objection by making
a day a long period. The biblical account makes vegetables appear on
the earth before the sun and moon and that is impossible by the
canons of ordinary experience and reason. Moreover, it is absurd to
think of the earth and the sky being created before the sun. There is
strictly speaking no sense at all in having day and night succeed each
other before the sun. But why dwell on this. In the light of modern
knowledge the Bible is full of demonstrably false statements such as
that the hare chews the cud.

I do not wish to argue matters of religion, but I must say you will
never get far with the modern age and temper if you ignore the fact
that on matters of science the Bible is antiquated. If you wish to
spread knowledge which is a very laudable objective, please don't repeat things on which many of us have been brought up and have rejected. You won't get any farther than your predecessors if your information is no better.

Please do not think that I am actuated by any hostile motive, on the contrary, I think you will be helped by giving attention to what I am urging on you.

With all good wishes,

Sincerely yours,
MORRIS R. COHEN

And to J. H. Berman in Joplin, Missouri:

January 11, 1937

Mr. J. H. Berman
111 Moffett Avenue,
Joplin, Mo.

Dear Mr. Berman:

I have your letter of January 7th asking me for my view on the question "Should the Jew be prominent in public life?"

My answer is that the Jew, as everyone else, should avoid notoriety or what Milton calls "bad eminence" but it would be disastrous for Jews to avoid taking their proper part in public life, and if they do their work with an excellence that makes them prominent, so much the better.

The notion that we will be safer by adopting a position of permanent inferiority has no support in history or human experience.

I shall be interested in learning what arguments are developed in your group against this position.

Sincerely yours,
MORRIS R. COHEN

Cohen was not a Zionist, and on that score has been condemned by some of his Zionist friends, although his antinationalist position was consistent with his liberal philosophy. He wrote in *A Dreamer's Journey*:

I could never bring myself to support efforts to establish a Jewish State which would not be in accord with the democratic principles of separation of Church and State and equality of civil, religious and economic rights to all inhabitants regardless of race and creed [p. 227].

But neither was he an anti-Zionist. He frequently expressed admiration for the way in which Jewish pioneers rescued the soil of Israel from long neglect, "the triumph of mind and soul over the desert."[9]

"Zionism," he wrote, "has rendered the supreme service of increasing men's self-respect, and has helped men to realize that they must be ready to give of their own past experience as well as to accept."[10] His hope for the land of Israel, expressed in 1946 in his last statement of his position, was for a "framework of a non-sectarian state that allows equal rights to all—Jews, Christians, Mohammedans, and atheists alike."[11]

Early in 1941, Cohen met Ben-Gurion in Brooklyn at the home of Dr. and Mrs. Shlomo Bardin, who had recently come from Palestine. Ben-Gurion and Cohen sat at opposite ends of the table, and as their remarks grew more and more heated, each banged harder and harder on the table. They soon woke up David, aged seven, for whom noise had special meaning—he'd been raised in Palestine. "Mommy," he called out, "who's being shot?"

But essentially, Cohen's attitude was not far from that of his friend Judah L. Magnes, first chancellor of the Hebrew University, who said in 1927:

. . . it would be a great honor to the Hebrew University if Professor Cohen were to consent to come to us and explain to us something about the Hebraic spirit which also courses through him in his passionate love of righteousness and of justice, that Hebraic spirit of which the Hebrew prophets were great proponents and of whom Professor Cohen is a worthy child.[12]

Cohen did become a member of the advisory board of the American Committee for a Department of Education at the Hebrew University in Jerusalem. He wanted to see the Hebrew University "become a beacon of light throughout the world."[13] When in 1935 he gave books to its library, Hugo Bergmann, the learned philosophical director of the Jewish National and University Library, wrote to Cohen from Jerusalem to thank him for his "valuable contribution . . . this token of interest in the development of the Library."

In a letter to Adolph Fraenkel at the Hebrew University in Jerusalem, Cohen alluded to his own position re Zionism.

February 23, 1938

Dear Professor Fraenkel:

It was very good of you to write me your lovely letter in regard to my retirement from the City College in order to give more time to the Conference on Jewish Relations. I do not recall what I said to you at our pleasant meeting in Harold Laski's home, but in regard to the fundamental question of the Jewish religion and Jewish nationalism, I am not aware that I have changed my views in the last forty years. My skepticism with regard to these two issues does not, however, blind me to the fact that there are Jews, and that they are entitled to live and to be protected against those who would degrade them.

The work of the Conference is primarily in the field of research, to act as a sort of intelligence Bureau to the Jewish people.

My absorption in the work of the Conference, which has now gone on for about four years, has made it difficult for me to follow the progress of mathematical thought in recent years. At the time I had the pleasure of meeting you, you were working on a new edition of your Mengenlehre. Did you bring out a new edition after 1930?

With kindest regards,

Cordially yours,

MORRIS R. COHEN

After Hitler's advent, world Jewry faced a grave crisis. It was urgent to discover what was happening to the Jews of Germany. By July of 1933 Cohen was in touch with a project of the New York Public Library to obtain firsthand source material on the subject. A few months later, he inquired of Manley O. Hudson, international-law expert at the Harvard Law School, whether there was anything "in international law which would justify a group of American jurists in issuing some kind of public protest against the method of the German Government of trying to control the actions of people outside of Germany by holding their relatives as hostages." Hudson offered no hope for such a course of action. But Cohen had already decided with his close friend, Arthur S. Meyer, to organize a research body to serve as an Intelligence Bureau for the defense of Jewry. Cohen sent out this preliminary letter:

June 5th, 1933.

You have doubtless been stirred, as most Americans have been, by the barbaric efforts in Germany to deprive the Jews of their essential human rights, and perhaps you have already taken part in some protest or contributed to some agency which is trying to relieve the terrible sufferings of the victims of this medieval oppression. My object in writing to you is to elicit your opinion as to whether we as American Jews can do anything of permanent value, in this situation.

No matter what the German government may now do or promise, the anti-Semitic propaganda which has been carried on for over twelve years by the party now in power is bound to have its vicious effects for years to come. Moreover, there is every indication that this anti-Semitic wave will spread in other countries, as it is in fact now spreading in Austria.

It occurs to me that some permanent organization of professional people, teachers, students, doctors, lawyers, artists, and other intellectual workers and educated people—all the classes that can, on the basis of their own experience, sympathetically understand what is now happening to our Jewish brethren—is needed to combat the permanent forces that are trying to destroy the Jewish people. So far as I know, there is now no organization of professional people for the purpose I have in mind, and in any case what I am thinking of is an organization of liberal men and women who will not let their differences in regard to religious orthodoxy, zionism, socialism, or communism hinder them from cooperating to prevent the permanent degradation of the Jews as human beings.

The work of the proposed society may take all sorts of forms, depending upon circumstances. It may try to enlighten public opinion, or it may supply needed books to Jewish students who cannot otherwise obtain them; it may aid diverse forms of necessary economic readjustment, or it may help gifted Jews to find positions for which they are eminently qualified. But you and others to whom I am writing will doubtless suggest so many other activities that properly fall within the scope of such a society that I need not at present give any longer list.

Please let me have your frank opinion as to the general possibilities and advisability of the plan. Would you yourself care to attend an informal meeting in your neighborhood to discuss the matter?

Faithfully yours,
MORRIS R. COHEN

By November 1933 the Conference on Jewish Relations came into being with high hopes and a thousand dollars donated by Meyer. Its aims were to conduct scholarly research on necessary Jewish problems, to publish and to hold conferences, to organize on a permanent institutional basis, and to bring together people otherwise divided by religion, culture, economics, and politics. The Conference, now called the Conference on Jewish Social Studies, is still in existence.

A modest chapter of *A Dreamer's Journey* tells about the Conference on Jewish Relations, but with too little indication of how radically it transformed Cohen's life. Not until 1937 was there an office other than the Cohen apartment, already crowded with his fabulous library. At first he did not even have clerical assistance. He carried on like a juggler keeping a good many balls in play. He became not only the Conference's chief planner but also its principal money raiser. He helped to guide research and to obtain sponsorship of research projects from universities, foundations, communities, and individuals of wealth. He organized meetings on crucial topics, tried to build up membership, sponsored publication of the research, helped maintain working relationships with other organizations in Jewish or social studies, wrote annual reports, and kept up with the correspondence and administrative detail. Beginning in 1939, there was considerably more.

Rushing from one appointment to another with no car at his disposal, he would sometimes keep a half-dozen appointments in one day. No rich Jew was safe from him. One day he stepped into the office of Joseph J. Klein, one of the trustees of The City College. Klein immediately pulled out his checkbook and asked, "How much is it this time, Morris?" Cohen protested. "Wait, Joe, I want to tell you about it." "It's not necessary, Morris. If you back it, it must be good."

Never an administrator, he took too many of the decisions, along with the work, upon himself, occasionally wounding the feelings of his collaborators, just as in the old Davidson days.

By 1937 the Conference's slate of officers consisted of: Cohen, president; vice presidents, Salo W. Baron, Edward Sapir, Israel S. Wechsler, Harry A. Wolfson; treasurer, Arthur S. Meyer; secretary of the board of directors, Harry N. Rosenfield; executive secretary, Melvin M. Fagen, with Miss Mina Wagman as his assistant. David Rosenstein was, and still is, one of the stalwarts.[14]

The following Conference correspondence affords a glimpse into the operation.

> 854 W. 181 Street
> New York City
> September 20, 1935

Dr. Samuel Rosenblatt
Baltimore, Md.

Dear Dr. Rosenblatt,

The Conference on Jewish Relations wishes to bring together a number of scholars to take counsel as to how we may best promote an understanding of the historical, psychologic, sociologic and economic conditions which have made and still make for anti-Semitism. The immediate object is the promotion of a more comprehensive view of the whole field on the part of the participants. . . . Those of us who have studied the problem from one angle or another, need the stimulus of exchanging views with those whose approach has been from a different angle. We hope, however, that this conference will prove a source of enlightenment not only to those who participate, but also to those interested in reading the reports and papers which the participants may care to have published in appropriate form. . . .

> MORRIS R. COHEN

> January 24, 1936

Professor Albert Einstein
112 Mercer Street
Princeton, New Jersey

Dear Professor Einstein:

I delayed answering your letter because I wanted to get in touch with Professor Morris Cohen. In order not to make this letter too lengthy, I shall give you a very brief outline of the work he is doing and hope you will afford me the opportunity to talk to you about it in person. If you desire, I could come to see you with Professor Cohen.

About two years ago Professor Cohen organized, under the name of Conference on Jewish Relations, a group of liberal and intellectual men and women to promote research on basic facts on which Jewish communal action must be based and to disseminate those facts to those who can best use them. A number of research projects have been undertaken and carried out. A year ago an economic conference was held, a number of eminent scholars contributed to the symposium and the proceedings were published. Last month a very important conference on the history of anti-semitism was held. Here, too, a number of eminent speakers made important contributions. Investigation as to Jews in colleges and professional schools is being carried on now. Much of the material which the High Commissioner of the League of Nations for Refugees, Mr. McDonald, incorporated in his report to the League and all of the facts of the supplementary report were gathered by the historian engaged for the purpose by Professor Cohen.

Many of us feel that the work of the Conference on Jewish Relations to which Professor Cohen has given unstintingly of his time and of his means is of great importance. We should like to enlist the aid of others in order to make it possible for Professor Cohen to go on with the work. It is for this purpose that I should like to come to see you to ask your advice and also your kind cooperation. The immediate project it to gather about fifty people at a dinner and outline the plan. I feel that your name and presence will be of great help.

Please convey my sincerest wishes to Mrs. Einstein and the hope that she will soon regain her health.

With kindest regards, I remain

Yours sincerely,

I. S. WECHSLER

[Dr. Israel S. Wechsler]

Conference on Jewish Relations, Inc.
854 West 181 Street
New York City

October 26, 1936

Mr. James N. Rosenberg,
165 Broadway,
New York City.

Dear Mr. Rosenberg:

In the past two years you have been intimately associated with certain important phases of our work; and I know of no one better qualified than yourself to judge whether our work ought to continue. I therefore turn to you for aid in dealing with the question of finances, on which depends our future existence.

Our membership is composed of a little over six hundred men and women and I think I may fairly say that they include some of the most distinguished Jewish scholars in this country. Men like Professors Albert Einstein at Princeton, Harry Wolfson and Felix Frankfurter of Harvard, Sapir of Yale, Sharfman of Michigan, Perlman of Wisconsin, Kandel, Baron, and Wechsler of Columbia, Dean Klapper of the City College, Dean Loeb of George Washington University, and Vice-President Deutsch and Prof. Max Radin of the University of California are a few of the names that come to mind. But as our members are all scientists, college teachers or engaged in other liberal professions, we cannot expect to raise the substantial sums of money needed for our research work. You have known this and you have not only generously contributed yourself but have helped us before to finance some of our most important investigations.

We feel that the growth of anti-Semitism in this as in other countries calls for the most careful study of all the factors on which our safety and that of our children depends. For the problems involved are not merely temporary but have their roots in history and are likely to remain serious not only during our lifetime but during that of our children. We must, therefore, take a long-range view of the situation and be thoroughly prepared with accurate and reliable knowledge for the various contingencies that are likely to arise. The movement for the emancipation of the Jews in liberal countries began in the 18th century. The pendulum is now swinging the other way and we see a reversal of the liberal trend in the spread of dictatorships and totalitarian states. The success of Hitlerism, founded in part on anti-Semitism, breeds crops of demogogues who hope to rise to power by similarly making anti-Semitism one of their chief weapons. From such appeals to prejudice there flows a steady stream of pseudo-scholarship as to race theories and as to the history and contemporary state of the Jews. These falsehoods cannot be met successfully except by accurate knowledge obtained by scholarly research as to the true state of Jewish social, economic, and political activities in the present as well as in the past. We do not wish to become a propaganda organization. We rather aim to make the results of our researches available to all people of good will whether Jews or Christians who can make proper use of the knowledge of the truth. In brief, we wish to organize an Intelligence Bureau for the Jewish people in their fight against the forces which would degrade them and deprive them of their human rights. To do this we must aim not only to meet false charges made against us but to promote a better understanding among ourselves as to the basic factors which determine the conditions of Jewish life. We need this knowledge also to strengthen our own resources and to assure that our general policies shall not be based on mere guess work. In view of the various divisions among Jews we are especially in need of the authority of the facts to guide us. For this purpose we have been carrying on studies (1) as to the position of the Jews in our educational system; what are the causes of discrimination and what are the factors by which better adjustments are effected, (2) studies of the Jews in the professions; what determines their opportunities, their difficulties, and the resulting ethical standards of practice, (3) the general geographic and economic distribution of the Jews as regards agriculture, industry, and commerce with a view of determining the current trends and the conditions for an optimum distribution, (4) intensive studies of the position of American Jews in small communities as well as in large cities with a view of determining the possibilities of a better geographic adjustment, and (5) researches into the historic, anthropologic, psychologic, economic and other social-political causes of anti-Semitism.

We have reason to believe that the result of these studies placed at the disposal of thoughtful people, will be enlightening to our Christian fellow citizens as well as to our own people. There is a growing interest in these problems today and we believe that we have the scholarly resources to meet this demand if we can secure the funds for the purpose. You have yourself seen at close range what careful and scholarly work Dr. Janowsky did on the petition to the League of Nations. I think you will find that all of our other work is of the same thorough and reliable character, as indeed one has a right to expect of men who have to maintain their standing as scholars.

As to the question of finances, it must be recognized that the number of people actively interested in scholarly research is necessarily small and that their financial resources are very much limited. I doubt, therefore, whether we can raise more than $5,000 a year through any intensive drive for a larger membership. We need, however, at least about $25,000 a year to carry on our work effectively. A minimum of $15,000 per year for three years would at least put us in a position of being able to demonstrate the importance of our plans. Therefore I express the earnest hope that you will aid us in bringing about this result.

I have not gone into great detail about our work because I am sure that you know from the contacts and participation in it in the past two years all its far-reaching and important implications. Should you, however, find that any of your friends wish further information, I shall be glad to put that at your or their disposal.

With high appreciation of your past services, I am

Faithfully yours,

MORRIS R. COHEN

October 27, 1936

Dear Professor Cohen:

The Conference on Jewish Relations has to my personal knowledge done work of great importance and of splendid quality. I am satisfied from my knowledge of your organization and its financial needs that it is vitally important that a minimum of $15,000. per year for three years be assured you in addition to your membership dues. I intend to try to raise this for you. Having in mind the old maxim that actions speak louder than words, I hereby personally pledge $1,000 per year for three years, the first $1,000. to be paid not later than December 31st of this year.

I am immediately communicating with various friends of mine urging them to do precisely what I have done.

Sincerely yours,

JAMES N. ROSENBERG

June 7, 1938

Dr. Benjamin R. Harris
885 Elm Place
Glencoe, Illinois

Dear Dr. Harris:

. . . I thoroughly agree with you that the acceptance of any quota for the Jewish people in regard to the professions would be a great calamity to liberal civilization. Indeed, I made that point four years ago in an address before the National Conference of Jewish Social Workers. . . .

I do not know whether you are acquainted with the work of the Conference on Jewish Relations, of which I have been Chairman. It undertakes to study the basic factors which determine the position of the Jews in the modern world, and their relation to their fellow citizens. If you are interested I shall be glad to have our literature sent to you, and I shall be happy to have you join us. . . .

Faithfully yours,

MORRIS R. COHEN

March 8, 1939

Dear Will:

There has been a good deal of talk about settling Jewish refugees in Alaska. To do so however we must find opportunities for employment there. This makes me wonder whether it would not be possible for the Hollander Company to set up a factory in Alaska itself. I know that there are a great many difficulties, but some of the refugees might be very useful in such an enterprise and it would be a God-send to find a place for them. . . .

With kindest remembrances to your good wife and yourself,

Cordially yours,

MORRIS R. COHEN

Mr. William J. Greenfield,
c/o Hollander and Company,
East Kinna Street, Newark, N.J.

Among the Conference's research projects[15] were studies of Jews in the legal profession in New York City, of the position of Jews in the American medical profession, and of Jewish occupational distribution in New York City. The Conference, a pioneer in Jewish population studies, promoted such projects in various cities throughout the nation. One Jewish community, as a result of such a survey, found it did not need the home for the aged that it had contemplated building. It saved about $1,000,000. (*Jewish Population Studies,* 1943, was edited by Sophia Robison and *Essays on Antisemitism,* 1942, by Koppel Pinson with a Foreword by Salo Baron.)

Research fellowships at universities were established or partially subsidized by the Conference. A survey of racial attitudes among college students, conducted by Eugene L. Horowitz under Robert Lynd, Ralph Linton, and Gardner Murphy, was sponsored jointly by the Conference and the Pi Lambda Phi Fraternity. Studies were made of "Jewish Workers in New York City Men's Clothing Industry," of "The Economic Structure of the Jewish Community in Detroit," and of "The Jews in the Waste Industry in Detroit."

In international affairs the record was brilliant. The Conference sent Oscar Janowsky to Europe to prepare a legal and factual report on what was happening to the guaranteed minority rights of Jews. The High Commissioner for German Refugees, James G. McDonald, made of his proposed letter of resignation a documentary analysis of Nazi crimes against non-Aryan citizens of Germany. The Conference sent Janowsky and Melvin M. Fagen to Europe to compile materials in support of the petition to the League of Nations, which backed the McDonald letter. The Janowsky-Fagen book, *International Aspects of German Racial Policies,* sponsored by the Conference and the American Jewish Committee, was published in 1937 with an Introduction by Rosenberg and Cohen. Janowsky's *People at Bay: The Jewish Problem in East Central Europe,* published in 1938 with a Preface by Cohen, was also sponsored by the Conference.

When Cohen was making plans to leave for the University of Chicago, in a moment of discouragement, or perhaps of clear-mindedness, he drew up what amounted to a letter of withdrawal from the active direction of the Conference. But "Draft not used" is scribbled in Cohen's handwriting in the corner. The unsent letter is reproduced in part.

Let me analyze what I regard as the fundamental weakness of our present organization. It has been, I may say without impropriety, too much of a one-man organization. That is, people have looked too much to the president for all sorts of determinations for which the responsibility should be more widely spread. This would not have been so serious an evil in the formative years of our organization if your president were a man of some executive ability. This, however, is not the case. Let me speak frankly. I am essentially of a reflective, or, if you prefer, scholarly point of view. I have no inclination to be a missionary, that is, to convert other people to my point of view. I not only am not a salesman, but I cannot get myself to wish to be one. I am a pluralist in ethics, and while devotion to the Conference seems to me a duty, I have no inclination to argue or persuade anyone who thinks that his line of duty is in some other direction. Moreover, either as a result of this or for other reasons, I entirely lack the ability to make other people work that I take to be the essence of leadership or executive ability, and in that sense the Conference is most unfortunate in having me as president. I do not wish to harp on a note of false modesty. I realize that lots of people have joined the Conference or contributed to it because of a certain prestige which I have acquired in an altogether different field of human achievement. But that, after all, will not enable the Conference to grow. Personal loyalties are an instrumentality, but they come and go, and no one person can be a foundation for an enduring enterprise affecting the welfare of as large and permanent groups as the Jewish people. In point of fact, the extent of my future services must, in the nature of things, be limited even if I should give up all my interests in philosophy and kindred studies,—an effort which, I must say frankly, it is impossible for me to make. For, as I look over my own life of the last four years and see what I have been able to do for the Conference and what I could otherwise have done in the way of what has hitherto been my life work, I feel that the old motto, "Shoemaker, stick to your last," is a wise one so far as I am concerned. I have never, since my early years in the Davidson Society, had any ambition for practical achievement. I have always been and still am convinced that theoretic life needs no justification and is its own good excuse for being; that the philosopher is under no obligation to do anything else but to philosophize. To the extent, therefore, that I have taken time out to help in the organization of the Conference, I must regard that as an interlude in my career. In brief, therefore, I must look forward in the remaining years of my life to gathering up the threads of my philosophic reflection and giving to the world the result of my life work in philosophy. I do not, of course, wish to desert the Conference. I am more persuaded than ever of its indispensability, but I think that I can do a great service to it by insisting that the burden be more widely distributed and that there be a more general recognition of the fact that my value to the Conference is much more my value as a critic of ideas rather than as an organizer or director.

Instead of following his own rational advice, Cohen sent a more restrained second draft that talked Conference and not Cohen, and went right on with Conference work, although at Chicago the work load was somewhat eased. An interview reported in the New York *World-Telegram* for December 21, 1937, shows a mood of buoyancy.

"I have put my four books by," said Dr. Cohen half humorously in the sunlit living room of his apartment on West 186 St., overlooking the Harlem river, "and how long it will be before I can return entirely to my own work again I do not know. I am going to engage in research with the Conference on Jewish Relations, sociological research into the status of the various Jewish groups in the United States, so that we may know how many there are, what their problems are and what are their relationships to the community at large." . . .

Dr. Cohen said that Jews were rapidly losing ground in the banking field. . . . [He] cited other fields in which he felt that opportunities for the Jews are limited—utilities and transportation among them. He said it was the purpose of the group with which he was associating himself merely to make the factual information available, not to take action. . . . "Our program must be in line with general scientific research. There is no reason why non-Jews should not co-operate with us. In fact, we have non-Jewish collaborators." . . .

Dr. Cohen could see in absolute pacifism no refuge for the intelligent man confronted by a world apparently about to go crazy for a second time.

A frank letter on the subject of propaganda shows Cohen's concern for truth regardless of the issue:

TO Mr. Jay Leo Rothschild
Law Offices, 22 E. 40th St.
New York City

February 1, 1939

Dear Mr. Rothschild:

On my return to the city I find your good letter, for which I am very grateful. It is encouraging to find that our work and plans interest you sufficiently to write as you do. The success of our program depends upon our receiving not only constructive suggestions but also pertinent dissents. For even when such dissent is based on misapprehension it gives us a chance to clarify our position.

The Conference on Jewish Relations is not a propaganda but a fact-finding institution. This is not because we regard propaganda as unnecessary but because we believe in the division of labor. (1) Effective propaganda requires far greater resources than our organization can possibly hope to acquire, while other organizations are in much better position to do it and are in fact doing so. We restrict ourselves to finding the facts and to make them available on the theory that all agencies of good will need to know the truth. (2) While so many are engaged in fighting anti-semitism, some attention must be devoted to careful study of our own strength and weakness and our Conference is devoted to this task so far as no other organization is doing it.

There have been objections to our program on the ground that we are bound to find facts unfavorable to us and that this would have a bad effect. I must say frankly that I regard this attitude as foolish, as the attitude of a man who is afraid to go to the doctor lest the latter find something wrong with him. When a ship is in the vicinity of rocks, the safest course is surely not to close our eyes and steer blindly.

But now comes the question of publication and a great many more people object to our publishing anything which shows our weakness. This objection does not seem to us well founded. (1) It is not possible for Jews to become informed of certain facts without others sooner or later learning about it. The notion, therefore, of gathering information and keeping it secret does not seem a very practical one. (2) If we do not publish the facts, our enemies are more likely to exaggerate rather than under-estimate our weakness and we have no way of refuting their lies. (3) Even from the point of view of effective propaganda it is well to note that if our publications are to carry any weight with fair-minded people (and we cannot hope to do much with the others) we must be 100% honest, i.e. we must tell the whole truth as we find it and not deliberately falsify the picture by leaving out the shadows. If we follow the latter course, the scientific character of our work will be rightly suspected, we shall become known as another propaganda institute, and we shall fail to reach those open-minded people whose support it is most urgent that we secure. In this connection it is well to remember that the core of our membership, as well as working force, comes from academic people who are located in all of our leading colleges and universities and who are in touch with the sentiment existing in these institutions. If educated America is to be favorably influenced toward a just attitude to us, I am confident that our procedure of including the unfavorable facts in their proper background is the most effective way of preventing the spread of unfavorable misinformation. (4) No one can well dispute the fact that if the Jewish people remain ignorant as to their own weakness[es] they will not be able to remedy them, and the danger of these weaknesses thus continuing and even growing is much greater than the chance that any of our publications will strengthen anti-semitism. Some chances everyone must take who wants to accomplish anything at all and wisdom consists in considering all the alternatives. Moreover, there is some justice in the view that we Jews today are too much concerned with what others think of us and not enough with the more important question as to what we ourselves should think of the situation. Self-respect and the strengthening of our own morale requires that we ourselves be bolder and more realistic in facing the situation before us with open eyes.

The foregoing does not ignore the fact that publication is a practical venture and must take into account both timeliness and the possibilities of our results being misunderstood. It is for that reason that I told you we would not publish our study on the status of Jewish lawyers before getting the judgment of a number of people whose judgment we valued. We did this after my visit to you and we are confident that the publication of the study will do the Jewish people more good than harm. The concensus of opinion among those that we consulted was that our study would tend to refute the gross exaggerations current as regard the weaknesses of the Jews in the legal profession in New York. Of course, there were a few dissenters. But can anything be done in this world if we wait for absolute unanimity?

As to the study of Jewish criminals in Illinois, it is to my mind a most effective refutation of the widespread error that the Jews specialize in certain fields of crime. It is silly for us to pretend that there are no Jewish criminals when everyone knows that the contrary is true. What is important is to establish the fact that we are a normal people and as regards criminality certainly no worse than the rest of the population.

Trusting that you will find this a clear statement of our policy, I am with kind remembrances,

Cordially yours,
MORRIS R. COHEN

And so the circus continued, except that three new rings were added. By 1939 the Conference launched its quarterly, *Jewish Social Studies,*[16] with Salo W. Baron, the authority on Jewish history, and Hans Kohn, the authority on nationalism, as coeditors with Cohen. First-rate scholars in the field served as managing editors, first Koppel S. Pinson, then Joshua Starr, followed by Theodor Gaster. From the start the periodical won the eminent name that it still enjoys.

Another offshoot of the Conference, the Jewish Occupational Council, also came into being in 1939. It gained the support of about a dozen of the leading Jewish organizations, some of which had not been previously on speaking terms. The Jewish Occupational Council became a favorite brain child of Cohen's. The Conference had proved a catalyst in this co-operative venture into Jewish vocational guidance.

The third project was a Committee on Peace Studies. Cohen had proved prescient in matters of war and peace. In 1937 he and Rosenberg had warned in their Introduction to *International Aspects of German Racial Policies:* "Policies of hatred or violence cannot be confined within any frontier and will not stop with Jews . . . internal persecutions bear the seeds of international conflict."

Early in World War II Cohen claimed that there would be peace as well as a war to be won, and that there would be applications to be made to the Jewish cause. Unlike most non-Jewish international specialists, he had profited by the lesson of how, despite "guaranteed" minority rights, the Jews had been degraded after World War I in countries like Poland and Romania. His last presidential report to the Conference on Jewish Relations, in January 1940, stressed the necessity of preparing for postwar studies on Jewish world problems. American Jewry, he realized, would have to bear the brunt of the burden in many ways.

By July, a month after the fall of France, Cohen had drawn up a statement of research necessary toward the protection of world Jewry in the postwar world. He sent a copy of it, marked "Strictly Confidential," to Einstein, along with the following letter:

July 11, 1940

Dear Professor Einstein:

Some time ago I wrote you about a plan of forming a committee to study the problems of possible peace. We have succeeded in setting up such a committee and I am enclosing a statement of its aims and scope. I am confident that we can obtain funds to enable us to pursue most of the studies outlined therein as well as the cooperation of all those who can help us with information and ideas.

I should be very grateful if you would return the statement with your comments.

With kindest regards, I am
Cordially yours,
MORRIS R. COHEN

The committee referred to in Cohen's letter was the Committee on Peace Studies chaired by him, under the auspices of the American Jewish Committee. By October 1940 that committee's report was adopted by the American Jewish Committee. The Research Institute on Peace and Post-War Studies was officially established by November 1, with Cohen as chairman to draw up the blueprints and Max Gottschalk, professor of international law, as director. Problems of three sorts were considered: relief and rehabilitation, migration and colonization, and vindication of Jewish rights, politically, economically, and culturally. For the *Contemporary Jewish Record,* April 1941, Cohen wrote "Jewish Studies of Peace and Post-War Problems." Reissued in pamphlet form by the American Jewish Committee in 1943, it was widely distributed. Cohen wrote:

Nevertheless, we must face the fact that hundreds of thousands, if not millions, of Jews will want or be compelled to leave Europe as soon as peace is declared. . . . it would hardly be possible to return the many homeless refugees to their former habitation and economic position [p. 8].

We shall therefore have to face the inescapable task of helping a large number, not only to leave Europe and transport themselves to other countries, but also to help them adjust themselves to make a living in their new homes [p.8].

Nor must we forget that the problem of five million Jews in Soviet Russia may become a burning one in the very near future. It will certainly be so if war breaks out between Germany and the Soviet Union. . . . At present we have inadequate knowledge of Jewish conditions in Russia [p. 14].

From Chicago, during his last quarter of teaching in the fall of 1941, Cohen wrote to Sidney Wallach.

November 4, 1941

Dear Sidney:

I think it of the utmost importance to call a meeting of the peace committee, if for no other reason to let them know that the peace studies are being continued and that their judgment as to what ought to be done is still desired. I am thinking, however, that it would be a very gracious thing if Mr. [Maurice] Wertheim [president of the American Jewish Committee] could come to the meeting, and get a line as to what it is that we are after. Even if he cannot make any commitment as to the future of the Committee, I think it would be not only a courtesy, but a very helpful move. . . .

On my way to New York, I expect to stop over at the University of Michigan and talk to Professors [William] Haber and [I. L.] Sharfman about the situation.

In connection with the meeting on the 17th, Dr. Gottschalk's staff and Mr. [Maurice] Hexter should prepare some data as to the number of Arabs in Trans-Jordania and Iraq, and something of the position of the Jews in Iraq as well as Syria. This, for the purpose of fortifying our own delegation in opposing any plan of mass transportation or transplantation of Arabs from Palestine into neighboring countries. For, if we approve the latter course, we shall be approving the uprooting of the millions of Jews in Europe.

With kind regards,

Cordially yours,
MORRIS R. COHEN

By the time he left the guidance of the Research Institute, late in 1941, in the competent hands of Dr. Gottschalk, the publication schedule was well under way.

On the subject of war and peace, Cohen wrote from Chicago:

November 11, 1941

Mr. Max Putzel
300 Riverside Drive
New York City

Dear Mr. Putzel:

I have your letter of November 3 and I thoroughly agree with you that the proportion of Jews in this country who are pro-intervention is about the same as of other Americans. Possibly it may be a little higher because after all the Jews have suffered more from Hitler than any other group of human beings.

I ought, however, to add that while I am opposed to war—and I do not know of anyone who genuinely wants it—I am not at all certain that we can manage to keep out of it. The Chinese have a proverb: "No man can enjoy more peace than his neighbors will allow him." If Mr. Hitler succeeds in eliminating the British Navy as a world force—and it seems to me there is a good chance of England's becoming empoverished through the continual sinking of their ships and the goods which they carry—then he will in all probability prepare to make war on the United States. The world has become too small to allow the United States to keep out of every field in which Germany is interested. The German militarists will not be able to satisfy the German people by the conquest of Europe alone. They will, therefore, be under necessity to conquer the United States either by military force or by diplomatically forcing us into a policy of appeasement which will mean the end of democracy in this country.

If Hitler keeps Norway and the coast of France, as well as the Danish and his own harbors, he will in the course of five years or so be able to build a navy much larger than the present United States navy. We shall, therefore, have to go in for a heavy program of arming and this again means the end of democracy as the history of Europe clearly indicates.

I mention these difficulties not because I am convinced that things will turn out that way, but because it seems to me that the opponents of war ought to meet these arguments and not merely shout that war is dreadful—something which is too true but not very helpful in deciding what we ought to do.

I retired from the service of the City College four years ago and I teach here for part of the year.

Sincerely yours,
MORRIS R. COHEN

One of Cohen's last major speeches was delivered before the Jewish Welfare Board in Chicago. It was seven months before Pearl Harbor. The subject was "American Democracy in the Present Emergency." As philosopher and Jew, he related "the Jewish problem" to the struggle of liberalism over totalitarianism.

I trust that we as Jews will cultivate a liberal attitude with regard to our own affairs and in regard to the vital differences which separate us. However deplorable any of us may regard it, no one can honestly deny the fact that we Jews are unalterably divided in regard to religion, in regard to Zionism or Diaspora nationalism, in regard to political theories and policies. . . .

In the world struggle which faces us . . . our only hope is the triumph of the liberal forces in our country and abroad. The liberals are our natural allies and the illiberals are our natural and relentless enemies.

. . . sooner or later, I believe we shall have to fight the totalitarian effort to control the whole world. . . .

The great desideratum today . . . is for us to hold on to the faith in American liberalism. . . . Those of us who realize the benefits which the democratic regime has accorded us, will not give up the fight.[17]

A little later, he wrote in the same vein to Wertheim, newly elected president of the American Jewish Committee:

I think we must emphasize the fact that we fight as American Jews for the maintenance of the fundamental basis of humane civilization, which liberated the Jews from the ghetto and gave them the opportunity to enjoy the glorious privileges which our country offers, because it is based on a philosophy of freedom. . . . we must fight the old fight for justice which the Hebrew prophets fought in their day and which all lovers of mankind have fought for through the ages.

Before the collapse of his health at the end of 1941, Cohen had accepted offices in the Jewish Social Research Council, the Joint Distribution Committee, the American Palestine Fund, and the American Jewish Committee. The ORT (Organization for Rehabilitation Through Training), of which he had long been a supporter, enlisted him in its Economic Research Committee. He was president of the Jewish Academy of Arts and Sciences since 1936. He did not lend his name only, but participated.

The philosopher, fully emerged from the ivory tower, had become a guide on public affairs as well as one of the country's leading research advisers on Jewish problems.

Cohen's affection for Yiddish, his mother tongue, never flagged. He saw in it a language eminently suited to "heimische" affection and ironic wit. His intimates knew that the surest way to soften him was to call him "Meishele." He could swap Yiddish jokes for hours on end with a friend like Adele Sutta, whose repertoire matched his.

Unlike many assimilated Jews, he had respect for the Yiddish tradition, and thought the Jewish community would be well advised to strengthen the movement for Yiddish education. Acquaintance with Yiddish literature is indispensable, he claimed, for immediate contact with Jewish life here and abroad, today and for centuries past.[18] He paid tribute to the Yiddish press.[19]

A Dreamer's Journey portrays Cohen's life as emblematic of a generation of Jewish immigrants to the land of promise. The Jewish newspaper, *The Day,* published the early portions, serially, in Yiddish translation. One of the happiest evenings of Cohen's years of retirement as an ailing widower was spent at the home of his former student, Ascher Achinstein, where several installments of the Yiddish translation were read with commentaries. My father laughed until the tears came to his eyes. Two days before Cohen died, his chapter on Davidson appeared in *The Day*. And so his last, like his first, publication was on his "Beloved Teacher," his last message in his first language.

Cohen had a deep attachment for the Hebrew language, the language of prayer. Despite his break with the ritual that is the core of practicing Judaism, he once confided to his brother, Sam, how dear to him were the prayers chanted by their parents, like "vivid illustrations in the book of my life."[20] Seders at the home of our maternal grandmother had been memorable experiences for the Cohen children. On the first Passover after her death in December 1917, we set about making in our home as good an imitation of Grandma's Seder as possible. Mother co-operated, but our father came first to scoff. In later years, however, the age-old family ritual came to mean much to him. This letter of his has since been read as part of the ceremony in the family Seders:

> [Chicago]
> Thursday, April 10, 1941

To the Israelites (namely Mary, Felix, Lucy, Leonora, Willie, Harry, Grace and Gene Maura,) celebrating the Passover Seder at the House of Solomon the Son of Moses the Cohen

Dear Folks:

When I was a boy in Russia, and saw the suffering of the Jews vividly before me—touching, indeed, my dear mother—I read the Hagadah with great feeling. When I came to this blessed land and the doors of opportunity were opened to me, the Seder ceremonies ceased to have much meaning to me. But while the tragic fate of millions of Jews in Europe in recent years, and our uncertain future even in America, have not made me go back to theologic supernaturalism, they have made vivid to me the need of trusting to the larger vision according to which calamities come and go, but the continuity of life and faith in its better possibilities survive. Let us therefore hope that we shall all meet together and celebrate more festivals in days when the world at large will be in a happier state than it is now. And let us not in this hope fail to enjoy the blessing of this day to the Cohen family.

With love to all of you—

> MORRIS (né Moses)

Each Jew has his own definition of what constitutes a good Jew. For some, it means belief; for others, the keeping of a kosher home or regular attendance at synagogue or temple. Still others might use the measure of a man's financial contribution to Jewish needs or his support of Israel. And some may judge by a man's readiness to stand up and be counted as a Jew when the going is tough.

There was no abstract doctrine of Judaism, Cohen felt, upon which all Jews can agree. "I have always been a Jew," he said, "because I was born and brought up in a Jewish family."[21]

Cohen once scribbled a draft of a letter to the editor of the *Herald Tribune* in which he expressed admiration for the way the philosopher

Henri Bergson, despite doctrinal differences with the religion of his ancestors, listed himself as a Jew in the days of Nazi domination over France.

Jan. 7, 1941

To the Editor of the Herald-Tribune:

Your editorial today on Henri Bergson concludes on a note that deserves and will bear frequent and emphatic repetition. Whatever the differences among philosophers as to Bergson's distinctive doctrines, no one can fail to be touched by his nobly heroic courage in refusing to be exempted from the harsh rules applicable to his fellow-Jews. In dark days we need to have examples of this sort before us to keep alive our faith in the better possibilities of human nature. And I may add that to accept rather than escape our common lot has been the attitude of great philosophers since the days of Socrates.

Cohen swam against two tides of his times—religiosity and Zionism—but he kept faith with his people. Does not the key to Cohen lie in his Jewishness, from his Litvak tongue and his wit to his concern with justice and ethics, his interest in things Jewish, both historic and contemporary? The very intensity of his devotion to learning followed the Hebraic tradition. Even his dissatisfaction with Dewey's instrumentalism, or subordination of abstract to practical thinking, may be viewed as the natural outcome of Cohen's prime orientation.

Cohen's agnosticism was deeply tinged with piety. He proclaimed faith not in established dogma and rites but in universal truth, the eternity of ideas, and humility before a cosmos bigger than man. He shared Spinoza's "amor Dei intellectualis" and admired the modern forms of Spinozistic spirituality exemplified in Santayana, F. H. Bradley, and Russell. These were the four philosophers for whom Cohen felt the greatest attraction. He would have been the last person to claim spirituality as exclusively Hebraic, but he did state that the "subordination of material things to spiritual values has made it possible for Jews to survive unprecedented calamities with dignity and self respect."[22]

For Cohen, philosophy took the place of religion. His philosophical other-worldliness, unassociated with belief in monotheism, resurrection, or a day of judgment, was impregnated with a concept of eternity. In consecrating his life to the search for the true and the good, he sought timeless values. A believer might discern in it, Epikoros or agnostic as he was, the quest for God.

It remained for a Texan, who to the best of my knowledge had never known Cohen, to draw the analogy once made by Judah Magnes. Levi A. Olan wrote in 1953:

The fact is that we need a Morris Raphael Cohen in our Jewish life to shake the smugness out of our religious, cultural and communal life. His writings may irritate many, but like those of the prophets, they are the words of a wise and thoughtful Jew.[23]

In the first act of Cohen's life, he was an orthodox Jew; in the second, a rebel. During the third act, his youthful reflections about giving himself to some humanitarian cause were kindled by Davidson, the flame nurtured by Mary. In his fourth act, he developed a spiritualized naturalism, reminiscent of Spinoza's. In the final act, he sacrificed the unfinished writings and the remainder of his days on the altar of the Jews.

To put it still more succinctly, the first and the last chapters in the book of his life were Jewish.

XIV. *Cohen and Frankfurter*

SHORTLY AFTER Felix S. Cohen's birth in 1907 Felix Frankfurter wired the Cohens, "Congratulations to you, good luck to the happy one." Felix Cohen's first grandchild, also Felix, was born in 1961 in Vienna, birthplace of Felix Frankfurter. The name goes on in the family.

Felix Frankfurter and Morris Cohen remained friends for more than forty years, since the days when they were first roommates at Harvard.

Throughout the years, the appearance of a Frankfurter letter was the occasion for joy. Morris and Mary Cohen would sit down together to decipher the hieroglyphics of his handwriting. The letters on both sides were cast, not in the guarded tone inevitably assumed for publication, but in the frank and spontaneous manner of two intimate friends who trusted each other.

The last visit between the two friends had taken place in my father's little apartment in Washington in the early fall of 1946. My father asked me to show Frankfurter the inscribed photograph of him that hung in the bedroom. Frankfurter murmured to us pensively, "Was I ever really that young?"

I called on Mr. Justice Frankfurter in his chambers at the Court, on November 23, 1954, to gain permission to use his letters to Cohen. I had boned up by rereading their correspondence. He reminisced to me about his friend and the issues they used to debate in the old days, expressing himself in the very words he had originally used in his letters. I could have finished the sentence for him, but I was remembering from my reading done the day before and he after the lapse of many years. It was an amazing demonstration of *le temps retrouvé*. Here was a living testimony of the ties of friendship.

These are the letters of their youth and of their maturity. Mr. Justice Frankfurter's letters cannot be reproduced *in toto* here for lack of space.

239

Those used have been selected for their bearing on Cohen. Their differences sparked and stimulated them both. Theirs is an epistolary record of a deep and lasting friendship. *Res ipsa loquitur.*

The Harvard Union

Dec. 10, 1905

My dear Morris,

The postmark "Lakewood" betokened good news and good sense. I am glad to hear you are coming round but I don't fully see the wisdom of coming back in a week in view of the approaching recess. Why not stay till after New Year? Do you wish me to call for the theses in the Philosophy Department . . . ?

With regards from a lot of boys and your success,

FELIX

1707 Cambridge St.
Cambridge, June 8, 1906

My dear Morris—

. . . I am sorry to learn of the day set for your wedding, as it will be impossible for me to be present. I have an examination the very day. . . .

I shall welcome with pleasure the visit of Herr Doktor und Frau Doktor Cohen.

With sincere regards,

FELIX

March 9, 1912

Dear Morris:

It is distinctly healthy to submit to analysis an institution that enjoys such uncontested acceptance as does the case system today. I am glad, therefore, you are applying your critical probe. But I agree with Pound in thinking "you do the case system an injustice." Undoubtedly, there is a humiliating lack of philosophic legal literature in this country, which reflects quite accurately the shabbiness of philosophic legal thinking. But I think your theory of causation is wrong in ascribing even a contributory influence to the case system for this condition.

The chief trouble is not with the case system of instruction, but with our Anglo-American case system of legal development. Precedents, not underlying philosophic principles, form our legal habit of thought. The old-fashioned text-book system of instruction, with its generalization from a surface consideration of cases, retarded any philosophic approach to the law. It is the case system, which is the empiric, scientific method, that gave us the necessary data and method, first, for a historic, and then for a sociological basis of the law. Of course, the university should react upon the development of jurisprudence, but you must remember that our law schools are professional schools, and their first business is to fit men for the practice of the profession. Cases are the raw stuff of the profession, and the case system must be judged, not by the legal literature that its exponents have produced but, by the alternative text-book system of education. Legal instruction and legal thinking before the days of Langdell and Ames were arid and empty. It is the case system which has given to us the great storehouse of historical data, now availed of by men like Wigmore, Pound, and others, in gradually stimulating philosophic thinking in the profession and the evolution of a philosophic jurisprudence.

I deplore with you most deeply that Dean Ames should have left behind no general treatises, but the blame lies not with the case system. Time exacted the heaviest toll from him, and no man ever paid it more cheerfully. I think you little realize the years of labor and untiring effort that were necessary to revolutionize legal instruction in this country. For years at Harvard, Langdell and Ames, and gradually Thayer, were the only exponents of the case system. Their own colleagues were opposed to it. Years and years were spent by Ames, with a scholarship fastidious to a fault, in producing really wonderful case books. During our time at Cambridge, he was about done with them. He told us once that the system was the fruitful instrument for the right kind of text-books. And I shall forever remember that wonderfully serene smile of his, with all the impersonal gladness of a child, as he joyously said "and you shall have them." I counted on ten years more of the most productive work from him, during which he would have given us at least one or two general treatises such as only his remarkable power could have produced.

He was deeply interested in the social and economic causes which shape our law, and nothing would have pleased his essentially intellectual mind more than indulgence in the luxury of philosophic generalization. Added to this, was his strong human interest. You speak, for instance, of having no book from him on Master and Servant. You will be interested to know that for years he was a student of workmen's compensation laws, and the whole relation of Master and Servant was a subject that frequently tempted him. But he was even more interested in his students, and to them he gave his time and thought with divine extravagance. I was constantly pained by the wasteful drain that was made upon him, but my regret was checked by the thought that he would rather have lightened the load of a single student, or permanently stimulated his interest, than to have written the most classic treatise.

You have opened up a line of inquiry about a subject that is most appealing to me professionally. But even at best down here, I have got to think in scraps and write in jerks. I did, however, want to enter a *caveat* on one or two of the points in your letter, if for no other reason than to invite your retort. You will remember that as far back as law-school days, I used to get my jurisprudence from you. I can't, however, let pass unnoticed your protestation of modesty that these waters are, perhaps, too deep for you. You know, neither modesty nor miracles among friends.

Yours, as ever,

FELIX

Law School of Harvard University
Cambridge, Mass.

July 23, '14

Dear Morris:

I happened to agree with the restrained judgment of The Green Bag on a certain paper, a juristic article recently written by a layman named Prof. Cohen, and three copies of The Green Bag will get to you before long.

The editorial committee of the Legal Philosophy Series has shown good sense in getting you to write the introductory article for their volume on Legal Method. You seem to me to be so admirably equipped to make philosophy and law a happy union—and thereby to give more bite and content to philosophy, and more reality and direction to law.

You would have reason to be pleased with my increased enthusiasm for doing the necessary work of hard-pan study. I have a woeful sense of my limitations and my ignorances. Sometimes it doesn't quite seem possible that I should have escaped knowing at least a few more things than I do. I can't help putting some of the blame on the college as she was, or regretting that I did not earlier meet somebody like Davidson, or for the matter of that, somebody like you. However, I am not wasting energy in crying over what is not. I only want you to know I am pretty actively alive to the job that is ahead of me. For the coming year I am up against the very practical proposition of giving three courses. I will have to pay my way, as it were, as I go along. It is fine to think that you and I will plow together a good deal in the same territory, and it's a mighty big comfort to me.

I will bear in mind the kind of material you are after. I wonder if it is possible for you to come up here and spend a week or so during the summer. We will work without interfering with one another, and still have good hours together. I have very comfortable quarters for you. We could even spend the week-end in the country with my friends the Kings, who have long been eager to know you. They are faithful readers of your favorite author. By the by, I met Prof. Tufts out there the other day and we had a good time together. I suppose you know that he expects some book-reviews from you for the first number of his Journal [*International Journal of Ethics*].

I am awaiting Kohler [*Philosophy of Law*, 1914, by Josef Kohler]. Thank you for sending it to me, and by gum I am going to learn French pretty quickly. Don't worry that I read too much German, but even the little that I do cries for a subtler antidote.

I am passing on your message to [Robert G.] Valentine, and I am looking eagerly for Felix's letter. Give all the children my very best. Tell Mary I found a new enthusiasm—Rose Schneiderman. Valentine and I dined with her the other night and she certainly has an effective, genuine personality.

I hope the summer is happy with you all.

As ever,

Yours,
FELIX

15, December 1914

Dear Morris:—

I have cabled to [Lord Eustace] Percy about [Eugen] Ehrlich. I like the brief way in which you dispose of statesmen. The Lord knows I have seen enough of their ineptitudes and still worse, their unimaginative timidities. I venture a guess, however, that not even you would substitute the present lot of statesmen with the present lot of professors. After all, Ehrlich looms big to you and Pound and me because that is at present one of the main items of our interest. On the other hand, the main job of the belligerent statesmen and diplomats is to be suspicious of every alien. Of course, the business of life,—even in times of war,—is to discriminate; but it takes a lot of time to discriminate and even statesmen have only twenty-four hours a day, even in war times. As a matter of fact, if you have been following the recent parliamentary debates you will know that the government was most criticized for its leniency toward Germans and Austrians in England. The Ehrlich performance is to me just as stupid as it is to you, only I want a philosopher to have some tolerant understanding of the rational basis of stupidity. My predominant emotion is immense regret that, at best, Ehrlich's trip will be much delayed.

I ought to go to Chicago [for the Conference on Legal and Social Philosophy] but I simply can't. I am fearfully short on time, and I simply have to stay on here and grub on a case book on Interstate Commerce Cases during the welcome Christmas recess. I have to be tied up more this year and next. By that time I will have a little bit of that sense of liberation of which you spoke. I am liking it here more and more and things go pretty well, I think. It is the deuce of a problem, however, to satisfy the four or five shifts of mentalities into which a big class divides itself and to satisfy, above all, one's own standards particularly when, as you know, I have a notion that it can't be that everybody else doesn't know all I know. However, I am gradually realizing that it isn't the business of a teacher to invent ideas wholly. A great deal of the job is to find acceptance for old wisdom and to give ferment to other minds. I suspect that is the direction in which I will be able to do something eventually. Incidentally, I begin to see what a high value you set upon "vitality" in teaching.

I hope all goes well with Mary and the children. My best to them!

Faithfully yours,

FELIX

P.S. (I almost forgot the most important thing. You know my notions about finance. If money is once out it is out and I do hope for dead sure that it is absolutely easy for you to have returned the check. If not, you are thoroughly disloyal not to tell me so and don't give the rest of it any thought whatever).

June 5, 1916

Dear Felix:—

One of the greatest needs of civilization today is the greater development of the science of ethics, the science which studies the principles of right and wrong as between different classes, such as employers and employees, men and women, etc. All practical discussion as to the conditions of a lasting peace between warring nations, the conflicting interests of social classes, or the right relation of an individual to his family or country, is based on the assumption that certain principles of justice have been satisfactorily established. Yet there can be no doubt that the study of such principles is the least advanced of the sciences today.

In these days when all the institutions of civilization are questioned, no one doubts the tremendous importance of science as an aid in building up a better human life. The physical sciences have increased manifold our control over nature, and the social sciences are slowly increasing our control over the social or human factors of life. The great need is that the science which integrates all these results and shows their bearings on daily life should make some corresponding advance.

The reasons for the backward condition of this important science are several. I am inclined to think the unfortunate conditions in the past, to have been the entangling alliances of ethics with different theologies. But the main fact which stands out today is that there is no organized body of investigators today who devote their main energy to promoting the science of ethics, as others do for physics or economics. The science of ethics can be substantially furthered only by an organization of trained scientific workers acting in co-operation. Modern physical science received its great impetus not from the universities but from the great scientific academies organized in the sixteenth and seventeenth centuries by enlightened powers. In our own day the Rockefeller, Carnegie and Gage foundations have encouraged scientific investigations in physical science, philanthropic effort and education. But the far-sighted person to endow specifically ethical research has not yet arisen.

An academy of ethical study could make a survey of what has actually been achieved in various fields so far, and encourage research along the lines that are likely to be most fruitful. It could efficiently cooperate with workers in the various physical and social sciences and stimulate them to undertake investigation problems, and establish a sort of intellectual clearing house. A great deal of scientific labor today is wasted because there is no agency for making generally available the results of specialists' studies.

How can such an academy be established? My answer is that the internationally distinguished body of men who composed the editorial board of the international Journal of Ethics already forms the nucleus of such an organization. Professor Dewey, Pound, Wigmore, Adler, Baizelotti, Hoffding and the others could, if they had the financial means, get the cooperation of all scientific men in a position to render any aid. I am not a believer in large endowments. What is needed is a start rather than a perpetual income. Five, ten, or twenty five thousand dollars a year, for five years would be sufficient to demonstrate the rich possibilities of such an undertaking. By that time the universities, or the educated public generally, will have realized the importance of such an organization, and will be ready to support it.

Sincerely yours,
MORRIS R. COHEN

[late September 1916]

Dear Felix,

I think Walter's [Lippmann] Hughes article illustrates Freudianism at its worst—the seeking of reasons in the subconscious for facts which are not facts at all. Walter makes the unfounded assumption that Hughes has not lived up to his record as Governor etc.—but the fact is that Hughes is saying precisely what he said in his campaign speeches in 1908—I remember them very well. Hughes, as I pointed out in my article is simply a lawyer, versed in commercial transactions but altogether innocent of the problems of statesmanship, and his campaign simply bears me out. I do not think that Hughes has any particular preference for the two-party system—he simply accepts it because he has never thought of anything else that might take its place—just as he has never thought of anything to take the place of our tariff system.

When I pointed that out to you last you said Hughes has grown; but the campaign so far has not demonstrated the latter fact.

I certainly think [Elihu] Root is a hypocrite—or as near to it as any man in public life today can come. He is morally indifferent to things which he pretends to defend—see for instance his N.Y. State Bar Association address that judges must not make the law, and the conclusion which shows that he *knows* better. Did he not say "Constructions can be found etc."? The more I think about him and the more I read of his utterance the more I am convinced that he literally is the most immoral man in public life—a thorough server of the particular class that happens to have employed him. If he thinks himself honest it is because a life of crooked dealings (as in the Whiskey Trust affairs) has dwarfed his moral perceptions.

Arthur [Meyer] and Marion's address is 604 W. 112 St. When you write to them please remember that they are not yet familiar with your not always easy handwriting.

College has begun and the grind is on. I am having trouble renewing my lease on my present house, but have not abandoned hope that I may be spared the trouble of moving. May and the kids are all well and send their best regards to you.

MORRIS

Emory Buckner was up here today and we had a lovely day walking in the woods. He joins in regards to you (and also in my estimate of Walter's Hughes).

October 3, 1916

Dear Morris,

As to Hughes, I do not know just where we join issue, but I smell differences between us. I agree with you that Walter may have been riding his Freudian hobby in seeking for an explanation of what I think on the surface presents a mystery, i.e., that Hughes' judicial work undoubtedly shows distinction, undoubtedly rises way above the average, whereas his campaign is totally devoid of distinction and intellectually wholly commonplace. Walter may or may not be right in his Freudian explanation. I agree with you, that another explanation lies ready to hand, namely that in his judicial work Hughes was giving us the result of painstaking craftsmanship. His political speeches are the commonplace repetitions of even a good mind that has not particularly thought about those things. Therefore I have thought that if Hughes would really be telling what is inside of him, he would say to the American people;—"I truly did not want to get off the bench. I liked my job. Maybe I was subject to the claim of ambition to be president, but being a Puritan, ambition would have to take a moral form. The moral form was my belief in the two-party system, and my conviction—enforced upon me by all the Republican leaders—that I was the only savior of the Republican Party at this contingency. I accepted the nomination but I have no views whatever that are entitled to expression on the issues of the campaign, for I have not thought about the things that as president I should have to think about. I have not thought about them, because all my energies were absorbed with my judicial work during the last six years. However, I should bring to the presidency two qualities: (1) The power to master the facts of even the most complicated situation, and reach a disinterested judgment thereon. (2) The courage to act on the conclusion I have so reached. Therefore I ask you to elect me president as an act of faith."

You see that I disagree with you in your opinion that Hughes does not care about the two party system. I believe he does, and does very vitally, even though he may never have thought of anything else that might take its place. I think in this regard you fail to give sufficient attention both to intellectual and emotional associations. The Republican or the Democratic Party means nothing to you or me. We have to work out an association with either, or neither, on purely rational grounds. Men like Hughes and Stimson are born to their association. Their fathers or their uncles, for one thing, fought in the

Civil War, and that tradition is a perfectly terrific force in binding them to the Party. It is a terrific force in making it unnecessary to think that there is any need for a substitute for the Republican Party. The force of this party pull I think you quite underestimate. Next time I see you I'll tell you how it operates, for instance, in the case of such scientifically-minded women as Miss Lathrop and Alice Hamilton.

As to our respective estimate of Hughes' ability, I suspect that we disagree, but I should like to know a little bit more just what you mean when you say he lacks statesmanship. If you mean that he is merely a good lawyer, "versed in commercial transactions," that he is without native ability of a high order to master the problems of statesmanship, I disagree with you. He has mastered some problems of statesmanship as to which he was completely innocent when he was Governor. He *is* subject to the impact of facts. Compare, for instance, his perfectly ignorant attitude as to national versus state power in his message against the income tax amendment—at which time he did not have the imagination to visualize the part the nation necessarily has to play in our community and individual lives—with his opinions in the Minnesota rate cases, (230 U.S.) and the Shreveport rate case, (234 U.S.), where he was made to see by the facts the necessary dominance, in certain fields, of the central government, and the mischief the selfish rule of the states could produce. That's a very striking illustration of where his accepted, untested theory was slain by the experience of convincing facts. Read his opinion in *Bailey* v. *Alabama* (219 U.S.) and see how much better a nose he had for the actual operation of peonage laws in the South than Holmes, whose opinion is much more brilliant as an intellectual distillation, but considerably moved from the realities of a modern commercial or agricultural community.

Of course Hughes carries a general stock of economic and social views with which he was inculcated at Brown thirty-odd years ago, except insofar as such views have been adjusted by specific problems of government and of life that he has had to face, but he has not a rigid, or a dull, or a commonplace mind; very much to the contrary. You may be right that he is merely a lawyer of large commercial experience, but against your impression is the testimony of Holmes, who sat with him for six years, and who says of Hughes that while he is not prepared to say that he is a great man, he "is a very considerable man, who has vistas." I confess he has not allowed us to see his vistas on the stump, and what Holmes doubtless means is that he is capable of deep conceptions when his mind actually gets busy on a problem. In other words, the analysis that Walter made is, I think, substantially correct. [Rest is missing.]

October 13, 1916

Dear Morris:

Next to the Dewey piece your essay on Royce is the best thing you have done for the New Republic. I liked it very thoroughly. It has that quality which makes one re-read it again and again. If you wrote that way when you were miserably sick, I hesitate to think—this being an ironical world—what you would have done if you had been well.

There are a lot of things to talk about as to some of which we might have the interest of differing in details. I have about made up my mind to vote for Wilson, but I do wish it were possible, in the interest of evidence, to have Hughes run the United States for the next four years, just to see what he would do with it. As I read your article, and find myself in emotional as well as intellectual agreement with what you say, about the lazy and soft shallowness of the present day so-called social sciences, and the unsatisfactoriness of catch-all phrases and starved positivism, and yet often find myself,—and give others the impression of being—eager for quick results, I feel that one must take a good many chances of guesswork in the daily con- duct of life, and in the field of action, which, on the Olympian heights of reason, would seem unjustified.

I remember Holmes' observation that the art of life is making cor- rect guesses on inadequate data. All of which only means that the duty of relentless thinking is all the greater, and just because this is a finite world, we need all the instruments we can possibly get for as near as possible correct thinking, i.e. thinking that takes all the rele- vant factors of life into account.

My best to you all,

Yours,

FELIX

Where and how have you moved?

THE ZIONIST ORGANISATION
Central Office

77, Great Russell Street,
London, W.C.1.
22nd July 1920.

Dear Morris,

Only a line for I am enslaved by the Zionist work, a work funda- mental of getting some unity out of the pluralism in Jewry.

The other day I had tea with Lord Haldane and he is keenly in-

terested in the intellectual manifestation in America. He said he had
seen something of your work and particularly extracts from it. He is
very anxious to have what papers of yours are available. I wish you
would send him as many of your papers as possible. If you choose
tell him you do so in response to his request communicated through
me. His address is: Right Hon. Viscount Haldane, 28 Queen Anne's
Gate, London.

How is your housing problem getting on? You will be interested
to know that my friend the Lord, namely, Eustace Percy, is spending
all his time on the housing problem of London, so you see the burdens of the world are world wide.

Literally I have been working night and day and I have seen very
very little even of Marion, but we are planning within a week or so
to go to Germany to be back here the 1st September. I hope May
and the children and you are very well.

Marion and I send our affectionate greetings,

Yours

FELIX

854 W 181st St.
Nov. 28/20

Dear Felix:

Of course it is not necessary for me to say that I am glad to hear
from you, but this trip it would be hard for me to exaggerate how
much I value this evidence that some one occasionally is mindful of
my existence. Living in the city sometimes emphasizes one's isolation.

In answer to your question as to what I am about these days, I
can only say that I am teaching at the City College (12 hours per
week), getting acclimatized to the noise of the city, and finding out
by reading Einstein how little mathematics I know. That man Einstein is the real thing in every way, but his mathematical knowledge
is more than I can attain unto. We never had a really thorough
course in mathematics at the City College in my student days, and
though I have picked up some bits in my irresponsible intellectual
wanderings, it has been too fragmentary and not sufficiently continuous
to carry me anywhere within hailing distance of the big issues in
mathematical physics which interest me—though they are beyond
my power.

In connection with a course I am giving in the College on the Philosophy of Civilization I am getting at new angles or points of view
from which to view the logic of social events and efforts. This makes
me feel that my book on Logic is what I ought to be writing—that
there are the distinctive contributions which I can possibly render in
the field of philosophy—but writing, I find, depends not on the mul-

titude or vigor of your ideas, but on the habit of writing, and I find it impossible this winter to acquire the habit of writing.

I have read both Hohfeld's paper and Kocourek's, and thoroughly agree with you as to [the] silly and dogmatic character of the judgments which the Yale school have passed on the so-called Hohfeld system. As a logician I naturally value some of Hohfeld's distinctions as aids to clear thinking, and I have no doubt that many legal problems are elucidated by his manner of analytic approach. But he falls into the natural dogmatism of the metaphysically untrained when he sets up convenient distinctions as absolutely valid for all inquirers, forgetting that because one kind of distinction is valuable for a certain purpose, it does not follow that other distinctions are not equally valuable for other purposes. Pound sometimes seems to me to fall into the same absolutism in conversation, though in writing he is more careful. I devoted several paragraphs to Hohfeld in a paper on Legal Method which I have never had the patience to finish. If you are interested I'll dig it out from my numerous papers and send it to you.

Mary and the boys are very well. Leonora is a little bit under the weather—takes school too intensely and nervously, but I guess she will soon be all right, especially if I can get her into a more congenial school.

With kindest regards to Marion,

MORRIS

March 4, 1921.

Dear Morris:

Your wishes have been fulfilled.

(1) A letter from the Faculty is going to Holmes [on his eightieth birthday].

(2) Brandeis has been tipped off long ago.

(3) The New Republic is carrying an article by Haldane.

(4) etc., etc., etc.

Of course, the old boy likes the appreciation, particularly from the youngsters. I think a volume from you is the thing to do. That is what I am planning to send him. But he is very sensitive about excessive expenditures on the part of those he knows cannot afford them. I, therefore, suggest that in what you send, you do not make him feel that you have splurged.

Now that spring is coming, I hope that we may see you before long,—although for myself, I live mostly on trains.

My very best to you.

Yours,

FELIX

April [1921]

Dear Morris,

I wrote to Judge [Julian] Mack about Einstein—your desire to have him at C.C.N.Y. There is a long story connected with his visit that I shall tell you next we meet. I'm glad the newspapers did get his sweet, childlike personality, tho Marion says nobody could miss it. I do hope he escapes all further press notices.

I'm glad your Hopkins experience was so stimulating. That money also resulted does not take away its exhilaration. And it *is* a joy to hear your own thinking germinated in the process. That's fine!

Marion and I are looking forward to a long, loafing, out-doorish summer. We're in quest of a quiet place and it looks as though we'd be lucky to get what we want. I'd have lots to say if I saw you.

Take care of yourself and my love to all of you

FELIX

Marion is fine, though working hard. She is fascinated by physiology, [illegible] the scientific process.

Dec. 2 [1921]

Dear Morris,

If you don't know you will want to that on December 8th (next Friday) Holmes will have served 20 years on the Supreme Court. Oh! for the mold that made him.

May would have been thrilled by a wonderful meeting last night, at Symphony Hall, for recognition of Russian Gov't—at which Borah was speaker and I presided. . . .

I am finely and at work

Always

F

Vassar College
Poughkeepsie, New York

Dec. 30/21

Dear Felix:

It's a shame, the way I have neglected to answer your last letter. But this is really the first chance I have had. Some four or five weeks ago at the beginning of the milk-strike in New York I got some milk into my system that has been working havoc with my digestive or undigestive works. Perhaps it's not the milk but something else. But the fact is that before that I was going well, and flattering myself that I was beginning to work—I had put in several good licks on my logic book—when all of a sudden I caved in and had to discontinue. But while I am knocked down I am not out. I am here attending the meeting of the Philosophical Association where I have had to read a paper on Myths and Science in Popular Philosophy. The paper was unusually well received which makes me think that after revision it may have some merit. . . .

I saw Herbert Croly a few days ago and he was very much in the dumps—discouraged is a mild word. Can't we arrange some sort of function to make him feel what a really substantial thing the New Republic has been in the intellectual life of the last decade?

You have a former pupil of mine [Nathan] Margold in one of your courses. He is a modest but a fine chap. Encourage him and also tell him to take care of himself physically.

May and the children are well—especially William who is a daily revelation to me of how genuine and deep the joy of growing life can be. He is . . . a continuous fountain of joy. Leonora is starring at the Ethical School and Felix at Townsend Harris Hall, and are both becoming quite mature—in fact too much so when they criticise some of my philosophic views on evolution, religion and the like. But as I have already crossed the 40 year line I ought not to be surprised at the possibility of my being considered an old fogey. But in my heart I am much younger than I was sixteen years ago.

My warmest affectionate greetings to Marion and yourself and hopes that the new year may bring us an opportunity of meeting in person—

MORRIS R.

May 3, 1923.

Dear Morris:

Just as I was on the point of writing you a further word, aroused in me by your fugitive comments the other day on Dewey, comes your letter.

(1) As to Dewey. . . . [See Chapter X.]

(2) As to the Storrs' lectures:

(a) Of course it is enough for me to know that you want to undertake them for me to exert myself to the utmost in that direction.

(b) I have not talked with Pound about the matter at all and, therefore, did not express his views.

(c) I have no reverence for the expert. My favorite formula is A. E.'s mot: "The expert should be on tap, but not on top." Without having analyzed my own attitude, I suppose it comes nearer to yours than to Pound's occasional expression of his own, in that I attach greater importance to the general ideas even without the content of the specific juristic material; though you, on the contrary, being human as well as a philosopher, are apt, like other mortals, to minimize the importance of what you haven't got. (In saying this I do not minimize the extraordinary amount of law you have "picked up" on the way.) On the other hand, I am also very keenly alive to the mischief done by "general ideas" without their test in the provocative variety of human manifestations. It is "general ideas" that give us things like the Minimum Wage decision: and I am not sure that you will transcend the limitations of the concrete experience, or the concrete thoughts out of which you build your general ideas, any more than Kant and Hegel did.

From which I hope you will not gather that I am unsympathetic to the significance of the organizing or the creative value of "general ideas." I am, however, profoundly impressed with the humility which we ought to feel towards them, and the tentative dominion they ought to hold over us. All of which calls for the elaboration of a talk.

(3) What you say about the [William James] Sidis boy arouses my intense curiosity, for the tragic comedy of the father of the boy being a psycho-pathologist could not but suggest itself to me.

(4) Tell me what answer you gave to your inquirers for a text book on logic.

By the way, I have been meaning to write you to disabuse your mind if it charges me with being the author of the editorial in the New Republic some weeks ago arguing against the constitutionality of the Borah proposal. I not only did not write it but I thoroughly dissent from its conclusions. So far as an interpretation of the Constitution goes, I am pretty sure that the Supreme Court will knock out a 6 to 3 or a 7 to 2 proposal, although I do not think they ought to. The remedy itself does not terribly excite me. The difficulty to be dealt with goes deeper than this remedy assumes.

Yours always,

F F

[no date]

Dear Felix:

Glad to get your letter and the enclosures which I just barely glanced through.

(1) As to my being too busy for a philosopher—Here's the cause: 3 different courses of three hours each at the C.C.N.Y. A weekly lecture at the New School which compels me to go over an enormous

mass of material that most men are supposed to have read but which I find that they who quote it have not.

(2) Your friend Hopkins [Ernest Martin Hopkins, president of Dartmouth College] embodies all the vices that he accuses the Liberals of—ungenerous, carping etc. He, doubtless, is a lovely man personally. But he is clearly no more open to argument than Upton Sinclair or a Mohammedan dervish. There comes a point in human relations when words become powerless against the incrustation of habit —and the presidency of a college makes a man care for "practical" results which are the very death of free inquiry. Why argue free thought with the Pope? I am not sufficiently pacifist to believe that the world can be readjusted by moral suasion. More anon.

As ever

MORRIS

October 28, 1927

Dear Morris:

There are no first year scholarships except as a result of a competitive examination which is due in a month or so. I assume your nephew [Henry Cohen] will appropriately apply for that, and here is hoping he will prevail.

[Professor Harry] Sheffer is still in a very bad way, but I have more hopes of a radical solution of his difficulties than ever before.

Your dinner certainly was the most significant thing of its kind that I have ever attended or heard about. And your own remarks were altogether beautiful, although you must have been under great pressure and subject to a great deal of weariness. It was in good truth a memorable occasion.

Always yours,

F F

May 14, 1929.

Dear Morris:

I enclose herewith a memorandum which will convey to you most vividly the condition of Holmes. Since then, he has maintained his beautiful serenity and power. I have a letter from Brandeis today in which he writes that Holmes "is in fine form again, working as of old." He has written some superb opinions. Holmes certainly has by the nature of his temperament, but still more by his achievement, the ultimate serenity and wisdom of life. I believe there never was a more beautiful exhibition of human dignity than the sight of Holmes walking up, unaided, the little hill at Arlington, where Mrs. Holmes was laid to rest, and then walking away from the grave again unaided.

In one of the last letters I had before his great grief, he referred to you. I had written him to tell him (having much delayed in doing so) of your election as President of the Philosophical Association. He replied, "Everything good that happens to Cohen is a joy to me." I think if during the next fortnight you could go to Washington on some pretext other than an especial visit to him (which would give him concern) he would enjoy a visit from you very much. I would let him know in advance when you are coming and let him fix the time for seeing you, indicating that you are going down on some other matter. Of course, you ought also to make it a point to see Brandeis.

I have not read Felix's [Felix Cohen] thesis, but both Sheffer and [Professor Sheldon] Glueck are most enthusiastic about it concerning the portions within their own special fields.

Yes, I wish we could see more of each other. Isn't Cambridge the more philosophical meeting ground? I am in process of putting a book through the press which [second page missing]

                                                    Dec. 21/30
Dear May,

I should think your household would be excited! Wasn't that sweet of the Einsteins and—fitting. He is such a beautifully sincere and unspoiled great man.

And well may you be proud of Felix' performance [victory in the Columbia Law School moot court trial before Judge Cardozo].

We're well—but have lived for months now in the twirl of the terrible Palestine situation. For weeks we have been on the water's edge —and I don't even now know whether any day I may not have to go abroad. In such uncertainty have I lived a "scholar's" life. Happily, Marion is very well—else the situation would have been intolerable.

I'm awaiting keenly Morris' book.

                                        Always yours
                                        FELIX
Love from us both

                                                    Jan. 29 [1931]
Dear Morris,

For your book reviews I'm willing to wait months. That's a perfectly beautiful commentary on Parrington—duly paying homage to his achievement, yet fitting it in its appropriate perspective. And I rejoiced over your insistence on the importances that transcend the

Evanescent—more or less—political issues. Parrington's labors I revere—for his great integrity and his scholarly *sitzfleisch*—when most modern academicians are salesmen or at least journalists, writing for the next edition of the paper. Which leads me to ask when your book will actually be out—held, as it were, in my hand.

I wired to ask if you ever wrote a specific piece on Holmes—I have a vague recollection you have and still cannot place it.

These have been—and are—hectic times for us but life goes well and fully. [Two words, illegible.]

Always,

FELIX

Feb. 2/31

Dear Felix:

May and I spent last week in Charlottesville, Va. I went there to give a lecture at the university and May and I enjoyed the vacation from the New York routine. Your telegram was relayed to me by William, but I could not quite make it out. Now that your letter and the original telegram are before me I can answer (as I have by telegram):

I wrote a note (editorial) in the *New Republic* a week or two after Holmes' *Natural Law* appeared in the Harvard Law Review in 1918, and a longer signed review of the *Collected Legal Papers,* in the *New Republic,* a few months after publication (1921). I do not know whether these can be called tributes, or whether they are suitable for the purpose you have in mind. I have no copies of them.

It is a genuine joy to me to receive your tribute to my piece on Parrington in the N.R., and for a number of reasons—principally because you have meant and still mean a great deal in my life. Writing reviews—principally for the *New Republic*—and getting commendatory letters from you is an old pleasure. I sometimes doubt whether the business of writing thick books is not something beyond my natural tempo, and whether I ought not to get back to the old habit of shorter flights.

Reason and Nature will be officially published on March 15, but a bound copy will be ready for Holmes on his birthday [his ninetieth, on March 8, 1931]. The book that I should be finishing now is on *Contemporary American Thought;* but I have not been able to do much since getting back from England.

Yesterday May and I, accompanied by Arthur Meyer, who was in Washington, had lunch with Holmes. He was in extraordinary good fettle and "a good time was had by all." After that we called on the Brandeises and they confirmed our impression that Holmes is really getting a new lease of life. (Incidentally Louis D. himself looked much better than when I last saw him.)

How are things in the Law School world? Is Pound back on the job? And how do things fare with Zach [Zechariah Chafee] and with T. R. Powell?

Our bestest to Marion

Affectionately
MORRIS

[Frankfurter asked Cohen on December 3 or 4 of 1932 whether he should accept the invitation of the City College's Associate Alumni to serve as one of the vice presidents of the association. The following letter is Cohen's answer. Frankfurter's class was 1902.]

Dec. 6/32

Dear Felix:

It is very hard for me to advise you as to the enclosed. If your acceptance involved your coming to attend a few meetings of the Board of Directors of the Alumni Ass'n I would say: by all means accept. There are many good men on the Board, but no one cares enough to do anything. A few words by someone with sense and courage might galvanize the dead body. Also as Robinson [Frederick B. Robinson, president of The City College] refers to you and to your friends as the Sacco-Vanzetti crowd there might be some value in impressing the Alumni body that the officers of the Alumni Association are not all Robinson satellites. On the other hand, why give your name if you cannot find the time to do anything, especially if you are going abroad? You might be in the position of *seeming* to approve of policies with which you are not in sympathy.

Moreover, I do not *want* to advise you, because I do not know enough about the situation in the Alumni Association. I became so disgusted with it a few years ago that I ceased paying dues, and have no information as to what is going on. I have confidence in Donald Roberts' integrity. He has real convictions and courage. But he does not seem to get results because he is an instructor at the College and that ties his hands. I suppose that he would have been promoted long ago if he were not one of the few men at the College who have opinions of their own.

I wish I could see you and talk C.C.N.Y. matters with you at some length. I am very much at sea about the situation myself.

Do you get the Columbia Law Review? I have an article there (in the November issue) which might interest you. I shall be glad to send you a copy if you want one. The volume of essays on legal philosophy is now in press and ought to be out within a few months. It won't, I dare say, add much to my reputation, but it will bring me some relief from the pressure to have this particular volume out of the way. There is one new piece in it, on Contract and Sovereignty, which I may print in the Yale or Harvard Law Review before the book appears.

My best to Marion and yourself,

As ever,

MORRIS.

P.S. If Abe Flexner's Institute of Higher Studies were to offer me three or four thousand dollars a year I would quit teaching here and devote myself to getting out some real books which I believe I still have in my system. Do you think that is even a remote possibility?

January 8, 1933

Dear Morris:

And the most affectionate good wishes from both of us to May and you and the children.

Secondly, Holmes is in fine spirits, but feeble of body. I saw him in Washington about a week ago, and remarked to myself that Holmes has a fourth wind. He is firmer in his interests, in his talk and in his spirit. He says "I am having a very pleasant time." But he has practically stopped writing letters—it is such physical torture to him. That accounts for his silence. If you plan to see him, or otherwise communicate with him, I suggest you write directly to his secretary, Donald Hiss.

Thirdly, I put your review of his grandfather into Julian Huxley's mind, to his great interest. If you happen to have an extra copy, send it to me, please.

Finally, it will be a delight to see you. Suppose we say Sunday the 15th. We can have a long stretch together, and in the afternoon when some of the boys come in it will be fine for them, perhaps also for you, to foregather.

Ever yours,

F F

March 1, 1933

Dear Morris:

It was kind of you to have [Osmond K.] Fraenkel write me on the City College business, and I am glad to have your further word. I don't have to tell you how the whole business makes my blood boil. I have, as you know, general deep feeling on such issues and that my own alma mater should be guilty of such brutal and stupid behavior intensifies my unhappiness.

Were I in New York, I might overcome the disabilities of other pressures and responsibilities for some public and private tasks outside of my academic work and start something. But if one is to attempt to lead such a fight one must be prepared to follow through. A single literary protest won't do. And by temperament, as you know, as well as by professional habit, I can't enter a fight unless I fully know what I am talking about and can operate from the basal supply of fact. But I can't do that, even though I have entire confidence, of course, in the accuracy of what Fraenkel and you and Felix and Margold tell me. Anything I say will bring forth a reply, and that will have to be dealt with and so on and so forth, and that process I cannot possibly pursue from Harvard Square.

Surely there must be resident graduates who care about good sense as well as the inculcation, by example, of a generous and wise-spirited youth. Cannot some of these be aroused? I shall be glad to join them in any round-robin statement or any form of collective action.

It was a great pleasure to see May and you at the New School, and of course I enjoyed my brush with you.

Always yours,
F F

April 6, 1933

Dear Morris:

I have some time followed Ort [ORT] and with the deepest sympathy. I wish I could express that by acceding to the wish you convey. You indeed have influence with me, and no one more influence than you in having taught me to bring some coherence to my life and not allow it to be torn into a thousand pieces. As it is, it is broken up into about 549. I have had to draw the line some time ago against the assumption of any further obligations. I could not possibly take on the Presidency of Ort. You and I know that merely giving one's name is giving nothing in these matters unless one actually directs— knows what's going on and makes the daily or the recurring decisions on the basis of knowledge. I simply cannot do this from a distance and in the light of the circumstances that confront me. Perhaps I am foolish in giving reasons because my conclusion is unalterable, even though you destroy my reasoning. I am very, very sorry but I simply cannot undertake the task. Why not Henry Moskowitz?—or some other prominent Jew of New York. Of whom there must be many who have free time on their hands.

As to educators, I would suggest Paul Kanaus, Abraham Flexner, Roger Lindsay and President Hutchins of Chicago if he will do it.

Ever yours,

FELIX

Yaddo, Saratoga, N.Y.
July 14/33

Dear Felix:

. . . You do not answer my inquiry as to Holmes and his general condition. I take it that he is going on as usual.

I am distressed by what you say of Pound. You may remember that I did not favor his taking the Deanship—on the general ground that scholars should keep out of administrative posts. . . .

I hope that you and Marion will have a restful as well as profitable time at Cornish. The idea of "burying" yourself until you finish a certain piece of work, like putting a seed in the ground and not disturbing it until it bears fruit, appeals to me very much, and I envy those who can do it. I can't do it myself, because of my ancient enemy—Poor Health. That is why I admire all the more those who *can* do it.

By the way, did you get a copy of my book on *Law and the Social Order?* I asked the publishers to send you one of the first copies off the press.

Always affectionately yours

MORRIS

30 Oct. 1934.

Dear Morris:

I have been in Washington, hence the delayed acknowledgement of your note. (The old gentleman was in one of his best moods, and Stone told me he was at his very best ten days ago, just as naughty as ever. I think it makes a lot of difference what time of day one goes to see him. His vitality is spent at the end of the afternoon.)

I am sorry that this weekend is also bad. How about Nov. 10. If you come up on the night train the night before, we can have the whole forenoon, say from 9:30–12 for talk.

But in any event, I hope that if you can't do that, you will put on paper what you think I could appropriately say at the Alumni dinner about present trends at C.C.N.Y. As I have indicated before, I don't want to turn a dinner into a fight, everything in its place, but on the other hand I should not hesitate to deliver my mind of truths that are vital particularly just now, and I trust to the felicity of the moment to say these things not too truculently.

If children constitute the greatest satisfaction of parents, Mary and you are indeed full of riches and justly proud. I am glad to hear about Leonora and William.

Always yours,

F F

13 Nov. 1934

Dear Morris:

Alas, I have a class on Saturday and therefore will get to New York only in time for the [alumni] dinner. I am sorry about that for I should like to pay my homage once more to your mother, the recollection of whom, and of your father, remain most vividly among all the vivid recollections of that extraordinary dinner in honor of their son. The fact of the matter is that I have not been uptown or downtown New York for ages. On the very rare occasions on which I go to New York, I practically always go ad hoc, and remain within a very confined area. My brothers will tell you that in order to see them from time to time we arrange to meet either at the Harvard Club or at the Bar Association.

Many thanks for your notes, which are precisely what I wanted and of which I hope to make good use. A thousand thanks!

Always yours,

FELIX

February 5, 1935

Dear Morris:

1. I have sent a small check to Arthur Meyer. I wish it could have been much larger.

2. I read the account of the Conference [on Jewish Relations] with interest and with hope. It proves anew that a government personality is an essential. Would that circumstances enabled you to give yourself more freely to this child of yours.

3. The enclosed copy of a letter speaks for itself, and I shall send you on the reply as soon as I have it. In any event a letter from Julian [Mack] this morning says that there is a good chance of raising the money for Janowsky.

I am very sorry to hear of Mary's illness and I hope she is now restored.

Affectionate greetings to both of you,

Always yours,

FELIX

[Attachment:]

Professor Salo Baron and Professor Morris Cohen do well to direct attention to the importance of the observations on minority rights made in the memorandum by Dr. Janowsky. Nothing less is at stake than the maintenance and promotion of those fundamental needs of man without which the individual is bereft of dignity and self-respect. The achievement of the claims which are sought to be protected by the devise of "minority rights" are thus a prerequisite to even a rudimentary level of civilization. Jewish interests happen to be the focal point of Dr. Janowsky's study, but the problems concern all races. They are neither parochial nor nationalistic, still less chauvinistic. These issues touch the well-being of Europe, and through their repercussions affect the whole world. No one has given more thoughtful consideration for these problems than Dr. Janowsky, and I feel grateful for the opportunity to associate myself with Professors Baron and Cohen in inviting careful study for Dr. Janowsky's paper.

FELIX FRANKFURTER

Triuna Is. Lake George
(P.O. Box 1, Bolton N.Y.)
July 23/35

Dear Felix:

I am glad to get your letter. Thinking highly, as I always have, of Margold I was naturally pained to receive a note from Learned Hand that Margold has got himself "thoroughly disliked" at Washington by his "arrogant and high-handed manner," though B himself had not noticed any such change in our friend. Apparently you do not share the supposed Washington opinion, and that is gratifying. (Incidentally I do think that Margold made a mistake in devoting so much attention to Glavis to the neglect of more important matters).

You are certainly right about English policy today being shortsighted. They are not doing anything to settle the great major issues, and I do not think Hitler will hesitate to double-cross Britain when it suits his purpose, which may happen as soon as he can link up with Japan against Russia.

As to the U.S. Supreme Court and the Constitution your position is to me entirely incomprehensible i.e. I do not see on what possible ground you can defend the present arrangement. Everyone of the points I made in my "dogmatic" statement in the *Nation* ("dogmatic" because of the necessity for brevity—I made all these points at greater length in my book on *Law and the Social Order*), you have yourself at one time or another endorsed; and the main point you have yourself made far more effectively than I have, namely that there is no use of talking of the Supreme Court being the guardian of our liberty or bulwark against hasty action, when in fact there are few (if any) instances where the Supreme Court did so save us, whereas there are many instances where the Supreme Court did the contrary because of devotion to traditional phrases and ignoring of the actual situation. And, indeed, the fiction that the court is passing on a point of law laid down in the Constitution prevents a procedure whereby the Court can adequately inform itself as to real factual economic and social issues involved. You remember what McReynolds said to you when you were arguing the minimum wage law. I can understand McReynolds position that all the decisions of the Court on which he agrees are logically necessitated by the Constitution; and I can understand the position of the Wall St lawyers who know better, but think the Supreme Court and the fiction good bulwarks against democratic legislation. But I can see no possible ground for your position—at least you failed to indicate it when you somewhat pontifically dismissed the suggestion of some method for the recall of judicial decisions.

In your letter you speak of a distinction between the national and the state interests in our economic life. I am confident that you will never be able to draw such a line—at least not to the satisfaction of any large body of economic students. Nor could you if you drew such a line prove to any large body of lawyers that that is the line which the Supreme Court is authorized to draw and has drawn. The Supreme Court makes constitutional law and the best anyone can do is to *guess* rightly what the next decision will be. No one really knows. The dicta of Gray and Pound still holds—Constitutional law is politics, and not very clean politics at that—for it deals in dishonest intellectual coinage hiding factual issues under false legal covers.

Your holding up Stone and Cardozo as great economists whose judgments ought to be the law of the land, does credit to your loyalty as a friend, but is hardly convincing. Stone began as a partner of Morgan's son-in-law and has never shown sign of having learned how the other half lives (see his book on *Law*). That it is possible for anyone to think him a liberal shows how extremely reactionary the Supreme Court is. Cardozo is an admirable person, and I love him as you do. But I have never seen any great economic insight in him, and some of his decisions in N.Y. on labor cases were extremely unfortunate. Brandeis is the only man on the Supreme Court who does understand the effects of economic factors in the lives of producers and consumers. But his fundamental faith in small enterprize is like that of the agrarians of the unreconstructed Tennesseeans, like Don Quixote trying to revive chivalry (an admirable institution in its day) or Mrs. Partington trying to sweep back the sea. Donald Richberg unconsciously proved it in the Brandeis volume which you got out.

I should be lacking in candor if I did not say frankly that the fundamental weakness of your position in this matter is due to your thinking in terms of personalities and neglecting ultimate issues. You think in terms of Holmes, Brandeis and Cardozo, and you think more men of that type would make the Supreme Court a good institution. In this you ignore the fact that it is only by accident that men of that type can get on the Supreme Court and that when they do they are more likely to be on the minority side than on the majority in any really important decision. But more important than that is the fact that the whole system is fundamentally dishonest in its pretensions (pretending to say what the Constitution lays down when they are in fact deciding what is good for the country), and the *worst possible form of government* for it separates power from responsibility. The Court has the last word (practically so, since a small fraction of the population can be used by the vested interests to block a constitutional amendment), but it is never held responsible for the harm which follows from such decisions, as on the minimum wage laws, on the child labor laws etc.

You may say: this is all too theoretical. But is not the present regime defended on purely theoretic grounds? And certainly bad theory at that! I am persuaded that if we are to emerge from the present economic and social chaos without resort to a communist revolution or a fascist dictatorship, it can only be by easing up the restraints which the present idolatry of the Constitution and the Courts puts in the way of national planning of production for use instead of for profit. It is because you ought to be with the forces of liberalism rather than against them, that I hope you will devote a little more attention to these issues than your expression hitherto seems to indicate.

With affectionate greetings to Marion and yourself,

As ever yours

MORRIS

192 Brattle Street
Cambridge, Mass.
August 8, 1935

Dear Morris:

Many thanks for taking the trouble of writing me your long letter. It was foolish of me to start this discussion—for it calls for full talk and I am so habituated to dictation that I am almost paralyzed when it comes to hand-writing, and my secretary is on leave. So I hope what follows will not seem ungracious and at worst will only suffer from appearing "dogmatic"—to quote your phrase—"because of the necessity for brevity."

(1) I did not defend "the present arrangement." I merely claimed that your account of it—and your remedy—were dogmatic, not so much because of what you said, but because of what you left unsaid. For after all your significance is that of a teacher and a Socrates.

(2) I don't think you will deem me arrogant if I say that there is nothing in your letter that I did not already know. From which it does not follow that I sin against the light. After all, I've been a student of Supreme Court opinions, from Jay down, and I have written predominantly against the Court's confusion between the majority's notion of policy and the requirements of the Constitution. But that is not the whole story of the Court's function and performance.

(3) Nor am I blinded by my personal attachment to Cardozo, Stone and Brandeis. But disagreements with their opinions do not justify the cavalier way in which you dispose of them. I did not say that Stone and Cardozo were "great economists," still less that their "judgments ought to be the law of the land." But it's really too childish to talk about Stone's bias as Morgan's son-in-law's partner in the light of his really first-rate and free-spirited, radical work in such testing economic-legal fields as taxation, valuation and corporate finance. You could hardly have written as you did about him had you read all these opinions of his. But then, why should you have? Similarly are you unfair in your comment on Cardozo's labor views—a subject about which also I happen to be not wholly uninformed.

(4) And your disposition of Brandeis, like Lerner's . . . characterization of him as "economic primitiveness," is merely a preference for your own judgment as to the play of economic forces, about which, I suspect, he knows as much as you do. I do not say you should surrender yours for his—I do say you should write as a teacher and tell your readers something about these issues.

(5) And the history of Canada, Australia, the U.S.A. and now the All-India Federation—on all of which I have put years of study and thinking—prove that there *are* problems of Federalism, problems of governing a Continent and at the same time avoiding the iron rule either of Germany or Russia. Your readers would never suspect that these are problems, and tough ones, from your Nation piece.

(6) I'm not saying the Supreme Court is in Washington and all's well with our world. You know that I think no such thing. I do, how-

ever, deprecate these easy answers to very difficult questions—and the assumption that amending the Constitution, stripping the Supreme Court of its powers, making of us, in essence, a unitary state are all a.b.c., so obvious that the implications and the cost need not be responsibly faced.

Perhaps the difference between fellows like you and Lerner and me is that I have spent half my life in the actual tasks of government and all of it in acquiring intimate knowledge of its practicalities. If I were you I would not be so cavalier!

Yours,

F F

P.S. Are you sure that the laws that we need to get us out of economic and social chaos are barred by the Constitution? Have you—or any one else—formulated these laws?

November 4, 1935

Dear Morris,

You know who Archie Mac Leish is—but you may not know him personally. He is not only a considerable poet, but he is a first-rate student of the law and at one time was elected to this faculty but preferred to live a literary life.

He is now one of the editors of Fortune, which is, as you know, a very influential publication, reaching as it does some hundred thousand substantial conservative subscribers.

He has been much troubled by what he believes to be a steady growth of anti-Semitism in this country and he is planning a series of articles for Fortune intending them to be as factual as possible with reference to the foundations of anti-Semitism and the position of Jews in American life. He plans to deal with the various professions, the arts, politics, business, etc., etc.

I told him that you are the first and the most important source of information to tap for the data which he is seeking to explore. And he will promptly try to get hold of you. You will find him not only a very intelligent and charming person, but truly civilized—the things of the spirit and the mind really matter to him. I want you to give him every possible assistance, to talk to him at length and to put him in possession of all the statistical sources that you have made available in your forethought during the last few years. *Verbum sap!*

Always yours,

FELIX

January 24, 1936

Dear Morris,

Thank you for your letter.

(1) It is not my habit to lay things up against people, especially such worthy people as Janowsky.

(2) I don't believe in weakening strong cases by weak arguments. If people with the predisposition of Judge Mack and myself thought the argument is no good, what do you expect of an international tribunal to which you address it to think about it? I have a prejudice against giving the enemy good openings, and I like to avoid, as far as possible, opportunities for the cuttlefish.

(3) Nor does your quotation from Cardozo alter my judgment on the particular point. Cardozo is a little inclined to rhetoric, particularly in his private correspondence, and I should not go to him for the best wisdom as to an effective way of pushing a case. I did not say that the materials of the legal argument should not be used; I indicated that they should be used persuasively, and in the form of a recognized legal right.

(4) Of course I am for any kind of impressive remonstrance, especially by people like the House of Bishops. By the way, have you read the recent discussion on this subject before the Church Assembly?

(5) I have been meaning to write you about another matter—the Rand [School Press] book on Lawless Judges [by Goldberg and Levenson] to which you wrote an introduction. Now you know full well that whatever else I may or may not think about the Supreme Court and the judicial function in general, the one thing I do deem profoundly important is a constant stream of criticism upon the work of courts and judges. But critics also have duties of decency, let alone a duty not to hurt their cause by unfairness and inaccuracy. I must say I was shocked to have the authors dispose of Holmes', Brandeis' and Stone's conduct, in connection with the Sacco-Vanzetti case, as "hypocritical," which was the "mildest" they could say about it. And I was only a little less shocked that you should put your imprimatur on a book that used such language about such men. Now in the first place, Brandeis took no action in the Sacco-Vanzetti case for the all-sufficient reason that through Mrs. Evans, who was practically a member of his household, he was judicially disqualified. And Holmes, far from sharing the Massachusetts prejudices, expressed himself to Thompson when he argued before him at Beverly Farms with the utmost freedom in condemnation of the trial. But he felt himself bound by rules that fettered his discourse. After all, let us remember, it was

Holmes who a few years previously had dissented in the Leo Frank case.

All this may seem to you a little thing in a crusade on behalf of a noble cause. I must say I don't feel that way about it. It seems to me that a symbol of reason and tolerance like yourself should not encourage the substitution of one set of untruth and intolerance for another.

Ever yours,

F F

January 27, 1936

Dear Felix,

I do not seem to have made the point of my last letter to you very clear. I was trying to explain the situation and not to argue. I know very little about International Law, and even if I knew as much as you, I should not be dogmatic because I am convinced that these are not matters which can be definitely settled on an objective basis. As to the substance of the issue, I do not see that you and I differ in any way. As I wrote to you (confidentially), Janowsky himself thought it was a mistake to introduce the argument as to the legal consequences of Germany's pledges.

As to the book on "Lawless Judges," please note that the term *imprimatur* does not apply to my introduction. An *imprimatur* is given only after an official *nihil obstat*. But I explicitly stated in my Introduction that I cannot agree with all its statements. I also intimated quite clearly that the authors had an unclear idea as to what is Law and were confused as to what they meant by the phrase *Lawless Judges*. Nevertheless, I see no reason for changing my view expressed in the Introduction, to wit: "That it renders a real service in challenging our traditional complacency in regard to the Judiciary." I thoroughly agree with you about the injustice of characterizing Holmes', Brandeis' and Stone's conduct as hypocritical, but that I think, is due to the fact that the authors have no clear idea as to the niceties of the legal system. I cannot, however, get excited about a transgression of this kind, which seems to me narrowness and bad manners. It may weaken the force of the book among certain legalists. But to those who, like myself, regard the judicial veto over legislation as a deadly cancer preventing a healthy political life in this country, there is less reason for judges refusing to intervene on behalf of Sacco and Vanzetti than for their actually intervening to kill the N.R.A. On that point, I am willing to go to bat with anyone, on grounds of pure logic. I understand your shock that I should have written an introduction to a book that contains such an uncomplimentary reference to men whom I reverence as much as Holmes and Brandeis, but I do not feel at all the way you do. Indeed, it seems to me that your own thinking on legal and political issues has suffered from the intensity of your personal loyalties. As an honor recipient of the latter, I confess I enjoy it immensely, but it seems to me that a little more abstract detachment from personalities is needed in judging great issues.

With affectionate regards, as ever,

MORRIS

[no date]

Dear Morris,

I am sorry to have taken so much time and energy from efforts that are more important and potentially more fruitful, probably, than were needed for your long letter to me about your introduction to the Goldberg volume. I should have made my point more clear at the outset.

Of course I was not shocked that you should write an introduction to a book with which you differ so much, and of course, also, I don't want you to wait for the book that attacks a profoundly important public problem with complete accuracy and fairness. What was in my mind was simply this. You are nothing if not an educator, you are the symbol of reason and the long view. As such I thought you might have told the authors that only its silliness saved their characterization of Holmes, and Brandeis and Stone from the crudest kind of arrogance. And so, you might have labored with them either to delete such obfuscating unreason, or explicitly dissociate yourself from it, not for moral but for educational reasons, in your preface. "General disclaimers of agreement" are not very effective. I shall leave you to decide whether I am too easily shocked, adding only that tolerance and compassion for our common human lot are one thing, but tolerance towards untruth and unfairness in the kind of people who generally are on our side, is quite a different thing.

Of course statements must be more illuminating if the chaos and complexities of life are at all to be understood. But one may be illuminating as Bertrand Russell was illuminating when some years ago here he gave a lecture on the current theories of physics. Whitehead was in the chair. At the conclusion of Russell's lecture, he (W) said: "I am sure we shall all remember what we have just heard as perhaps the most memorable lecture any of us ever has had the privilege to hear. And not the least extraordinary quality of this extraordinary performance is that he made as clear as he could what could be made clear and left the surrounding darkness of the subject unobscured." Marion said "clearer than truth" not "clearer than insight warrants"

Always yours,
FELIX

P.S. The enclosed correspondence may interest you. If you have time for comments at all, I should be grateful.

January 31, 1936

Dear Felix,

I emphatically do *not* differ from you in deploring the uncalled-for attack on Holmes, Brandeis and Stone in the Goldberg volume, "not only as a matter of fairness but also in the interest of a more accurate, and therefore more convincing, analysis of the problem." How can any reasonable man differ on this point? Where I do differ from you is in not being as "shocked" by it as you declared yourself to be in your first letter. I do not expect as much as you do from human nature. Possibly, also, you may still be shocked that I should write an introduction to a book with which I differ so much. But here again it is a question of a choice between two evils, and I am not sure that anyone is in a position to be certain which is the lesser evil. My first impression of course was to refuse to have anything to do with a volume which is so sloppy as to its fundamental conception of law and lawlessness. But then I reflected that if I waited for a book that was free from fault, I should wait in vain forever, and that meanwhile many books less honest would continue to be published to strengthen the evil against which Mr. Goldberg protests. Then I began to make a list of the points in the volume with which I disagreed. But that not only became too long, but I was afraid it was not long enough and that the enumeration of my dissenting points would be interpreted as approval of all the rest. Hence I chose to enter a general denial of agreement with the authors and a commendation of the point for which it seems to me the book is to be commended. If anyone thinks that I chose unwisely, I have no defense except my general scepticism as to whether anyone is in a position to decide a matter of that sort authoritatively on objective or compelling evidence. I confess that I think such scepticism which makes people feel lighthearted about moral responsibility in such cases, seems to me rather wholesome. I always recoil from the attitude of the late Felix Adler who thought there was a definite moral imperative in all these cases, the same for all human beings. However, I grant to others the right to be shocked at this moral indifference of mine.

I see no connection, as you seem to in your postscript, between the absence of an objective basis for settling such questions as those of International Law, and the question of detachment from personal loyalties in determining general issues. International Law is largely a matter of opinion and modifiable convention. The opinion of a man like Grotius commends itself to some people by its seeming plausibility. But if you are trained in mathematics and learn to distrust self-evident principles, you cannot regard such opinions as decisive. Likewise, when practices are accepted in part, but modified to some extent under changing conditions, it is vain to pretend that on questions of this sort there is just one correct answer and all others are incorrect. Under the circumstances the proper thing seems to me to recognize that certain doctrines or attitudes are more or less established while others are less likely to find favor. But it is vain to pretend to definitive solutions where the data or the evidences are insufficient in the nature of the case. My reference to your intense personal loyalties hampering your analysis of legal and political issues, refers to something altogether different. It refers to your occasionally using arguments which are quite definitely fallacious, and which you would recognize as fallacious if you were not personally involved. If you wish to, I will recall to you instances, but I do not think that is important and I certainly did not mean to admonish you on that score. For I believe that we must all pay dearly for our virtues. I regard your personal loyalties as great virtues (you know how I admire Bret Harte's *Tennessee's Partner* and similar stories). I suppose that I too pay for my effort to disregard personal considerations in the analysis of general issues, but that seems to me unavoidable. The gods will not allow us to have all the virtues. So I think we should cultivate those which come easiest to us as the natural gifts of the gods, and not take our limitations too much to heart.

In regard to Marion's observation that some statements are clearer than the truth, there are two things to be said. It is well to distrust clear statements about complicated issues for they are generally attained by pseudo-simplicity, by ignoring actual and complicated factors. There is, however, another observation which is equally important and not so often noticed, and that is that all human discourse to be effective must be simpler and clearer than the living situations to which they point. How can statements be illuminating if they are as complicated as life itself? Indeed, to illumine an object is to throw artificial light on it. But that is too long a topic to dispose of in a personal letter. I try to touch on it in my paper on Some Absolutisms in Legal Thought which the Harvard Law Review rejected and which the Pennsylvania Law Review will print in April.

With affectionate regards,

As ever,
MORRIS

February 4, 1936

Dear Felix,

Our correspondence in regard to the Goldberg volume has been very illuminating to me in confirming my doctrine that most human differences hinge on questions of emphasis or preferences, which really cannot be settled on an objective basis, and therefore cause (except for very reasonable people like you and me) intense irritation and heat. You attach great importance to effectiveness, and are not satisfied with general disclaimers. You would therefore write to the authors or make a specific disclaimer. I have no objection to that but I am not impressed with the urgency of the matter as you are. Of course, if I had nothing else to do, I would do what you suggest, but I think that I probably spent my time doing something else which seemed at the time more urgent. I am not sure either way. But if anyone is certain that I did wrong, I think he is certain too easily. I may also add that "tolerance towards untruth and unfairness in the kind of people who generally are on our side," is not my chief weakness, and I see no point in your addressing that remark to me. On the contrary, I am apt to err the other way, and have often been accused of being ineffective because I am a lone fighter.

In regard to your correspondence with [Henry Sloan] Coffin, I entirely agree with you, though I should put my reasons in somewhat different terms. There is a certain duplicity about liberalism which shocks intellectually conscientious people. Thus, the broad church in England claims to be broad enough to include everybody, but when it comes to electing Bishops, the standards are very narrow. My friend Dr. [Mordecai] Kaplan wants a broad Judaism to include all Jews, but only those who are religious in his sense should be put in positions of authority and trust. This is the case with our Universities. They claim to stand for universal truth, but in the end they do not want to get away from certain sectarian and partisan commitments. I have no objection to Yale University insisting that it is a white, Protestant organization and acting accordingly*; but it should make some effort at consistency. What arouses my irritation at the University Club is not that it excludes Jews, but that it calls itself a "University

* as it used to in regard to compulsory chapel.

Club." But we are dealing here with one of the root evils of human nature, the desire to eat our cake and have it, an evil which I suppose will continue to plague the human race long after you and I are gone. The only hope that I can see in this particular case is for a concerted movement on the part of the American Association of University Professors to attach a certain discredit to sectarian scholarships as well as to endowments for the teaching of sectarian doctrines. In recent years several universities have had the courage to refuse gifts for the teaching of specific doctrines. Some agitation to extend this to sectarian scholarships may gather headway. Unfortunately, however, the precedents and the sentiments are against us. That does not make the fight less urgent but the prospects of victory are very remote.

With kindest regards,

Affectionately yours,
MORRIS R. COHEN

5 Feb. [1936]

Dear Morris,

Many thanks for your letter—which I much cherish. I know I have a simple, even naïve side, and Marion has extended the boundaries of my wisdom by making me even more aware of it. But I really believe that you and I are "very reasonable people"—we can talk over differences that matter to us, without it mattering between us!

Your analysis of the Coffin-University matter strikes deep responses in all. Could you without too much trouble put together for me or have put together a list with chapter and verse, of the instances in which universities have "refused gifts for the teaching of specific doctrines."

The enclosed correspondence with Alfred Cook [City College '92] please return.

Yours ever,
FELIX

February 7, 1936

Dear Felix,

I am returning herewith your correspondence with Cook, and am enclosing some of my own with that worthy. Perhaps a few words are necessary to clarify the latter correspondence.

I have never been active in Alumni affairs, and have made every effort to keep out of the fight over the Report of the Special Committee (if I had participated the Majority Report would not have contained so many unfounded i.e., false tributes to Robinson). But as my nephew Henry [Cohen] works for Cook, and as I have been trying to get the latter to help me in the Conference on Jewish Relations, I could not well refuse the invitation to come to his house and explain to him the C.C.N.Y. situation—to the extent that he would allow me. He seemed very courteous and respectful to me, and I thought that I had impressed him with the fact that I had nothing to do with the Alumni Report. However, some of Robinson's henchmen succeeded in drilling into Cook's mind the idea that all this fight against Robinson was a Cohen affair. On Friday the 24th, Cook called me up and asked me to agree to some compromise proposition. I told him that this was none of my business and that it would be improper for me to intervene actively. I also told him that he was mistaken in his assumption that this was a Cohen-Robinson fight. Cook thereupon terminated the conversation in a huff. The next morning I wrote him the enclosed letter. He did not reply at first, but in his address at the Alumni, he insinuated his belief that I was back of the opposition. Apparently he has difficulty in believing that my present and former students may respect me even though I have neither the opportunity nor the desire to spend my time influencing them to the extent of telling them how to vote. I suppose there is nothing that I can do about it, and normally I shouldn't care. I am, however, a bit concerned about the fact that in his fear of anti-Semitism, Cook himself raised the Jewish issue at the meeting of the Alumni and he seems now quite peeved at his failure to swing his plans, and he threatens to rouse up a great deal of opposition against the College. Somebody should talk to him and impress upon him that there is still a good deal to be learned about the situation. Possibly Judge Lehman or somebody of that type.

As soon as I can, I shall hunt up the instances of Universities refusing to accept endowments for sectarian teaching. Perhaps you can [get] at the information more expeditiously by writing to W. H. Tyler, the general secretary of the American Association of University Professors. A minor but troublesome surgical operation has worked havoc with my spare time.

As ever,

Affectionately yours,
MORRIS

February 10, 1936

Dear Morris,

I am more sorry than I can tell you that your strength should have been so needlessly and brutally drained by Alfred Cook. I have known him a good many years and your letter to him does your Spinozian qualities high credit. . . .

Ever yours,
F F

P.S. Whitehead will be 75 on Saturday (15th) week. His address is 984 Memorial Drive, Cambridge.

February 14, 1936

Dear Felix,

Cook did take up a good deal of my time and energy, but I would rather write an ineffective letter that you regard as Spinozian than many effective ones that are of a different quality. You know my motto, "The means are as important as the end." I trust all is well with you and Marion.

Affectionately,
MORRIS R. COHEN

[Written at the bottom of above letter]
Morris,

I'm often of the opinion that they [the means] are even *more* important—for we can often judge the validity of "means" more than we can appraise "ends." And even Spinoza ought not to waste your strength.

Ever
F

May 22, 1936

Dear Felix:

I was delighted to see you in such good physical fettle a week ago in New York. Your stay in the South seems to have done you good and I hope that you will not let the more active and cold North wear off the Southern bloom.

To the many compliments which you must have received as to the charm of your address at the Lawyers' Club, let me add a note of my own bewilderment as to the meaning of your address. I could not at all make out your reference to the Constitution as a legal rather than a political document. I cannot for the life of me see that any of the issues that you mentioned are anything but political; and if a few old men are to decide these issues under the fiction that they are interpreting a legal document of "the will of the people," then why on earth talk about democracy?

Also may I ask whether it has never occurred to you that the issue between federalism and centralism is just as much a shibboleth as that between individualism and socialism? Our Supreme Court knocks down state boundaries without the least hesitation when it comes to the regulation of interstate commerce (so far as the interests of corporations are concerned, at any rate) and under guise of interpreting the 14th Amendment abolishes the one virtue of federalism, namely, the power of the individual states to experiment in social legislation.

Also, is not the United States Senate actually a federal council in which every state is represented, the smaller states much more so than the bigger states? Surely the questions of adjustment between various states are political and a federal council rather than a purely legal body or court would seem to be the logical way to deal with the situation.

With affectionate regards to Marion and yourself,

Faithfully yours,

MORRIS

May 22, 1936

Dear Morris,

Why the delay in your letter? I expected your affectionate castigation not later than by Monday last. And you tell me nothing I did not know.

Believe it or not, it cannot be less than a quarter of a century since I became aware of all that you now tell me. This, I am afraid, will only add to your bewilderment, inasmuch as you probably do not share the belief of Socrates that by sinning against the light there is a brighter hope for my reform. I know I should have made a great hit with you if I had told those lawyers "Abolish the Supreme Court and to Hell with the Constitution." But then, I am not a philosopher; I am merely an empiric lawyer.

Let me deal with your three specific points. The situation is not quite so simple as one might suspect from your comments:

(1) Of course the Constitution may fairly be called "a political document," but "political" is not one of those crystal clear words with a single, inescapable meaning. When I characterized the Constitution as "a legal document" in juxtaposition to political, I had in mind that philosophy about judicial review which is represented by James Bradley Thayer's writings and Holmes' opinions. And you ought not to throw Thayer and Holmes too casually out of the window. *Their* conception of the Constitution would enable this country to move

rather easily within the framework of the Constitution towards ends that you and I care about. Such a view is neither logically foolish nor, as a matter of history, wholly futile, howsoever much you and I may agree on some recent events.

(2) Federalism v. centralism may become just as much of a shibboleth as individualism v. socialism. And I also know that the Supreme Court can play ducks and drakes with its professed devotion to federalism. But that does not disprove the idea itself—it is merely reason for challenging their misuse of the idea. It is not accident that Australia and Canada and the United States and now India are federalisms. Turn this country into a unitary state, and I think you would make inevitable a denial of that life of reason about which you care most.

(3) Granted a federalism in which accommodations have to be made in the inevitable conflicts as between the central government and its constituents, it seems to me fantastic to expect the United States Senate to make those adjustments in the hundreds of minor cases involving federalism which come before the Supreme Court that never get into the newspapers and which not even you ever read.

At the moment, I am in the midst of finishing an essay on Waite, and so must stop.

Marion was delighted that you approved of my looks if not of my law.

Ever yours,
FELIX

June 10, 1936

Dear Morris,

(1) It wasn't pride at all Morris; it was a confession of the extent of my intellectual depravity. Besides, I wasn't writing to a pupil; I was writing to one of my teachers.

(2) I didn't, of course, profess to quote Socrates nor to speak with literal accuracy. I thought you and I could indulge in playful ping-pong. But, am I wrong in believing that Socrates somewhere in effect says that to know one is doing wrong makes reform more hopeful than to sin in ignorance.

(3) Don't take me too literally, Morris, but if you did not want me to show up the Court and the Constitution, what did you want me to do?

(4) All public law is political in the Aristotelian sense. Of course the elements that go into a decision in constitutional law are much more reflective of matters of policy than is true in private law. But

Thayer's writings and Holmes' adjudications are based on the assumption that the application of the Constitution may be a domain of law and very different from what we ordinarily understand by politics. To be sure it differs—in degree. But as Holmes used to say, it is none the worse for that. The difference is one that matters.

(5) "The idea" of federalism—once you accept that idea, then there must be some arbiter for the inevitable conflicts in the application of the distribution of political power between two governments.

(6) We apparently are at one in not wanting a unitary state and in wanting opportunity for social experiments.

(7) I am not defending the Court for this, that or the other thing, and I should be much surprised if you and I differed about any particular case. But it does seem to me fantastic to suggest that, as you have done, the United States Senate should make the adjustments as between state and federal power. And I would like you to draw an Amendment that would provide that the Court may decide in "minor" cases but not in major cases. If you mean to imply, as Holmes did in his 1913 speech, that the Union would not come to an end if the power to pass on Congressional legislation were taken away from the Supreme Court, that is a different story, and there is a great deal to be said for it. Or if you were to suggest that the due process clause should be repealed, that is also a different story and a good deal is to be said for it; although I notice that some of my friends are keen about the due process clause when situations like the Scottsboro case come up. If you tell me that the due process clause should be restricted to its historical procedural function, I can understand that, and again say there is much to be said for it.

I am neither boasting, nor unappreciative of your wisdom, when I say I am familiar with all the criticisms of the Court, for I have made them myself for now nearly thirty years. I am also familiar with the practical difficulties of the various devices for dealing with these difficulties, and the evil ends to which gadgets like 7–2 requirement, and judicial recall, etc. may be put. Above all, I realize as I realize, and speak as I speak, in the light of my convictions as to the state of intellectual unpreparedness of even informed Americans for dealing with these problems.

Ever yours,
FELIX

October 29, 1936

Dear Felix:

Your comments on the enclosed are too hasty:

(1) In the spring of 1933 a number of people, Arthur Burns

among them, did decidedly agree with me that the four die-hards would not be budged and that there was more than an even chance that one of the others would join them to kill the main progressive measures, so that the only safe course was to appoint at once four additional judges who were alive to the needs of their times. It did not require much wisdom to see this and one who couldn't see it was no fit leader for a great people in time of crisis.

The common prejudice against "packing" the Supreme Court (like the House of Lords) as in any way unfair or "indirect" rests on fictions and I am surprised that you should fall for it. Can you mention a single good reason in support of your preference? Of course, ultimately we must amend the Constitution, as I indicated; but you know that this is a long process and that it is silly to ignore the element of time in human affairs. An amendment can for a long time be blocked by a small minority in Congress or in the States. Why should the majority not avail itself of its power to do what is necessary to get rid of the atrocious abuses of child labor, of exploiting men and women by wages below the minimum of decent subsistence?

If a man is running away from a fire or other danger, and meets a huge rock in his way, he is wise to run around it. What should be thought of the advice to follow the more "straightforward" way and push the rock out of the way? Sooner or later he may return to do it, but not when getting away from danger. A very serious doubt could have been raised as to the constitutional right of the President to declare a bank holiday. But the urgency of the time demanded that it be done first and doubts be attended to later. *Until* the Constitution is changed so as to make it more responsive to popular needs there is nothing dishonorable in using the combined constitutional power of the legislative and executive to overcome the obstinacy of a few old men. To sacrifice the welfare of millions for a polite fiction seems to me indefensible.

I venture to add that if Roberts had voted with the minority in the Gold case, the President would have had the country with him if he had refused to follow the Supreme Court's decision, just as Jackson once did and as Lincoln did when he refused to honor Taney's writ of habeas corpus.

(2) Article III, Section 2, paragraph 2, second sentence expressly gives Congress the power to regulate the appelate jurisdiction of the Supreme Court. This has actually been used on a famous occasion to prevent the Supreme Court from passing on a given statute after the Civil War. You can also create a new court for such cases as

occur, appoint proper judges, and prevent appeal to the Supreme Court.

I think that the popular veneration for the Constitution is much less than our politicians and newspapers pretend. For Congress did for ten years refuse to obey the mandate of the Constitution to apportion representation according to the last census and no one cared. There were no popular protests or anything of the sort. A little courage and imagination ought to be exercised by liberals once in a while and not left to the Hitlers and Mussolinis.

Affectionately yours,
MORRIS

January 1, 1937

Dear Felix:

On my return home I find your touching letter in regard to your and my mother and the qualities which their generation represented. It moves me profoundly and the fact that you feel that way is one of the deep bonds that attaches me to you.

In my profound admiration for the men and women of their type I do not believe that I am unjust to the younger generation, which includes my children and my pupils. Our parents were a selected group that stood up under the trying conditions involved in uprooting their lives in their old homes and coming to make new homes and raise their children in a strange land.

This has been brought home to me most vividly in the last few years when my mother came to live with me. Deprived of the companionship of the one who had been her husband for 67 years, suffering from a confining and fatal heart disease, with few of her friends left to come to see her as she was approaching her 90th year, she was naturally dependent on my companionship which, alas, could not be adequate. Yet she bore her lot with a dignity and graciousness that was most inspiring.

Now, I believe that many of the younger generation following us are capable of the same serene fortitude. It is only the conditions which have become more easy and our system of education which has grown to be rather lax that seems to make the difference in the total impression. Perhaps the younger generation has less reverence, but I think that on the whole it is much better so. It will mean less of the conventional hypocricy which pretends to be shocked when some prominent person does publicly what a large proportion, if not a majority, of our fellow men and women do privately.

When I called on you yesterday I was very anxious to discuss some of the affairs of the Conference on Jewish Relations and some of my personal plans growing out of my prospective retirement from City College. In regard to the former, I am enclosing two documents which I should like you to read and return with any comments which occur to you. My personal problems can wait.

I thought both you and Marion seemed in very good condition, though your tendency to raise your voice seems to me indicative of a nervous tension which a more relaxed life can probably eliminate with great profit to your health.

With best wishes for the new year and at all times,

Ever affectionately yours,

MORRIS

January 2, 1937

Dear Felix:

After leaving your house on Thursday I spoke to Mrs. Whitehead about an unusually gifted student of mine who cannot find enough money to enable him to pursue graduate studies at Columbia. Mrs. Whitehead thereupon volunteered to contribute $25 or $50 and suggested that you have ways and means of reaching people who can contribute more.

I should hesitate to ask you if it weren't for the fact that those on whom I usually rely for such purposes, such as Julian Mack, seem unable to help me at this juncture.

The student to whom I refer has as an undergraduate done work every bit as good as that of Paul Weiss, Ernest Nagel, Sidney Hook, Joseph Ratner or any of those of my former students who have since achieved distinction in Philosophy. Of course one can never be certain of the future. But since my past investments along this line have more than made good, I think that this one is worth trying.

As ever,

MORRIS

January 13, 1937

Dear Morris:

1. I wish it could be more but it just can't. I don't have to tell you the demands that are made on one these days.

2. Let me reiterate on paper what I said to you face to face about your review of Thurman Arnold's book. To me it was completely satisfying, just to the fresh critical considerations in Arnold's book, but also regardful of the profounder philosophic and logical factors that Thurman, and so many like him, so blithely disregard. These are

great days for throwing the baby out with the bath. If you have an extra copy of that review, I shall be grateful to you for it.

Ever yours,

F F

January 23, 1937

Dear Morris:

1. I can hardly believe that Hitler will be able to float a loan here, but I am trying to make soundings and give warning. This takes care also of your inquiries regarding exchange controls.

2. Thurman Arnold is an unusually nice fellow, but, as you indicate, like so many others, he thinks the world was born yesterday.

I know it will be quite a wrench for you not to teach at City College, but the chances are good that after a while you will find the conditions of your life serener, and increasing rather than diminished opportunities from the kind of stimulations that you so uniquely give.

Ever yours,

FELIX

DAY LETTER

Washington, D.C.
May 14, 1938

Dr. Stephen F. Duggan
Care of Mrs. Alfred Weld
Greenwich, Connecticut

Heartbroken that I cannot express at the dinner, howsoever inadequately, the deep sense of pride that all of us feel for Morris Cohen's enduring contributions as a teacher and as a thinker. He is as significant an example of the ministry of the teacher as anyone I have known anything about since Socrates. May he long continue to discharge that ministry, whatever the form in which he chooses to do so. Though the range of his services is the world of reason, as City College men we take special pride in him and I send the affectionate greetings of a devoted friend.

FELIX FRANKFURTER.

Heath, Mass.
July 12 [1938]

Dear Morris,

1. It certainly will do no harm to send Janowsky's book to the President—Whether he will find time to read it, I know not.

2. Send copies to
   (1) Hon. George S. Messersmitt
       State Department
       Washington, D.C.
   (2) Irving Dilliard
       St. Louis Post-Dispatch
       St. Louis, Mo.
   (3) Frank W. Buxton
       Boston Herald, Boston
   (4) Geoffrey Parsons
       N. Y. Herald-Tribune
   (5) Wm. A. White
       Emporia Gazette
       Emporia, Kan.
   (6) Hon. Herbert Hoover
       (through Lewis Strauss)
   (7) Henry G. Leach
       c/o Forum
   (8) C. C. Burlingham
       Black Point, Conn.
   (9) Charles A. Beard
       New Milford

3. I am very glad that you wrote Pound about that mischievously silly "Marxian."

4. What about Eugene Meyer? Have you done anything with him? Fondest regards to Mary and you.

Ever yours
FELIX

October 4, 1938

Dear Morris:

1. I think that your program of lectures is admirable. Inasmuch, however, as I assume you will want to tap the law students primarily I suggest that we hold these lectures in the Court-room because, while it may seem a little thing, it will make all the difference in the world in the attendance of law students whether they can go from their various places of work in and about the law buildings to the Court-room or have to go to the New Lecture Hall.

2. I think your proposed seminar on Legal Thought is just right, but hope you will concentrate on the problem which "is to be found in every branch of the law," rather than give it the emphasis which you do in the tail end of your letter by concerning yourself primarily with the question of making "constitutional law less uncertain." What do you say to this?

3. I have in addition a very personal problem. I want to attend your seminar, but, in view of various commitments that I have already, I cannot set aside another evening. Would you be agreeable to an afternoon meeting? If not I will have to drop out of it.

4. Which brings me to another personal problem. For reasons completely beyond my control I am more enslaved as to time than I have been at any period of my life, which explains why I haven't seen Mary and you as yet.

Ever yours,

F F

475 West 186 Street
January 2, 1939

Dear Felix:

I was deeply touched by your very generous reference at the Z.B.T. luncheon to our old friendship. It is a friendship which has meant a great deal in my life and I cannot hide the fact that in recent years you have done or left undone things which would give most people the impression that not only I but even Mary (who has for a third of a century shown unquestioning devotion to you) have lost our place in your regard. I do not say this by way of complaint for I realize that the tides of life are stronger than any of us can control and I am sufficiently philosophic to accept the result. In any case, nothing that you have done or can do can efface from my memory what you did for me in that horrible winter of 1905–6 when I was at the end of my tether physically and morally (bankrupt). Your patience and sweetness have been an inspiration to me which no difference of opinion as to political and economic affairs can erase.

The New Year naturally suggests reflection. Some years ago you wrote to me that I was the only one who did not take you merely for granted but treated you as a real friend and talked to you freely as one. This induces me to render you the service of friendship, of giving you the gift of seeing yourself as others see you.

I am a pluralist and do not believe that there is any one form of behavior which is imperative on all men. I believe in the biblical saying "In my father's house are many mansions." It takes all sorts of men to make a world. Nevertheless, it is an advantage to see ourselves as others see us (occasionally) and I have a suspicion that few people render you that service, a suspicion founded on a letter which you once wrote me to the effect that other people take you for granted and do not take the trouble, as I did occasionally, to point out whither you are drifting. . . . [End of letter is missing.]

Washington, D.C.
May 5, 1939

Dear Morris:

I do think it would be worthwhile to write a note of correction to the members of your Conference regarding the Harvard Report.

Your shrewd discernment that the routine here would of necessity transform my habits, is likely to be vindicated. For the first time in my life almost—at least since the early days in New York—I am a prisoner in my routine with all the compensating advantages it brings. However, what with my gregarious nature and the number of people who steadily stream through Washington whom I happen to know, life is not too easy.

I met a man the other day who reminded me not a little of Einstein in his simplicity and sweetness, to wit: Niels Bohr.

And what are your plans ahead? Aren't you going to do some more writing? I hope so very much.

In not many weeks we shall be out of here, and the summer will be relatively quiet, punctuated with hundreds of certiorari. I am planning to do a great deal of reading in branches of the law to which I have heretofore paid no attention, such as patents.

With affectionate regards to Mary and yourself,

Ever yours,
FELIX

Heath, Mass.
July 25 [1940]

Dear Morris,

If I'm not wrong, today is your 60th birthday. All cosmic or general reflections which naturally aroused by this new evidence of the flight of time are subordinate to my thought of you and the quality of your life and its rich achievements. That the world is so far from the life of reason, which is yours, is surely not your fault. And so I send you my affectionate fond wishes—and Marion joins.

Ever yours
FELIX

Supreme Court of the United States
Washington, D.C.

November 19, 1940

Dear Morris:

I rejoice over your election as Carus Lecturer. I have some notion of the implications of that Lecture in your chosen field. After all, what matters most apart from one's own consciousness of doing one's utmost, is the judgment of one's peers. That is what the Carus Lectureship implies. I warmly congratulate you and congratulate all of us that this stimulus has been given you for your book on a Liberal Philosophy of History.

Not only have I been crowded for various reasons touching the work of the Court at the beginning of the Term, but my back has been giving me much trouble with resulting heavy inroads on my time and energy. But if you will come down for a day I will somehow manage to see you.

Ever yours,

FELIX

January 30, 1941

Dear Morris:

This is a belated acknowledgment of your admirable letter to Burlingham. What is happening in C.C.N.Y. affairs?

Whatever may befall me I hope I shall never lose my eagerness for candor. And so I am grateful for your personal letter even though I do not enter upon a discussion of what you write. Were the time mine I would do so but the themes to open up are too complicated to be disposed of in a single letter and it would hardly be profitable to discuss the complexities of human relations in a syncopated way.

Believe me,

Ever yours,

F F

February 5, 1941

Dear Morris:

I have taken the most effective step to carry weight with Lauson Stone. In other words, the Justice will write to his son about you.

Perhaps the best thing to do is to get men on the Board [of Higher Education] whom you know to ask me about [Dean R.] McKeon. To have one's opinion solicited is always more effective than to offer free advice.

It is very sweet of you to say what you do about our personal relations. I can assure you I reciprocate both the delicacy of feeling and the loyalty which possesses you. I know this is what Holmes used to call "tall talk" but I think it is an accurate revelation of at least the conscious inner feeling.

With warmest regards to Mary,

Ever yours,

FELIX

March 4, 1942

Dear Morris:

I wish you had been in Court not so many days ago when a little ceremony took place which gave me much pleasure and which would have warmed your heart even more than it did mine—and it warmed mine a good deal. Your Felix moved Henry Cohen for admission to our bar. What a lot of reflections swiftly passed through my head as I saw those two boys! Indeed not only their lives but almost all of mine quickly passed in review.

And you have also been in my mind, as it were, professionally, for I have been dipping into a book by M. C. Otto of Wisconsin, called The Human Enterprise. I wonder if you have seen it and if someday you will tell me what you think about it.

I hear that you will be under wraps for a little while—that you will be compelled to be dormant. I do not know anyone better equipped to endure the confinement to which you are now subjected by the hard experience of his life—you have had much too much illness and drain on your strength all these decades—as well as by the discipline of his mind and the mastery of his soul. I sometimes wish that I had a mild kind of longish illness during which I could enjoy such thoughts as flicker from time to time in my mind and perchance could live in the world of books for a long stretch of time. Instead the grind of the Court is greater than ever. However, I try not to be wholly unmindful of your wise admonition. Incidentally I was surprised to notice in Holmes' letters, even in the early days, a sense of constant pressure. But then you have often told me that the intellectual occupation of a philosopher and a philosophic spirit are two very different things.

I wish it were true that science has eliminated distance for then I would see you—briefly or at length as circumstances permitted. But this brings you my affectionate good wishes and the warm regards of both of us.

Ever yours,
FELIX

June 19/42

Dear Felix,

I was very much touched by your sweet letter which I have not answered sooner because I have not yet overcome many obstacles. Since you wrote the letter Mary has passed away. You who knew how much she meant to me will understand the void in my heart, particularly the absence of that zest for life which was her great gift. I shall try to be as brave as possible, but her absence is a loss which nothing can replace. I console myself with the thought that nothing was spared to make her passage as free from pain as possible—also that her last moments were peaceful in the deepest sense. She passed away with a song for humanity on her lips. I shall try to carry on as best I can, in which I expect the children to help me, for they are all brave and devoted to her memory.

Ever yours,

M. R. C.

per L. C. R.

3708 Oliver Street,
Washington, D.C.,
April 28, 1943.

Dear Felix,

I have just heard the devastating news of the death of your brother Paul, and hasten to send you my heartfelt sympathy.

I did not see much of him in recent years, but I had grown to esteem him very highly. Mary also developed a high opinion of his wife.

I trust Paul had made some provision for her and her daughters' maintenance.

With kindest regards to Ella, Stella and Marion,

Devotedly yours,

MORRIS R. COHEN

1511 30th
Friday

Dear Morris,

You bring whatever comfort a dear old friendship can give to grief. Poor Paul has had the fates against him for some time—a few years [ago] lovely Fanny died suddenly and luck in all sorts of ways told against him. And now he was stricken almost overnight. His two daughters—charming girls—are happily married.

I have been silent, but not indifferent. You have often and much been in my thoughts. But this has been an especially imprisoning year for me. I hope for some relief before very long.

My affectionate regards and fond wishes to you, in which Marion joins.

Ever yours

FELIX

2617—39th Street, N.W.,
Washington, D.C.,
September 28, 1944.

Dear Felix:

My very kind secretary, Mrs. Fischer, tells me that she and her husband the Major occasionally see you. This suggests to me that you may be inclined to grant me similar privileges for the sake of old times when you were my room mate and when you took part in the testimonial which City College gave in my honor. I still count myself one of your devoted friends, and I should be happy if you felt the same way about me.

You will be interested to learn that with the help of my son Felix I have finished two books, one a logic book and the other a collection of essays under the title, The Faith of a Liberal, both soon to be published by Henry Holt and Company. I am also working on my Carus Lectures, on The Meaning of Human History.

My best to Marion and your dear self.

As ever, yours
MORRIS R. COHEN

2617—39th Street, N.W.,
Washington, D.C.
October 9, 1944

Mrs. Felix Frankfurter,
c/o Mr. Justice Frankfurter,
The Supreme Court.

Dear Marion:

This afternoon my son and I enjoyed a delightful visit to your Felix. We were, however, disappointed at the report of your difficulties following your surgical operation. We trust your recovery will be rapid.

About the time of Mary's death I myself suffered a devastating illness from which I have not recovered as yet. I have not as yet regained normal powers of speech. Your Felix has ample evidence of that.

Meanwhile, my intellectual life continues with moderate success. I have just been scheduled to deliver the Carus lectures before the American Philosophical Association. I expect my son Felix will read the lectures that I can't well give myself.

With cordial greetings, I am

Ever yours,
MORRIS R. COHEN

[1944]

Dear Felix;

I was grieved to learn of the death of Quezon, the President of the Philippines.

I remember the handsome way in which he apologized to you and told you that he had been mistaken in thinking you were a tool of General Edward.

Would that our Southern Democrats could learn that magnanimous conduct is not restricted by color or race.

You may be interested in learning of the fact that I have recently completed two books that Henry Holt is soon to bring out—*A Preface to Logic* and *The Faith of a Liberal*.

My best to Marion and yourself.

Ever yours,
MORRIS per L. C. R.

Oct. 17/46

Dear Morris—

It warmed my heart—as it would have yours—to hear the affectionate response which your telegram to the C.C.N.Y. [alumni] dinner evoked from the 2500 diners.

This little piece of mine I send—because I want to send it, not because it is important.

My devoted regards,

FELIX

February 1, 1947

Dear Alvin [Johnson]:

My enforced absence from tomorrow's meeting of farewell to Morris Cohen adds to my grief. When death comes to an intimate, much of one's self goes. And Morris was a friend who tied me to life by a deep as well as a long friendship. Of this personal relation it will not do to speak, so close was it, except to say that the most intimate scrutiny only enhanced my admiration for his motives and his purposes, his fortitude and his serenity. To preach the philosophic temper as beautifully and as persuasively as he did, in itself confers a great boon on men. To maintain it as consistently as he did is a greater achievement. Fundamentally, of course, Morris Cohen gave his life to contemplation, and to an extraordinary degree he strengthened the taste and the talent for contemplation in others. And contemplation, in his preaching and his practice, was not an evasion of life but a realization of one of its deepest aspects.

All his life he knew the blows of fortune as well as its mercies. But his fortitude seemed to become sweeter and more serene when the blows came heaviest. I think I am not romanticizing when I attribute the extent to which he was able to keep a stout heart, through all the darkness of recent years, to the fact that Morris Cohen really disciplined himself to live the truth, that it makes all the difference in the world whether we put truth in the first place or in the second.

A great teacher has left us. But as is true of all great teachers, Morris Cohen will live on in the minds of men, and in the minds of men of generations to come.

Very sincerely yours,

FELIX FRANKFURTER

XV. *Letters on Law*

To his diary, Cohen confessed as a young man:

> Curious that I who have found the taming of the emotions such an impossible task should be the one to preach a rigorous intellectualism which assumes that we can suppress, encourage and manage our emotions any way we think we *ought*.
>
> The real fact is duality. Yet when I come to describe it to others I identify myself with the dark heroic philosopher [c. 1902].

His inner emotionalism sometimes showed through, even in his philosophy of legal thought. The intensity of his interest in jurisprudence and constitutional law was a measure of his concern with making the law a more scientific, rational, and effective tool for social justice. In the pursuit of that cause he found fellowship among a good many kindred souls. His correspondence with some of them is sampled here—Judge, later Justice, Benjamin N. Cardozo; Judge Learned Hand; and Professor, later Dean, Roscoe Pound. With a host of other judges and lawyers too, Cohen sought to view the implications of the law in the light of philosophical perspective.

Benjamin N. Cardozo

February 17, 1926

My dear Professor Cohen,

. . . I read your articles from time to time, my dear Professor Cohen, with a growing and deepening sense of the range of your knowledge and the breadth of your thought. . . .

Faithfully yours,

BENJAMIN N. CARDOZO[1]

Allenhurst, N.J.
August 25, 1927

Dear Professor Cohen,

The syllabus of your lectures and the additional articles reached me safely this morning.

I have run over the syllabus and am greedy for the published volume. It will be an event of the first importance in legal philosophy. I am sorry we shall have to wait so long for it.

I have read with delight and interest the articles that you left with me last week. I am left a little depressed, none the less, by the range of your learning and accomplishments. It seems as if a mere amateur like myself might as well hold his peace and be silent.

I will take good care of "Jus Naturale Redivivum" and send it back to you when I am in town.

With best wishes for a pleasant vacation (if vacation there is to be) and for the speedy and triumphant completion of the *magnum opus* now taking shape under your hands,

I am faithfully yours,
BENJAMIN N. CARDOZO

Sixteen West Seventy-Fifth Street
March 9, 1931

Dear Professor Cohen,

I am thankful to you for a reprint of your address, Vision and Technique in Philosophy, which was handed to me this morning by your nephew [Henry Cohen].

What you say is not altogether palatable to sciolists and amateurs (I fly their banner without shame), but palatable or unpalatable, I am sure it is a needed bolas.

Never was a bolas more skilfully concealed in a sugar coating thick enough to conceal the medicine within until mastication reached the centre. The form is admirable—an amateur and sciolist does not dare to judge the substance.

I am excited about the publication of your new book, for which I have already put in an order. Do follow it up soon with a book on jurisprudence.

As ever faithfully yours,
BENJAMIN N. CARDOZO

Dec. 27, 1932
2101 Connecticut Ave.

Dear Prof. and Mrs. Cohen,

I prize your message of good will.

In my place of exile at Washington I think of you often.

You will visit me, of course, if you find yourselves in Washington. With every good wish for the New Year,

I am faithfully yours,
BENJAMIN N. CARDOZO

April 29, 1933

Dear Professor Cohen

. . . Herman Oliphant called on me yesterday and spoke in glowing terms of your son's book [*Ethical Systems and Legal Ideals*]. I haven't seen it yet. What is the title? I'll get a copy at once.

Every now and then I read some striking article from your pen and get a new sense of your omniscience.

Faithfully yours,
BENJAMIN N. CARDOZO

Rye, N.Y.
Sept. 7, 1933

Dear Philosopher,

It will be a joy to see you tomorrow, Friday. . . .

I expect you to let me know the latest frills in the fashions for philosophers; I am sadly out of date.

Faithfully yours
BENJAMIN N. CARDOZO

Learned Hand

Judge Learned Hand's Chambers

Dear Cohen

Your note was friendly. Maybe I stole the idea from you; I did steal some of it anyway. Having stolen it, I suppose my sub-conscious self has been saying to me that it is not original. By the way, so far as I can learn, the sub-conscious self is always a rotter, doing the most shameful things, a kind of half-man, clutching homo sapiens around the neck. If so, he must have told me this merely out of savage spite, not because he has any modesty; or does he hate homo sapiens so much that he wants to queer all he does.

As ever
L. H.

Jan. 15, 1916

My dear Cohen:

I have yours with the time table enclosed, which I shall keep, and hope to be able to get out, perhaps of a Sunday. I am much obliged for the tip about Ulpian as against Justinian. I thought the Pandects began that way. I am sorry that you have forgotten the two unimportant ones. Perhaps it will help you to bring them to mind when I tell you that the other two marks are opposite the following phrases: "It would as eagerly encourage judicial initiative if the laws were framed by labor unions as it insists upon rigid obedience in a system framed for the main part for the protection of property and for the prevention of thorough-going social regulation." The second is, "All this has changed. The profession is still drawn, and so far as we can see will always be drawn, from the same economic class as before."

I suppose that you object to the last on the ground that the lawyers are by no means all drawn from the capitalist classes. If that be your objection I am inclined to disagree. There are a good many who get in who are in no true sense from the capitalist class, but I should think the proportion very small and outside of a city like New York, almost negligible. Perhaps that is not the objection.

Faithfully yours,
LEARNED HAND

February 1, 1916.

Judge Learned Hand's Chambers
April 25, 1923

Dear Cohen

I am all for your proposal. Why shouldn't we have an evening together at the Century some evening. . . . how would May 7th do? Would you rather meet me here or there? It is better two wise men should be alone cerebrating than that they should suffer the irrelevancies of Frauen und Kindern.

L. H.

[When Hand came to dinner at the Cohens' in 1915, we children, banished to a bedroom, raised such Cain that he never again came to the house. I remember screaming at the top of my lungs.]

February 25, 1926.

Dear Morris

I should not want to bind myself to be in the neighborhood of Cambridge on the second week of September. I cannot tell just what I shall be doing then; I may be in the West for all I know and up in Canada. My plans have to be kept pretty fluid as I have three young women and a wife with whom I should like to have part of my vacation.

However, this will not forbid my getting ready some kind of paper on the philosophy of law and, accepting your assurance that I can do so, I will. If I am within range I will come and read it myself; if I am not, perhaps it will be as well to let someone else read it, who may not feel so responsible for its shortcomings.

Now then, so committed, advise me how long they generally are. About thirty to forty minutes I suppose. Yes, it would be good if you are hereabouts say at lunch hour for you to come in and guide my nascent steps as a legal philosopher.

Faithfully yours
LEARNED HAND

Roscoe Pound

Law School of Harvard University
Cambridge, Mass.

24th February 1912.

Professor Morris R. Cohen,
College of the City of New York
St. Nicholas Terrace and 139th Street,
New York City.

Dear Mr. Cohen:

I am sending you the reprints requested.

I do not know enough in the way of philosophy to be entitled to hold opinions of consequence on such subjects, but I really should like to see Professor Dewey, or someone of his way of thinking, attack some of the problems of the philosophy of law. With all my admiration for Kohler I cannot by any means subscribe to his system. The very points which he makes against Jhering, whom he is fond of saying was absolutely unphilosophical, seem to me to mark the difference between a type of legal thinking of which we have had altogether too much, and a type which we very much need.

Yours very truly,
ROSCOE POUND

The College of the City of New York

March 7, 1912.

My dear Prof. Pound:

When I was a student at Cambridge, I frequently missed a lecture in metaphysics by James or Royce to take in a lesson in law by Dean Ames or Judge Smith. Hence I do not need to be assured of the thorough excellence of the case system as taught "on its native heath."

Nevertheless I think that the introduction of the case system in this country has been distinctly unfavorable to the growth of any philosophy of law, primarily because it has tended to emphasize precedent above social reasons. It is, of course, true that the doctrine of stare decisis is fundamental to the common law, and that all common law lawyers must argue from past decisions where the continental lawyer can argue from principles. But the case system of instruction has tended to unduly emphasize empiricism in the law.

In view of my limited knowledge of legal literature I suppose that I have no right to express or even entertain any opinion on this matter. But the reading of the works of Langdell, Ames and Gray has produced upon me the very decided impression that the three of them were decidedly handicapped in their outlook by an over-devotion to the case system. As a layman I cannot but marvel at the learning and thoroughness of Prof. Gray's Rule against Perpetuities. But there is not in it, so far as I remember, any indication that this rule grew up in any definite economic environment or that in the history of its development it had any connection with any social ends. So far as its method is concerned, one can imagine it to have been written in some monastery as a scholastic exercise. Both Langdell and Ames seem to me to have wasted wonderful mental power in devising subtle reasons to justify decisions of deservedly obscure judges. Dean Ames, in particular, seems to me to have had great powers in the direction of a constructive philosophy of law, and in several of his articles in the Harvard Law Review he shows appreciation of the fact that jurisprudence is not a Laputan dealing with concepts, but rather a science of human adjustments. Yet in spite of his remarkable powers must we not say that his contribution to the philosophy of law is, under the circumstances, disappointing? Dean Ames, of course, rendered invaluable service to the legal profession by his numerous case-books, but a professional philosopher may be pardoned for thinking it unfortunate that a man of Dean Ames' power could not have given us general treatises on such topics as the theory of Criminal Law, Torts, or even on such topics as Master and Servant.

It is at any rate a most significant fact that the first thirteen volumes of the Modern Legal Philosophy series are all translations into English. To what do you yourself attribute this fact? In this connection it is interesting to remember that the English speaking community where the doctrine of stare decisis never had the same hold as it has on us—viz. Scotland—has always been able to maintain a vigorous interest in the philosophy of law. This is shown not only in its books but also in its legal periodicals. Has the case system of instruction been making any progress recently in Scotland? They used to drill them pretty thoroughly on text-books in the old days at Edinburgh.

Yours very truly,

MORRIS R. COHEN

March 20, 1912.

Dear Mr. Cohen:—

I can not think that the Case system of instruction has anything to do with the status of philosophy of law in Anglo-American countries. Certainly things are quite as bad in England where they use text books as in this country where we use Case books.

The situation in Scotland is due to two things:—first, the general Scotch taste for philosophy, and second, the circumstance that Scotland received the Roman law in the 17th century and consequently Scotch institutional books were filled with the ideas of the philosophical school upon the continent.

Scotch law for a long time has been Roman only in terminology. Moreover, I submit that there is quite as much philosophy of law to be found in Mr. Justice Holmes' opinions as in text books, and it is usually infinitely sounder. Please look at Robinson's "Elements of American Jurisprudence," Andrew's "American Law," Smith's "Elementary Law," et id genus omne, and ask yourself whether philosophical instruction with respect to law from these books could possibly be profitable. Undoubtedly our Anglo-American judicial empiricism has neglected matters which the social-philosophical school is now compelling jurists to consider. In this respect, however, I am bound to say that many of our teachers who employ the method of instruction by cases are doing much more for the law than any text writers of whom I know.

Very truly yours,

ROSCOE POUND

11 March 1914.

Dear Cohen:

Don't you think that one who endeavors to be scientific may be orthodox once in a while? Really, insurgency ought not to be practised for its own sake and after all many of the orthodox ideas in jurisprudence represent a deal of experience which, off-hand, insurgents are sometimes likely to throw over on quite insufficient *a priori* grounds.

Seriously, I think you will find there is no conflict between the paper on common law and legislation and my remarks as to legislative justice. Judicial handling of the materials provided by legislative law making is one thing and the relative advantages of judicial and legislative handling of concrete causes is quite another. I have found nothing in the history of legislative justice to indicate that it can be made to administer justice according to law. Possibly a very enlightened legislative body might do so but the chances of liberalizing judicial administration of justice seem to me much greater than those of introducing a proper stability and uniformity into legislative justice.

After all, judicial justice is not justice of the cloister. If you know many judges, you will soon perceive that on the whole they see more and know more of life than almost any other class of men. The jurist, rather than the judge, is the man of the cloister. You must be careful not to let your reading of Continental literature on this subject mislead you. The Anglo-American judge is a very different person from the Continental magistrate. In continental Europe the judicial magistrate is a mere cog in the vast administrative machine. He becomes involved in an amount of red tape on one side of his activities which is quite as bad as the procedural red tape in which our judges have been involved on another side. Most of the talk about bringing the administration of justice into accord with life which you find in the Continental books refers to a situation which you will hardly find in our nisi prius courts at all. It is not merely that the jury correct this in courts of law, in courts of equity it is corrected by the viva voce trial and the oral examination and cross-examination of witnesses. The Continental system of deciding by proofs rather than upon trial in civil cases is largely responsible for the condition of which Continental writers complain.

As to caveat emptor, my notion is that that represents the stage of the strict law. The strict law does not know of anything in the nature of an implied warranty and conceives that every man must look out for himself and protect himself by express provisions in the contract. The notion of duties of good faith and of warranties involved in a transaction, or as we should say, implied therein, comes in the stage of equity or natural law. Caveat emptor in our law of sales has really been nothing but a memory for a long time. I do not think that any important change has gone on in our law of sales of chattels in this respect except that some of our American courts were apt to ignore the equitable side of things and try to deal with them very much in the spirit of the strict law. This was mostly due to the mental limitations of mediocre judges elected for short terms in our state courts. If you will read, for instance, Williston, On Sales, on the subject of implied warranties in the sale of chattels, I think you will come to this conclusion.

Very truly yours,

ROSCOE POUND

16 March 1914.

Dear Cohen:

I dislike very much to undertake a paper for the conference as my hands are more than full. I have an address before the bar association at Cleveland on the fourth of April, I have another address in May and still a third in June and there are limitations to one's productivity. What I should like to do if I had the time would be to go into the general subject of rule and discretion in the administration of justice pretty thoroughly. Possibly I could outline my views for the conference but it would hardly be possible to do more than that. Would you be satisfied with such an outline taking, say, twenty minutes for delivery? [Pound read his "Rule and Discretion in the Administration of Justice" in April 1914 for the Chicago meeting of the Conference on Legal and Social Philosophy held in conjunction with the Western Philosophical Association.]

I agree with you that the New York Court of Appeals is still pretty backward. But courts the country over have been changing very fast, sometimes I fear somewhat too fast. We must be careful in our eagerness to liberalize the law not to destroy other features of the legal system which are no less important. One reason why legislatures have appeared more liberal than courts has been that they have felt they could shirk responsibility by enacting statutes in the full confidence that courts would pronounce them invalid. I am pretty confident that a great deal of social legislation would never have gone through legislatures if those who voted for it had believed that legislative enactment would be final. Nevertheless I regard legislation as a very important agency in the effort to improve the law and want very much to see our courts adopt a proper attitude toward it. It is quite another thing, however, to turn the application of the law over to non-judicial bodies. I do not believe we could make a greater mistake. In impatience at the strict law the seventeenth century turned to arbitrary power. In the same way we are turning for a season to arbitrary power and arbitrary power is quite as likely to be used by bad men for bad purposes as by good men for good purposes. Experience with the initiative and referendum and recall in some of our western states, which are finding to their surprise that the professional politician can use these weapons quite as effectively as the reformers, indicates what is likely to happen with our boards and special commissions as politicians learn to use them. I think we ought to be careful not to be like the end in the football game who loses sight of the ball in his mad endeavor to tackle somebody. I have long found myself in the peculiar position of being branded a dangerous radical by one party and a reactionary by the other. This does not disturb me very much because I have long felt that most of our progressive friends were anything but scientific. The heart rather than the head governs a great deal which they do.

Very truly yours,
ROSCOE POUND

4th April 1916.

Dear Cohen:

I agree that the work suggested in your second proposition would be very profitable if well carried out. But why must people be subsidized to do things like this which ought to be done for their own sake? Perhaps this is an irrelevant question in the present connection, where the whole point is that something is to be subsidized, and the question is what shall it be. It would be quite possible with the material we have in our library here for such an ethical survey as you propose to be carried out very thoroughly provided the right man did it. Every man, however, cannot handle statutes intelligently. It is quite futile generally for a man without some legal training to expect to understand what he is using. I do not know any student here at the moment who has the requisite combination of ethical and legal training. If you have anybody in mind I should think the money would be indeed well spent in putting him upon such work.

What I have feared about Mr. De Coppet's plan was that his money would be frittered away in a half a dozen different lines of research leading nowhere in particular. If we are in the nature of Trustees are we not bound to see that his benefaction is so administered as to make the most out of it that is possible, and can the most be made out of it unless we limit ourselves to taking up two or three things that we can make effective and doing them as thoroughly as possible? Very likely you have hit upon one of those two or three things. I confess nothing so good has occurred to me.

As to the matter of statistics there is very little in the way of legal statistics available that has much of any value. The German judicial statistics are very good. The English judicial statistics are also good though for quite different purposes. In this country, outside of the publications of some of our municipal courts, judicial statistics are quite barren of value. I have kept track of this matter for years and have on hand myself about all the material that seemed worth while. I doubt if students of moral science as yet can make much out of it.

Yours very truly,

ROSCOE POUND

In other words I think your second proposition a very good one. It promises a great deal, if well executed. Cf. the Vergleichende Darstellung which the Germans got out as the basis of a new penal code.

30th December 1918.

Dear Cohen:

I had not seen your paper on Mechanism and Causality in Physics and shall be glad to have the reprint. I have just finished reading the Parmenides in the original and must confess it has changed my views about Plato considerably. I think the difficulty was that I started out reading the Phaedo in college and then read in college the Protagoras and the Gorgias and then afterwards read every dialogue through the colored spectacles acquired in college. My last re-reading of the Parmenides has shaken my notions completely. I now seem to see that Plato was not at all a dogmatic teacher but more than anything else was an inquirer who wanted us above all things to understand both sides and all the possible objections and then was willing to concede to us the liberty of forming tentative opinions as to the best solutions at which we could arrive. If this is not what the Parmenides really means I do not know what it does mean. After reading Burnett, and Benn and Grote on the subject, on top of the original I am not disposed to alter this view. I am going to read the Republic over again this winter—but that is a long job.

With cordial regards

Yours very truly,

ROSCOE POUND

24th January 1921.

Dear Cohen:

I ought to have acknowledged your cordial note long ago. But you know something of the condition of things in this office, and it has been worse than ever this year. I have barely been able to keep up with the daily grist of letters calling for immediate business attention.

I am learning a good deal from the seminar in the Philosophy department, the opening of which you attended, and indeed wish that you could be present and take part. Few of those who attend have any real knowledge of the legal problems which are brought up and unless a number of men who have both a legal and philosophical equipment take part in such an exercise a good deal of the benefit that might be derived is missed.

With cordial regards

Yours very truly,
ROSCOE POUND

9th February 1923

Dear Cohen:

Many thanks for sending me the proof of your review. I should have sent this back to you long before but I loaned it to one of my colleagues who has only just returned it. I should, however, have had no time to look at it until this morning in any case.

I think one who puts his notions in print ought to be judged by what he prints and not by what he may hold as the views behind the print. Hence I am quite content to abide your judgment of what is in print. . . . On one or two points, however, I think some suggestions might be made. In note 1 on the first galley you speak of the age of Coke as the age of Marlowe, Shakspeare and Ben Jonson; but the age of Coke in legal history is the age of the Long Parliament. Coke's great legal influence was established as Chief Justice under James and in opposition in Parliament under Charles. The book of all books which has influenced American law was Coke's Second Institute published by order of the Long Parliament as part of the struggle between Parliament and the Stuarts. The book became, therefore, an orthodox legal oracle of the Puritans. In other words, the age of Coke legally is a generation later than the one of which you speak.

Also in the matter of the economic interpretation, it is not merely Brooks Adams that I have in mind, but a series of authors of whom he is perhaps only the most vigorous. The economic interpretation had a great run in legal literature in this country during the era of Rooseveltian progressivism. Just as we must distinguish between history and the historical school, I think we must distinguish between a proper use of economics and the so-called economic interpretation. I remember somewhere Macaulay in speaking of a book written by Dean Sherlock in the theological controversies of the seventeenth century says that in his zeal against the Socinian heresy he seemed to get over on to the other side of the road into the Arrian heresy. Very likely I may have done the same thing. It is hard to steer between heresies, and in hitting at one, one might very likely step back across the line into the other.

Very likely in the same way I may have made myself to appear Hegelian in my protest against ignoring the factor of legal ideas in actually shaping our legal materials. Kohler seems to me to be a man who with a Hegelian apparatus is in general anything but Hegelian in his actual treatment of legal problems. He knows more law than all the other writers on the subject combined—with a liberal margin over. Consequently he is immensely useful when one has a real legal problem before him.

I might say also that in my lectures at Cambridge just published by the Cambridge University Press, I took up under the head "The Great-Lawyer Interpretation" the influence of masterful personalities in legal development.

I would say to you, do not change anything but receive my suggestions for your private eye. Perhaps, however, I might urge on you to consider whether what you say about Kohler and Berolzheimer at the end of the paragraph at the top of galley 34 is really in good taste. I can duplicate these foolish remarks from every English and French jurist who wrote during and just before the war. Throwing such things about seems to me to belong to an era through which I hope we have passed. Everybody has been saying foolish things, and the fact that he has said them does not detract in the least from the valuable work that he may have done. I do not think I could demolish Inge's book on Plotinus by quoting the ridiculous things that he says there about Hegel. Neither do I think that one demolishes Kohler or Berolzheimer by pointing out that either of them may have indulged in remarks of this sort outside of the immediate scope of their work. What I object to about this sort of thing is that the average reader says: Berolzheimer said so and so, Pound quotes Berolzheimer, ergo. While you are above this your readers are not, and I suspect a good many of your friends will take it that you are making exactly that sort of argument.

Yours very truly,
ROSCOE POUND

15th December 1924

Dear Cohen:

I do not know anything about Petrashitzky. What I do know is at second hand purely. The impression which I had received was that he was a notable person.

As to German and Austrian scholars who might be invited to the Congress, I suppose it would be important to have different types of thinkers represented. From that standpoint one would think at once

of Radbruch, either Wenger or Klein, and Cathrein. I suppose Stammler is too old to come over here. If he could be induced to come I
should prefer him to all the rest put together.

As to Vienna, I do not know much about any one but Kelsen, and
I suppose he would not exactly be rated as a philosopher.

If you put the matter to me simply for my judgment from the
standpoint of fruitful contributions for *juristic* purposes, I should be
inclined to say Stammler, Kantorowicz and Kelsen. That would give
you three important philosophical juristic points of view. But perhaps
the juristic tail would be wagging the philosophical dog.

With best regards

Yours very truly,
ROSCOE POUND

25th August 1931

Dear Cohen:

I have just been reading "Reason and Nature." I had already read
some parts of it in different periodicals with great interest and profit.
But the book as a whole fills me with rejoicing. It is indeed a remarkable contribution, and I am sure will have a permanent place in
the literature of philosophy. It is tonic to find a thinker preserving
his balance during a riot of unbalance. But what is more to the point,
your theory of polarity seems to me exactly what we have been needing in social and legal philosophy. I rejoice to have the matter so well
presented in a form in which I can think about it and apply it, and to
which also I may refer students.

With best regards

Yours very truly,
ROSCOE POUND

1st May 1933

Dear Cohen:

I am indeed most obliged by your sending me your book "Law
and the Social Order." I read the articles reprinted therein as they
came out, but I am sure it will do me good to read them again, and
I am rejoiced to have them in this permanent form.

Things have moved swiftly in Jurisprudence in the present century,
and those of us who wrote much in the era of emancipation may perhaps some day be thankful for the statute of limitations. But I remember your papers read in the days of our conferences on legal and

social philosophy as things of permanent value which the feverish movements of today cannot replace.

Yours very truly,
ROSCOE POUND

July 9, 1938

Dear Pound:

Permit me to call your attention to two points in the report of the Committee on Administrative Law of the American Bar Association.

1. The first point, a minor one but still of some significance, is the omission of initials in the footnote reference to Dr. F. S. Cohen's article on Transcendental Nonsense, etc. There are a number of Cohens today writing on legal topics, and it would prevent misunderstanding if you indicated the initials. I should not myself, for instance, want to be given credit (positive or negative) for my son's brilliant writings. While I naturally admire them immensely I am certainly not always in agreement.

2. More serious is the characterization "Marxian" applied to the view that administrative law is what administrative officials do. There is nothing particularly Marxian about that view. It is simply the "realistic" position held by all the so-called realists in this country, who generally, like Llewellyn, draw their inspiration from Ehrlich rather than Marx. Nor does the fact—if it is a fact—that a certain view is held in Russia prove that it is Marxian. Many things in Russia are very far from being Marxian.

I must confess that in insisting on the latter point I am not only interested in accuracy for its own sake but also because I feel that for many members of the American Bar Association the characterization of any view as Marxian is itself a judgment of condemnation, and that, I am sure you will agree, is unfortunate. No intellectual gain is achieved by using vague labels like Marxian in connections of this sort, and I trust you will see your way to correct the misimpression.

With kind regards,

Sincerely yours,
MORRIS R. COHEN

15th September 1938

Dear Cohen:

Your letter of July 9 came while I was in South America.

As to the reference to Felix Cohen's article, I can quite see your point. Lawyers are in the habit of making citations so as to identify the article rather than with reference to identification of the author. In other words, the idea is to enable the reader to find the article cited. I suppose the Committee used the legal form as a matter of course without thinking that laymen would make such a mistake as you suggest.

As to the other point, I confess it did not occur to me that the characterization of any view today as Marxian necessarily involved condemnation. With all respect to your suggestion, I cannot recede from the proposition that the idea of law as something required by a division of society into classes and the institution of property, which will disappear with the abolition of property and disappearance of a class organization of society, and its corollary of administrative absolutism as to matters not involving proprietary relations, is Marxian. I have read Marx, Engels and their orthodox interpreters on this point thoroughly and repeatedly. I am aware that in Russia recently the exigencies of the dominant regime have led to a partial repudiation of this, and a new orthodox interpretation of Marx's views. But I see no reason for accepting this as something binding upon the rest of the world.

May I suggest to you that the unwillingness of American so-called legal realists to admit the Marxian pedigree of many of their ideas is no valid reason why those of us who are not willing to go to the radical extremes to which many of them go should ignore the plain facts.

Yours very truly,
ROSCOE POUND

September 20, 1938

Dear Pound:

I have your letter of September 15 and am glad to note that you are back in Cambridge, after visiting foreign lands. I hope I shall have a chance to see you when I get to Cambridge.

As to the connection between legal realism and Marxism, the position of your committee seems to me quite untenable. Legal realism descends from Hobbes and earlier still from Bodin, not to go back to what you yourself have called "Byzantism." To call it Marxism seems to me to confuse matters. And I think it is very unfortunate because Marxism and Russia are used by a great many members of the legal profession as condemnatory labels. As you know, I am willing to break a lance with the legal realists on any proper occasion, but I think it quite unfair to try to create any prejudice against them by associating them with Russia and Marx. I am sure that Messrs. Frank, Llewellyn and Moore can in no way be charged with being Marxists.

With kind regards,

Cordially yours,
MORRIS R. COHEN

22nd September 1938

Dear Cohen:

I know it is quite unprofitable to engage in epistolary argument, but I still think you miss the point. The line of realism (if you like to call it that) which comes from the law books of the late Empire through Bodin and Hobbes thinks of laws as commands of a sovereign lawmaker. That seems to me quite a different thing from the idea of particular orders in particular cases not in accordance with rule or precept, but as a product of the individual action of an individual official at the moment and under what he chooses to consider as the circumstances of the moment. You will recollect that there was a serious discussion in the Roman law books as to whether the princeps was legibus solutus. If he acted as magistrate he was expected to act according to law and his decisions were supposed to be interpretations of the law. That is a very different doctrine from the doctrine that what is done officially is law because it is done officially, and that whatever is done in the adjustment of relations or disputes is law. That doctrine I still think is immediately connected with the notion of disappearance of law (in the sense of a body of authoritative precepts) with the abolition of property and of the classes which are taken to result from the institution of property. What the committee is talking about is administrative absolutism and the juristic theories upon which it rests.

I do not find anything in Bingham's writings to indicate that he is a believer in administrative absolutism. As to Moore, he has not written on the subject. As to Frank and Llewellyn, you can prove almost anything out of their writings, but Frank seems to me to stand definitely for administrative absolutism both in the judicial and in the administrative process as the only thing which is psychologically possible. Nevertheless, passages can be found in his book which indicate an assumption that a settled course of judicial decision can be called law.

I doubt if any one who has not given a great deal of attention to the decisions of courts upon administrative rules throughout the English-speaking world, and to the action of current administrative bodies in the last ten years has any conception of the extent to which administrative absolutism has gone not merely in this country but in England and Australia.

Yours very truly,
ROSCOE POUND

Sept. 25, 1938

Dear Pound:

You are perfectly right about the unprofitable character of epistolatory argument. I cannot for the life of me see that administrative absolutism or legal realism is in any way identical with Marxism or Russian in origin.

Faithfully yours
MORRIS R. COHEN

Varia

November 7, 1941

Professor Hessel E. Yntema
Michigan Law School
Ann Arbor, Michigan

Dear Yntema:

Let me, in the first place, thank you for your kindness in sending me a copy of the May number of the Michigan Law Review containing your article "Jurisprudence on Parade." There is one point in it with which I heartily agree. It is the distinction (pp. 1164–1165) between jurisprudence which is concerned with the normal, necessary attitude of the judge and practitioner and of those who train lawyers and jurisprudence as an anthropologic examination of the behavior of lawyers and judges. This is precisely what I have always insisted upon against Underhill Moore and other realists who (despite your disavowal) have persistently denied that the former can be (and should be) carried on scientifically. In none of my writings have I ever opposed a scientific anthropology of law, but I do think it should be left to competent anthropologists. Law teachers are not generally trained in sound anthropologic methods of investigation and one cannot become a scientist merely by announcing that fact.

Your references to me in this as in previous articles of yours impress me as remarkable feats of misunderstanding, but I enjoy fiction even about myself.

Kind remembrances,

Sincerely yours,
MORRIS R. COHEN

P.S. Should you care to modify your opinion of what I stand for, you might read my review of Fuller's book in the June number of the Illinois Law Review. You might see there how mistaken you are in putting me in the same category with Fuller.

Behavioristic passages in the writings of Underhill Moore, Oliphant, and some of your own earlier tilts against the *ought* element in the law is surely the essence of positivism, in the usual meaning of that word. The perversity is not on my side.

TO Julius Hochfelder,
Patent Lawyer,
Glendale, California

January 24, 1942

Dear Major Hochfelder:

Like yourself I have been impressed with the absurd lack of intelligence on the part of our municipal, state and federal legislators, but for many weighty reasons I cannot agree that your proposed remedy would be an improvement.

(1) In the first place my acquaintance with academic people does not lead me to expect much more intelligence from those who have an academic degree than from those without it. Even professors of the social "sciences" do not as a body show more general intelligence about public affairs than the average. At any rate, they differ about proposed legislation as much as the rest of the population or the members of their income-group.

(2) No matter how educated a legislator may be, he will be ignorant about most of the issues that come up. The proper remedy, therefore, is to provide legislators with all possible facilities for acquiring the relevant knowledge about the special issues that come up. Our provisions for public hearings and for legislative reference bureaus are better calculated to bring about intelligent legislation than any of the provisions you propose for the qualification of legislators.

(3) Everyone of the qualifications you propose is subject to grave abuses:

(a) Academic degrees from many of our colleges represent merely several years leisure and ability to pay tuition and maintenance expense.

(b) Who is to test the knowledge of the various subjects you propose?

(c) Who is to test the candidate's "excellent character, integrity and loyalty?" And his devotion to the democratic form of government? The terms will, if we judge from recent experience, be certainly used to disqualify representatives of all sorts of progressive groups.

(d) No salary is high enough to guard anyone against temptation if he is the kind of man that can be tempted. Some
of our bank presidents receiving very high salaries have
not been able to resist such temptations. Most of the
trouble is with the bribe *givers*.

(4) Any restriction on the choice of legislators or representatives
is essentially anti-democratic and has been used for anti-democratic
purposes. A democratic legislature should be a fair cross-section of
the people whom it represents. History shows that intellectual aristoc-
racies such as the scholars of Imperial China or the bureaucracy of
old Germany (most of whom had Ph.D.'s or J.D.) produced highly
undesirable results compared with unrestricted popular elections—
just as the jury system is better than judgment by trained judges alone.
If you study the administration of New York State, you will find
that highly educated governors such as Charles Evans Hughes and
F. D. Roosevelt did not do as well as the uneducated Alfred E. Smith
or the Republican politician B. Odell. I am not suggesting that college
education is always a disadvantage, but rather that we should be
somewhat sceptical as to its universal adequacy. The fact is that our
educators are far from omniscient and there is very little science or
demonstrable knowledge about human affairs. Between two men of
equally good native judgment, the better educated man is, of course,
preferable. But the electorate should have the final say as to who has
the better judgment.

I am convinced that your proposal would, if adopted, do more
harm than good.

Sincerely yours,
MORRIS R. COHEN

XVI. *The Holmes-Cohen Correspondence*

THE VOLUME *Morris Raphael Cohen, Teacher and Philosopher,* contains this message:

> Nothing could give me more pleasure than to join as I do in this expression of honor to Professor Cohen. I have read his writings with admiration and great profit. I have enjoyed his conversation with equal profit, affection and reverence. I am proud that he calls me friend. I envy the youth who sit at his feet.
>
> Very truly yours,
> O. W. HOLMES.

To his last days Morris R. Cohen kept on his bedroom wall the treasured picture of Justice Oliver Wendell Holmes. The story of their friendship is told best in their long and warm correspondence.[1]

The College of the City of New York
Department of Philosophy
St. Nicholas Terrace and 139th Street

April 10, 1915

My dear Justice Holmes:

Mr. Frankfurter has forwarded to me your kind letter with reference to my paper on *History vs. Value.** It is, of course, always gratifying to have one's intellectual output appreciated; but in this case, I assure

* Published in *Journal of Philosophy,* Vol. 11 (Dec. 17, 1914), p. 701. This was originally delivered as an address before the American Philosophical Association in December 1913. It was subsequently published as a chapter of *Reason and Nature,* 1931.

you, it is unusually gratifying, since it makes me feel that I have been able in some slight measure to repay for the great pleasure I have derived from reading your *Common Law,* your articles in the Harvard Law Review, and your published decisions or dissents. Not being a lawyer, the latter do not lose their value to me by the accidental fact that the majority of the court do not always see the truth as you do.

I have taken the liberty of sending you some more of my fugitive papers, as a token of my indebtedness for intellectual stimulus derived from your writings. Needless to add, this does not involve any obligation on your part to read any of these papers which are for the most part of purely technical interest.

Respectfully yours,

MORRIS R. COHEN

April 12, 1915

My dear Mr. Cohen:

Your letter and the accompanying articles gave me much pleasure —although of course as yet I have only noted their subjects. I have just sent to Wigmore at his request a few lines*—a page or two—or three—written currente calamo—repeating some of my chestnuts that I have not printed before—apropos of the theme of Ideals—suggested by your article and Del Vecchio's book† (—I merely refer to your article as an excellent one—) I adverted some years ago in noticing Holdsworth's History** to how little as yet with their preoccupation with the embryology of legal ideas, people had had to say concerning the worth of those ideas.

I am glad that a philosopher is interested in the law—I hardly should be interested in it—if it did not open a wide door to philosophizing—and enable me to illustrate another of my chestnuts that the chief end of man is to frame general ideas—and that no general idea is worth a straw—

If you come to Washington I hope I shall see you.

Very sincerely yours,

O. W. HOLMES

* "Ideals and Doubts," *Illinois Law Review,* Vol. 10 (May 1915), p. 1, reprinted in *Collected Legal Papers,* 1920, p. 303.

† Del Vecchio, *Formal Bases of Law,* 1914, Modern Legal Philosophy Series, Vol. 10.

** Holmes reviewed Holdsworth's *History of English Law,* 1909, in *Law Quarterly Review,* 1909, p. 412, reprinted in *Collected Legal Papers,* p. 285.

Supreme Court of the United States
Washington, D.C.

May 15, 1915

My dear Professor Cohen:

Here are a few chestnuts that I was stimulated to scribble off and print, by the joint effect of a request from my friend Wigmore and reading your article. I say chestnuts, because they mostly are old formulas of mine, but I hope they may be less so to others. At all events they will be evidence of my regard for your writing and you.

Very sincerely yours,

O. W. HOLMES

No need to say anything.

March 9, 1916

Dear Professor Cohen:

Your kind letter gives me great pleasure and I thank you for it. I have a constant reminder of you in a volume of your essays that I have had bound and that bears your name upon the back. But I am grateful for this one of later date, and really pleased to think that you still remember me.

Sincerely yours,

O. W. HOLMES

Nov. 17, 1916

Dear Mr. Cohen:

You will be welcome whenever you come* and I hope it may be at a moment when I am not too driven by work to get all the pleasure and profit I should expect from meeting you. I thank you for the articles which delighted me. I do not always have time to read the New Republic but whatever bears your signature I read unless it escapes my eye. I am conscious of so much agreement that I rise in my own opinion as I read.

Sincerely yours,

O. W. HOLMES

May 27, 1917

Dear Mr. Cohen:

Would that you might embody any of your opinions in a booklet or a folio if you prefer. I am sure we should be the wiser for them. My

---

* Letter missing from Cohen to Holmes between March 9, 1916, and November 17, 1916. Where letters later are referred to but omitted, they, too, are missing.

pleasure in meeting you was as great as yours could have been and I only regretted that the time was so short. I think we are at one in not believing that man can swallow the universe.* I at least go on very comfortably without the belief that I am in on the ground floor with God or that the cosmos, whether it wears a beard or not, needs me in order to know itself. I suppose it needs me as it needs any grain of sand, because I am here. And the whole, if there is a whole, would be I know not how much other, if an atom were subtracted from it, but I do not believe that a shudder would go through the sky if our whole ant heap were kerosened. But then it might—in short my only belief is that I know nothing about it. Truth may be cosmically ultimate for all I know. I merely surmise that our last word probably is not *the* last word, any more than that of horses or dogs. It is our last word nonetheless. And I don't see why we shouldn't do our job in the station in which we were born without waiting for an angel to assure us that it is the jobbest job in jobdom. But we are all like the old Knights who wouldn't be satisfied with your admission that their girl was a very nice girl, but would knock your head off if you didn't admit that she was the best ever—bar the Virgin Mary, perhaps.

I must shut up as I have other things to do but this will assure you of my great satisfaction at having met you and my hope that it was not the last time.

Sincerely yours,
O. W. HOLMES

Littleton, N.H.
Sept. 5, 1917

My dear Mrs. Holmes:

Permit me to express to you again my delight at finding that you are a granddaughter of the Nathaniel Bowditch to whom I am so greatly indebted personally. To the exoteric public, mathematics is a cold dehumanized game with symbols, but to the initiated it is a celestial music that ennobles and makes worth while the pains of existence. LaPlace's Mécanique Celeste is one of those noble celestial symphonies that is made audible to lesser mathematical spirits like myself by your grandfather's great commentary. Many otherwise weary hours have been brightened for me by the lone volume of the Mécanique Celeste which my College possesses. I dare not say this to the Judge—he looks so sternly at me whenever I speak of mathe-

---

* *Cf.* Holmes, "Natural Law," *Harvard Law Review,* Vol. 32 (1918), pp. 32, 40, 43, reprinted in *Collected Legal Papers,* pp. 310, 315.

matics that I'm afraid he will call me sentimental as well as good. But you as the granddaughter of a great mathematician will understand.

Permit me to add that among the many delights of my visit to Beverly Farm that of seeing your beautiful plants and flowers was not lost.

With kind regards,

MORRIS R. COHEN

Jan. 5, 1918

Dear Mr. Cohen:

Except in the news of trouble in your family your letter gives me great pleasure, as has everything that I have seen of or heard from you. If I had not been breathlessly busy I should have written to you to express my delight at your recent article in the N.R.* pointing out that the assumption of quantitatively fixed relatives as uniform in similar sequences was itself more or less of a fiction—(I hope I don't make you shudder at this attempt to recall your theme by an act of distracted memory and to put it in a phrase—as other people always do, when they purport to repeat what one has said.) Still as a bettabilitarian I should lean to that as against any single system of the interstitial miraculous based on your doubt. I should like to sit and talk with you—but pressed as I am I can do no more than thank you for your letter and reciprocate every good wish.

Sincerely yours,

O. W. HOLMES

Beverly Farms

Aug. 31, 1918

My dear Cohen:

Frankfurter read to my wife and me just now your article Rewards, Penalties and Plato,† and I just write a line to say with what delight we listened. It is "Acme—A.1." in my humble judgment—uniting learning wit profundity and deuced good writing. Accept my envying felicitations.

Ever sincerely yours,

O. W. HOLMES

* The reference seems to be a review of Emile Boutroux, *The Contingency of the Laws of Nature*, in *The New Republic*, Vol. 13 (Dec. 15, 1917), p. 191, reprinted in *The Faith of a Liberal*, p. 430.

† A review of Paul Elmer More, *Platonism*, in *The New Republic*, Vol. 17 (Aug. 31, 1918), p. 130, reprinted in *The Faith of a Liberal*, p. 72.

Sept. 3, 1918

Dear Mr. Cohen:

Your letter has just been received. I should be delighted to see you and can put you up if you can stop over night as I hope. Evidently you haven't received my second letter expressing my delight at your piece in the New Republic about Plato and a book—as I am having a button sewed on—I was about to say I couldn't stop to get the title but it is done. Still however I remember that I can't, because my N.R. hasn't come. The privileged Frankfurter read it to me. It was ripping. I have been moved by a book on Natural Law (which I don't think much of) to write a few words for the Harvard Law Rev. i.e. Laski* impounded them to that end. I say nothing that I haven't said a thousand times in conversation but one rather likes to see one's fundamentals in print. So I wound up with a nice twist at the tail of the cosmos—agreeing with the Natural Lawyers that we have to come back to them. I should like to read it to you—it is short. Our feeding hours are 1 p.m. and 7 p.m. (breakfast 8:30 or later).

In hopes of seeing you,

Ever sincerely yours,
O. W. HOLMES

Sept. 10, 1918

Dear Mr. Cohen:

If you come not much later than the 22d we can put you up and shall be glad to see you. On the 28th we leave and in view of the nearness of time I consulted my wife to know whether it would be all right. She says yes. So I still shall hope to see you. Please let me know the exact time. If there is no change the trains leave Boston at 10^{45} a.m. (in time for the midday meal at 1), 2^{20}, 3^{15}, 4^{27} (qu. 4^{25}?) a good train—5^{02} etc. Other trains in addition Saturday. So if I know the date and train I will tell the stable man to meet you. I have just been reading Bertrand Russell's Mysticism and Logic with much less liking for A Free Man's Worship than, I gather from Laski, you feel. It seems to me no better than shaking your fist at the sky. It presupposes a ποὺ στῶ outside the universe. Also I inferred from our former talk and your writing that you would agree with him in thinking reason paramount to the universe. Whereas I don't see that it stands any differently from my preference of champagne to ditch water. It is one of my Can't Helps, and no doubt is paramount in my universe, but as a bettabilitarian, I bet there is (with apologies to the unknown for even that predicate) a universe of which mine is only a very inadequate aspect, from which my Can't Helps come and that

* Laski was Book Review Editor of the *Harvard Law Review* during the academic year 1917–18.

may or may not be superior to them. I admit that it is among the non apparentibus as to which speculation is useless but we all like to try a twist at the tail of the cosmos (as I believe I said before). If you come you shall expound and I will listen. I venture another remark on B. R.—Mathematics is a tool with which to work on given premises. The premises are a matter of insight—not of mathematics —and I have thought that some mathematicians were not so strong on them as they were in handling their tool. But I wish I knew their beastly language, as I feel very helpless when they sail off on the aeroplane of their calculus. But in general it requires a tough fibre not to repine at spending one's energies on the transitory law when you fellows are shaping the (relatively) eternal. But the transitory also shapes the eternal as Mons. Jourdain talked prose, without knowing it.

Sincerely yours,

O. W. HOLMES

Sept. 28, 1918

Dear Mr. Cohen:

It was a disappointment not to see you and a pleasure to read your article.* I have felt but never so articulately expressed to myself the confusion between logical relations and the psychological process of discovering them. As to certainty, by a coincidence, in the article I handed to Laski the other day, I said certitude is not a test of certainty†—explaining by adding that we all have been cocksure of things that were not so. This week ends my vacation and, I fear, my chance for philosophical reading. I have bored myself by trying to improve my mind and have been repaid by reflections when the dull books were read. I shrink somewhat from novels, which I used to devour, partly perhaps because time grows more precious. Is it a parodox to call it precious when the damned worm is gnawing away while one sleeps to consume one's vitals?

Well, I trust that I shall survive to have another good talk with you, and hope that every day will see an improvement in your health.

Sincerely yours,

O. W. HOLMES

I turned two pages
instead of one but
don't stop to copy.

* "The Subject Matter of Formal Logic," *Journal of Philosophy,* Vol. 15 (Dec. 5, 1918), p. 673, originally delivered as an address before the American Philosophical Association in December 1917 and appearing subsequently as the first chapter of *Preface to Logic,* 1944.

† "Natural Law," *op. cit., Collected Legal Papers,* p. 311.

21 Coburn St.,
Yonkers N.Y.
Dec. 9, 1918

Dear Justice Holmes:

I received your note and the extract from the Harvard Law Review on Natural Law which I read with profound admiration and delight. All of the things you say I agree to, though I could never say them as well; and if I find certain logical qualifications necessary, to put a beard on your doctrine (to use your own words), that only means that you and I have somewhat different styles of fighting for the same good cause. I hope you are not averse to my regarding myself as a companion in arms.

I am hoping to be able to come to Washington the New Year's week, and I hope to have a chance to make up for the conversation I lost last September.

With kind remembrance to Mrs. Holmes,

Sincerely yours,

MORRIS R. COHEN

Supreme Court of the United States
Washington, D.C.

Feb. 3, 1919

Dear Mr. Cohen:

The Subject Matter of Formal Logic is received and has been read with the usual pleasure I have in reading what you write. It found me ready to accept your view, which, indeed, I don't see how anyone can quarrel with. And it makes me feel like a worm because of my ignorance of mathematics. How I wish I knew what the non-Euclidean geometry is! I don't understand the sentence p. 677 "2+2+4 is impossible therefore" etc.* If you know some golden book, not too long, philosophic, sociologic or otherwise calculated to expand the judicial mind sit down at once and name it and stick it in an envelope directed to me—for I have the promise of a little leisure beginning today and I want to make the most of it. Alas! I am, what I think ominous for significance, I am industrious—I have bought a little etching by Ostade that I think fit to make one cry.

Yours ever,

O. W. HOLMES

---

* As it originally appeared, the passage ran: "2 + 2 $\neq$ 4 is impossible, in any universe, in which 2, 4, and $\neq$ have the meanings assigned in our arithmetic." Justice Holmes apparently misread the inequality sign, $\neq$.

Feb. 5, 1919

Dear Mr. Cohen:

Oh no—it was not Voltaire*—it was the influence of the scientific way of looking at the world—that made the change to which I referred. My father was brought up scientifically—i.e. he studied medicine in France—and I was not. Yet there was with him as with the rest of his generation a certain softness of attitude toward the interstitial miracle—the phenomenon without phenomenal antecedents, that I did not feel. The difference was in the air, although perhaps only the few of my time felt it. The Origin of Species I think came out while I was in college—† H. Spencer had announced his intention to put the universe into our pockets—I hadn't read either of them to be sure, but as I say it was in the air. I did read Buckle—now almost forgotten —but making a noise in his day, but I could refer to no book as the specific cause—I never have read much of Voltaire and probably at that time had read nothing. Emerson and Ruskin were the men that set me on fire. Probably a sceptical temperament that I got from my mother had something to do with my way of thinking. Then I was in with the abolitionists, some or many of whom were sceptics as well as dogmatists. But I think science was at the bottom. Of course my father was by no means orthodox, but like other even lax Unitarians there were questions that he didn't like to have asked—and he always spoke of keeping his mind open on matters like spiritualism or whether Bacon wrote Shakespeare—so that when I wanted to be disagreeable I told him that he straddled, in order to be able to say, whatever might be accepted, well I always have recognized etc., which was not just on my part.

I wrote to you yesterday, before the arrival of your letter—I had perceived this similarity of your article to what I read last summer but could not remember accurately and so said nothing about it. The second reading gave me the pleasure I expected—and it would be nonetheless if it was true as it is not that the article is of no use. The useless is the ideal expression of man. Doing a stunt in vacuo—like going to the North Pole is the final expression of man's contribution

* Holmes had remarked that of all the intellectual gaps between generations the gap between his own and his father's appeared to him the widest. In a missing letter received by Holmes on February 4 or 5 Cohen had asked whether this intellectual shift might be ascribed to Voltaire.

† Holmes was at Harvard College from the fall of 1857 to April 1861. *The Origin of Species* was published in 1859. Herbert Spencer published his *Social Statics* in 1850 and *Synthetic Philosophy* in 1860. In 1905 Justice Holmes made his famous comment: "The Fourteenth Amendment does not enact Mr. Herbert Spencer's Social Statics," in his dissenting opinion in *Lochner* v. *New York,* 198 U.S. 45, 75–76. The dissent has since become the law.

to morality which as my father used to say of the atmosphere is an empirical mixture. —Woman, the mother, contributing living for others, man, the fighter, contributing achievement. This profound generalization I worked off on my wife at Niagara Falls many years ago when I was just too late to see a man drowned in going through the rapids, and my wife said sadly, if it had been of any use. But I must deny you that highest praise because the article is a real help towards understanding our thinking. By the by—did I ever mention— probably I have—the anticipation of Bergson in Rejected Addresses —"Thinking is but an idle waste of thought?"

Sincerely yours,
O. W. HOLMES

I repeat from yesterday that I should be glad to know of some book to read that will illumine a darkened soul.

Feb. 11, 1919

Dear Mr. Cohen:

The books have arrived this morning. It is most kind of you but of course I didn't mean to ask you to be at that trouble. Being here I shall hang on to most of them as long as I have a chance to read them. At the moment I am expecting an assignment of cases to write, but it will go hard if I have not some time before the adjournment ends. Two or three I shall return ὡς τάχιστα as I have read them. The other day I took from the shelves and began to read Plato's Phaedo. I found on it my note Feb. 3, 1860.* It was fifty-nine years almost to a day since I last read it! What a queer thing to hear people talk of the "inexorable logic" by which Socrates led to his conclusions. You could drive a six mule team through the gaps—but it is wonderfully taking literature even when you rebel or rather smile at the admissions that this that and the other is evident from the proof.

Yours sincerely,
O. W. HOLMES

March 7, 1919

My dear Justice Holmes:

March 8 is, I believe, your birthday and so I take this occasion to express my heartiest congratulations and best wishes. I cannot subscribe altogether to your father's dictum "Old Time is a liar," but I have never seen the spirit of man defy time so chivalrously as in your

---

* In October 1860 Holmes's undergraduate essay *Plato* had been published in *The University Quarterly,* Vol. 4, p. 205.

case. Every time I read what you write or have the good fortune to see you personally I feel refreshed and rejuvenated. I hope that both you and Mrs. Holmes will continue to enjoy for many more years the wise happiness which comes with ripe experience.

Sincerely yours,

MORRIS R. COHEN

P.S. I ought to have answered your last letter which came with the returned books; but the illness of my children distracted me somewhat. . . . The Davidson Society is still in existence, though in financial difficulties. As to Joachim of Fiore I am not sure that your question was a call for cold information. Briefly, Joachim was a Calabrian monk of the 12th century who wrote many commentaries on the prophets and prophecies of his own. His main idea seems to have been that there was to be a third dispensation following the first dispensation under the Old Testament (God the Father) and the second dispensation of the New Testament (God the Son). The third dispensation was to be of the Holy Ghost, and a regime of mystic monks was to succeed the temporal and ecclesiastical hierarchies. Joachim died in the year 1202 or 1207 but in 1256 some monk wrote a liber introductorius ad evangelium aeternum in which Joachim's ideas were developed with little regard to the feeling of those who value the temporal interpretation of Christianity, the Papacy etc. It caused considerable trouble in the Franciscan order and Dante who was a Franciscan lay brother seems to have been very much influenced by it. Davidson used to talk to me a great deal about the matter, but after digging for myself on the basis of Renan's study of Joachim (in his Nouvelles Etudes de l'hist. rel. pp. 217–322) I found that there was no earthly nourishment in the whole business except to explain Dante's line, 140–141 in the Paradiso XII. Joachim's works were printed in Venice early in the 16th century, but are difficult to obtain now, and I doubt very much whether they would interest you in the least.

M. R. C.

Washington, D.C.
Nov. 23, 1919

My dear Cohen:

No letter accompanies your proofs* so I assume they are to be read and returned. I like your discourse immensely and I think there

* "Communal Ghosts and Other Perils in Social Philosophy," *Journal of Philosophy*, Vol. XVI (Dec. 4, 1919), p. 673. The substance of this article constitutes Book III, Chap. 3, of *Reason and Nature*.

is not a word in it with which I do not heartily agree. I always have told our beloved Laski that his are counsels of perfection not true theories of divided sovereignty. As long as law means force—(and when it means anything else I don't care who makes it and will do as I damn choose—) force means an army and this army will belong to the territorial club. Therefore the territorial club will have the last word—subject to the knowledge that if it does too much there will be a war in which it may go under in its present form. Also I am with you in your partially expressed rebellion against the notion that something particular has happened and that all our old ideas are upset— Even Pound sometimes talks as if it were a recent discovery that social considerations are paramount when you come to a final issue. I am thoroughly with your defense of the philosophic attitude, and so I might go on. . . .

I didn't answer your former letter as to my little contribution*— the only thing to say is that it only inadequately expresses my sense of the value of your thinking to the world.

Queer—yesterday morning before receiving your proofs I was writing to an English friend of mine on his theme how few were detached in their thinking.

Ever sincerely yours,
O. W. HOLMES

Nov. 26, 1919

My dear Cohen:

Your article had been read and returned with my hearty agreement before your letter came. When I go out this morning I shall get the photographer to do up a photograph and shall send it to you as you request. It makes me vain that you should want it.

Ever sincerely yours,
O. W. HOLMES

21 Vista Ave., Yonkers
Dec. 4, 1919

My dear Justice Holmes:

I have been away from home for a few days, and am glad to find that your letter and photograph arrived while I was away. My grati-

---

* In his autobiography, *A Dreamer's Journey*, 1949, Morris R. Cohen refers to the contribution of which Justice Holmes speaks: "My dream of publishing a treatise on scientific method had taken on new life in 1919. In that year Justice Holmes, Judge Mack and other good friends had helped me over a period of vast discouragement and financial difficulty by subsidizing a sabbatical year in which I was able to devote myself to reading and writing without the distraction of college classes." *Cf. Reason and Nature,* p. xvi.

tude is enhanced by the reading of the dissenting opinion in the Abrams case.* I have seldom read anything which seemed to me to [be] so timely and yet of such permanent importance, so courageous and yet so just to all the relevant considerations.

I am very sorry to hear from Frankfurter of Mrs. Holmes' ill health. I ardently hope that she will soon regain her strength.

Gratefully yours,
MORRIS R. COHEN

July 21, 1920

My dear Cohen:

Your papers† came in due time and I have read them indeed had read most of them before. As to Einstein I shdnt like to be called on to recite, but as to the philosophers I think you are very sound—except that I wonder in what sense you accept pragmatism and reserve the doubt of ignorance as to Charles Peirce. It always seems to me that one must remember that W. James was in large part an Irishman and as such of course was stronger on aperçus of human nature than in continuously sustained logical thought. The modest place given to C. J. Marshall (by implication) when you get into the [word blotted and illegible] rather tickles me—of course it is quite right. If you were comparing men as totals he would stand a good deal higher, though I never have *worshipped* at his shrine. I was reading Hoernlé's book** the other day and found it intelligent but not specially illuminating—I don't see why anyone should bother over the suggestion that consciousness is an epiphenomenon—It is the way the cosmos acts when it gets a certain knot in its guts—and I don't perceive why there is any more right to think away consciousness than there is to think away nerve tissue—the total is the datum. And you can take it or leave it—but you can't take part and say that the rest is cosmically unnecessary—because, (salva reverentia,) you dont know anything about cosmic necessities. But that is only one of several cases in which the philosophers seem to me to make needless trouble—Achilles and the tortoise is another—Your postulate is that whatever sort of an infinite you get up it has got to go into five minutes and half a mile

---

* *Abrams v. United States,* 250 U.S. 616, 624 (Nov. 10, 1919).

† Apparently the enclosures included a series of articles "On American Philosophy" in *The New Republic,* devoted to Royce, Vol. 20 (1919), p. 148; James, Vol. 20 (1919), p. 255; Dewey, Vol. 22 (1920), p. 82; and Santayana, Vol. 23 (1920), p. 221; and also a series of two articles on "Einstein's Theory of Relativity" appearing in *The New Republic,* Vol. 21 (Jan. 21, 1920), p. 228, and Vol. 21 (Feb. 18, 1920), p. 341.

** Hoernlé, R. F. A., *Studies in Contemporary Metaphysics,* 1920.

—and then you (not you, Cohen,) say I have an infinite ∴ it must take eternity. But I speak timidly on such themes to you—As to pragmatism I must quote something I said in 1891 before I ever heard of it. Of course I recognize that the utilitarian pragmatic tests are more exquisite than my words. "I do not believe that the justification of science and philosophy is to be found in improved machinery and good conduct. Science and philosophy are themselves necessaries of life. By producing them civilization sufficiently accounts for itself, if it were not absurd to call the inevitable to account."* I had previously said that the passionate pursuit of the mystery was self justifying & the satisfaction of it an end in itself. Your insistence on similar views always gives me great pleasure. I am sorry the meeting didnt come off and sorry for your troubles—better luck perhaps later.

Yours sincerely,
O. W. HOLMES

Aug. 7, 1920

My dear Justice Holmes:

Your good letter of July 21 has just reached me, owing to my absence from the city. What you say about philosophy delights me, even though you pass over the matter on which I was most anxious to get your opinion—the Einstein articles. For some years I have been planning a book on the foundations of physical science, and as a preliminary exercise have undertaken to write a more or less popular book explaining my main points. The two Einstein articles are part of this plan and I was anxious to get your reaction, because of the remarkable diversity of opinion as to their intelligibility which has reached me—some thinking them remarkably luminous and others remarkably not so.

My agreement with pragmatism extends to the main point made by Peirce, viz. that the way to make our ideas clear is to examine their *possible* consequences, or in technical language, all their possible implications. It is an attempt to extend the experimental method to the handling of ideas, and very fruitful if used logically, for the essence of intellectual liberality consists in the realization that what is familiar to us is only one of a number of possibilities. Logical pragmatism as a method of exploring the field of logical possibilities is, therefore, of the highest value. This aspect however, has not been developed by James or Dewey because they are not interested in logic and metaphysics but only in psychology.

What you say about Hoernlé's book seems to me very true. I should

---

* Speech to Yale Alumni, February 3, 1891, *Speeches,* 1913, pp. 4, 5.

go further and say that Hoernlé and his master Bosanquet are peculiarly insensible to the vast penumbras and vaster darkness that surrounds even our clearest ideas. Their philosophy thus lacks any of the spirit of resolute adventure which makes the human glory of philosophy. Starting with the assumption that everything is ultimately known or knowable, they cannot possibly do much for the genuine extension of the realm of human knowledge. —I hope to have time to write a review of Hoernlé's book and will try to explain my attitude a little more fully.

I expect to be in Boston on Tuesday or Wednesday and hope to enjoy some oral exchange of opinions at Beverly Farms.

With kindest regards to Mrs. Holmes,

Sincerely yours,

MORRIS R. COHEN

Aug. 23, 1920

My dear Cohen:

This is an explosion of delight. Tourtoulon came the other day and I am now almost exactly half through him. I was reading just now and stopped because I must tell you what joy I was getting. It seems to me that I hear him saying lots of things that I thought few knew except myself—others that I never knew and that make me sit up— and all with such wise and cautious scepticism. One or two little places seemed to me not quite up to the mark but they were slight. I havent had such pleasure from a book for a long time—I must have his volume for my own. Cant I pay whoever owns this and get it? or must it be returned? I feel as if I wanted to have it by my side for-ever more—meaning by forever such months or years as I stick it out *ici bas!*

I dont dare direct simply to West Springfield and therefore write to your locus. I want to make notes on the flyleaf and little √ in the margin, but have strictly respected the virginity of what is not my own. Please when you answer be as simple as I am in my avowal of my wishes and say you cant have it or you may have it for $x & y cents and add another to the favors that you have done me.

Ever sincerely yours,

O. W. HOLMES

August 31, 1920

My dear Cohen:

Of course it is a pride and pleasure to have Tourtoulon as a gift from you—It is only my sense of Justice that rebels. I asked for it and it seems that you bought it—I thought you said that you had two copies and therefore inferred that you could part with one. I think I ought to pay for it but I leave it to you. I value what you say very greatly but it reminds me of a case I argued when young—A man sued for salvage of a boat in which he had sailed two or three thousand miles from a sinking ship—Lowell J. said that as the boat seemed to have saved the man as much as the man the boat he thought that account was in aequilibrio. I wrote to Laski that I wished that he might read Tourtoulon—that there was a little more distinguishing and systematizing than I care for but that I thought it the best corrective I know for people who were astraddle of a formula like the Webbs or Cole (Social Theory), wh. Laski has a little tendency to be. Systems are forgotten—only a man's aperçus are remembered. I used to say extravagantly of course that Kant could have told his main points to a young lady in ten minutes after dinner. Isn't there some truth in it? I have finished reading the book but shall go over it again —(after finishing Dumas' Les Quarante Cinq—) I followed it with a book of selections of early English prose that I happened to see in the shelves and was delighted with the simplicity and force of some of the writing—very different from Milton when he is not soaring—Well—I thank you with all my heart—

Sincerely yours,

O. W. HOLMES

I shall look with eagerness for your book on legal philosophy*—my chief interest in the law has been in the effort to show the universal in the particular—That has kept me alive—whatever the result may have been.

West Springfield, N.H.

Sept. 1, 1920

Dear Justice Holmes:

I hope your sense of justice will not continue to rebel when you learn that I had been intending to present the Tourtoulon volume to you from the beginning; but owing to my timidity about asking people to invest their time in reading a new book, I manoeuvered to have you ask for it so that in case you did not find it interesting you would have been free to drop it. The other copy I am using in revising the English translation which is to appear soon in the Legal Philosophy Series.

* A projected treatise on Law and Justice was never completed, but fragments of it were embodied in two volumes of legal essays, *Law and the Social Order*, 1933, and *Reason and Law, Studies in Juristic Philosophy*, 1950.

Of course I thoroughly agree with you as to the relative importance of insight (aperçus) and system. I used to illustrate it with the names of Plato and Aristotle—though that is a trifle unfair to the latter who was not devoid of insight of his own apart from that which he utilized from Plato. But in recent years I have been impressed more and more with the tragic ineffectiveness of insight that is not properly uniformed, housed, advertised or as the modern phrase goes properly capitalized and "sold" to the public. It takes a great deal of wisdom and experience to recognize insight in its raw state, and all sorts of social institutions, red tape, symbols and ceremonies are necessary to emphasize the importance of things which the multitude would not notice otherwise. A great deal of Kant's insight, for instance, is to be found in the Cambridge Platonists, but they never impressed the philosophic world because they had not the imposing apparatus and machinery. The tendency of American life seems to me to emphasize beyond any reasonable limit the role of the promoter, the popularizer or distributor rather than the creator or inventor—to glorify Edison and Marconi and to ignore Willard Gibbs and Theobald Smith. But after all it is of importance not only that wireless electric waves should be discovered but also that they should be commercially exploited. I am saying all this because I am beginning to feel that the arts of system-building, rhetorical and formalistic persuasion and the like, are of the utmost importance in preparing the soil from which the tall trees of intellectual genius arise. The law does a great deal to interfere with the expression of rare individuality, but it also compensates this destructive tendency by creating favorable soil for future growth.

With kindest regards to Mrs. Holmes,

Sincerely yours,

MORRIS R. COHEN

Sept. 6, 1920

My dear Cohen:

The Tourtoulon incident is closed by your reassuring statement and once more I thank you for the most stimulating book I have read for a long time. Now I write to fire off a suggestion but with the real timidity with which I always should offer a philosophic thought to you. It is this. Man is like a strawberry plant, the shoots that he throws out take root and become independent centres. And one illustration of the tendency is the transformation of means into ends. A man begins a pursuit as a means of keeping alive—he ends by following it at the cost of life. A miser is an example—but so is the man who makes righteousness his end. Morality is simply another means of living but the saints make it an end in itself. Until just now it never occurred to me I think that the same is true of philosophy or art. Philosophy as a fellow once said to me is only thinking. Thinking is an instrument of adjustment to the conditions of life—but it becomes an end in itself. So that we can see how man is inevitably an idealist of some sort, but whatever his ideal and however ultimate to himself, all that he can say to anyone else is—Je suis comme ça. But he can admit that a person who lives in a certain emotional sphere should be indifferent to intellectual justifications although he reserves to himself his advantage of believing that he can explain the other and that this other can't explain him.

That is all I wanted to say but I will add apropos of the acquired superiority of means to ends—that we think the statesman better than the man who simply eats his dinner, travels to and fro and begets— yet the statesman is only a means to his doing so. Also an anecdote of when I was young—a man who called himself a juridical traveller said: We speak of the Remorse of Conscience—a thousand years ago more or less we said The Ayen Bite of Inwit—the image is the same —biting back on oneself—and is equally intelligible to you or me— but the introduction of a dead language has made it unintelligible to the man in the street—And so by the mere force of language (he concluded) we are creating a spiritual aristocracy. The answer again is that the derivation has got new roots—that we no more think of the image than does the man in the street—and that he knows what remorse means as well as we do.

I think the best in age for man is an electric light—the spark feels isolated and independent but really is only a moment in a current.

Have I talked banalities or was it worth saying?

Yours ever,

O. W. HOLMES

Sept. 11, 1920

My dear Justice Holmes:

I am very much interested and, indeed, delighted with your figure of the strawberry shoots to illustrate the relation of means to ends in human affairs. But though I agree with the main contention and all the practical or concrete applications I prefer my own way of underpinning these results. I am sceptical for instance, about your assertion that "thinking is [originally] an instrument of adjustment to the conditions of life." Thinking *may* be just an accident which has become *partly* adjusted to the conditions of life and in part not so—if we interpret life narrowly or biologically. The relation of means to ends does not seem to me a very fundamental part of nature. It is just our way of picking certain threads of relation between things that interest us. Nature in itself is not a prudent artisan, but just prolificates in all the possible ways. The primary relation is not that of means to ends but of blind impulse in all possible directions. In the helter skelter of impulses many defeat themselves, and many get so adapted to conditions, and flow in regular grooves or channels, that we associate their happy endings with their origin. They become illumined and we call them rational. But the fact that impulses and tendencies not conducive to the prolongation of life tend to eliminate themselves, does not mean that our nature is originally or even now free from them. For the most obvious fact at which most philosophies blink is that death—not only the death of the moment or individual but also of the species and of the physical system—is just as natural and just as prevalent as life. It is only in the order of preference that one of these towers above the other.

This being my general background I never can look at any "means" as *merely* means. Each impulse that is subordinated to the attainment of another is like a servant who subordinates himself to his master, but *always* maintains a life of his own in some respect. As we become enlightened we realize more that the choice of ends includes that of means, and hence the sterility of the old casuistic problem, Does the end justify the means? An end that includes certain means, like a household that includes certain kinds of servants, becomes *ipso facto* undesirable.

Of course the life of man compared with that of the larger whole in which he figures is like that of an electric spark. But the latter might speak up: Why do you say I am *only* an electric spark? I am a full royal electric spark, and there are no electric currents without me or the like of me.

I shall lecture in Baltimore in February and March [Johns Hopkins University] and hope to be able to visit Washington several times this winter.

With kindest regards to Mrs. Holmes and yourself,

MORRIS R. COHEN

Sept. 14, 1920

My dear Cohen:

Many thanks for your letter—I have no disposition to disagree with anything in it. Only I think we are not quite *ad idem*. In my image of the electric spark I was not lapsing into what we both contemn, the notion that consciousness is an epiphenomenon, but endeavoring to illustrate what I live on a good deal, that whereas personality presents itself as isolated and over against the universe, it really is a moment in the intersection of currents that come from and go out beyond it—that man is a cosmic ganglion and inseparable from his time and place—

As to means and ends I was not going beyond the sphere of conscious thought. As to the function of that I was merely firing a Bergsonian snap shot and for my purposes did not care very much whether the analysis was correct or not—the point was simply that miser, saint, philosopher, painter all illustrate the so to speak physiological destiny of man to live to ends outside himself and so to be an idealist and a martyr, while most of the misers saints and the rest don't recognize that they are examples of the same thing. Of course what you say as to nature not being a prudent artisan and as to blind impulses seems to me O.K. but not quite relevant to what I had in view. This is not to bother you for an answer but simply to limit the scope of what I wrote before. I hope I shall see you next February—a month in which I generally have more leisure than before or after.

Sincerely yours,

O. W. HOLMES

I am puzzled about direction—your envelope says Springfield—the postmark is East S. Your former letter said West. I shall stick to the old address.

Nov. 29, 1920

My dear Justice Holmes:

I have received a copy of your book* from the publishers and wish to thank you heartily. I expect to write a review of it for the New Republic, and if you don't object I'll send it to you before printing.

I hope that both Mrs. Holmes and yourself are enjoying good health.

With kind regards.

Sincerely yours,

MORRIS R. COHEN

Jan. 5, 1921

Dear Cohen:

It gives me very great joy to know that you have received this item of recognition [in January 1921 Cohen was appointed full professor, after eight years of teaching in the philosophy department of The

* *Collected Legal Papers,* 1920.

City College] small in comparison with what you deserve. I send every good wish for you and yours for the New Year.

I don't know whether you adhere to your notion of reviewing my book—which I hardly need say I should be proud if you did. I shouldn't want to see it before it came out and should wish you to be perfectly free. I do feel at liberty to mention what you wouldn't be likely to know, that Maitland called the Early English Equity epoch making and that among the researches that it started Barbour on the History of Contract in Early English Equity in 4 Oxford Studies in Social & Legal History seems to me to confirm what I ventured to reconstruct from a bone and a scale—He doesn't say much about my essay in his book, but an article before his lamented death gave me full credit for starting the whole business.

The articles on agency have been most criticized—but they were honest work and I think at least followed one strand of the development. I don't at all assume that you will stick to your intention, or press it in any way or mean to do more than state facts that are a little out of your line.

Sincerely yours,

O. W. HOLMES

I am rather driven and have to cut this short.

Jan. 30, 1921

My dear Cohen:

Your generous notice of my book* touches and moves me deeply. There is no-one whom I was more anxious about—for there are very few for whose judgment I care so much. But I wanted you to feel free to "pass with your best violence" and so did not want you to show me what you wrote before it appeared. I will not expatiate on the happiness it gives me to read what you say. It makes life easier. An odd phrase for a man who will be 80 in March. It seems as if at that date one might tie up the past into a neat package, insure it with Cohen as valuable, and take an irresponsible rest. But as soon as a corner is turned the road stretches away again and ambition to go farther returns—if only to be carried in a civic procession as a survivor, which, when I was a small boy and saw the veterans of the past carried in a barge, seemed to me a wonderful thing. With regard to your criticisms I may not have expressed in writing the reserve that I often have expressed in talk—that I was speaking only of the

---

* Cohen's review of Holmes's *Collected Legal Papers* appeared in *The New Republic*, Vol. 25 (Feb. 2, 1921), p. 294, and was later reprinted in *Law and the Social Order*, p. 363.

economic aspects of the regime of private property. I always have recognized that there might be an emotional issue and that people might say I don't like it and I want a change even if it costs me more —What I think a mistake is the giving of an emotional attitude the aspect of an economic one. That I believe to be a humbug and while I fully agree that it involves an issue of fact I have not failed to talk with some economists who could give me light and for thirty years have expressed to more than one of them the wish that we might be furnished diagrams—expressed in money, labor hours or by whatever unit was best of the different consumptions

R R Travel	Meat
Cereals	Luxuries of the few as I believe it would turn out, &c. &c.

As to the purposes of the cosmos—on the last page but one (bottom) I leave open whether there is a plan of campaign—But as I dont believe that I am a little god, I do in a sense worship the inevitable—although in an unpublished speech at the Tavern Club (for Paul Bourget) I spoke of "man's most peculiar power—the power to deny the actual and to perish"—

Of course you are right in taking me up on everything being connected with everything else—I know that you have your reserves on that and are far more competent to speak than I am—I know that the hypothesis is not proved—but it seems to me that it is almost the postulate in thinking about the universe and that the great advances in thought have come from betting that there is more connection than has been established up to that moment—

But I bow to you on that. Also I think it likely that early associations affect my emotional attitude toward the mystery of the world. Well—I expect a fall soon—for I begin today proud—I hope to avert the irony of fate by recognizing that self feelings are a bait by which nature gets our work out of us, but still I am very proud of such words from a philosopher whom I so deeply respect.

Ever sincerely yours,

O. W. HOLMES

854 W 181st St., New York

Feb. 14, 1921

My dear Justice Holmes:

Your very good letter expressing your appreciation of my review reached me some time ago, but this is the first chance I have to acknowledge it. The ill-health of my wife and youngest boy left me little freedom.

Your kind words are a great source of pride and joy to me. It would be difficult for me to say more, because in the whole of my career I have not received any recognition which has meant more to me than your generous estimate as to the value of my intellectual efforts.

When you say that the unity and connectedness of things is a postulate of thought and that all progress results from betting that it will be found in hitherto unknown regions, I thoroughly subscribe. Only I add that we can also safely bet that all unity and connectedness of things will be found on closer scrutiny to be full of unbridgeable gaps. Newton may find a law of gravitation to connect hitherto disconnected portions of the universe (the stars and terrestrial objects) but the progress of science is bound to show lacunae in his formula, and discrepancies between it and facts. Unity and diversity are the two blades of the shears with which we try to cut out a pattern of the universe, and it is only our human weakness that makes us emphasize one of these blades at a time.

I expect to be in Washington next Saturday and Sunday and shall be delighted to call on you and Mrs. Holmes if you are free.

With kindest regards,

Sincerely yours,
MORRIS R. COHEN

March 2, 1921

My dear Cohen:

In answer to your inquiry let me say that recently I read Mr. Lowie's book on Primitive Society and read it with unqualified admiration. It seemed to me to unite in an extraordinary way practical experience, learning and insight, and, so far as one not a specialist on the subject could judge, to represent a most characteristically modern and real advance upon the earlier and too easy generalizations that stimulated this next step. The book convinced me at once that Mr. Lowie is a real force in the present world of thought.

Sincerely yours,
O. W. HOLMES

854 W. 181st, N.Y.
March 7, 1921

My dear Justice Holmes:

Please accept my heartiest congratulations on your eightieth birthday. On this occasion you must permit me also to say what I have

perhaps said before, viz. that you have taught me how little do courage and serenity depend on the years and how much they are rather
the result of heroic devotion. You have made me realize that the
heroic spirit is a real divine element *in* the cosmos.

I hope also that at least for the next four years [President Harding
had taken office three days earlier] you will not be induced by anyone to abandon the bench—not even for the sake of philosophic writing. When I was younger I thought you might do well to leave to
others the decision of mundane cases and devote more of your time to
settling or unsettling the universe. But I see more clearly now that the
universe can be dealt with in legal decisions also.

With best wishes for many happy returns of the day,

Sincerely yours,

MORRIS R. COHEN

March 9, 1921

My dear Cohen:

For the books I thank you and for the letter I love you—As I have
told you before you pump new courage into me—I delight to think—
oh what a descent—that I have my mathematical friend. You say
80th birthday. birthdays 1^{born} $2^{1 year}$—$10^{9 years}$—$80^{79 years}$—$81^{80 years}$
Hein?—Shall I parody Rousseau's lady and say learn mathematics
and study Philosophy? Whatever you do if I can understand it I shall
profit by it and always shall be your obliged and sincere friend.

O. W. HOLMES

Salmon Lake House and Camps
North Belgrade, Maine

August 12, 1921

My dear Justice Holmes:

It is many weeks since I received your very kind letter of congratu-
lation on the occasion of my fifteenth [wedding] anniversary. All sorts
of domestic cares, and the nursing of my daughter back to strength
after a tonsils operation prevented me from writing to you at the time.
I want to express to you my deep appreciation of your very beautiful
letter to me and also my appreciation of what your friendship has
meant to my husband. Owing to his conscientiousness in not publishing anything which does not conform to his own high standard, he
has not received the general recognition which I think his attainments
merit. This makes him care all the more for the interest and appreciation which a few discerning minds express in regard to his work.
Nothing, in recent years, has given him so much joy and courage as

the expression of regard from you and from Prof. Einstein.

Your photograph, with its inscription, is one of our dearest possessions, and I may add that your friendship for my husband has been inspiring not only to him but also to me and our children.

With sincere regards to you and to Mrs. Holmes, from Mr. Cohen and myself, I am,

Yours gratefully,
MARY R. COHEN

Beverly Farms
Aug. 31, 1921

My dear Cohen:

Your Later Philosophy* was read from cover to cover by me today on my way to town—and delightfully lifted me out of the cares and annoyances of business. I think it admirable—as well as most interesting and instructive—I don't wonder Santayana was pleased at your handling of him—though I think he deserves it. But to all you are equally just and appreciative. I was much touched by a letter from your wife some time ago in answer to mine—My compliments to her. I have had a little excursus into philosophy this summer.

Haldane—Relativity (not very well understood as the words bother me) Hegel—Logic—Wallace trans. I still don't see how he gets out of logic into time—as I used to put it. H. can't persuade me that a syllogism can wag its tail. Aristotle—Metaphysics—divided between eternal truth and laboriously discussing quibbles to which the sufficient answer was oh pooh—(as it seemed to me). Bergson Creative Evolution—3d time as easy seeming now as once it appeared difficult—but I don't believe him any more and suspect he is less original than he seems to an outsider at first reading. Plato—Timaeus—with a remarkable introduction by Archer Hind—& with him adieu to the theme. I have read a lot of other stuff of course but don't go into that —as the vacation seems beginning and is nearly over.

Sincerely yours,
O. W. HOLMES

854 W. 181st
March 7, 1922

My dear Justice Holmes:

On the occasion of your eighty-first birthday anniversary I wish to express my heartiest congratulations and best wishes, and my trust

---

* "Later Philosophy" constitutes Chapter 17 in the *Cambridge History of American Literature*, 1921, Vol. III, pp. 226–65.

that you will long continue to regard the Cosmos with that resolute youthfulness which time can only confirm.

With kindest remembrances to Mrs. Holmes,

Sincerely yours,

MORRIS R. COHEN

Hinsdale, Mass.
August 8, 1922

My dear Justice Holmes:

I was sorry to learn that you chose a hospital to spend part of your summer in, but I am gratified to learn from Felix that you expect to be back on the bench in Washington when the parade of cases begins in October. I hope that, with soldierly courage and judicial discretion, you will long continue to defy Time as that ancient bully ought to be defied by wise men.

Two books have lately stirred me very much. One of them is by your old friend John Chipman Gray, On the Nature and Sources of the Law. I am reviewing the second edition of it for the New Republic and the re-reading impresses me with the solid wisdom that is unostentatiously crammed away in almost every page. I am particularly impressed with the homely illustrations with which he confronts all the grand principles. I think Gray's view of the law is rather limited by his pre-occupation with the law of real property—and he does not deal adequately with the grand policies of the law as they actually operate. But his wisdom is mature, generated by long familiarity and grappling with problems, rather than by clever devices for ignoring difficulties.

The other book is by a still older writer by the name of Shakespeare. It is a play called Hamlet. I do not care much for the libretto, the action is rather melodramatic and the characters, outside of Hamlet, decidedly stereotyped. But the depth of human sympathy and the wonderful music of the language seems to me, after about seventy-five readings, one of the most marvellous achievements of the human genius.

With kindest remembrances to Mrs. Holmes,

Sincerely yours,

MORRIS R. COHEN

Aug. 10, [1922]

My dear Cohen:

Your letter came just as I had been thinking about you—and is most welcome of course. I can't write more than a bulletin—but that is a good one—the doctor came in in the last sentence and told me I might go out for a little dinner—the first after confusion, oblivion and getting into a routine that has superseded life—

I have suspended intellectual functions during this, as I believe, rather big hospital job—but I have only partially realized what was going on and have come out smiling. I agree about Gray & won't fight today about Hamlet—The most heartbreaking pathos is in Antony & Cleopatra, I think—I am reading, sometimes too hastily to understand, Santayana's Soliloquies—(Soliquities, a nurse called it). His scepticisms seem all right, his dogmatisms comic—his total not quite charming and yet nearer to my way of thinking (I guess) than either of his former associates [at Harvard, James and Royce]—But this is as far as I can swim with a lead pencil and on my back—wherefore adieu—with real thanks for your remembering me.

Sincerely yours,

O. W. HOLMES

January 2, 1923

My dear Justice Holmes:

I have been very deeply stirred recently by the re-reading of Spinoza's works (in connection with a paper I have been writing* on his Amor Dei Intellectualis) and I cannot better express my appreciation of the intellectual integrity which your work on the bench continues to exemplify than by sending you a copy of Santayana's edition of Spinoza's *Ethics* and *Improvement of the Understanding*. Please accept the same with the expression of the best wishes for the New Year to you and to Mrs. Holmes.

Ever faithfully yours,

MORRIS R. COHEN

Washington, D.C.
April 9, 1923

Dear Cohen:

A second time I have read one, a first the other of your two papers†—with much pleasure and high appreciation. —They are mighty good and justify what I hear Bertrand Russell says (that you are the first living philosopher of America). They came this morning

---

* Read before the American Philosophical Association in December 1922, reprinted partially in *The Faith of a Liberal*.

† One of the papers was Cohen's review of Pound's *The Spirit of the Common Law*, in *Journal of Philosophy*, Vol. 20 (Mar. 15, 1923), p. 155, reprinted in *Law and the Social Order*, p. 327.

and your reference (Journ. of Philos. 164) to "essentially vague terms like due process" tickle me as I was about to deliver a dissent in the minimum wage case*—in which I spoke of "the vague contours of the Fifth Amendment" and made a few remarks on Liberty of Contract. The other dissenters thought I went too far and I flocked alone—

Perhaps I shall venture to send you the case when I get it.

Meantime I am

Ever sincerely yours,
O. W. HOLMES

Blue Mountain Lake, N.Y.
July 31, 1923

My dear Justice Holmes:

After a rather strenuous time at Chicago—teaching philosophy to eager and too unsophisticated westerners—I come here for a little vacation and am regaled by your introduction to the last volume of the Legal Philosophy Series. I am very glad, indeed, that you took the trouble to write it, not only for the weighty words of wisdom which it contains, but also because it seems to me especially calculated to make our over-hasty brethren on the right and on the left pause for a little reflection.

While I thoroughly agree with you that our reformers need above all to think of the cost which their pet schemes will involve, I should (as a resolute, unabashed theorist) insist on the absolute necessity for questioning first principles—as, indeed, you yourself have elsewhere insisted. I say this because the fear of passing judgment on the work of the gods (and goddesses) ought not, it seems to me, frighten us; though, in practice it is well to calculate our limited strength before trying to resist the tides of destiny.

I hope soon to gather together some papers of mine—old and new —into a volume on *Reason and Nature* to be published next fall, and I hope you will allow me to dedicate the volume to you.† For I am sure that without the encouraging words which you passed on some of the papers already printed, I should not have ventured to publish them at this stage.

With kindest regards to Mrs. Holmes as well as yourself,

Sincerely yours,
MORRIS R. COHEN

* *Adkins v. Children's Hospital*, 261 U.S. 525 (1923).

† The volume, dedicated "To Mr. Justice Oliver Wendell Holmes, the Courageous Thinker and Loyal Friend," was actually published in 1931. See Holmes's letter of March 14, 1931, p. 358.

Aug. 3, 1923

My dear Cohen:

The suggestion that you dedicate your book to me gives me the greatest pride and pleasure. There are few things that could please me so much. I thank you for the rest of your letter—Of course I agree with you as to questioning first principles—They are like what an old Frenchman in a forgotten novel by F. Soulié says as to courage—It is never proved but always to be proved. But alas fools who are incompetent to question anything take advantage of the fact. I haven't seen the book yet to which I wrote the introduction except the galley proofs in which there were frightful typographical &c errors—I trust corrected. Rather dull stuff I thought most of it. If I had not been asked to do it before I was ill last summer I should have backed out. I still avoid all extra taxes on my strength, keep as quiet as possible, see almost no one—and don't bother even about improving my mind. My only reading is Sainte Beuve's Causeries, an occasional detective story and just now because of burning words from Laski Jane Austen's Pride and Prejudice—I confess in a whisper to having found her rather a bore heretofore. I hope you are accumulating strength and not over working.

Ever sincerely yours,
O. W. HOLMES

Sept. 14, 1923

My dear Cohen:

Peirce's Chance, Love, & Logic came here three or four nights ago, I assume from you and I send you very hearty thanks. I have just finished reading it—just running my eye over the mathematical parts without understanding them and doubting if I understood some other of his arguments—I feel Peirce's originality and depth—but he does not move me greatly—I do not sympathize with his pontifical self satisfaction. He believes that he can, or could if you gave him time, explain the universe. He sees cosmic principles when I should not dare to see more than the limit of our capacities, and his reasoning in the direction of religion &c seems to me to reflect what he wants to believe—in spite of his devotion to logic. That we could not assert necessity of the order of the universe I learned to believe from Chauncey Wright long ago. I suspect C.S.P. got it from the same source.

I don't know that I understand Peirce's views of space and time—for having resolved that I would devote this vacation to leisure and the vacation having but one week more, I gave but a limited time to my readings—but I can't help doubting whether they are anything more than human ultimates—and whether speculations as to how the uni-

verse was, before the monuments that we can see, are not futile—
Somehow I cannot believe that time is to be applied to it except for
our limited purposes.

Your introduction is an admirable bit of work, as usual—I thank
you once again—shall read Sainte Beuve's Causeries for one week
more—and then with a wild shriek plunge into the gulf of work that I
expect to find waiting for me in Washington.

Ever sincerely yours,
O. W. HOLMES

I hope you have got rested and into good shape—.

Nov. 29, 1923

Dear Cohen:

Your article* was duly received and read—somewhat hurriedly of
necessity—but with profit and appreciation—I have more respect for
the universe now that I know that there is a place in it for $\sqrt{-1}$. You
are illuminating as always—and I shall try not to forget the lesson.

Ever sincerely yours,
O. W. HOLMES

June 11, 1924

Dear Cohen:

Your letter comes just as I am leaving—so I must send you only
hurried thanks. You bring a sinister grin to my mug. The book came
too and without opening it I told my messenger to send it on by book
post to Beverly Farms where I shall find it awaiting me and laboriously extract improvement from it. But I am trying to realize that it
is too late to bother longer about my immortal soul and that it is lawful to seek amusement. But again I am glad to have a pièce de résis-
tance. A dame has just sent me Ouspensky Tertium Organum—with
demand for an appreciation. I am suspicious—and should be glad of a
hint from you as I gather from a glance that salvation lies in the fourth
dimension—which is a hard look out for me. Well—I must stop. I
am thankful for your friendship—My compliments to your wife whom
we were very glad to meet at last.

Yours ever,
O. W. HOLMES

* "On the Logic of Fiction," in *Journal of Philosophy*, Vol. 20 (Aug. 30,
1923), p. 477, subsequently appearing as Chapter 5 of *A Preface to Logic*.

June 13, 1924

Dear Justice Holmes:

Teachers and judges have this in common: they must learn to read or listen to a great deal of inexcusable foolishness. I flatter myself that while my flesh is weak I have developed great patience in listening to foolish argument of students and in wading through numerous pages of nonsense to get at a possible idea or aperçu on which confused minds sometimes stumble. Ouspensky's book, however, has tried my patience beyond the three (or is it eight?) mile limit. The man has some sort of intelligence; and if he had only taken the ordinary trouble of informing himself about modern mathematics he might readily have learned how nonsensical are the things which he has put down in this Tertium Organum. But, alas! The charm of speculating about the incomprehensible is one of the inescapable allurements of human life.

Spengler's *Untergang des Abendlandes* [*The Decline of the West*] is not a book for the improvement of the mind, but for lawful amusement. He has a great trick of generalizing in a way to make the facts irrelevant. But I found it very stimulating; for he opens vistas of possibility to a thinking reader who is ready to play with the author and, independently, with the subject matter.

I trust that you have now got rid of the cold and cough which you had in Washington and that you are facing the gods as erect as usual.

With kindest regards in which my wife joins,

Sincerely yours,

MORRIS R. COHEN

Beverly Farms
June 15, 1924

Dear Cohen:

Your letter greets my first morning here just as I was regretting my stupidity in leaving your last in Washington. Spengler met me on my arrival last night. You relieve my mind by what you say about him and confirm an impression from my first glance. I have read far enough in Ouspensky to believe that I shall not get much from him. He has all the earmarks of what I don't believe. He interests me mainly by recalling a talk I had with Count Schouvaloff when the Grand Duke came to Boston almost or quite before you were born— He worked off on me things that I had not heard before—the notion of a being living only on a plane—(is that from Helmholz?) and the suggestion that a point $\times$ infinity took us into a new and from the point's outlook unimaginable novelty; the line—& so the line to the plane—and the plane to the solid—whether the solid $\times \infty$ led to the 4th dimension or what, I don't remember. Of course you have got to multiply in a particular way to get the result—but it tickled me. I am hardly oriented here yet, but I had to let off a line to you and not wait to send a solid.

Yours ever,

O. W. HOLMES

Beverly Farms
June 19, 1924

Dear Cohen:

One additional word as to Spengler, to thank you and tell you how he tickles me. I read slowly as I can give only a limited time to the book and have to use the dictionary—though N.B. it is wise not to bother too much or one loses the general thought in the detail. I have read only 60 pages—but you may imagine that I chuckled at es gibt keine ewigen Wahrheiten. He gets nearer to being able to smile at himself than most Germans, though I doubt if he can—well, this is only a grunt after an hour, a happy hour, with this book—and now I must take my very modest constitutional walk—

Yours ever,

O. W. HOLMES

Beverly Farms,
Massachusetts
July 14, 1924

My dear Cohen:

This moment sees the finishing of Spengler—Damn him—he has been my task and duty since I have been here—a duty not too assiduously pursued, you can see from the time taken, even though I had constantly to turn to the dictionary. The swine has given me my money's worth—for I haven't read anything so suggestive and stimulating for a long time, from its abundant aperçus in spite of excessive repetition—I don't believe his most fundamental propositions, but I feel a lot of new light on the different *Kults* that he discusses. I infer that he is not so strong on the natural sciences as he is on mathematics, music and art—Were he not a German I should be surprised at his dogmatism in statement, when his general view is so sceptical. In spite of his scepticism he seems to feel an inward demand for absolute truth and to be disappointed at the conclusion that he can't scoop up the universe. As I read I often wished that I could consult you. I don't understand his distinction between the realms of space & cause and effect and of time and Schicksal. What is cause and effect outside of time—and what is Schicksal if not the working of cause and effect? I don't doubt that you could explain—I am perfectly willing to believe that he can't say experimentally that cause and effect are exactly equivalent—For the matter of that I have often said that if causes suddenly ceased to produce effects—or phenomena appeared without cause—and I was not too scared to think—I should simply say—Tired so soon? I thought you would last my time—But I make more modest demands of the cosmos than those who are disposed to think that it wears a beard—I might ramble on—but I just want to tell you that I have read the book—with a good deal of intellectual emotion and am deeply obliged to you for sending it to me—while my feeling toward the writer is not unmixed with malevolence—Following your intimation, which accorded with my impression from 80 pages, I have felt warranted in letting Tertium Organum wait for better days. Now that I have finished Spengler and sent off some accounts that are the bore of July 1, I feel the man of leisure unless you set me another task—which I shouldn't promise to perform. I hope all is well with you—my compliments to your wife whom I was so glad to meet—

Sincerely yours,
O. W. HOLMES

Colony Hall
Peterboro, New Hampshire

August 13, 1924

Dear Justice Holmes:

Your very good letter of the 14th of July has just reached me—the mail clerk at the City College kept it there four weeks. —I am naturally delighted that you liked the book and differed as much from Spengler's fundamental dogmas as I did. Spengler is a good deal of a journalist,—he is weak on the facts, in mathematics as well as in the natural sciences and also—I am informed by specialists—in art. But he has a very suggestive way of bringing together things which are not generally thought of together. He thus helps to build up new vistas or at least perspectives in which we see things in new lights. Would you like to have me send you the second volume which deals with the perspectives of world history?

Your question about the difference between the realm of causality and the realm of *Schicksal* is to be answered by reference to the German (Kant & Schopenhauer) distinction between the phenomenal and the real or noumenal realm. Causality applies only to phenomena, the noumenal realm is governed, or more accurately *is* Schicksal. I am not myself in sympathy with this. The world behind the veil of phenomena is too much like a world where you can have your cake and eat it too. But there is something in it of the old Heracleitean identification of Fate and Character.

I fear I am even more heterodox as to causes than you are. I would not be in the least surprised if things happened without any causes. Indeed I frequently do see things happen the causes of which I know nothing about, and it is only a maxim of prudence that makes me believe that a cause is there and worth while seeking for. I have touched upon that in my book on Nature and Reason which I hope will be actually published within a few months.

If you find yourself still curious as to whether there are some new or old books worth looking into I think I can venture to send you something.

With kindest regards to Mrs. Holmes and yourself.

Sincerely yours,
MORRIS R. COHEN

Beverly Farms
Aug. 15, 1924

My dear Cohen:

Your letter gives me pleasure and comfort—The further I get away from Spengler the freer I feel to decline his dogmas—but the stimulus was worth the trouble of reading him. I doubt as to Vol. 2. I very much should like to look it over—but I doubt if I should work through it—and if you meant me to keep Vol. 1 I don't want you to make another gift—and on the other hand I always am worried by books to be returned until I have seen them dispatched by mail. I should be grateful for any suggestions such as you intimate that you have up your sleeve. If Schicksal is in the realm of the ding an sich— much as I believe in it—I leave speculation about it to other hands. As to causality I think I have said before that if phenomena appeared without causes and I wasn't too scared to think, I simply should smile and say: Tired so soon? I thought you would last my time—I always surmise that just as objects of sight or hearing can be expressed in other terms which make them finite, it well may be that Time is a mode of the finite—and that if the cosmos wears a beard its mode of consciousness may be in some other unimaginable form. I find it hard to believe that infinite time is an ultimate, although it is so for me— After Spengler I read Thucydides the most important books 1, 2 & 7 in Greek the rest mainly in translation—It was my last Day of Judgment book and I can die more easily. I think the English make too much row about him, although of course he was the first in his line. I can get more eternal truths for less money elsewhere. I was moved but it gave me pleasure to think that Socrates was jawing away while the empire fell—and that after it fell it became the leader of the world in philosophy—I noted with interest what always strikes me in the Greek Choruses—the absence of politeness as we understand it—and the kindred absence of the hypocritic Christian sanction in political communications. They come down to hard facts without veils. Since then I have read Marius the Epicurean—curious product of the old Oxford exquisiteness—from a scholar and a gentleman who never has come in contact with the grind of affairs—and to my mind a futile importation of Pater's spiritual experiences into a time and mind to which they were impossible—Now I am reading La Guerre et la Paix —A long novel ought to be thin, like Dumas—It is an imposition to take so much of a reader's time with thick fiction—when every sentence requires notice, but Tolstoy was a giant—little as I care for what he thought. Please remember me to your wife.

> Sincerely yours,
> O. W. HOLMES

> Keene, New York
> August 18, 1924

Dear Justice Holmes:

I have sent you some books on which you will (in all human probability) not be examined at any day of judgment, but which you may be interested to page through and perhaps taste here and there. Simmel has some interesting comments on Art and on Rodin which may provoke some reaction from you. The book on Nietzsche by Salter is an uncommonly conscientious one, and does more justice to Nietzsche than most enthusiastic disciples or opponents manage to do. The pamphlet on The Unknowable by Santayana contains more than his book on Scepticism.

You need be under no compulsion or hurry to return these books. The two belonging to the N.Y. City College library you may return at your leisure. The others, you may keep with my high regards. The second volume of Spengler I have not with me but I think I can have it sent up from New York. I happen to have an extra copy of it at the College.

Your judgment about Socrates seems to me a little harsh. Socrates was by all accounts a brave soldier, and his refusal to obey the mob's demand to violate the law in the case of the five generals (or admirals) ought to make him an honorary member of all those associations which really believe that law should be enforced while it is on the books.

Tolstoi's *War and Peace* and his *Sebastopol* are more than fiction. They seem to me classics (especially the latter) of human endurance under hardship.

With kindest regards to Mrs. Holmes,

Sincerely yours,
MORRIS R. COHEN

Beverly Farms
Aug. 24, 1924

Dear Cohen:

You seemed to be in transitu when you wrote—so this to the College. I write only to say two things. You misapprehended the emphasis of my remark that as Athens was losing her Empire Socrates was jawing in the streets. I didn't dream of implying a criticism on the old soldier—I meant only that it comforted me to think that just when Athens seemed to be going to ruin she was opening what perhaps was her fairest flower and beginning her rule in the kingdom of philosophy. After War & Peace I read Butler's Way of All Flesh—He has many keen insights—I have suspected that he had not such a central one as coordinated them into a philosophy. —Now I am in Salter's Nietzsche—When years ago I read translations of N. he seemed to me to be writing in a less emancip[at]ed atmosphere and to think and ask us to think that he was a Hell of a Fellow because he didn't believe what his neighbors did—but I shall read Salter with a reasonably docile mind—I think I have read Santayana's book—but have not yet examined it.

They shall be returned within a reasonable time—if I live so long.

Yours ever,
O. W. HOLMES

Beverly Farms
Aug. 28, 1924

Dear Cohen:

By this mail the Nietzsche is returned to you—the others will follow later. You always enrich me by your sendings and this book is no exception. I am very glad to have read it. There is much that I long have believed, after or independently of him—much that I don't care for. He never, it seems to me, got away from his theological start—and must see man as a little god to be happy—and, perhaps because of his nerves, he is in such a touse about his beliefs—I prefer more serenity. But he had real insights and it is pleasant and instructive to read so conscientious a study of him.

Sincerely yours,

O. W. HOLMES

Beverly Farms

Sept. 8, 1924

My dear Cohen:

By this post the remaining three books: Santayana, Scepticism & Animal Faith and The Unknowable and Simmel, Mélanges de Phil. Relativiste are sent to you, to the same address as this letter. Salter's Nietzsche was sent some days ago. Santayana improved somewhat on rereading—as a careful stopping of rat holes though it hardly seems to me novel and seems to me verbose through his desire to make literature. Perhaps his Catholic antecedents make him like to use words that trail rainbows but disguise his meaning, esp. spirit and essence—His literary turn often has a similar effect upon me—Simmel seems to me rather a dull maker of superfluous categories—some of the later pieces seemed to me the best. I was pleased however to see him emphasize experiences that fill the field of consciousness to the exclusion of the antithesis of ego and nonego. I used to dwell on that as a partial explanation of sympathy, e.g. pain—the suggestion of it tends to fill the field and it is a second thought that the pain is that of the other fellow not of you—but the suggestion never seems to have impressed anyone. I should be glad if you would acknowledge receipt of the books—as I worry over such things. They were a benefaction to me—A letter I wrote to you at Peterboro was returned—I suppose you had flitted. I said then that I was glad to see Santayana say a good word for Spencer in the pamphlet. There also were his arabesques of words that hardly pay to unravel.

Sincerely yours,

O. W. HOLMES

Sept. 12, 1924

My dear Justice Holmes:

Your letters of August 24, 28 and Sept. 8 and the book-parcels all duly reached the City College. But this is the first opportunity I have of acknowledging the receipt, as they were not forwarded to Keene,

N.Y., whither I vainly fled from New Hampshire to escape the hay-fever.

I am glad to find that your judgment of Socrates is not what I had misunderstood it to be, and also that you think that Butler had not such control of his insight as to make a coordinated philosophy of them. Butler (and in a measure his imitator Shaw) always seemed to me like a clever and skillful boxer, able to make many telling points, but, withal, devoid of real vitality and strength. With your judgments on the other books I am also in agreement. I am especially delighted with your appreciation of Salter's book on Nietzsche. That book caused me to revise my estimate of Nietzsche in several regards and it is a pleasure to find that you also found it seriously worth while.

As soon as the hay-fever season ends, I hope to finish the book on Reason and Nature about which I wrote to you last summer, and I hope you will not regret to have your name associated with it.

With kind remembrances to Mrs. Holmes

Sincerely yours,

MORRIS R. COHEN

Feb. 16, 1925

Dear Cohen:

Your discourse on Spinoza has come today and I have read it with delight. I am grateful for everything that gives me new reason to love and admire that great man, and also I take in with predetermined assent the collateral criticisms. I think what you say about James* is wholly correct. It was an early and abiding difference between us. I remember writing to him that one of his Essays would please the Unitarian parsons and the ladies. I never supposed him to be sacrificing to a desire for popularity—but I rather thought I saw the Irishman—so visible in his father's work—coming out—great keenness in seeing into the corners of the human heart but impatience of and incapacity for the sustained continuous thinking that makes a philosopher—a great psychologist—not a great philosopher, I always have thought him.

Also I warm up with your tribute to Bradley.† I followed your advice and got the Essays on Truth & Reality and read them. There were passages that I didn't understand that I didn't bother about because I thought that like others who have got into the Hegelian system he continued to swing round in circles as it seems to me all Hegelians do.

* See The Faith of a Liberal, p. 310.
† Ibid., p. 319.

But I was deeply moved by the intensity and persistence of his thought —It makes most other things seem common—and I was delighted by his insistence (I suppose Hegelian in his case) on the inseparability of man and the universe. I think the failure to see this—and the setting up of man as a little God over against the big one, or the cosmos from which the big one has disappeared, is the sin against the Holy Ghost.

Yours ever,
O. W. HOLMES

March 7, 1925

My dear Justice Holmes:

I had hoped that my book on *Reason and Nature* would be finished in time to enable me to present it to you, with its dedication, on your eighty-fourth birthday. But the fates have delayed me, and I herewith offer you the first installment of it.* Being an introductory chapter it is rather thin, and in the endeavor to sound the dominant note of the book it is rather one-sided. But you have always been generous in seeking for my ideas behind the utterances; and if the high regard and affection which makes me send this to you will make your birthday happier, I shall feel rewarded to an unusually high degree.

With heartiest congratulations and best wishes to Mrs. Holmes and yourself,

Sincerely yours,
MORRIS R. COHEN

March 13, 1925

Dear Cohen:

Now I have read your article and am as much pleased by it as I expected to be—I think it admirable for truth and timeliness—As you know, I reserve a theoretic doubt as to the cosmic ultimateness of our can't helps—but I have no doubt that they are our can't helps and govern our world. I regard the will to believe as of a piece with the insistence on the discontinuity of the universe which Bill James shares with Cardinal Newman, and which I suspect as induced by the wish to leave room for the interstitial miracle. When we were in our 20s W. James said to me (in substance) that spiritualism was the last chance to spiritualize or idealize the world. I then and ever since have regarded that as a carnal and superficial view. As to the will to believe

* "The Insurgence against Reason," *Journal of Philosophy,* Vol. 22 (Feb. 26, 1925), p. 113, the substance of which constitutes Chapter 1 of *Reason and Nature.*

why may we not ask on what ground it is recommended except some
assumed can't help to which we all must yield—Otherwise why would
it not be a sufficient answer to say I don't want to? This whole business that you attack seems to me like modernism in art or skirt
dancing—devices of those who don't want to take the trouble and to
go through the long labor necessary to do the regular thing to substitute a high kick and a suggestion that you are going to see something that you *aint*—with which indecency I leave you and hope that
the book will come out soon. I think you are a rational man in the
best sense of the word and I rejoice in you.

Sincerely yours,

O. W. HOLMES

Supreme Court of the United States,
Washington, D.C.

May 25, 1925

Dear Cohen:

Again my thanks for a new pleasure, a pleasure that I mean to renew in a few days as soon as leisure comes again. I have had and have
some work on hand and so have read the two articles* only once and
they need a second squeezing for me to get all their juice. They seem
to me full of wisdom and sound views. I will not attempt to expatiate
now as I have to go to Court presently and fire off some opinions.

Ever sincerely yours,

O. W. HOLMES

Oct. 3, 1925

My Dear Cohen:

Many thanks for your line—We have just got here and I am in
work up to my eyes but expect that order and breathing time will
come out of the chaos. We had a delightful quiet vacation and I acquired some chunks of culture almost forgotten already. We both
are well—and we shall hope to see you. At present we go to taverns
for our victuals as the servants don't come till Oct. twenty some-
thingth—but later we furnish them and almost always are at home
in the evenings.

Sincerely yours,

O. W. HOLMES

We will twist the tail of the cosmos till it squeaks.

* "The Rivals and Substitutes for Reason," subsequently reprinted as Chapter
2 of *Reason and Nature*.

Jan. 24, 1926

My dear Cohen:

Your letter, as always, gives me a glow. I thank you and wish you and yours a happy New Year. I had a letter from Laski the other day in which he said that Bertrand Russell again expressed the opinion that you were the most significant philosopher that we had in the U.S.—I turn back to the words—beginning with Sir Maurice Amos "I was interested to find that he, like I, was more impressed by Morris Cohen than by any other of the academic people he met, for sanity of judgment not less than width of learning. Ben Huebsch, the publisher, who was in here on Tuesday, said practically the same thing—that he felt there was no wiser counsellor in life than Morris Cohen—And on Friday B. Russell was discussing with me the significant American philosophers. Someone there said he supposed Dewey was the outstanding figure. Russell at once said with great emphasis that he thought Morris infinitely more important than Dewey. It is good to think that he is getting this recognition from men of such varied types and opinions"—I thought to write this to you before but the preoccupation of the moment put it off until now. The letter made me rejoice.

Now I have taken a dry dive into a month's sitting and shall breathe only law for a time—but not deeply enough to prevent my delight when I hear good words of you.

Ever sincerely yours,
O. W. HOLMES

Nov. 29, 1926

My dear Cohen:

Many thanks for your article on Bacon*—It says what I long have believed, but says it with a learning and authority that gives me much pleasure. I was tickled too by what you said about the effect of his writing—It so happens that I just have reread his essays and they led me to repeat that the first cause of the survival of a great work is its *sound*—Without the song of his words Shakespeare would not be read as he is—Bacon's Essays with necessary dross have many shrewd remarks—but they are ABC to us and we shouldn't read them if they didn't sound so well—we should get more mental stimulus from a number of the New Republic.

I hope all is well with you—It is with me. I am very busy and therefore write short—I have had some cases that in minor ways opened speculative vistas—which is a joy.

Ever sincerely yours,
O. W. HOLMES

* "Myth About Bacon and the Inductive Method," *Scientific Monthly,* Vol. 23 (1926), p. 50, reprinted in *Studies in Philosophy and Science,* 1949.

Beverly Farms
Sept. 21, 1927

My dear Cohen:

Many thanks for the volume of Robinson's poems—How often have I been indebted to you for new impressions—This time I think rather less than on some previous occasions. I do not readily fall in with American adoption of Arthurian magic. R. has a poetic gift and his words leave an echo—but it seems to me the echo of an echo— His music on the mystery of life does not quite enchant me—and I suspect, though this should be said with trembling, that he is a little too serious about man for an ultimate. Still I am very much obliged to you for the introduction. I have not been wholly unmoved and I shall read more. We are just preparing for our migration and next week I hope to go to Washington. I have no magnum opus mastered as an achievement of vacation, but I have read some things and a little philosophy. The result has been to add to my bill of rights this: No man shall be held to master a system of philosophy that is 50 years old—The comment is that all that anyone, philosopher as well as others, has to contribute is a small number of aperçus—But he constructs a system (which never lasts) and a later generation, if it wants to read his insights at first hand, always probably familiar with them, has to wash two tons of sand for a tablespoon full of gold—The experienced, if they do it, know what they are about, but the young think that the system is the thing and that they must master that— which older fellows regard simply as a bore to be sifted. This was suggested by Spinoza's Ethics, with memory of Kant & Hegel. I don't believe his postulate or yield to his logic—yet I immensely value his sense of the continuity of the universe and his superhuman view of good and evil.

The demands of life shut me up—I must stop—but I am

Ever sincerely yours,
O. W. HOLMES

April 1, 1928

My dear Cohen:

The minute before this marks the closing of your MS. volume,* read. It impresses me very greatly and I long to see the whole thing in print, though I fear that it would contain passages that I did not understand. The general bias of your thought commands my enthusiastic assent—as you have known before now. If when the book

* This was a preliminary draft of *Reason and Nature*.

comes out it still bears my name in the dedication I shall think it one of the greatest honors I ever have received.

I have been very constantly and pretty hard at work—and the crevices have been filled by what I curse you for! For did not one of the essays that you sent crack up Demogue Notions Fondamentales du Droit Privé so much that I felt bound to take it from the Cong. Library and begin it at once? And having begun it I had not the moral force to send it back unfinished—Well, yes—it is a good book—I think I see why you liked it—but I dont think it told me anything that I didnt know although no doubt it emphasized and directed more thought to some things than I had given to them before—I am glad that I have read it that I may not be bullied when some one sits up and says Demogue—but I could ill afford the times it took out of me—and the dislike of having in my house books that dont belong to me gave it a right of way that I greatly grudged—If you go blowing the horn of another law book please put in a footnote Holmes need not read this—unless it is essential to salvation.

With this I return to my labors—30 new applications for certiorari —that I must consider—

I took it that you meant me to keep the MS vol. you sent to me— but if you need it I have it safe in my shelves—And you have my grateful thanks.

> Sincerely yours,
> O. W. HOLMES

> Washington, D.C.
> January 3, 1929

My dear Cohen:

Of course any honor to you delights me—I don't know about the American Philosophical Association [Cohen was elected president for 1929], (to my shame) but I assume that the election sanctions the proposition that you are It, and I rejoice. With my advent to the place of Oldest Ever I also have had some things that pleased me—but they have made me think of Finis with some anxiety as to my duty—So, as I wrote to someone yesterday, I am happy, melancholy and gay—the happier for your letter. A happy New Year to you.

> Ever yours,
> O. W. HOLMES

> Jan. 15, 1930

My dear Cohen:

This is only a line of thanks too long delayed by incessant occupation, for the Faith of a Logician.* I can't go into critical remarks just now. I have a surmise that you believe our ultimates to be *the* ultimates more strongly than I do but I don't know. I always think of Caesar's "Et superest ager" after the divisions of which he speaks. As a bettabilitarian I bet the cosmos has in it a somewhat that would strike us as pretty queer if we were capable of being struck by it with our present faculties. But I am swamped in the law.

Affectionately yours,
O. W. HOLMES

Beverly Farms,
Massachusetts
July 8, 1930

My dear Cohen:

By some fatality, I know not what, your article on Vision & Technique etc.† escaped me until today. I have just read it with the usual pleasure that I expect from anything of yours. With hearty agreement also, bar a very few sentences which I did not know enough to understand. I suspect that I should stop, with avowed ignorance, a little earlier than you would—perhaps because you know more about the subject—perhaps merely by temperament—and perhaps it isn't true.

I hope all is going well with you. I am in my vacation, in these days not unpursued by court work, but getting some time not only for drives and sleep, but even for reading. My sec'y is reading Trotsky's autobiography to me now. Laski imposed it on me and I shouldn't be happy not to finish it, but I don't like the man, or see the evidence that he incarnated a great truth, and his life calls up all the ultimately critical judgments that I got from early association with the abolitionists.

Ever sincerely yours,
O. W. HOLMES

Oct. 9, 1930

My dear Cohen:

Thank you for your letter and the good news that it gives. You don't tell about yourself but I infer that all is well with you. The first

---

* Cohen's statement of his philosophical position, in *Contemporary American Philosophy,* edited by Adams and Montague, 1930, Vol. I, p. 219.

† "Vision and Technique in Philosophy," Cohen's presidential address delivered before the American Philosophical Association; reprinted in *The Faith of a Liberal,* p. 365.

days of a term have a lot of confused work before we settle down to our Court—but everything is in good shape with me and I am well as far as heard from. The possibility of unforeseen accident looms larger than in youth but I hope to reach 90 and still to be able to call myself

Your affectionate friend,
O. W. HOLMES

February 28, 1931

My dear Justice Holmes:

May I visit you on Sunday March 8 and bring you the first copy of my book on *Nature and Reason?* I should also like to bring my son who as editor of the Columbia Law Review wants to present you a copy of the March number of that publication which is dedicated to you.

Trusting that the cosmos will continue to present twistable ends, when we meet again, I am

Affectionately yours,
MORRIS R. COHEN

March 2, 1931

My dear Cohen:

It will be a delight and pride to see you, your book and your son. My only regret is that I can't ask you to feed with me. Duties and preemptions have filled my table at luncheon and at supper I shall be so tired that I shall ask no one except Laski who will pass the night with me. If the day is fair I shall try to get a drive from 3 to 4 p.m. After that, and in the morning from 11^{30} to 1 I shall be accessible and be looking forward to your visit. I suppose that between 4 and 5 there may be a number of people here.

Affectionately yours,
O. W. HOLMES

854 W. 181st
March 8, 1931

Dear Justice Holmes:

Knowing the multitude of letters that reach you on your birthday and your anxiety about answering them, I am loath to add to your burden. Yet I cannot forbear to express my profound gratification that you have been permitted by the fates to hold your post so long and so well. Recently some of my friends have argued before your court and they have reenforced the impression that your written opinions make on me, which makes me hope most ardently that you will continue on the bench for some years to come. One who thinks clearly and courageously must be prepared to be in advance of the main army which moves more slowly. But, within a few years, I am sure that many of your views which have not yet prevailed will become the dominating forces which they deserve to be.

With all best wishes,

Affectionately yours,
MORRIS R. COHEN

March 14, 1931

My dear Cohen:

There has been no time yet to thank you for your book and re-membrances, but I rely upon your understanding and forgiving. It will be my first serious reading and I don't doubt will fortify you in your great place in the philosophic world. Your place in friendship needs no fortification (nor does the other, for the matter of that). I look on the visit from you and your son as only deferred.

Affectionately yours,
O. W. HOLMES

Beverly Farms, Mass.
July 13, 1931

My dear Cohen:

Thank you from my heart for your picture.* It is admirable—better than a photograph from life it gives the acumen of the subject and his goodness. Your work will outlive the canvas but while it or any repro-duction of it remains it will be confirmatory evidence of what the books prove. Anyone who sees it will say There was a wonderful man.

Affectionately yours,
O. W. HOLMES

My best remembrances to Mrs. Cohen.

Colony Hall,
Peterboro, N.H.
July 17, 1931

Dear Justice Holmes:

It is naturally difficult for me to agree entirely to your extraordi-narily generous tribute to my character and achievements. But I am

* A photographic reproduction of the oil painting by Joseph Margulies. See page 102.

stirred to my depths by your extreme kindness, and I am quite proud to have drawn this tribute from you. That is itself an achievement that makes me feel that my life and struggles have been worth while. I shall treasure it for the rest of my life and I think that my children will do likewise.

Gratefully and affectionately yours,
MORRIS R. COHEN

854 W. 181st
Jan. 13, 1932

Dear Justice Holmes:

As a citizen I regret to hear that your wise counsel will no longer be heard in the conferences of the justices of the Supreme Court and that our country will no longer have the benefit of your services as a judge, except to the extent that your past decisions and other writings may continue to point the true way. But as a friend I trust that you will find joy in your increased leisure and twist the tail of the cosmos with a freedom which your previous duties did not allow.

My wife joins in cordial regards and best wishes.

Ever affectionately yours,
MORRIS R. COHEN

Beverly Farms,
Massachusetts
July 26, 1932

My dear Professor Cohen:

Mr. Justice Holmes has asked me to thank you for sending to him your paper on Hegel's Rationalism,* and to tell you that he very much enjoyed reading it. He finds it a little difficult to write himself, and he does not therefore undertake a critical discussion, but sends to you his very good wishes. I am

Very sincerely yours,
HORACE CHAPMAN ROSE
Secretary to Mr. Justice Holmes

854 W. 181st
March 7, 1934

My dear Justice Holmes:

I am grateful to you for having a birthday at least once a year—for it gives me an opportunity to express my affectionate homage. As a

* "Hegel's Rationalism," in *Philosophical Review*, Vol. 41 (May 1932), p. 283; reprinted in *Studies in Philosophy and Science*, 1949.

token of it I have sent you a book on *Logic and Scientific Method* written by a former student and myself. It is a book primarily for college students, and its subject-matter is proverbially dry. But a good deal of the life-blood of one of your ardent friends has gone into the work of which this book is the outcome.

With best wishes for *many* happy returns of the day,

Affectionately yours,

MORRIS R. COHEN

P.S. The Italians have a pleasant and happy custom of saluting one who has a birthday by saying: "May you live one hundred years more." One (American?) lady who was permitted to congratulate Pope Leo XIII on his ninetieth birthday, thought that this meant: may you live to be one hundred years old, and by simple arithmetic concluded that she ought to say to the Pope: "May you live ten years more." Whereupon the Pope replied: "Madam, why do you limit the bounty of God." That is why I underscored the word *many* above.[2]

XVII. *Friendship, Issues, and Ideas*

ON A WALK through the Westchester hills, Cohen once confided to a friend, Mrs. Harold Beckman, "Well, I'll never be a great philosopher."

"Why not?" she queried.

"Because people mean too much to me. I want to like people and I want them to like me."

Cohen's correspondence reveals his gift for friendship. He made friends with ordinary people as well as with the intellectual giants of his day, with women and men, children and grownups. He could quiet a baby's crying when nobody else could and gained the confidence of many a small child. The only time in his life that I knew him to dance was at the bidding of his first grandchild, Gene Maura.

Cohen even made friends of his own three children. Although he believed in and practiced parental discipline, he brought us up not to be conventional, once inviting us, if we wished, to call him Morris, which we refused to do. He was proud of his children. When his friends and colleagues chided him for being overboastful of his first-born, beautiful and bright Felix, he protested, "Everybody *thinks* that his child is the best. The only difference is, mine *really* is."

His children were, inevitably, influenced by his philosophical mind. He acknowledged proudly to his logic class at the College that Felix, at two and a half, had bested him in logic. It seemed that one evening when he came home he found Felix in distress.

"I lost my ball."

"Don't worry, I'll find it for you."

"You mean you'll look for it."

"All right, I'll look for it. But I'm a little tired now. After supper."

"Papa, does that mean as soon as supper is over?"

361

The youngest child, Willie, proved that he, too, was his father's skeptical son. It was Thanksgiving, 1915, in the big old-fashioned kitchen of the Cohen home in Nepperhan Heights, Yonkers. The cat was in hiding under the coal stove. Willie, aged four, took the poker and tried to rustle her out. Eight-year-old Felix tried to wrest the poker away from his younger brother.

"The Good Book says to be kind to dumb animals," Felix argued. But Willie answered, "Daddy says not to believe everything you read."

The most radiantly happy expressions I ever saw on my father's face were when his boys used to sing and he would smile at Mother. He confided to his student, Hodes, who came to the house with his fiancée, "My three children mean more to me than my work."

Of his children, he said he had a thinker, Felix; a dreamer, Leonora; and a doer, Victor William; but that he ought to change their names from Felix S. to Felix Sweet, from Leonora D. to Leonora Darling, from William J. to William Joy. A year before his death he dedicated his *Faith of a Liberal* "To the ever-blessed memory of Mary Ryshpan Cohen, the dear companion of my life's journey and to our children, who, in life's diverse paths, have remained loyal to the liberal faith in which they were nurtured."

Felix Cohen turned out to be an inestimable boon to his father. Independent as were their minds, their relationship was one of rare understanding. Felix's prodding and assistance helped him produce *Reason and Nature*. Felix directed the flow of Morris Cohen's posthumous books with selfless drive, devoted skill, and scrupulous regard for his father's words.

Cohen's solicitude for his children's intellectual development did not dampen the warmth of his love, as his letters showed.

[early spring 1930]

Dearest Leonora:

I have no clear idea of what you want me to do for you in regard to your essay on the theology of Plato and Aristotle. I am sending you under separate cover Caird's book on the subject. If you take Jowett's Plato, last volume, you will find in the Index sufficient references to your theme under the heading God pp. 421–3. Read the most promising references, especially those to the Timaeus and you will need no other material—though the references in Benn, Zeller, and Gomperz may aid you after you get your material together. Plato was steeped in the popular theology of his day. Always speaks with reverence of sacrifices, the oracle at Delphi etc. Yet in trying to uphold the old orthodoxy he has to banish superstition and so refines the notion of the Godhead until it departs from the popular view very far indeed. Hence he is both full of popular superstition and of philosophic view of Deity in which the popular mind cannot participate—because the anthropomorphic form is banished altogether.

Aristotle's theology is not so readily gathered from his work. Read Zeller's Aristotle ch. 16 (vol. II, pp. 325 ff.). The following appended notes may be of some suggestion to you.

It would be nice if you could come home next weekend.

Your loving Father

[He appended this note:]

Aristotle's View of the Gods

God or the gods according to Aristotle (it makes no difference which you use) cannot be said to create the world. For to create is to *do* something (in time) and one does that only to improve his condition. But the gods must be supposed to be happy (supremely so) all the time. Hence to ascribe any act of creation, or interference in earthly affairs, is blasphemous. The same result is achieved by looking at the processes of the world itself. All these processes involve changes of matter in accordance with certain forms e.g. acorns grow into oaks and these give rise to other acorns, so that there is a cycle through which the matter passes. Matter itself and form itself are thus eternal and uncreated. And God is thus not their creator. Nevertheless God is the unmoved mover of everything in nature, just as a good man without taking part in the affairs of his neighbors may influence them by setting a model for them to imitate.

You can see this more in detail as follows:

Considered in itself matter is mere possibility. It becomes something e.g. marble or a brick if it assumes a definite form. The marble may assume the form of a statue through the act of the sculptor, or the brick the form of a house through the act of the mason. But when we get to the organic field, the form poses itself on the matter. And when we come to thought the sensations of things become definite ideas by taking on rational form. But the most creative thought (or creative reason) is that which gives form to the whole of nature. Now God is the form of forms or the thought of all thinking. The gods thus think not of anything material or barely possible, but they are most active in thinking of the ultimate reality which is their own nature.

The moment of creative insight is a great thrill in the life of the individual philosopher. But the gods have that supreme bliss all the time. Thus the gods are supremely happy, make everything in the world strive for perfection, and yet are not themselves active or engaged in any activity except that of contemplation.

Aristotle's God is not much different from Dante's God as portrayed in Dante's Paradiso. God is a point outside of the universe. The crystalline sphere that encloses the one containing the fixed stars moves so as to have all its parts within the wonderful light of that Divine point. The sphere of the fixed stars revolves so as to be within the light of the *primum mobile,* and so on to the moon which is its lowest planet. The earth is fixed because Satan the centre of darkness is the very antithesis of God. This is Dante's picture, and is Aristotelian in the sense that God described in the last canto of the Paradiso is not doing anything [but] strive to be within His light.

Aristotle states his view clearest in the 7th chapter of the eleventh book of his Metaphysics (Book Λ).

Feb. 14/41

Dear Sweet Child:

Mother (and I too) will be made very happy if you accept the enclosed token of our love on your birthday. Mother and I are highly appreciative of your wonderful devotion to us all these years and especially since Mother's illness. Mother would have bought you a present, but since she could not do so she thinks a reversion to the custom [gift-giving] when you were a little girl would be most appropriate. I hope you will agree with her and thus add to her gratitude.

Ever your loving
DAD

The University of Chicago
Department of Philosophy
April 11/41

Dearest Lealie:

I was glad to get your sweet letter and the pleasant review of your book. . . .

I do not know of any Balzac story that I have not seen in print, and therefore will not be new to your audience. Moreover those stories that I recollect may not be accurate. Thus I vaguely remember that Alexandre Dumas (who was not generous to other novelists) said to some great literary "shot" as Balzac was dying: We are losing the greatest mind (or literary figure?) in Europe. But the exact wording I cannot guarantee. The one sentence *in* Balzac that I remember and can place in its context is a statement in the story called Honorine: "Frenchmen do not travel. They live in France." But I have

a book at home called *Wit and Wisdom of Balzac* [by Harry Rickel].
It is in the hall opposite the closets amidst a number of books on
French and Italian literature. Some extracts from it would best
serve your purpose.

Vaudrin [editor, Oxford University Press] wrote me about my book
on American Thought which he wants to publish. I told him that it
would be considerable time before I get to *write* that book in its final
form.

I have engaged rooms in the Saranac Apartment Hotel where we
stayed in 1938 and 1939. They provide maid service and Mother
does not have to do any household work except prepare meals when
we do not care to go out. In the past that has not been any strain on
Mahi.

Love to you, to Mother, Felix, Willie, Harry, Lucy, Grace and
Gene Maura.

DAD

The Saranac Hotel
5541 S. Everett St.
[Chicago]
4/26/41

Dearest Lealie:

It was a very sweet letter that you sent me to Oberlin—where,
incidentally, I had a very quiet and pleasant time.

I spoke to the editor of *Modern Philology* (Dr. Crane) and he
said he would see that your book receives a review. I received a letter
from Mrs. Balz in which she said that her husband [Professor A. G.
A. Balz, Philosophy Department, University of Virginia] "enjoyed receiving your daughter's book and spoke of it in most glowing terms
—" which is not at all displeasing to the father of the author. . . .

With love to you both
DAD

Friday
[November 1941]

Darlingest Léali:

I was happy to get your good letter, the post card and the coat
and delighted of course to have Harry call me up and speak to me
from Michigan. . . .

The election of Wright [to the presidency of The City College]
was not unexpected on my part. It is rather a come down from such
a man as [Dean Carl] Wittke or [Dean Richard] McKeon, but better

than others who have been considered. No really good man was willing to take the presidency under the present set-up, with the witch-hunting still going on in the form of trials. Let us hope that better days are coming.

Don't catch cold before the Christmas vacation and be sure to go out of town for a good rest during that week. I shall probably see you on Friday the 19th.

Lovingly
DAD

My love to Harry, too.

Albert Einstein

Cohen met Einstein for the first time in 1921. Dr. Reinhardt Wetzel of The City College physics department went to the ship to meet Einstein when he landed in America for the first time, evidently the only person who had come to greet him. He invited him to lecture at the College. He had no money to offer, but that didn't matter to Einstein. Cohen met Einstein for the first time at that lecture. A College photograph taken right after the talk shows Einstein in the company of Cohen and other host professors. Einstein spoke no English, and so Cohen, who knew German and enough physics to have published in *The New Republic* two papers on Einstein's exciting new theories of relativity, reported the lecture for *The Campus*. Einstein was pleased and made plans to meet him again.

It was spring, and Einstein told Cohen how much he would like to see the country outside of New York. Cohen arranged with a friend for a car and chauffeur, and on a sunny Sunday Einstein with Morris and Mary Cohen set out for the Westchester hills and woods. We children had come along before the trip began to be introduced to Einstein; he was waiting, playing with a group of rather ragged little boys, laughing and waving his cane. Afterward as we Cohen children walked home, we overtook the boys. "I know who he is," said one of them, "he's the musician from the Colosseum." The Colosseum was the local cinema. None of us told the boys whom they had really met.

To commemorate that visit, the Einsteins sent gifts—a jewel box for my mother, a photograph for my father, inscribed in German, "To the philosopher and warm friend, Albert Einstein." A correspondence began between the two men, or more properly between the two families since the wives also wrote.

Einstein was the indirect cause of Morris Cohen's sole visit to the movies. A special showing was held for Cohen, and he was paid a hundred dollars for his review of a film on Einstein's physics. (When chided as to why he did not attend the cinema, Cohen used to answer that he would, under similar conditions.) Here is part of his review for *Vanity Fair* (August 1923):

Einstein in the Movies

I confess that before actually seeing it the idea of putting Einstein's theory on a film struck me as painfully absurd, almost as indecorous as that of a bishop appearing in a cabaret performance. But a little child has led me to change this attitude. I have a boy of 11 attending one of those modern schools that do not overemphasize reading, writing, and such other high-brow stuff; and so when he came home one day all full of enthusiasm for the Einstein movie which they had shown him I pricked up my ears. I found that the little fellow had really learned something in an enjoyable way and I became rather anxious to see for myself how much of the relativity theory could possibly be illustrated in the cinema.

. . . gave me the opportunity to see how much more suitable moving pictures are than mere words or fixed diagrams to represent physical happenings. The moving picture adds the dimension of time to the picture and is thus a more adequate representation of actual physical events.

. . . the Einstein film is well worth while. . . .

On the Einsteins' second visit to this country, 1930–31, they spent only a few days in the East, but asked to see the Cohens. So at the dinner given by Dr. Leonor Michaelis, distinguished biochemist of the Rockefeller Institute, the Cohens were present, along with Dr. Bela Schick.

After Hitler's accession to power, the Einsteins again arrived in America, this time to settle down for good at Princeton, where he became director of the school of mathematics at the Institute for Advanced Study. In the late fall of 1933, they invited the Cohen family for luncheon at their home in Princeton. The economist Dr. Otto Nathan, who soon became Dr. Einstein's closest friend in America, was the sole other guest at the luncheon. My brother Victor William, who was already an experimental physicist, was taking his doctorate at Columbia and studying under Dr. I. I. Rabi, the future Nobel-prize winner. Einstein was much interested to hear of my brother's experiments in measuring the nuclear spin of the sodium atom. *"Ja, ja,"* said Einstein, "even though I'm a theoretical physicist, I sometimes like to experiment in a laboratory. I've tried my hand at some experiments in ferromagnetism."

Mrs. Einstein confided to my mother that of all their worldly possessions that had been confiscated in Germany what they most regretted losing was their sailboat, for sailing was her husband's greatest relaxation.

The return visit was a luncheon for the Einsteins at the Cohens in early January 1934. My brother Bill took a photograph that shows a radiantly smiling Einstein and his wife, Elsa, with the Cohens. Though Einstein's long hair was already gray, his mustache was still dark, and his unlined face free of that air of sadness that haunts his later pictures. Einstein was going from our house to Steinway Hall, to rehearse for a violin concert he was giving for some Jewish benefit. "Those who come to see me instead of to listen to the music should pay double!" he said. I was invited to ride downtown and stepped into the car, which was crowded with Einstein's friends. "Why don't you take *das schöne Kind* on your lap?" someone asked. And that is how, for a short time, I sat on Einstein's lap!

Once at a dinner party where the Cohens were present with the Einsteins, Mother was not feeling too well, and, finding it chilly, said, "Morris dear, would you please go upstairs and bring me down my stole?" Elsa Einstein turned to her friend and asked in perplexity, "How can you ask your husband to bring you something from upstairs? He is a great professor, not a servant. I would never dream of asking such a thing of *meinen Mann*."

A year or two thereafter Mrs. Einstein was dying. Cohen had just written a review of Einstein's *The World As I See It* but had not yet published the piece, which was somewhat critical of Einstein's views on Jewish and world problems. Professor Otto Nathan came to the house to make a plea, in the circumstances, for a more gentle criticism. My father was always loath to let personal considerations sway him in his value judgments. I remember my mother trying, gently as always, to persuade him. He did slightly modify some of the most critical remarks, and sent a copy of the proofs to Einstein, who suggested only a few technical corrections.

Not long thereafter, Einstein was scheduled to speak at a dinner to organize support for my father's brain child, the Conference on Jewish Relations. My husband, Harry N. Rosenfield, borrowed his father's car to bring Einstein to New York. It was bitter winter, but when he arrived in Princeton, Einstein was not only hatless, he was coatless and without socks.

My husband was stern. "Professor Einstein, you must wear a coat."

"Oh, I'm not cold," he replied.

"Professor Einstein," said my husband. "I can't assume the responsibility of bringing you out in this weather unless you put on an overcoat." Finally, Einstein's faithful secretary, Miss Helen Dukas, came to the rescue and brought a coat, which Einstein dutifully put on.

My husband was still not satisfied. "How about socks?"

"I never wear them," Einstein replied.

"Why not?"

"They only get holes and then somebody has to mend them. It's less trouble not to bother."

Along the way, Einstein, perplexed, asked my husband: "Why do people want to see me?" He was too deeply modest to be spoiled by his fame.

As the letters below indicate, Einstein sent two manuscripts, handwritten in German, to Cohen. They constitute Einstein's mark of esteem for the intellectual companionship with Cohen, with whom he enjoyed "unforgettable conversations." The manuscripts of 1930 have never been published; in fact, they were the sole copies. The more important of the two, "Kaluza's Theory of the Relation between Gravitation and Electricity (Second Communication)" is a different paper from an earlier one of the same name (published in 1927 by the *Preussische Akademie der Wissenschaften*), evidently a sequel, as "Second Communication" indicates. Einstein, in this general statement of his theory of space and matter, reached into the philosophy of science, just as Cohen the philosopher reached a comprehension of the implications of Einstein's unified mathematical concept of the physical world. Cohen expressed in his autobiography how his contact with Einstein stimulated his philosophy.[1]

June 6/21

Dear Professor Einstein:

It was difficult for me to express to you orally and in a foreign language the joy and courage which my meeting you has afforded me. Poor health, too much drudgery, and a scattering of my mental efforts to the four corners of the intellectual world—law, mathematics, history of civilization, and philosophy—have prevented me from as yet accomplishing any of the things for which I have been striving. The kind and friendly interest which you expressed in my work has, therefore, meant much more encouragement to me than you can readily imagine. I hope that you will remember, when you read the several re-prints of mine that you took along, that they were written years ago and that they were addressed to fellow-philosophers. I can only hope that some of the things which I hope to print soon will be of greater value and will interest you more. I ardently hope that you will find it possible to accept the Columbia offer. If you decide to do so, please let me or Mr. Gano Dunn know. I am sure that we can secure similar offers from neighboring Universities. If you come for scientific purposes it will not be necessary for you to live in New York hotels. Arrangements can be made for you and Mrs. Einstein to live in some quiet neighborhood where you can meet the people you want and have your privacy respected.

With warmest regards to you and to Mrs. Einstein, in which my wife joins,

Faithfully yours,
MORRIS R. COHEN

P.S. I enclose a German translation of this letter, but I don't know which you will find easier to read.

New York, July 22/21

Dear Prof. Einstein:

Through the courtesy of Mr. Perleberg I have just received the two gifts which you and your wife were so kind to send us. Mrs. Cohen is away in the country but I am sure she will be as pleased and grateful as I am to be so sweetly remembered by you. Perhaps you can form a better idea of how thankful I am by reading the enclosed letter which I wrote a few days after you left New York. It came back to me some time ago and I was wondering where to address you when good fortune brought Mr. Perleberg.

I had been hoping to send you some portions of my book on the logic of mathematical physics. But the American Association of Law Schools has put me on an editorial committee to prepare books on Legal Philosophy (Rechtsphilosophie) and this will keep me busy for some time. However, I am not altogether out of touch with physical philosophy. A popular review [by Cohen in *The New Republic*] of eleven books on relativity, which I am sending you under separate cover, may contain some remarks of interest to you. Have you read Prof. Whitehead's two recent books? There is some talk of having him come over to America next winter to lecture. You might visit him at Columbia if you decide to come.

With gratitude and heartiest best wishes to you and Mrs. Einstein,

Faithfully yours,

MORRIS R. COHEN

June 23/22

My dear Professor Einstein:

Realizing that European scholars cannot at present afford to buy books printed in English, the American Philosophical Association has appropriated some money for the purpose of buying philosophic books and journals, and sending them *gratis* to European libraries and scholars that need them. As Vice-President of the American Philosophical Association and as a member of this committee I am very anxious to get into personal correspondence with German philosophers who can advise me as to what books are most needed and to whom they ought to be sent. Though I know many German philosophers by their works I know none of them personally. I should, therefore, appreciate it very much if you could send me the names of any philosophers that you know at Berlin or elsewhere and to whom you would be willing to recommend me as a trustworthy person. I make this request of you because I know your intense interest in the cause of international intellectual cooperation.

The Princeton University Press is announcing the forthcoming publication of your four lectures on *Relativity,* and I am hoping that you will soon have the opportunity of writing out the lecture on *Quanta and Radiation* which you promised to this College. Sommerfeld's *Atombau und Spektrallinien* is making a great stir among our physicists and the publication of a lecture of yours on the theory of quanta, or on any other phase of the subject, would be of great help to American physics and especially to the City College and to myself.

Please convey my kind remembrance to your wife, and believe me,

Sincerely yours

MORRIS R. COHEN

Radiogram, Berlin, Oct. 15, 1927
Dinner Professor Cohen Hotel Astor New York City
Remembering unforgettable conversations I send best wishes.

ALBERT EINSTEIN

Berlin W.—May 10, 1928
Haberland Str. 5.

My highly esteemed and dear Mr. Cohen,

On a recent visit Mr. Wind brought me the chapters which I have already read in part with great interest. Best of all, he could tell me directly of you and your activities, which he did with great warmth and understanding. He also mentioned that you suffer from nationalism, a state of affairs I know only too well from past experience. But it might console you to know that this suffering has almost ceased, since as time passes people have the laudable urge to turn again to new follies. —I repeatedly think of you, whenever I carry your handsome leather briefcase, filled with music, to the homes of friends to play music.

Our physics has at present again become quite interesting, since it doubts the possibility of the application of causality, in the usual sense, to space and time. If this interests you, you may orient yourself by reading a beautifully and lucidly written essay by Nils Bohr, which appeared recently in *Naturwissenschaften* and probably also in *Nature.* Still, I must admit that I hardly believe in the finality of this change.

With cordial greetings
Your

A. EINSTEIN

P.S. This is not in my handwriting, because at present I am sick.

N.Y. Dec. 16 –'30

Dear Dr. Einstein:

My husband, Morris R. Cohen, is sending you a brief-case as a very slight token of his love for you. He asks me to tell you that when the old one is worn out and you no longer have any use for it, he would be happy if you would give it to him as a most precious keepsake. It would be handed down as a most precious heirloom from generation to generation in the Cohen family, superior to diamonds and jewels.

Thanking you from my heart for that unforgettable visit of last Thursday at the home of Prof. and Mrs. Michaelis, and wishing you a happy journey, I am,

Yours forever grateful,
MARY R. COHEN

[December 1930]

My dear Mrs. Einstein:

My husband, Morris R. Cohen, and I wish to thank you from our hearts for the great joy and the great honor you conferred upon us by inviting us to spend the evening with you at Prof. and Mrs. Michaelis' home on last Thursday evening. It is one of the greatest honors ever received in the Cohen family.

If I had had the German language at my command I would have liked to tell your illustrious husband how we treasure his utterances not only in mathematics and physics (for that is understood only by two members of the family) but in regard to:

1. International peace and understanding

2. The duty of America to lead the way for the genuine outlawry of war and to find an intelligent way out of the economic depression of the entire world.

3. His mighty helpfulness to our people in Eastern Europe (the Ort [ORT]) and in Palestine.

4. [words missing] views on religion which seem to me as [words missing] to-day as were those of Isaiah for the people of his generation.

It is for these timely messages to a sorely tried humanity that all the world loves your husband and is on the way to worship at his feet.

I hope that at some future time when entirely convenient to you, you will give us the great joy and honor to visit us at our home to meet our children, Dr. Felix Cohen, philosopher and lawyer who hopes to mould law in America nearer to a true ideal of justice for the down-trodden, William who is specializing in physics, and mathematics and hopes to follow in the footsteps of your great husband and

Leonora who is studying at Columbia University.

May you have a happy, restful voyage and many happy years ahead of you.

Always gratefully yours,
MARY R. COHEN

December 17, 1930

My dear Mrs. Cohen,

I hope that the letter I have written you a few days ago and which Mrs. Michaelis wanted to deliver has reached you. I must tell you once again how much I value your kind attention and how grateful I am for it. The beautiful brief case which you have given my husband 10 years ago at the farewell in New York was taken good care of in spite of zealous use and was handled with great care. Once it has served its time it will pass into your hands alone or into those of your children. This I solemnly promise you right now. But its time has not yet come. It still serves faithfully and has a sturdy and beautiful look. So the wonderful new briefcase will lie around for a little while.

I am happy that you value my husband so much, I even may say that you love him. And you and your dear husband must feel yourselves the strength of my husband's feeling for your excellent husband. It is my desire to do something nice for you and so it is my intention to present you, after having returned home in good health, some manuscript notes of my husband which I consider important.

I greet you from my whole heart

Your

ELSA EINSTEIN

P.S. In the past days, my husband has produced a work about the present state of his theory. We have gladly decided to present it to you. We send it enclosed, and hope that it will reach you undamaged.

December 18, 1930

Dear Mrs. Cohen,

I was so glad to have met the two of you in a congenial (gemütlich) atmosphere, and have felt how close we are to each other. Your husband's essays I have already read to a large extent and with great interest. As a souvenir you will receive a small manuscript I have recently written, and which may, on account of the general nature of its contents, interest your husband.

With best wishes

Your

A. EINSTEIN

March 11, 1931

My dear Mrs. Cohen!

As often as I write you I have to thank you for some kindness that you have shown to us; this time in the form of wonderful candies. I thank you from all my heart for all the good things that you had let us have in such great quantity and in so charming a manner.

Unfortunately the wretched manuscript could not be found yet. I will personally complain in Berlin to the Foreign Office since if an ambassador is entrusted personally with such a valuable manuscript he is also responsible for its proper delivery. A registered letter does not get lost.

Be greeted from all my heart

Your

ELSA EINSTEIN

On Kaluza's Theory of the Relation between Gravitation and Electricity (second communication) by A. Einstein

[To his manuscript, handwritten in German, Einstein appended these notes to Cohen, which Dr. S. A. Goudsmit, physicist at the Brookhaven National Laboratory, has kindly translated:]

My efforts deal with a mathematical physical theory of space and matter. It is an attempt to extend Maxwell's field theory in the sense that the theory of gravitation, electricity and matter is based upon a unified mathematical concept.

I am of the opinion that the English Government has not acted in accordance with the duties it has taken upon itself. Yet I believe and hope that it will seek and find ways to influence the development of Palestine in the future in such a way that the true interests of Arabs and Jews, as well as English interests are served. On the other hand I believe also that the Jews must seek to make such contacts with the Arab people, that Jews and Arabs do not continually get into such a position that the English administration has to be called upon as arbiter. Because a healthy and satisfying development is only feasible on the basis of an independent agreement between the principal participants.

["The other manuscript," adds Dr. Goudsmit, "is a so-called popular paper *Old and New on Field Theory.* . . . Einstein tries to use words instead of differential geometry, but gives up on page 9."]

N.Y. Jan. 3,–'32

Dear Friends:

Accept our heartiest thanks for your wonderful gift to us—the two precious manuscripts and the two lovely letters that came with them. The Cohen family were overjoyed when the lost letters finally arrived. We have already decided to whom to leave the manuscripts when we make our will. They are to go to our youngest son who is now doing interesting research in physics. He is measuring the magnetic moment of the nucleus of an atom. When he has an opportunity to meet you again he will tell you about it.

May the New Year be a very happy one to you and your dear ones. With high esteem and deep affection,

Yours cordially,

MARY R. COHEN

The Institute for Advanced Study
School of Mathematics
Fine Hall
Princeton, N.J.

December 10, 1933

Dear and honored Mr. Morris Cohen!—

I have received your book on the philosophy of law, but so far I have read too little of it to venture an opinion on the subject. But I was pleased to note that in your book you properly defend reason which has been so discredited in our time of decay. I am convinced that this child of your spirit, too, will delight me like all the earlier ones.

My most cordial thanks, and greetings—

Your

A. EINSTEIN

Feb. 21/34

Dearly beloved Albert Einstein:

I have been urged to ask you to write a letter stating the grievances of intellectual workers against the barbarities of the Hitler regime. This letter is to be read at the meeting on March 7 devoted to the *Cause of Civilization against Hitler*. Although you have on previous occasions already indicated your attitude to what is now going on in Germany, a renewed expression of yours as to what the present German government is doing to the Arts and sciences would, I am sure, carry weight and help to make the meeting effective.

In collaboration with a former pupil of mine, Dr. Nagel, I have recently published an elementary text-book on *Logic and Scientific Method*. I have asked the publishers to send you a copy. I cannot flatter myself that it is worth your while to look into it. And yet there may be some points about modern logic which may interest you. In any case I hope you will accept it with my affectionate regard.

With cordial greetings to your good wife,

Faithfully yours
MORRIS R. COHEN

Einstein forwarded to Cohen a plea from Professor Anton Lampa about Dr. Ludwig Mach (the son of the philosopher Ernst Mach) who was in very straitened circumstances. The thought was to set up Ernst Mach Archives, with the son in charge.

9 December 1935

Dear Morris Cohen:

Last summer, Mrs. Carola Hauschka-Spaeth did one of the best drawings of me which exists today. To my knowledge, this has not yet appeared in the press. The best would be for you to contact Mrs. Hauschka for this drawing: 34, Vandeventer Ave. Princeton N.J.

Another delicate matter. I have received the enclosed desperate letter of a trusted old friend from Vienna who was my colleague in Prague [Dr. Lampa]. The matter appears to me not wholly hopeless, insofar as people *here* do have a certain appreciation for relics of significant men. Now I should like to ask you whether among the libraries or learned societies in this country there might possibly be one to which I might turn in this matter with some prospect of success. [Ernst] Mach certainly belongs to those men who decisively influenced the intellectual development towards the end of the last century.

My wife is already feeling better, giving me hope that she will return to somewhat improved health.

Hoping to see you soon again, with cordial greetings,

Your
A. EINSTEIN

January 2, 1936

Dear Albert Einstein:

I am enclosing a check of $35 for Dr. Ludwig Mach. I am hopeful of being able to raise some more money soon. When you send it to Dr. Mach, you may do that in the name of Professor Robert Lowie and friends.

Trusting Mrs. Einstein is completely recovering her health, and with most cordial good wishes for the New Year,

Sincerely yours,

MORRIS R. COHEN

June 3, 1936

Dear Albert Einstein:

The Pan-American University of Lima, Peru wishes to engage two or three teachers of Mathematics and I have been assured that there will be no objection to Jewish young men. The salary to begin with will be about *$2,500* which is fairly good, considering the low cost of living. Do you know any young men such as Mr. Zippen, who would care to apply for such a position? If you do, please tell them to get in touch with *Mr. Lyon, Secretary to Dr. Kennedy,* the President of the University, now *temporarily staying* at the Grand Hotel, Broadway & 31 Str., New York City. This seems a good opportunity for a Jewish young man not otherwise placed.

With kindest remembrances to your wife, whose health I trust is improving,

Cordially yours,

MORRIS R. COHEN

A. Einstein
112 Mercer Street
Princeton, N.J.
June 9, 1936

Dear Professor Cohen:

You sent me highly enjoyable news. If I have been slow to reply, it was because I meant to be thoroughly informed. And then there was the difficulty of my not knowing whether only pure mathematicians or also mathematical physicists might be considered. Let me name, first of all, three pure mathematicians:

Dr. Reinhold Baer
Dr. Zorn
Dr. Schilling

Baer and Zorn are German Jews, Schilling (also from Germany) is not Jewish.

The mathematical physicists are:

Dr. Nordheim
Dr. Cornel Lanczos
Dr. Stobbe

All three are from Germany, and Lanczos, for one year my former assistant, left for America before the time of Hitler. Nordheim, with considerable achievements to his name, has a temporary position, about to terminate, at an American university. The most reliable report on him can be furnished by Professor Karl Herzfeld of Johns Hopkins University in Baltimore. —I also consider Dr. Stobbe to be really gifted. He is at present at the Institute for Advanced Study of Princeton. Unlike the other two, he is not Jewish, but he lost his position in Germany for refusing to take over in Göttingen the lectures of Professor Born who had been expelled. Dr. Lanczos who at the moment is at Purdue University in Lafayette, Ind., is also an excellent man capable of original research. At the place just mentioned, he has a temporary position which, as he recently wrote me, is endangered.

I am firmly convinced that each one of these would acquit himself admirably. It is, of course, despicable that one should have to go to any pains in locating a field of activity for such excellent men.

Cordial greetings

Your

A. EINSTEIN

P.S. Schilling, too, lives here because he is anti-fascist. Depending on your more thorough information, I could aid you in the further narrowing of the choice.

November 25, 1937

Dear Professor Cohen:

It is extraordinarily good of you to wish to do something for my son. For about three weeks he stayed with me, and beginning this month he started by car on an extensive trip to hydraulic institutes throughout the country. Around New Year's he probably will have to go back to Switzerland. If there still should be time after his return, I should so like him to get to know you, and less for practical than for purely human reasons.

Meanwhile, my cordial greetings to you and your loved ones.

Your

A. EINSTEIN

December 30, 1938

Mr. Harold H. Levin
27 William Street
New York City

Dear Mr. Levin:—

Despite my high esteem and sympathy for the person and achievement of Professor Cohen, I shall not be able to attend the [Y.M.H.A.]

dinner on February 1st. Weakened health and the variety of demands on my time unfortunately force me to forego all occasions of this nature.

However, it is a pleasure to call attention to the significant service of Professor Cohen as a philosopher and teacher. His presentations of the most varied philosophic disciplines are distinguished by an exemplary lucidity and acuity of thought. He has the rare gift of rendering clear and simple the most complicated chains of reasoning, and he combines an uncommon grasp of literature with refreshing originality. He is stimulating, yet admits no vagueness, and this has lastingly and in a healthy fashion influenced philosophic thought in this country. I have always particularly admired his deep knowledge of the most diverse fields of specialized scientific inquiry. This is by no means true of all renowned philosophers, many of whom resemble the botanist who has never met a living plant face to face.

Your group should note with no less gratitude Professor Cohen's untiring effort in the interests of the Jewish community. We all know his refreshingly dispassionate devotion to its problems. His spirited wit never fails to enliven work on a serious subject, and he escapes the "brutish heaviness" that frequently and characteristically marks academicians.

I wish you a happy and stimulating evening. May it leave a lasting impression.

Yours, most sincerely
A. EINSTEIN

October 31, 1951

Mr. David Rosenstein, Chairman
Conference on Jewish Relations
1841 Broadway
New York 23, N.Y.

Dear Mr. Rosenstein:

I have received your book "Freedom and Reason" and have studied a good deal of it. It is really a worthy monument to the life-work and personality of Morris R. Cohen whom I consider as one of the most efficient teachers in clear thinking this country has ever had. The publication of this book shows the fruitfulness of Cohen's foundation, the Conference on Jewish Relations, which extends far beyond investigation of and public information about the social problems of Jewish Life.

Sincerely yours,
A. EINSTEIN

I knew him well as an extraordinarily helpful, conscientious man of unusually independent character and I rather frequently had the pleasure of discussing with him problems of common interest. But when I occasionally tried to tell something about his spiritual personality, I realized painfully that I was not acquainted enough with the working of his mind.

To fill this lacuna—at least scantily—I took his book *Logic and Scientific Method,* which he had published jointly with Ernest Nagel. . . . I became so fascinated that the external occasion for my reading receded somewhat into the background.

When, after several hours, I came to myself again, I asked myself what it was that had so fascinated me. The answer is simple. The results were not presented as ready-made, but scientific curiosity was first aroused by presenting contrasting possibilities of conceiving the matter. Only then the attempt was made to clarify the issue by thorough argument. The intellectual honesty of the author makes us share the inner struggle in his mind. It is this which is the mark of the born teacher. Knowledge exists in two forms—lifeless, stored in books, and alive in the consciousness of men. The second form of existence is after all the essential one; the first, indispensable as it may be, occupies only an inferior position.[2]

Santayana

At a time when Santayana was less widely known and admired than at present, Cohen promoted acclaim for him. His 1920 piece on Santayana for *The New Republic* (which pleased Santayana very much, according to C. A. Strong), his tribute to him in "Later Philosophy," published in 1921 in *The Cambridge History of American Literature,* his choice of Santayana as the subject of his Hopkins seminar in 1921, his use of Santayana's *The Life of Reason* as his text in his philosophy of civilization courses, his homage to Santayana in the Preface of *Reason and Nature,* all helped call attention to the philosophic charm of this "great and neglected figure," as he called him in *Chance, Love, and Logic.*

Cohen never met Santayana, whom he so admired intellectually, but cherished this letter from him and, I think, profited by its criticism in composing the "architecture" of his later books. Since Santayana did not keep letters to him, there is no record of any response by Cohen.

Rome, May 11, 1931

My dear Professor Cohen,

Let me send you my best thanks for your *Reason & Nature.* I find nothing in the book with which I don't agree, and a great deal that demolishes prevalent idols of the cave and of the theatre. You exhibit most valiantly the weaknesses of James, Dewey & Co. and honourably defend good sense and clear thinking against often cowardly, because convenient, confusions. Living as you do in the midst of morally rather intolerant currents, it is wonderful that you can swim so stoutly and successfully against the stream. Where you seem to me—I stand on the shore—to yield a little to insidious academic influences is in the distribution of your subject-matter. You discuss many points which—though perhaps socially worth straightening out—are of no importance in themselves. And your book in consequence takes rather the form of a running review or *mise-au-point* of contemporary disputes, and misses the architectural impressiveness which greater concentration might have given it. For instance, I hope you may find occasion before long to clear up and emphasize the *ubiquitous directness* of the dependence of mind on organic life, and the *non-existence of mental machinery*. Isn't it grotesque to suppose one idea capable of generating another, as if in music one note were asked to produce another note? On pages 70 and 71 you seem to me to accomodate your language too much to popular metaphors. In discourse relevant ideas are "chosen" because, the bodily and psychic (not mental) reactions being determined by inheritance, training, and circumstances, only relevant ideas *can* arise. And it is the physiological incidence of relaxation and play that brings with it innocent, wild, and perhaps pleasant fancies. It would be gratuitous in a pure spirit either to like rest or to indulge in vagaries. Another point to which I should be glad to see you return is the "reality" of universals. When an essence or a trope (if I may use my lingo) is exemplified in events, it becomes a part of their essence; but I should hardly say (would you?) that even the whole essence or description of a natural fact *was* that fact. The universal merely defines the fact, and is true of it; but the fact is more than its essence; it exists by being generated, situated, and sustained in the midst of nature by the flow of substance into that form at that juncture. Otherwise, your universals couldn't define existence, but only themselves. Am I wrong?

Yours sincerely

G. SANTAYANA

Harold Laski

Good spirits (no liquor however), good food, and even better talk were the mark of the Cohen dinner or luncheon or just plain conversation parties. No occasions were more sparkling than those at which Harold Laski starred or, once with Felix Frankfurter, costarred. Inspired by his appreciative audience, Laski seemed occasionally to "embroider." He told us one day of being presented at the Court of St. James's. While waiting, he started to file his nails. Suddenly it was his turn to make his bow. In his haste, the file slipped to the floor. His Majesty King George V bent down, picked it up, and handing it to him said, "Allow me, Mr. Laski."

Harold Laski, the book collector, told us also of a visit to the basement of Filene's in Boston, where he picked up a rare book at a bargain price. He asked to see Mr. Filene and announced that he had a valuable book that the firm might be interested in purchasing. "I sold it to Mr. Filene," he told us, "for a hundred times what I paid for it. Then I told him how I'd come by it."

In 1930, on Cohen's way back from Oxford, where he had read a paper at the 7th International Congress of Philosophy, he stayed with the Laskis in London. He asked Laski's advice about a gift for Mary. Laski took him to Liberty's of London, and there he bought three beautiful shawls. Shortly after Mary's death he spread one of those shawls across his knees, and called it his lifesaver.

As soon as possible after the war, in September of 1946, Laski came to America, where he had such close ties, and paid his final visit to his old friend.

After Cohen's death the Laskis still came to see the family on their trips to the States. In 1948 Laski told us of his visit with Stalin in the Kremlin. Knowing that he would have to imbibe vodka, he took the precaution of coating his stomach by partaking in advance of mineral oil and ham sandwiches. "Mr. Laski," said Stalin, "for a small man you have quite a capacity."

Laski once recited Mother Goose rhymes to our small daughter—Mother Goose with a strangely unfamiliar air. In that precise British accent of his he counted out on Marianne's fingers: "Eeny, meeny, miney, mo, Catch old Churchill by the toe, If he hollers, let him go, Eeny, meeny, miney, mo." I began to see what "old Churchill" had been up against in 1945, when Laski, as chairman of the British Labour Party, defeated him.

Harold's last visit to us was in the early spring of 1949. He was coughing, speaking in a hoarse voice, and looked not as chipper as in the old days. He was full of stories touching on Jewish affairs. Shortly after Hitler's rise to power, a German Jew approached Laski to urge him to help get out of Germany Jewish communal records that went back hundreds of years. Harold went straight to the most prominent leader of British Jewry, only to be rebuffed in these terms: "But I have nothing against Hitler except for the fact that he's anti-Semitic."

As Harold rose to leave, I said how grateful we were for his continuing to come to see us even though my father was gone. He took my hand and answered with great earnestness, "I couldn't come to this country and not see you. This is a sort of shrine to me. Morris and Mary were two of my three real friends in America."

A year later came the sad news of his premature death.

Cohen saved Laski's letters, but at the time of the Blitz in London, Cohen's letters, which Laski had saved, had to be burned along with other combustibles. One only was left. Here is enough of the Laski-Cohen correspondence, however, to give an idea of their relationship, its genuineness, its loyalty, its mutual respect and deep affection.

McGill University
Montreal

December 5, 1915

Faculty of Arts
Department of History

Dear Mr. Cohen,

I hope this is what you want. I, too, wish I had the opportunity to see more of you—in fact I wished the Conference [on Legal and Social Philosophy] had been twice as long. I enjoyed it immensely— not least your own contribution. . . .

I want to meet you again. I am trying to get a post at the Columbia Summer School—would that mean meeting you in New York? If the fates are kind I shall migrate to civilised regions next year and then maybe I shall be within what the strategists call striking distance.

Good wishes for your health—

Very cordially yours,
HAROLD J. LASKI

Rockport, Massachusetts
Sept. 10, 1918

Dear Morris,

. . . It would be tempting to accept your challenge about Oxford. But I am afraid that underlying it is less a desire for conversion than a symptom of your incurable eagerness for conflict. I go through life trying to avoid it and so you must forgive my refusal to join issue.

Yours very sincerely,
HAROLD J. LASKI

116 Warwick Gardens
W. 14
16.1.22

My dear Morris,

. . . How are you these days? I read with great joy your piece in the Cambridge American Literature—a masterpiece of summary. If you had reprints I wish you would send one to old [Samuel] Alexander at Manchester who spoke of it to me with real admiration. I find, indeed, that you are a person of high esteem with all I care about—Haldane, Alexander, B. Russell, and even Bosanquet.

I am fearfully busy. I shall send you, one of these days, a little piece on Karl Marx; but mainly Im trying to do a big work on the state from which communal ghosts are absent.

Where is "From Pythagoras to Einstein?" I look for its announcement weekly.

Our warm regards to all of you,

Very sincerely yours,
HAROLD J. LASKI

116 Warwick Gardens
London W. 14
21.VIII.25

My dear Morris,

Many thanks for sending me those papers; they make me look forward eagerly to the book. As always you teach me what no other American does in quite the same way, for there is an edge in your thinking that makes even agreement a source of intellectual striving.

You will perhaps see that in a new book of mine [*A Grammar of Politics*] I have noted a debt of gratitude to you. What one cant put on paper is the sense of a friendship which goes deeper than distance can destroy.

Ever yours,
HAROLD J. LASKI

*The London School of Economics and
Political Science*

21st Feb. 1928:

My dear Morris,

The paper on Property [and Sovereignty] is a remarkable thing and I am glad to have it; but I would give fifty like it for that report of the Cohen Dinner which went to my heart. I do wish I could have been there, and I do even more wish that I could have said what Maurice Amos and I were saying to each other last Tuesday—that both in Philosophy and Jurisprudence there are no people in America with half the significance that you have or half the amazing quality of saying in a dozen pages what other people blunderingly try to say in a whole volume. And how I wish, too, that I could talk over with you fifty problems on the verge of my mind.

I hoped that I should have been able to get over this Spring, but at the moment there is no money in the exchequer and your Foundations naturally invite safe people like Graham Wallas who can be trusted to supplement mild progressivism with unctuosity. However, one day it will be possible. . . .

My very warm greetings,

Ever yours,

H. J. L.

June 23/32

Dear Harold:

Please accept my heartfelt thanks for your very generous and really high-minded review of my book [*Reason and Nature*] in the Yale Law Journal. Of course I cannot help feeling that your friendship has made you over-generous in your general estimate; and I must add that failure to take Book I and Book II into fuller account has made you misjudge somewhat the objectives of Book III. But the latter point needs more time for development than I can give it now. I must say, however, that I was especially gratified by your brief but very penetrating description of my chapter on *History vs. Value* as an attack on "the notion that historic analysis can of itself give rise to value." Several poor "simps," like the one who reviewed my book for the *Times Literary Supplement,* thought that I was attacking history in the interests of mathematics.

My reason for hurrying to get this letter off is that I am anxious to recommend to you as strongly as I can my friend and former pupil, Dr. Richard B. Morris, who is sailing to London to study the City Court Records (or borough court records) and who will doubtless want to consult you and Plucknett. Dr. Morris has done amazingly interesting pioneer work on American Colonial legal history. Felix Frankfurter, John Dickinson and others share my profound admiration for the work he has already done. In addition he is a very charming fellow personally. I regret that I do not know his young bride, not having had any chance to meet her. They have just got married and their stay in London will be part of their honey-moon.

Please convey my very warm regards to Frida and to Diana [their daughter], and believe me to be

Ever affectionately yours,

MORRIS

22/5/34

Dear Morris,

I have two things to thank you for. One, your book on Logic. It seems to me the best introduction that I, certainly, have ever read, and two, for asking me to write to Abe F. [Flexner] about you.

I told him long ago that if I were doing what he is doing, you of all people would be the person whose interest I should seek to enlist, and you tell me that you agree with this, that re-enforces my own judgment.

I hope, with luck, to come over to America next Easter. If I do you may be sure that I shall come as fast as I can to see you and Mary.

Our love to you both.

Yours ever,

HAROLD J. LASKI

4.7.34

Dear Morris,

When I got back from Russia the other day, I found the enclosed from Flexner. As you will see it is not very hopeful. From what I hear he has become very difficult about the whole of his Institute [for Advanced Study], and I fear that it will be difficult to do anything with him. However you might be able to do something through Felix.

Love to you both,

Yours ever,

HAROLD J. LASKI

Aug. 6, 1942

Dear Harold,

You will be pained to hear that my wife died last June. You who have known her will not need to be told how great is my loss.

It seems petty when death is visiting old and young to be mourning for one individual, but such is life. It is hard for me to learn to bear it. My children have stood the test nobly and they are all a great comfort to me.

Still I feel lonesome and a nice letter from old friends would be very welcome. I have been seriously sick and am now slowly recovering. Please write me about yourself, Frida and Diana. How is fate treating you? And what is the outlook for a better world order?

I am sending you a little package of food because we are told here that the English people find it difficult to purchase certain commodities to which we've all been accustomed.

With best regards to Frida and Diana,

Ever faithfully yours,

M. R. C. (per L. C. R.)

Manor Cottage,
Little Bardfield,
Braintree, Essex.

Great Bardfield 86

8.9.45

My very dear Morris,

It was exciting beyond words to open an envelope and, after this epoch of agony and silence, find a word of greeting and affection from you. It was hardly less exciting to hear that you are writing books on just the things I should wish to hear you comment on.

It is only a very few weeks ago that I heard from a passing American here of Mary's death. I know what that must have meant to you, for it left an ache in me. I shall never forget her infinite kindness to me, her unending interest in life, and that remarkable fund of good-will she expended with both hands. Sympathy is of no avail to any one who loses a comrade like that; so I say no more than that Mary remains part of the experience of the good that I cherish as the most intimate part of myself.

And what of you, dear Morris? How are Felix and your learned daughter? I read her book with great interest, and wrote to her about it, but, as I did not hear from her, I imagine the letter was sent by some boat which fell to a submarine. Anyhow, if you or one of them has a half-hour, please let us have all news in detail. We are hungry for it.

We are all well, if a little dazed at being alive. We have had our experiences. The house was blasted twice, once when we were there, though it is now in good order; and I was badly blitzed in 1941, though hardly even scratched. We are both very well. Diana is in grand form, even hoping that her husband (Robin Mathewson, classics) may be demobilised by December. At present, she and her two sons, (four and four months respectively) are living in Oxford, where they have been throughout the war. But they have bought a house in London, and will come back there as soon as the army allows Robin to return to civil life.

These have been pretty hard years, physically as well as spiritually. To combine academic work, some politics, and war-duties for nearly six years of the black-out is like feeling one's way through a fog to an unknown destination. Anyway, we have, like Sièyes, survived, though the destination still seems as unknown as before. It is a pretty grim Europe, ravaged, bewildered, unhappy, rather like, I imagine, what it was in 1848, gleams of great hope here, passionate reaction there, and, underneath it all, a vast volcano smouldering angrily. It's a world in which there is an immense opportunity for great creative

action, but, also, one in which the men of privilege and routine and
dead tradition are helped by the armies of occupation to keep their
hands on the levers of power. But there are immense stirrings, and if
we survive this dread winter that approaches, I suspect that we shall
begin to learn what the war was really about. All I know so far is that
it was a necessary as well as a famous victory. I only began to realise
on VE day what an immense shadow had been lifted from our lives.
I understood that better after I had seen the first tragic Jews out of
Belsen and Buchenwald. I know now what it means to sit down and
weep by Babylonian waters.

Frida and I both ache for the sight of America, though I doubt
whether the chances are high for any foreseeable future. It was all
very well for Emerson to bid one become a Nonconformist; he did
not know either what an exit permit was or that an academic outcast
like me would strike horror in the breast of any decent American
college president. So we watch the long procession of politicians,
business men, journalists, radio-stars, "safe" professors, aristocrats,
step jauntily with their priority-passages on to planes, while we sit
hungrily here saying that, perhaps five years from now, people will be
able to hear of the Socialist Gestapo without horror, and we can begin
to talk again with you and Felix F. [Frankfurter] in Washington, with
Alfred Cohn and Ben Huebsch in New York. America was never so
near England, and, yet, curiously, never so distant from me. I wish
someone at Harvard or Yale or Columbia would understand that it is
possible to be radical without being septic.

But it was a great election; and there is a real satisfaction in seeing
one's party come to ideas one has been preaching for twenty-five years
without knowing whether one satisfied anything but one's own conscience. I don't pretend to know whether the new government will
succeed. It has men of quality, a good programme, a grand set of
back-bench supporters. It all turns on courage, especially the courage
to satisfy our friends instead of appeasing those enemies of ours who
cannot be appeased. Anyway, the opportunity is there; and our people
have shown that first virtue of a mature politics, the power to be un-
grateful on principle. I deeply regretted that it had to take the form
of so personal a defeat for Churchill, who did a supreme war job; but
he chose the time, and he chose the battle-ground, and it was a clear
case of suicide and not of murder. Not even he could convince sober
people that I have enough importance to be made a vital election
issue after ten years of a political truce; and not even he could persuade the ordinary voter that behind the comatose visage of a dull
university teacher there lurked mysterious powers like those of Himm-
ler. Dr. Johnson was right when he said that no man was ever

written down except by himself. But I would have given much to have had him end a great career greatly and not pitifully.

It's a long time since the spring of 1939, when you took me back to the subway near 180th Street after some magic hours of talk. But believe me, dear Morris, this is one house where you are never forgotten and where, always, the memories round your name and work are always fresh and inspiring. The years change; but Frida and I do not change our friendships. One day, somebody, somewhere, will wave a magic wand, and we shall knock at your door to go on talking where we left off on that yesterday that is in another epoch.

Meanwhile, we all send our deep affection to you. To see you again is one of the best reasons for staying alive.

Yours, as always,

HAROLD J. LASKI

Edwin Arlington Robinson

In *The North American Review* for September 1916, Robinson spoke of a "mystical touch" about the MacDowell Colony that "compels a man to work out the best that is in him." Beginning in 1924, Cohen spent many fruitful summers there in Peterborough, New Hampshire. Mrs. Marian MacDowell, the composer's widow, saw to it that Cohen was housed next to Robinson in Colony Hall. Their bedrooms opened on to a common small sitting room. The two suitemates developed an understanding friendship for each other, terminated only by Robinson's death in 1935. As Cohen wrote in the Preface of *Reason and Nature:* "All great philosophers have something in common with the poets and prophets."

Despite Robinson's extreme reticence in *propria persona,* which Amy Lowell noted in *The Dial* for February 1922, he made Cohen his confidant in literature and religion. Hermann Hagedorn, who thanked Cohen in his biography, *Edwin Arlington Robinson,* for "penetrating analyses of Robinson's mental processes," has told me: "E A was a supremely lonely man all his life. A few people meant much to him—the Frasers, the Ledoux, the Isaacs, and your father."

In 1925 M. Charles Cestre, professor of American civilization at the Sorbonne, came to America to lecture on Robinson at Bryn Mawr. (In 1930, his *Introduction to E. A. Robinson* appeared in print.) Robinson confided to Cohen that in his youth he had been obsessed by the fear that he would die before he had fully expressed what was in him, but he said of Cestre, "I am glad I have carried my work far enough so that someone can discuss it."

99 St. Botolph St.
Boston, Oct. 30, 1925

Dear Mr. Cohen,

Thank you for your kind letters. It doesn't look now as if I shall get to New York much before the middle of November, but I expect to see M. Cestre sometime tomorrow. Please tell him for me how much I appreciate the active interest in my work—and don't forget that I shall be in New York before long. My address will be 328 E. 42.

With my best wishes for you and Mrs. Cohen

Yours very sincerely,

E. A. ROBINSON

Robinson's *The Glory of the Nightingales* elicited from some of the younger critics reviews that got under his skin. He wrote Cohen:

39 Ipswich Street
Boston, November 6, 1930

Dear Mr. Cohen

Let me thank you and Mrs. Cohen for your friendly letters about the book, which in spite of some incredibly stupid and misleading "reviews" (mostly by the younger fry) and almost no advertising, appears to be making its way. I'm glad to know that you like it.

I have been pretty well out of commission since my summer's work and have had fair warning not to do it again. I hope to see you this winter.

I trust that you enjoyed your trip abroad and found the philosophers all friendly.

Yours very truly

E. A. ROBINSON

Cohen has stated in notes on Robinson for Hagedorn that since E A had sent him copies of his successive volumes of verse, he wanted to send him a copy of his first book, *Reason and Nature,* completed at the MacDowell Colony. But Robinson did not collect books, and Cohen accompanied his gift with a letter to the effect that he felt a little conscience-stricken to be sending a book that might be a burden. Robinson replied:

Peterborough, N.H.
September 6, 1931

Dear Dr. Cohen

It would be foolish for me to compare your book with the work of your contemporaries, for you know that I am not sufficiently familiar with what they have done. But I am pretty sure that none of them have your incisive and confident clarity of expression in dealing with abstractions, or your full cup of fortifying rational juice to keep the thing going. Of course I am not rational, but I can appreciate your attitude and congratulate you on your achievement. I don't see how your book can fail to become a landmark, or some sort of mark, in the philosophers' world. I must still have my mystery, which you are good enough not to take away from me—though I fancy that you think me rather [not?] much at ease as at home in it.

At the end of this month I shall be sending a less profound and less rational book of another nature entirely—which you will be under no sort of obligation to read if it doesn't take you with it.

With my best wishes to you all,

Yours very truly,

E. A. ROBINSON

Your book goes with this, or in a day or two.

(Robinson's book was undoubtedly *Mathias at the Door,* published on September 15, 1931, in a limited edition of five hundred autographed copies.)

Cohen noted that in spite of "Robinson's aversion to abstract thought," he followed his reasoning. The two had a certain affinity with respect to mysticism. Robinson was glad that, despite his emphasis on reason, Cohen did not remove mysticism from the universe. Cohen wrote in his notes:

Robinson's religion, such as it was, was remote from accepted religious conceptions. A mystic is a man who recognizes that there is something beyond mundane existence but knows that it is beyond and doesn't try to describe it. Robinson, in that regard, was a true mystic.

In a sense he was in his spiritual life nearer the ancient stoics than to conventional Christianity.

The sustaining element in his spiritual life was a sense of fortitude as its own reward. He had an intense feeling that there was a beyond but didn't pretend to know what it was. . . .

If he can be called a mystic he is certainly no obscurantist. His vision is persistent and penetrating and unlike poets like Browning he never accepts easy optimistic solutions. He has the supreme courage to look into the darkness that surrounds the human scene, supported by the strength which comes from seeing things under the aspect of eternity. . . .

[He] strains to catch what little light a purified and courageous vision may gather.

Cohen's last note on Robinson seems to be the draft of a letter to him:

You put it in concrete, poetic and at times highly dramatic form and I put it in abstract formulae. But on essentials I cannot but pay my tribute to your vision of things. And the very fact that you have been able to persist in your work despite the wear of the years seems to me evidence of the fact that your vision of things is the fruit of fortitude rather than of ease.

This draft seems to imply a parallel quest by each of them for the essence of existence. Each portrayed the play of light and shadow over the human arena. The poet envisioned "the Children of the Night" groping their way toward a glimmering of light. For the philosopher, hopes, like stars, "pierce the infinite darkness which envelopes the human scene." Cohen as literary critic stressed Robinson's universality, for poetry, like philosophical truth and the Platonic *eidos,* transcends time.

Ernest Nagel

Of all Cohen's students, Ernest Nagel was the one to whom Cohen felt the closest. He seemed almost a son to him.

> Colony Hall
> Peterboro, N.H.
> June 20/28

Dear Ernest:
   Mrs. Cohen, Felix and I would very much like to have you come up and stay with us at our house in Lake Placid from July 15 to August 15. You can go out with the boys mountain climbing, swimming or canoeing, talk philosophy to me, or read and write in your own room. But the air in Placid is lovely and quiet and I think that you will like it. I very much hope that your plans will not interfere so as to prevent your acceptance. If you have committed yourself to teach in the summer my urgent advice to you is to get a substitute. It will be much better if you get a rest and begin on your doctor's dissertation.
   Talk it over with your mother and let me know as soon as you can. Trusting that you are all well, I am, with best wishes,

> Cordially yours,
> MORRIS R. COHEN

> Yaddo
> Saratoga Springs, N.Y.
> July 25/29

Dear Earnest [sic]:
   I am sorry that I cannot give you categoric advice. . . . I think you ought not to jeopardize your completion of your doctor's dis-

sertation. That must come first. If you can do it at Princeton go by all means. It will make the possibility of a desirable situation at C.C.N.Y. better next year.

Let me also say that while I have not because of all sorts of unforseen mishaps, been able to raise the $2500 *I expect* to be able to do so before the middle of September. But I might die before then, my friend whom I asked to raise it may go bankrupt, and you may find yourself in a hole. So it is well to nurse the Princeton proposition if there is anything in it. I will write to my friend Spaulding and let you know.

My kindest regards to your mother and yourself. Felix joins me in cordial greetings.

MORRIS R. COHEN

Colony Hall
Peterboro, N.H.
Sept. 6/29

Dear Ernest:

I left New York a little worried about your health. I trust it is better now after your little vacation.

Could you please call up Dr. A. A. Himwich, 1871 Madison Ave. Tel. Harlem 2115 and ask whether he received vol. 1 of Nature and Reason in *Ms.* I gave it to Paul Weiss to read, and told him to leave it with Dr. Himwich but have not heard from either. Dr. Himwich is not only my personal physician but a dear friend. He is well worth meeting, being especially interested in mathematical physics.

You will be glad to know that my own health is much improved.

With kindest regards to your mother,

Sincerely yours,
MORRIS R. COHEN

Peterboro N.H.
Sept. 10/29

Dear Ernest:

Enclosed are two checks for $1250. You will get the other half of the year's stipend in February. I trust all is well with you.

Give my kindest regards to your mother and sister.

Cordially yours,
MORRIS R. COHEN

[Peterborough, N.H.]
Aug. 1 [1931]

Dear Ernest:

I am sorry about the matter of publication of your thesis—very sorry that I could not have pushed it over last winter. However the loss of $210 while very serious to you now will not loom so large ten or more years hence.

I am sorry that my figure of speech about philosophic palaces[3] was so obscure that even you did not get the exact shade of meaning intended. I was concerned with the difficulty (which troubles me a good deal) between the need of *formulating* a philosophy on definite principles and the rain [?] of factual existence which always remains larger than anything we can get hold of or encompass. . . .

My kindest regards to your folks and to yourself.

Cordially,

MORRIS R. COHEN

The MacDowell Colony
Peterborough, New Hampshire
August 29/32

Dear Ernest:

I am very sorry that all my efforts to arrange for your coming here are in vain. The best thing for you to do I think is to drop the logic book at this point and let me work at it for the next few months. . . . When I get over my disappointment I shall write you more. . . .

Cordially yours,

MORRIS R. COHEN

c/o American Express Company,
Vienna, Austria
September 14, 1934

Dear Professor Cohen,

I am writing from a little town in Czechoslovakia where I am visiting my grandfather until Monday. I arrived shortly after the close of the Congress in Prague and am going on to Vienna for about a month, then to Warsaw, back again to Prague, and later if finances permit to Istanbul.

The Congress was as dull as only such things can be, and except for the opportunity of meeting about half a dozen worthwhile people it seems to me silly to travel long distances to attend one. There were a few tense meetings when some of the German or Italian representatives spoke, but no explosions. According to T. V. Smith, Kelsen had been invited to speak, but the invitation had been withdrawn (the official invitation had never been sent him—that is the official explanation) when some of the German delegates protested. Smith was of course very angry, and said some sharp things in his paper; but it was in English, and very few people understood it. Montague managed to have a very harmless resolution accepted about the right to free speech and criticism, for which even the Italian delegates voted.

Nevertheless, I found the trip to Prague very worthwhile, for I was able to meet Reichenbach, Carnap, and the Polish logicians, and even make arrangements to see them again in their home universities. Reichenbach is a splendid person, and I shall try hard to visit him in Istanbul. He has finished his book on probability, and it will be published in Holland in October, in German of course. He would like to have it appear in English also, and already has a translator but alas no publisher. I told him I would write to Harcourt & Brace, and that moreover I would ask you to use your influence in his behalf. He told me of the contents of the book, and on the basis of his description as well as his published writings, I think it to be an important work. R. also thinks the book could be used as a text-book in probability. If the request is not too presumptious, will you not please let me know what the possibilities are of the book finding an American publisher —I promised R. to write him when I heard from you.

I spoke to Radl and N. Hartmann, and gave them your regards. They were both sorry not to find you present, and each sends their warm greetings. Radl said he promised to send you an article for your magazine (is it The Philos. of Science?) but that he would not get around to it for a long time because he was both tired and busy with other matters. Many other people with whom I spoke knew of you through Reason and Nature. They had been both gratified and flattered to receive copies of the book, and uniformly spoke highly of it. Grelling was also present, and told me that the translation is of course all off. He is a Jew, but still in Germany and finds it very difficult to make ends meet. Indeed, the saddest sight in Prague was the many German refugees and the young German students who still are in Germany but find no intellectual nourishment at home. Reichenbach must learn Turkish within 2 years, and meanwhile carries on by having a native translate his lectures sentence by sentence.

I hope this letter finds you in good health, and hope also that you will be kind enough to write me once in a long while. My mother as well as I send our warmest regards and best wishes to you and Mrs. Cohen.

Cordially yours,
ERNEST NAGEL

Oct. 26/34

Dear Ernest:

Enclosed is the check from the publishers of the Logic Book. The second installment will reach you a little after Christmas. When you are financially on easy street we shall begin to discuss the question of how to divide the royalties. For the present it is not in order.

You will be glad to learn that not only is Willie independent now, drawing a salary at Iowa State University, but Leonora is instructor of French at Smith College.

There is no news otherwise. There is a new row at the College here, but that is nothing really new. I am planning a paper on the Statistical View of the Universe and one on Legal Philosophy. With regular classes and the New School, and the accumulating duties of the Conference on Jewish Relations that is about as much as I can hope to achieve before New Years.

Please write to me even if I do not seem to be a very responsible correspondent. With all good wishes,

Cordially,

MORRIS R. COHEN

Prof. Hope of Pittsburgh University has printed a pamphlet of questions and exercises on our logic text.

Prague, November 28, 1934

Dear Professor Cohen,

. . . I want to thank you again for your kindness, and meanwhile shall keep a faithful account of all the royalties you send me for the day of reckoning.

Since my last letter I made a one week visit to Lwow. . . . the Poles I met . . . take philosophy to be a serious business. They regard logic to be the analysis of linguistic forms, just as does Carnap here, and I am a little regretful that we did not identify in our text the proposition with the *sentence*—I think it would have made Chapter II more easily understood, without requiring any change in fundamental doctrine.

The saddest thing to me in Poland is the plight of the Jewish students, and it is surprising what a consciousness of being a Jew one develops in that place. They have practically no future in the universities, even though they are frequently the outstanding scholars. Both Lukasiewicz in Warsaw and Chwistek in Lwow commented upon the, to them, hardly explicable zeal of their students, almost all of whom are Jewish, who continue to study in spite of abject poverty and without any hope of social recognition. . . .

I have been enjoying Prague very much. Carnap has been most generous with his time, and both he and his wife are among the friendliest people I know. His latest book, *Die Logische Syntax Der Sprache,* I think to be a very important work, and it and my discussions with him have been a great help to me. An English translation is under way, and it should do much to introduce the study of logical semantics into America. . . .

I hope your paper on statistics is in good shape already. . . .

With kindest regards and best wishes, to yourself and Mrs. Cohen,

ERNEST NAGEL

Dec. 24/34

Dear Ernest:

The enclosed has just come and I hasten to send it to you with the hope that the exchange will become more favorable for you.

I was very much interested in your last letter. As you know the subject of symbolism has interested me very much for a number of years. While it would be at first simpler to identify propositions with the symbols or signs for them, in the end the distinction has to be made. For one proposition follows from the other only by virtue of the subject matter involved. This is just a dogmatic statement because I am not in a position just now to write a really respectable letter to you. I have not been well and hardly at peace at C.C.N.Y. But I shall write you very soon.

My wife joins in affectionate greetings to you.

MORRIS R. COHEN

Rome, March 31, 1935

Dear Professor Cohen,

The copy of the logic text-book which you asked Harcourt Brace to send me, as well as a check for $462.87 on royalties up to the end of the last year reached me here within the last two weeks. Thank you very much for both; I will try not to use the latter. As to the text-book, I cannot think of any changes which I would like to propose without having to read the book once more; and at present I feel I would like to be doing other things. Please let me know what changes you are contemplating; perhaps there is time for me to check them in my copy of the book before the next printing is made.

I have been here in Rome for the last month, and am enjoying the relatively warm weather of an early spring. The art museums are a great joy, and I have gotten a great kick out of the Greek sculptures.

Paintings interest me less, but the Michael Angelo and Raphael frescoes impressed me a good deal. I had a sense of relief to know that I reacted positively to other forms of art than music.

I have seen both Enriques and Santayana. Enriques is a pleasant man in his middle sixties, and though he talks a wretched German and I a still worse French we managed to make ourselves understood. As you know from his books he is not a philosophic heavy-weight. He still believes that laws of logic are laws of thought, and in general has changed no part of the creed contained in Problems of Science. His interest in foundation problems in mathematics is only mild when it isn't specialized, and on the whole he distrusts both the Russell as well as the Hilbert approach while at the same time he regards Brouwer's claims as exaggerated. His bête noire is formalism which to him is the gateway to scholasticism, which, finally, he regards as "dangerous" because barren and theological. On the other hand, he has a keen interest in the history of science, and is at work on a series of volumes, the first of which appeared in 1932. I met the mathematicians G. Fano and Levi-Civita at his home. . . . The professional mathematician who is troubled by fundamental questions is a rare bird; all that Levi-Civita could tell me was that he tried to find out what the issues in the present Grundlagenstreit were, but that he didn't succeed.

Santayana I have seen only once, though his assistant Daniel Cory quite frequently. He gave me a whole afternoon, and after an elegant lunch we walked all over the Capitoline Hill until dusk and talked everything from politics to essences. He is a most amazing man, and I had the impression of talking to [a] creature from another world. He is a wise man unmistakably, and even his personal foibles seem to have a rational justification. His political conservatism (if one can call his sentimental attachment to the Church that) is very mellow, and is an expression of his resigned evaluation of human capacities. His interest in America seems to be confined to Harvard College, for which he has a romantic love. He has just finished his novel, "The Last Puritan," it is about a thousand pages long and took him forty five years to write; and is working on Realm of Truth and Realm of Spirit. The afternoon was a very memorable one for me, and I was left quite bewitched.

I expect to leave Rome shortly, perhaps take a flying trip to Sicily, and then spend about two weeks in Florence, Venice, and Fiume (where I have an uncle). I hope to be able to see C. A. Strong in Fiesole. I understand he is quite aged now, and Santayana told me that he lost all his money and hasn't anything to bless himself with. In any case, I want to be out of Italy by the end of April, and then go on to England via Holland, where I want to look up some of Brouwer's followers. I plan to be home sometime in August.

I had an unusually cordial note from Professor Overstreet, in which he assured me that there would be place for me at the College next year. Since there seems to be no prospect of salary increases at Columbia, to say nothing of promotion, that makes me feel quite a bit easier.

Have you had a chance to read Reichenbach's Wahrscheinlichkeitslehre? I have not penetrated very deeply yet, but it seems first rate.

With warmest regards to Mrs. Cohen and yourself,

Yours always,
ERNEST NAGEL

I can always be reached through the American Express Co., Paris, France.

Cambridge, England.
June 4, 1935

Dear Professor Cohen,

Since I last wrote you I have covered much ground, and it has been physically impossible to write you as I would have liked. I went to Holland from Italy, in order to see some of the intuitionist crowd. Brouwer was away in Sweden, so that I was unable to meet him. But I did talk at length with Heyting, his most prominent disciple, and had a brief conversation with Mannoury. The latter is an old man, very set in his ideas and ways, and I was unable to get anything from him. The articles he wrote on "significs" mean as little to me as did his verbal comments. Heyting is devoting himself to build up as much of mathematics as possible on the Brouwerian base. There is something sound in the approach, and one can understand approximately what the school is trying to do. But the philosophic premises seem to me a quagmire; when they can formulate them it is a species of Kant, with the arithmetic of integers constituting the apriori frame.

Here at Cambridge I met Miss Alice Ambrose, who told me she corresponds with you, and who is taking Langford's place next year. She hopes to be able to meet you when she passes through New York early in September. She is working on the intuitionist logic for her dissertation toward her degree here, and has considerable sympathy for the position. Part of her essay is now appearing in *Mind,* and although she manages to cut away some of the rotten timber and exhibit the justifiable aspects of Brouwer, I have not yet been convinced.

I have arrived in Cambridge in time to attend some of the lectures. I made a vain attempt to be admitted to Wittgenstein's class, and went to see him for the purpose. He tore his hair, said it was impossible, that I couldn't possibly understand anything, that I was a tourist and he didn't like tourists, that he wouldn't be able to lecture with a strange face in the room, and that I should "spare him" that suffering. But I have been able to learn something about what he is doing from some of the students and certain mimeographed lectures which he had distributed. He has changed his position enormously since the *Tractatus,* and now is interested in "dissolving" philosophic problems by showing that they arise from violating the grammar of language. He thus tries to establish the meaning of words by examining, and artificially constructing, the usages in which they occur; and apparently shows that the "problems" arise because one meaning of the term, as exhibited in one usage, is transferred by analogy to another and different usage. What I have seen and heard is very interesting, but not so novel or revolutionary as the students and dons here seem to think. His almost pathological personality has seized the imagination of almost everyone here, and Wittgenstein is the main oracle to which the faithful gather.

I heard some of the lectures of Broad, Moore and Wisdom. Broad . . . reads from manuscript, and repeats each sentence three times so that no crumb of wisdom be lost. I came in time to hear him say something about Schopenhauer and also on the "good"; but I did not find the endless distinctions he makes any more illuminating than in his books. Wisdom is a young man, very keen like everybody here, but also very thin. Moore's lectures were the most exciting. He is an amazing person, unusually honest intellectually, very cautious and careful in everything he says. But the method he employs has its drawbacks; he whittles away so much that nothing of the stick gets left. There is a sort of intellectual myopia which seizes everyone here, so much concern with refining the instrument of analysis that the day of employing it never comes. As you see, I am a little disappointed with what I have found in Cambridge. It used to be the philosophic Mecca for me, and perhaps in the days when Russell was here it may have been worth the pilgrimage. I still find the atmosphere invigorating. . . . But I am hankering for thicker air than is to be found here, and for subject matter that is a little bit more "concrete."

It is of course no news to you that McKeon has gone to Chicago for good. I heard of it about three weeks ago from Schneider [Professor Herbert Schneider of Columbia]. He wrote me that McKeon had participated in the legal philosophy seminar with Patterson, and asked whether I would replace him (McKeon). Schneider advised me to do so, and I agreed. I feel a bit foolish in having done so, for I can do nothing more than exhibit my ignorance of the law. But I think I'll be able to stick it for this year at any rate.

I shall remain in Cambridge until the end of the month, and then go to London to attend the Joint Session of the Mind and Aristotelian societies. I have seen Miss Stebbing twice, for a brief time each. She is very hard worked, has seventeen hours of lecturing a week, besides a number [of] college duties. But I think in July she will be freer, and perhaps will then have time for some good discussions.

I hope the summer finds you in good health. Please give my cordial greetings to Mrs. Cohen.

With warmest regards and best wishes,

ERNEST NAGEL

South Wardsboro, Vermont
August 1, 1937

Dear Professor Cohen,

. . . Have you heard from Gail Kennedy? Before I left the city the steering committee (of which I am a member) for the group which met at the New School last May, considered a program for the next meeting, to be held some time in November. We thought we would have a symposium on the nature of physical law. Kennedy was asked to write to you whether you would not lead off the discussion, Einstein was to be the second symposiast [the Conference on Methods in Philosophy and the Sciences, held on November 28, 1937, at the New School for Social Research]. . . .

Always yours,
ERNEST NAGEL

En Route, Union Pacific, Post Card

Sept. 11, 1937

Have been too busy to write but hope to find lots of time to talk to you when we reach New York. I have just heard of a vacancy in Illinois which Sidney [Hook] might get if Dewey will back him. Please communicate this to him. I shall be back in New York on Wednesday evening the 15th. Affectionately,

MORRIS

The University of Chicago
Department of Philosophy

5/5/38

Dear Ernest:

. . . I am glad that you are gratified at having written the Logic book. Recently I attended the meeting of the Western Philosophical Ass'n and almost everyone sang its praises. This means that the book is being used by small colleges throughout the West where students do not often have opportunity to see wide vistas of scientific method from masters of special sciences. It is a comfort that we did nothing to cheapen the book in order to appeal to a wider audience. The book is valued for its substance. Prof. Morris Ginsberg of the London School of Economics rightly criticized the section on the comparative method as too negative and as missing the positive values of that procedure.

If you are free on Friday evening (May 13) please come over to 475 W. 186 (with Edith, of course). We shall be at home and we can talk over C.C.N.Y. and other matters.

I saw Klapper [president of Queens College] before I left town and told him that he failed as an educator if he did not realize that former pupils grow up to be men of attainments and are no longer the undeveloped boys that we knew at college. I think that he was impressed by my account of your philosophic achievements, and he promised to speak and correct his former remarks. . . .

My wife joins me in affectionate regards to you and to Edith.

MORRIS R. COHEN

Law School of Harvard University
Cambridge, Mass.

October 28, 1938

Dear Ernest:

I have your very pleasant letter and the enclosed check. Though I am rather more busy than usual since I am working in two places and trying to finish a paper on Philosophies of Jewish History, I would still give a good deal to have a pleasant talk with you, for I, too, feel that it has been a very long time since we had one.

I was in New York on the 21st and 22nd but had to attend to so many things that I could not get a chance to call you up. I am scheduled to come to New York on Friday, November 11th and I may stay over till Monday noon, the 14th. I hope we shall have a chance to get together.

I certainly should be glad to meet Philip Frank and will be obliged to you if you can help to arrange it for me.

The New Republic asked me to review Dewey's book but I told them that I am tied up for the rest of this year and that they had better give the book to you or to Paul Weiss. Perhaps they have already given it to someone else.

Woodbridge's tendency to go off the handle and to judge books and other intellectual movements by some personal overtones was always characteristic of his buoyant temperament and constituted one of the charms of conversation with him. As you know I have found the Einstein-Infeld book very clear and straightforward and my only quarrel with it is their uncritical acceptance of the notion that the Greeks did not know experimental science and their accepting the somewhat mythical account of Galileo's dropping two bodies of unequal weight and thereby proving the law of falling bodies, or anything else for that matter. Incidentally, my reply to Edith's contention that mass does not enter into the formula for friction in the air, is that friction is a force or has to be overcome by a force and that the mass of a falling body enters into the force which overcomes the friction of the air. When the force of gravity and the resistance or friction become equal the body ceases to be accelerated in its fall and that is what frequently happens.

My wife joins me in affectionate regards to Edith and yourself.

Cordially,

MORRIS R. COHEN

The University of Chicago
Department of Philosophy

April 28, 1939

Dear Ernest:

You need not apologize for "breaking in" upon me. Your letter is most welcome quite apart from the enclosed check. I knew of your promotion before the receipt of your letter, but was told to keep it confidential. You may be sure, however, that I rejoice with you and that I am convinced that it was richly deserved. I do not know why you should have been shocked or depressed by it. I, for one, know of no one else in American philosophy today who is so logically entitled to promotion. . . .

I am very glad that you are continuing on the history of logic. In connection with theories of induction, I wonder whether you have considered the theory of Apelt of the Frisian school. His theory of induction, so far as I can make out, approaches in some respects very close to our own, to wit, as a form of eliminating false hypotheses. As to the problem of the external world—I gave it up long ago. I am not impressed at all with anything that Russell has written on the subject. I do not believe there is such a thing as an external world in the sense that it is external to the mind, for I do not believe that there is a mind that is external to the world. The relation of externality (which I judge to be symmetrical) holds only between physical bodies that are impenetrable to each other. To apply it to the relation between an individual and the objects he knows involves a metaphor, and to take the metaphor literally is a source of confusion. This confusion serves many causes. For example, Berkeley's *Refutation of Materialism in the Interests of Theism,* or Anatole France's *Impressionistic Criticism* as against Brunetière's *Classical Authoritarianism.* It plays, of course, a large part in such issues as the relation of the individual to the government and the constitution of public opinion. But on the strictly intellectual side any clear formulation of the issue shows that there is no serious problem involved.

This is a cryptic statement, but if you really want me to develop it, I will be glad to do so.

. . . During the last week, for instance, I have been reading Veblen's *Economic Papers* and am profoundly impressed with the intellectual havoc which he has produced among American economists by his essentially confused idea as to what is scientific method.

My wife joins me in affectionate regards to you and Edith. We expect to be in New York by June 11, and hope very much that we will have a chance to see you before you leave for Vermont. Please remember me kindly to Sidney [Hook] when you see him.

Cordially yours,
MORRIS R. COHEN

[May 11, 1939]

Dear Earnest:

Please accept my genuine thanks for the reprint of your review of Reichenbach. That it should be inscribed "with affectionate regards" means more to me than I can readily indicate.

An exhaustive review and detailed analysis of a position like Reichenbach's is undoubtedly a great service to philosophy. But I wonder whether you could not be even more useful by giving your own systematic exposition of the issues, regardless of Mr. Reichenbach's utterances which are, after all, not as important as the subject itself. . . .

Yours, as ever
MORRIS R. COHEN

May 28/39

Dear Earnest:

Thanks a lot for your good letter of the 15th which I should have answered before today; but I have been below par. I trust that you have fully recovered from the grippe.

In regard to your comments on my paper on Scientific Method, there is no real difference of opinion between us. (a) The fact that Bacon assumes that the perceiving mind is a *tabula rasa* does not prevent him from assuming that the number of forms in nature is limited.

(b) I should still insist that verification differs from confirmation in excluding some alternative. The case you have in mind of a man working with *one* hypothesis is no exception. An experiment can verify a single hypothesis only if the result is inconsistent with the hypothesis being false. No number of experiments on the hypothesis that everything happens according to the will of Allah, the subconscious mind etc. really verifies or even increases its scientific probability, precisely because no experiment can be inconsistent with it.

We expect to be in New York and hope to see you and Edith before you go to Vt.

My wife joins in affectionate greetings to Edith and your good self.

As ever

MORRIS

July 11, 1939.

Dear Ernest:

It was good to get your letter and its pleasant enclosure,—pleasant because it is a reminder of the fact that the effort in writing the logic book is appreciated, as is shown by the extent to which the book is used.

My wife and I have been in the city since June 11th and have been fairly comfortable. Willie, as you may know, is teaching at the C.C.N.Y. summer school, in addition to carrying on some experimental work at Columbia; and so far we have found 475 West 186 Street a pleasant place to spend the summer. I suppose that I shall have to run away by the 10th of August to avoid the hay fever season. If I could only be sure that your part of Vermont will give me some relief, I should be glad to locate somewhere in your neighborhood.

I am not sure as to whether I shall go to Harvard in September. At one time I thought of preparing a paper on Verification. But I have been crowded with so many other matters that I think it best not to commit myself to something that has to be finished by a given time. Time is not to me a logical category, and to terminate a logical inquiry by considerations of the revolution of the earth around its axis and around the sun is becoming to me more and more distasteful. However, I may come around to hear Tarski and a few others. Also, it will be a good opportunity to revisit Cambridge where I had such a pleasant time last winter. Just now I am finishing a paper on the Criminal Law, after which I shall try to get out the one on Interpretations of the History of Science. I shall write the Dewey paper some time or other but I do not think it will be very important. I do not find that on the questions in which I am most interested Dewey's position is clear enough to make a statement of my differences from him very significant. He seems to me to be systematically evasive on all the important cosmologic problems.

You are perfectly right about the need for a book on Metaphysics. Despite the fact that I have a trunkful of notes, I am not sure that I can within a year or so get the book into shape. I am committed to giving a course on Law and Ethics at the University of Chicago Law School and I want to put some of my ideas into print for the use of my classes; and that, I imagine will occupy whatever time is left over after the Conference matters are attended to. There are also various parts of my book on the development of American thought which I want to get into shape so that if I pass away before finishing it, my literary executor might be able to publish parts of it. . . .

Hempel called me up the other day and told me that he is going to do some work at the City College and I am indeed glad to know that. . . .

The question of a successor to Overstreet and Cohen at C.C.N.Y. is one about which [Acting President] Mead spoke to me a few weeks ago. When I see you, I would like to discuss the matter with you.

With affectionate greetings to Edith and yourself, in which my wife cordially joins,

Faithfully yours,
MORRIS R. COHEN

South Salem, N.Y.
Aug. 18/39

Dear Ernest:

I am sorry that you have worried about my phrase that I might "pass away" before finishing my book on American Thought. Death is not "an abstract possibility" but a grounded one and one of the most certain of empirical propositions (i.e. those for which there is what you call "material evidence"). But I suppose that I ought to tell you what made me put that phrase into my last letter.

You know, of course, that I have always been more or less of an invalid for the last forty years, and never was really robust. Something is wrong with my pneumo-gastric nerve which makes my heart and stomach misbehave; and once in a while I have very distressing symptoms of death gripping me. One would suppose that having had them so often one would get accustomed to them. But that is not the case. In 1905–1906 I was knocked out for almost the whole year and it took me several years before I could recover. The same thing happened in 1915–1916 and I had to stop teaching at C.C.N.Y. for part of the first semester and the whole of the second. By means of excessive attention to my diet and other physical affairs I have been able to get along more or less—with only occasional distress. Last spring I strained my heart by going home too rapidly (a distance of over a mile) to avoid catching cold, and I am getting over the resulting depression rather slowly. I may live thirty years more or I may pass away any day if some unusual strain or aggravation hits me. But that, of course, is likely to happen to anyone. And you know that I do not consider it logically safe to make confident predictions about a single individual from theorems of probability.

The specific thing that made me put in the phrase about my possible passing away before I finish the book on American Thought is that I recently made a catalogue of the different books which at diverse times I started and which are thus in diverse states of incompletion. There are thirteen of them. And as manifestations of American Thought keep on appearing faster than I can write about them, you can see why a man of 59 may not feel too confident of finishing. But be assured I am not worrying about the matter. I do what I can without straining myself and when I'm gone the world will have to take care of itself as it did for a long time before I got on the scene.

You will be glad to hear that stimulated by one of your letters (the one before the last) I have gathered together several hundred pages of notes on metaphysics (my own views, not comments on the views of others) and had them typewritten. When I complete them they will constitute a dry, scholastic text-book on *Metaphysics*. Meanwhile there are a number of other projects which *must* be gotten under way—one of them an article on Dewey's philosophy (for the Am. Phil. Ass'n) which will compel me to read several of Dewey's books (including the *Logic*). I at first refused to undertake it but yielded because I fear that the cannonization of Dewey's empiricistic and moralistic philosophy will choke the speculative urge which seems to me the life blood of philosophy.

Since the end of July we have been here, 51 miles from New York, in a lovely house with hundreds of acres of ground around us. It has been both restful and not lonesome since the children come out here every weekend. We have about seven bedrooms and can accomodate any guests like Edith and your good self if you ever come this way. . . .

I expect to go to Cambridge on Sept 3, and hope to see you there— unless by good luck you can come here before then.

Please remember me most kindly to Sidney and his wife, and of course our best to Edith and your good self.

As ever

MORRIS R. COHEN

William T. Harris

At Harris' death in 1936, Cohen delivered the obituary address for the American Philosophical Association. He had frequently referred to him with admiration, though he never adopted his idealism. In *A Dreamer's Journey,* Cohen calls Harris a saint. Harris was also a Hegelian, the editor for over a quarter of a century of *The Journal of Speculative Philosophy,* the first journal in English devoted exclusively to philosophy, and the chief organizer of the Concord School of Philosophy. Through loyalty to Davidson, with whom he had been associated in the St. Louis group, Harris took an interest in The Breadwinners' College. While in Washington as United States Commissioner of Education, he directed its philosophy class through correspondence with M. R. Cohen, who was its secretary.

They first met in 1902 and became good friends. When Cohen went out from Harvard looking for a place in philosophy, Harris wrote a letter of recommendation for him, all the more strategic in that he was the leader of the educational profession in this country.

Breadwinners College
166 Madison St.
N.Y. Dec. 20, 1900

Dr. William T. Harris,

Dear Sir:

The advice which you were kind enough to communicate to us in your letter of the 26th of November, has been gratefully accepted by our philosophy class. We have decided on beginning our study of

Aristotle with that of the *Metaphysics,* paying special attention to the eleventh book, of which there is a translation by our beloved teacher, Thomas Davidson.

Our last meeting was, in accordance with your suggestion, set aside for the discussion of the tenth book of Plato's *Laws.* Though the point of greatest speculative importance, the priority of the self-moved was not new to us, having met it in the Phaedrus, there were several difficulties suggested.

In the first place, it is difficult to see what is the exact purpose of Plato in introducing the first eight kind[s] of motions. Would not his argument have been just as complete if he had introduced only the last two kinds of motion? It is difficult to see the principle *divisions* of Plato's classification of the first eight kinds of motion. The various kinds of motion do not seem to exclude each other, e.g. separation and locomotion, decay and corruption or destruction, etc.; besides, the ninth seems to include all the first eight.

Next came the difficulty of understanding what Plato meant by the expression: the self-caused motion is prior to the determined motion. Does he mean prior *in time* or does he mean *logically* prior? His illustration would tend to show that he means a chronological priority, but of course it might be doubted whether everything ever was in total rest. If we abstract motion from the universe, there would not be everything left. Nor is logical priority free from difficulty. The thing moved is just as necessary a condition of the motion as the mover.

In fact the difficulty lies in seeing just what is the distinction between self-caused motion and motion caused by others—a difficulty which is due to the vagueness of our causal concept. If I throw a stone in the air, what do I mean by saying that the motion of the stone is caused? So far as I can see it is simply this—that the stone flies when released from the moving hand. And the fact that the stone never does move unless some moving body come in contact with it, does not throw light, since all it shows is that the stone moves under some conditions and does not move under other conditions. And is not all motion of the same kind? Do not the stars or living organisms move under some conditions and do not move under others? To be sure there is a difference in the determining conditions, in some being few and therefore simple and universal, in others many, complex and therefore not as general. But that would introduce differences of degree only and not generic differences.

Then Plato's identification of the self-moved with the soul through the middle term *life,* is not altogether free from [a blot here—word may be "objection"]—jection. In the first place our consciousness refuses to look upon itself as a motion of any kind; neither our thoughts, our emotions nor our volitions have anything in common with motion. It, therefore, seems an empty figure to compare the soul with circular motion.

The statement that art is prior to nature, that the attributes of the soul are prior to attributes of physical body, might also be objected to. Art is impossible without nature which is the material of art, and such things as *opinion, care, law,* etc, are not prior to things *hard* and *soft, heavy* and *light* etc., since the former have no meaning unless they are ultimately referred back to the latter, whereas the latter do not imply the former.

Besides these intellectual difficulties, there were some moral difficulties for us in that book. A law enforcing religious conformity by force is not likely to agree with the temper of young men at the end of the nineteenth century. Some of Plato's doctrines in the *Republic* would come in under the head of the second heresy, and Plato himself in proposing the third law departed from the religious opinions of the Athenians, and thus contradicting himself. On the whole, the spirit of superiority and intolerance which Plato shows in this book— would as one of our members suggested, have been more worthy of the accusers of a Socrates than of Plato's Master. But I do not think these moral difficulties have kept us from *trying* to give due weight to his arguments. If the difficulties thus far suggested seem trivial, I beg of you to consider that they are given here just as they occurred to us, without much deliberation on them.

With the next year we begin the study of Aristotle.

Yours very truly
Secretary MORRIS R. COHEN

Breadwinners' College
166 Madison St., N.Y.
Jan. 31, 1900
[actually 1901]

Dr. William T. Harris

Dear Sir:

Your letter of Jan. 3 was received and discussed by our philosophic class. We deferred answering it until we should take up Aristotle's statement of the same problem. We have now studied Aristotle's doctrine of motion sufficiently, I think, to see that his standpoint is a continuation of that of Plato, viz. that all motion must ultimately be traced back to a first cause which is itself unmoved by others. But though Aristotle's statement of the problem involves us in new difficulties, it has not, so far, justified to us the fundamental assumption in which he follows Plato.

Probably I did not in my last letter clearly indicate the main difficulty which we find in adopting Plato's doctrine of motion as stated in the tenth book of the *Laws*. You seem to think that our difficulty consists in conceiving self-activity and independent being. Instead I should say that it is rather in conceiving *dependent* being. To be more exact, we do not see the validity of the distinction between independent and dependent being. It seems to me that all beings are, in a sense, independent subsisting by their own right, and yet all are dependent since no one could develop, i.e. could *be* in its dynamic sense, without the presence of others. But that does not mean that we can split up our universe into the moved and the mover.

You say "there are possible two kinds of being, one of them that being that is made what it is through other being, i.e. dependent being, and second, being that is independent or which has its marks and attributes, its constitution and nature all through itself." Now the difficulty consists in seeing anything in our universe corresponding to *either* of these two kinds of being. You give as a substratum of perfect (independent) being "the contents of the mind of Morris Cohen which are due to his self activity of intellect and will." But could these contents be what they are without the help of other beings, his parents, teachers, etc. and a whole social organism which enables him to be helped by the experience of countless individuals who have lived in the past? The truth seems to be that it is utterly impossible to conceive any being that is absolutely independent. On the other hand it is even more difficult to conceive anything corresponding to what you call dependent being. In order that there should be any borrowing of being there must be *something that borrows,* and is thus independent of your perfect being. If perfect being were to lend being to nothing, the being thus lent would be a part of the perfect being and therefore just as independent, since the whole is not independent of the parts, any more than the parts are independent of the whole. By making his perfect beings (Ideas) independent of the world of change that we know, Plato put himself in a position where he could not explain the relation between the world of Ideas and the world that we know; since no relation can be established between two being[s] one of which is entirely independent of the other.

With sincere gratitude for your kind interest in our work, I remain,

Yours respectfully

Secretary M R C

Feb. 25, 1900
[actually 1901]

Dr. William T. Harris

Dear Sir:

Your letter of ᾿ the ninth inst. and the thirteen copies of your pamphlet were received, and we return many thanks. Contrary to your expectation the argument in the latter did appeal to us. We read and discussed it᾿at our last special meeting and found no serious difficulty in following out the whole argument. We have studied philosophy sufficiently to see that spontaneity freedom or self-activity is at the heart of existence and the essence of every being or individual. But we cannot see how any being can be absolutely independent or absolutely dependent. You are certainly right when you say: "You have nothing whatever presented to your mind except through its self-activity. Somebody else cannot think for you."

But does that prove that this self-activity can go on without aid from and independent of parents, teachers, social organism etc.? To us it seems utterly inconceivable. What would be the use of education if it were so?

Again the relation of the thinker to the thought does not seem to offer an example of either dependent or independent being. It seems to us a return of the whole to a part. . . .

It may be that we have no thought corresponding to Plato's thought of his Ideas. But is [it] not an argument against these Ideas that their absolute independence make[s] Plato unable to find any relation between these ideas and the world of phenomena and therefore unable to explain the world of phenomena? And what is the point of the first part of the Parmenides if not just this—that the absolute unity and transcendence of the Ideas makes participation or imitation or any other mode of connection between the world of Ideas and the world of phenomena impossible? It would be very instructive for us to see how else that famous dialogue can be interpreted.

On Sunday March 3, our circle will have its first *annual* meeting, which will be devoted to the discussion of the meaning and function of philosophy. If possible a brief communication from you on that occasion would be highly appreciated.

Yours sincerely
Secretary M. R. C.

Sidney Hook

In his relations with his students, Cohen found affection no bar to criticism. Conversely, when they criticized him, he did not grow any the less fond of them, nor was he less fond because he was critical.

When Cohen disagreed with Hook, he said so, and vice versa. When he approved, he expressed himself with equal forthrightness.

Cohen's review of Hook's book, *Toward the Understanding of Karl Marx,* stirred up a lively exchange that did not seem to have affected their friendship. When Cohen became ill on December 30, 1941, at the Vassar meeting of the American Philosophical Association, it was Sidney Hook who called the doctor and looked after his old teacher.

Dec. 15/34

Dear Sidney:

I am unusually pressed for time, working with my very limited energy on a number of tasks which must be finished within a given time-limit. But I have managed to look up every one of your charges that my notes in the Student Outlook attribute to you views not contained in your book. My general reply—and it is only a very general one that I have time for now—is that you are the best judge of what you *intended* to say; and as I have no desire to commit you to my particular position, I can only express my sincere regret that my understanding of your book departed from your intention. At the same time I should insist that what seem to you errors are quite natural interpretations of your text—interpretations which would occur to any well disposed reader with no more intelligence than yours truly. I can cite many passages to bear me out. Remember that an author sees his text in a somewhat different light than does the reader. For this reason I can understand your disappointment, but I can not at all agree that there is anything strange in the manner or substance of my notes. I do not find myself guilty on any of your specified counts except not seeing your text with your eyes.

When I have time, or when you can come to see me, I shall be glad to furnish you a detailed [word missing] to every one of the points you make in your letter.

Cordially yours,
MORRIS R. COHEN

November 8, 1939

Dear Sidney:

I have just received the copy of your book on John Dewey and wish to thank you cordially for it. I borrowed the book last night from Ernest [Nagel] and read several chapters, which means that I found it interesting and well done though, as you might expect, it has not yet converted me or convinced me that my interpretation of Dewey is erroneous. But I am a pluralist and I am genuinely glad to see Dewey's point of view so vigorously defended.

We expect to be in town for the next few months and I shall be glad if you can come around to see us some time when you are at leisure and can engage in irresponsible and useless talk.

With kind regards,

Cordially yours,
MORRIS R. COHEN

3708—Oliver Street, N.W.
Washington, D.C.
March 1, 1943

Dear Sidney:

Some time ago Felix [Cohen] read to me your essay on "Failure of Nerve." He commented, "This is worthy of a pupil of Morris Cohen." I don't quite agree with him. You have other and more important claim to distinction on your own account, but the essay is good and I am glad to bask in its glory if only vicariously.

I wish the fates could send you to Washington before the war is over. I am truly lonesome, for although my children live in the same city with me, I see very little of them. Willie is working for the Navy, and like all Navy men he cultivates remarkable taciturnity. Leonora has given birth to a baby girl, and, like all mothers, is entirely absorbed in taking care of the infant. Felix is quite busy in the Interior Department but finds time occasionally to help me in some of the work that I am trying to continue, such as my Carus Lectures and a group of essays on "Prolegomena to Logic." However, his own work must necessarily receive priority. I expected when I came to Washington where so many of my former pupils are located that I would be overwhelmed with visitors. But long working hours, poor transportation, and miserable weather all militate against the best intentions. So I am back most of the time with my own loneliness. A letter from you would help a great deal.

Sincerely yours,
MORRIS R. COHEN

March 7, 1943

Dear Sidney,

I was very glad to receive your letter of March 5th. I have not yet received the copy of your review on Meiklejohn's book, but I suppose it was delayed in the mail.

I am awaiting anxiously the copy of your book "The Hero in History." I always remember Hegel's dictum: "No man is a hero to his valet, not because the hero is not a hero, but because the valet is a valet."

It is good to receive the assurance of your faith in me as a possible ally in the cause of naturalism and liberalism. Perhaps I shall be able to justify your faith with my return to normal health.

I should love to receive additional information about your doings and your prospects.

As ever

Cordially yours,

MORRIS

March 24th, 1943

Dear Morris:—

I recall the events you ask me about as follows:

You took sick the evening of December 30th, 1941 at Vassar, Poughkeepsie, an hour or so after the Association dinner. You had heard Mrs. de Laguna read her Presidential address. You liked it, you said to me, but were not overimpressed with it. The main points had been made before, some in *Reason and Nature,* etc. About 10:30 or so, someone told me that you had retired for the night and that you weren't feeling very well. I went down to your room to see how you were and found you in bed. You were restless and at the same time were very tired. You did not seem to be feverish to the touch but complained about general discomfort. You approved of the suggestion that a doctor be called. Your hands shook a little bit and your eyelids fluttered when you closed them. You weren't very much in the mood for talking but appeared glad to have someone in the room with you. You explained your condition as due to a lack of sleep and said you had been worried about Mrs. Cohen. You acted just a little bit frightened and seemed aware of it. You observed—with a wry smile—that you always got alarmed "under these circumstances" even when you didn't want to which was one of the reasons you could never believe in freedom of the will. I asked you if you ever had spells of this kind before and you said yes.

The physician whom Otis Lee called,—I don't remember his name —was the Roosevelt's family physician when they were at Hyde Park. When he came, you volunteered the information to him that you had told me. He found your temperature normal, pulse regular, and said that you were suffering from over-tiredness together with lack of fresh air and exercise as a result of being cooped up all day in association meetings. He attributed your discomfort to gas pains. He gave you a pill (aspirin?), told you not to worry, assured you that you would sleep through the night, and recommended a walk in the morning after breakfast. (He charged you $5.00)

You seemed to be greatly relieved by his presence, and when I looked in on you again after walking the doctor to his car, you said you felt much better and were ready to go to bed. I accompanied the doctor to his car in order to find out whether there was anything else he had found that he didn't want to tell you. But he repeated to me what he had told you, and assured me you would be all right the next morning. Everybody was glad to hear that there was nothing seriously the matter.

The next morning you were not in your room when I came by and I didn't see you until the very end of the morning session at which Glenn Morrow, Northrop and I read papers on "The Philosophical Presuppositions of Democracy." You came in during the discussion period just as Blanshard was denouncing all naturalists as people who had no right to be democrats, etc. Later you told me that you had been out walking, that you had had a good night's rest. But I remember that you weren't looking well, didn't speak much to people (which was unusual), and gave the impression of being low in spirits. You weren't sure whether you were going to return to N.Y. that afternoon or not. I have a vague impression that you were planning to go to Cambridge or New Haven or some place, other than New York, to which you had been invited.

That's about all I can recall. Maybe more will come back later. I hope this will be useful.

Cordially,
SIDNEY HOOK

October 28, 1943

Dear Sidney:

My secretary has just read to me your review of Beard's "The Republic: Conversations on Fundamentals" in the current number of the Nation.

I say "Damned good,"—meaning "Them is my own sentiments" better expressed than I could do myself.

Cordially yours,
MORRIS

Arthur S. Meyer

Cohen got to know Meyer through Leo Mayer, Cohen's Harvard friend and a cousin of Arthur Meyer. Meyer's generosity to the Cohens was particularly crucial in the days when financial troubles plagued even a philosopher who prided himself on being above such cares.

Cohen used to read his manuscripts at Sunday-night supper meetings at our home to a circle of Meyer's friends, including the wives: Osmond Fraenkel, Walter Pollak, Clarence Lewis, Walter Jonas, Jerome Michael, Harold Beckman, and others. Cohen was particularly close to Fraenkel, who read *Reason and Nature* in manuscript for him.

Arthur avowed to my father that, marriage aside, his friendship with him was the brightest part of his life.

> Mamaroneck and Garden Road
> Scarsdale
> July 20, 1930

Dear Morris,

Pollock's "Land Laws" reached me last Wednesday. Have I already thanked you? . . .

Just now I am deep in Shakespeare. Forty plays in as many days is a huge assignment. . . . it is still a stimulating experience. . . . Practically all of the students are teachers studying for credits or to gather notes for their own courses and ninety percent of them belong to the—in a manner of speaking—fair sex. Their society is a little depressing and, as I told Marion, I have not felt so bewomanned since the last time I was in a Macy elevator. . . .

This morning I . . . read Hook's essay on Morris Cohen in the New Republic. Notwithstanding a genuine admiration for an article so succinct and accurate, the thought would obtrude that, even with the advantages of our many talks and your patient explanations, some portions of the article eluded me; and then followed the query: Is it perhaps regrettable that Hook refused the opportunity of compromising somewhat with the untechnical audience who are the larger part of the readers of The New Republic? I know your feeling against thin gruel philosophy to appease the unphilosophical—but that, I take it, is because the pap is not philosophy at all but something spurious and unwholesome. An explanation of your view of life, somewhat less recondite (and though perhaps somewhat less exact, still sound within its limits) was not, I believe, utterly beyond the bounds of possibility.

. . . the best [news] was the progress of your book and the rapid completion of your Oxford article.

The Meyer family, serene if not boisterously happy, on this hot midsummer afternoon, join me in sending fondest love to Felix and to you.

> As ever,
> ARTHUR

Blue Mt. Lake, N.Y.
August 30/36

Dear Arthur and Marion:

Leonard [the Meyers' younger son] came here yesterday as per schedule. . . .

We had a long talk yesterday and I find myself heartily in agreement with his general point of view viz. to concentrate on music and art and get the needed *discipline* (on the necessity of which he agrees with you and me) from the centre of his interest rather than from outer indifferent activities. For this reason I went over the Bard College Catalogue and found myself much more sympathetic to the idea of letting him try it—at least for a year. The Faculty of Bard College does not inspire me with great hopes (though I personally know only one man on it), but the plan of its work seems to me sound and it may be just what Leonard needs. The whole business of education is involved in so many uncertainties that unless there is some insurmountable reason to the contrary a boy of Leonard's maturity and generally sound instincts should be allowed to follow his inclinations.

. . . needless to add, we all genuinely enjoy having Leonard here. . . . We all send our fond love to you,

As ever,
MORRIS

Inverness, Cal.
7/31/37

Dearest Arthur:

I received the photograph of Margulies' pastel of you, and I like it immensely. . . . It seems to me that he has caught the essential of ASM—the sympathetic intelligence which makes him such a good negotiator . . . and, above all, the spiritual quality which . . . may be, at times, covered over by other traits but which has been active enough to maintain a free companionship for over thirty years with a severe intellectualist like MRC. That, I think, is the true function of a portrait as distinct from a photograph—I mean the function of revealing inner character.

I am, of course, distressed to hear of your painful experience with your leg, and I hope that you will get accustomed very soon to go without cigarettes. After all, you are no longer officially in the tobacco business. . . .

May and I have been having a wonderful time here. May enjoys the scenery, the quiet, the people, everything—and I am having the kind of vacation that I should prescribe for myself (except the [Stanford] logic class which pays for it all). I am enjoying the opportunity of both quiet and library facilities. I have not done much writing, but I am catching up on some reading which I should have done long ago. The only thing that I would want to add would be that you and Marion could come out here and relax as we are doing.

With affectionate greetings,

MORRIS

The University of Chicago
Department of Philosophy

[April 1938]

Dear Arthur:

Unless my memory plays me false April 24 is your birthday and I wish to take the opportunity to express my abiding love and best wishes for many happy returns of the day. The years are stealing up on us and the prospects for the world at large are not as bright as they seemed when we first met or used to take our Sunday walks. But the blessings of true friendship do not wither while life lasts.

Ever affectionately yours,

MORRIS

May 31, 1938

Dear Morris,

. . . Marion kept your birthday letter and gave it to me early on the morning of the 24th. I have often called to mind your thought that friendship is one of the few certain goods that the world offers; and as other goods evanesce and other securities weaken, the certainty of our love becomes ever more precious.

ARTHUR

Blue Mountain Lake, N.Y.
August 30, 1938

Dear Arthur:

You have probably heard of Mussolini's flirtations with Hitler in regard to anti-semitism, and you probably know that nothing serious is going to happen to the 40,000 Italian Jews as a result of it. There is, however, a rather serious aspect to the situation which few people have paid any attention to. And that is the influence of Mussolini's utterances on the relations between Jews and Italians in this country.

It would be a major calamity if the Italians in large numbers joined the Germans in fostering anti-Jewish attitudes, in New York and other cities.

I mention this to you to show the importance of a judiciously minded man as chairman of this new committee. Whatever the shortcomings of the people on it (which shortcomings you find in all political bodies) a man of your equipment can certainly prevent a great deal of hasty and injudicious action on the part of our own people. A boycott, for instance, against Italy would be almost fatal to the Jews here, in view of Italian-Jewish relations in the clothing and other industries and in the general political situation.

Have you been asked to become acting chairman? Much love from all of us, to Marion and yourself,

As ever,
MORRIS

Blue Mt. Lake, N.Y.
Sept 6/38

Dear Arthur:

Imitation or flattery of Hitler is not the only cause of Mussolini's anti-Jewish drive. He has to pose as a friend of the Arabs to assure his African possessions. Also there are about 40,000 *German* Jews in Italy, most of them in Trieste, the old Austrian port which Italy annexed after the war. Naturally these Jews are not sufficiently friendly to Hitler to please the fascists. But above all Mussolini needs a diversion—the people are tired of the Spanish adventure and the military psychology cannot work without an enemy. The Jews are a convenient target.

Still I do not think that the Italians will ever go as far as the Germans in their anti-Jewish drive. There is not the age-long background of popular anti-Semitism and government policy in that direction. Anti-Semitism in Germany goes back to the Crusades and almost every distinguished philosopher of that country has supported it more or less. That is not the case in Italy. They cannot even get their anthropologists to endorse the government policies, and so the official justifying report was anonymous. Of course the Jews will suffer and the example is worse. But I still hold to my original view.

We all send our love to Marion and your good self.

As ever,
MORRIS

The University of Chicago
Department of Philosophy

May 22, 1939

Dearest Arthur:

. . . My routine work here has, because of a misunderstanding on my part, turned out to be much heavier than I expected; and while it is far from unpleasant it has kept my nose to the grindstone pretty constantly. . . .

As next Wednesday is your birthday I cannot refrain from taking this occasion to express to you my abiding love which the lengthening chain of years has only served to strengthen.

Mary also joins me in love to Marion and the children,

As ever,
MORRIS

Apr. 27—43

Dear Arthur and Marion,

I had a pleasant visit from Dan [the Meyers' older son] and Jerry [Professor Jerome Michael, Arthur's brother-in-law]. They told me that you were back in town. I suppose you cut your visit short I trust for not unpleasant reasons.

All goes as usual with the Cohens. Harry is busy with his garden and Leonora is busy with Marianne. William was away for more than a week on government business and just got back much to Grace's comfort and happiness. Felix is working hard drafting a statute for Porto Rico to set up self-government for the people of that island; and he is helping me to put final shape to the Prolegomena to Logic. He seems to have an extraordinary capacity for work. Little Genie inherits his temper and some of the characteristics that made Felix' mother so proud of him.

My own health is developing as was to be expected. I am slowly regaining my strength, though I am still far from having recovered my old-time health. The warm weather helps me a good deal. I am able to take considerable walking trips around the block, but I still am lonesome. The people I know in Washington work hard and are too busy to visit me.

How are you all,—Carolyn [the Meyers' daughter] and your dear selves? How is Leonard? Has he adjusted himself to his new position? I am writing this to induce you to send me a letter, for that is one of the few means of keeping in touch with the few friends who are dear to me. . . .

The apple blossoms are out in full force in our yard. I suppose the same is true in yours, or soon will be.

This is hardly a letter, but it sends you my dearest love and good wishes.

As ever,

MORRIS R. COHEN.

Varia

The following single letters give an idea of the diversity of Cohen's friendships.

Sept. 18/30

Dear Mr. [Edward S.] Greenbaum:

I have just got back from Europe and am shocked and grieved that your father [Judge Samuel Greenbaum] has passed away. I knew of course of his poor health, having met him several times last year on the Riverside Drive. But it is difficult for me to realize that his vigorous mind is no longer functioning amongst us.

I first met your father about thirty years ago, when I was trying to run the Davidson School as a branch of the Educational Alliance. He impressed me then and ever after as a man of remarkable clarity and fairness of mind. This and his great kindness to me when I was young and inexperienced made him one of the great figures in my life. It is a painful reminder of the transitoriness of human life to learn of his death, though it is a source of pride to me that I knew him and had his regard.

Please accept, on behalf of yourself and your two sisters that I know, the expression of my heartfelt sympathy and condolence.

Sincerely yours,

MORRIS R. COHEN

76 Grozier Rd.
Cambridge, Mass.
December 1/38

Dear Mr. [Sol] Strook:

I was very sorry, indeed, to hear of your ill-health which I imagine is in large part due to worry and over-work growing out of the terrible situation abroad. I am glad, however, to hear that you are making a good recovery and I hope that you will take good care of yourself when you return to your usual duties. The number of good men in this world is, alas, limited and their mere existence is (to a philosopher at least) more important than the amount of work they do. You are an older and wiser man than I am and it ill behooves me to give you any advice. But my observation indicates that the men who take good care of themselves accomplish more in the long run. With warm regards and all good wishes,

Cordially yours,

MORRIS R. COHEN

December 27, 1937

Dear Dr. Elliott:

I shall be glad indeed to join the Committee to sponsor the dinner for Stanley Isaacs. He has indeed been a friend of underprivileged children, and is entitled to the homage of his fellow citizens.

I wish I could see you some time personally. The years are creeping up and you may have seen in the papers that I am retiring from active teaching and have, indeed, been made Professor Emeritus (to begin on February 1st). It seems only yesterday when the boys gave me a dinner and you read that lovely letter of Felix Adler. Since then both of my parents and many of the most distinguished sponsors of that dinner have, like Felix Adler, left this human scene; but the good fight is being carried on even though the clouds look threatening.

My wife joins in warm regards,

Cordially yours,

MORRIS R. COHEN

Dr. John Lovejoy Elliott

March 9, 1938

Dr. Alberto C. Bonaschi [Commissioner]
Board of Education
500 Park Avenue
New York, N.Y.

Dear Dr. Bonaschi:

I wish to thank you for your kindness in sending me your most interesting article on Italian Currents in English Literature. What you say about Chaucer is, to me, most illuminating.

I also wish to express my profound gratitude for the very kind words which you spread on the minutes of the Retirement Board on the occasion of my retirement from the College of the City of New York. If my services have been of any value to New York City it is, after all, a very small return on the generous investment by New York City in the education of an immigrant boy. It has always seemed to me that the generosity of this city in matters of education makes it unique in the history of civilization; and it is my profound hope that this generosity will continue to express a temper of wise tolerance and liberality calculated to save liberal civilization from the dark forces which threaten it.

With kind regards and best wishes,

Faithfully yours,

MORRIS R. COHEN

August 4, 1938

[To Professor Theresa Wolfson Wood]

Dear Tess:

I am genuinely pained to hear of the death of your father. While I did not have the pleasure of meeting him, I think I know his type —the hardy pioneers who uprooted themselves from the old country and with little resources but their indomitable courage made a new home in this country and brought up their children to enjoy the best —at least in the intellectual field—that this country affords. We shall be happy if our children will show something of that tenacity, though I hope they will not be put to such severe tests as our parents were.

Though my father died four years ago, I still feel the vacancy in my life which his departure brought about. But we have to carry on and do our share of the work.

May and I enjoyed Chicago immensely. The people there were most kind to us and made our stay so agreeable that we are both looking forward to next spring as our real vacation. May is now in Blue Mountain Lake (N.Y.) and I expect to join her tomorrow, to return to the city on September 15, after which we go to Harvard (September 25) for the winter term. I hope we shall be able to see you and Austin, and possibly the children. Are they not old enough now to come to see us?

My best wishes for a pleasant and restful summer vacation and affectionate greetings, in which May would surely join me if she were here.

Faithfully yours,

MORRIS R. COHEN

August 4, 1938

Dear Dr. [Isidore] Silver:

It is extraordinarily sweet of you to send me your book [*The Pindaric Odes of Ronsard*] and your very gracious letter. I confess I am at times somewhat embarrassed to receive these gracious tributes from former students for what they think I have done for them. I know how much more my students were entitled to than what I could offer them. However, I have the standard excuse, I did my best.

> With all good wishes,
> Faithfully yours,
> MORRIS R. COHEN

December 23, 1935

Dear [Frederick J. E.] Woodbridge,

You remember Emerson's lines, "Nor knowest thou what argument Thy life to thy neighbor's creed has lent." I therefore want you to know how much my own faith has been strengthened by the reports which I have been receiving through Friess and Edman of your magnificent courage in continuing to meet your class despite your great loss and your physical handicap. We talk in our philosophic jargon about spirit and nature, but a concrete embodiment of human fortitude over adverse circumstance, illumines the meaning of life as well as strengthens our faith in noble effort.

Years ago, you taught me the meaning of the clear-eyed Hellenic attitude to life, but you are now showing the meaning of true courage.

While nothing can atone for your loss in the passing of Mrs. Woodbridge, it must be a comfort to you to reflect that after her experience in passing through the valley years ago in the Adirondacks, she lived to see her children married. Please accept both my heartfelt condolence and the hope that you will long be able to continue to set a noble example of how philosophy can enoble life.

> [MORRIS R. COHEN]

Conclusion

The Animateur

ON A FAMILY WALK one day, Morris Cohen recounted to Lucy Kramer, his daughter-in-law-elect, an incident that had occurred some twenty-five years earlier. Mary, who had come along, was startled. "You never told me that, Morris!" He answered calmly, "Give me time, May dear, give me time."

Given time, Cohen may be viewed in fresh perspectives. The more we learn about him—the more we uncover of the ideas he sparked, the fields he invigorated, the causes he advanced, the caliber as well as the number of minds that he stirred—the more clearly he emerges as a great *animateur* of America in the first half of our century. He was commonly known piece-meal. Yet the sum total of his accomplishments is a richer legacy than any of his single deeds.

The destructive side of Cohen's teaching was thrown into a spotlight that left in shadow his constructive side. He smashed sanctimonious com-placencies, petrified orthodoxies, idols of the day. So arose the legend of a purely negativistic philosopher, bent on destroying but not on replacing the old myths with anything constructive. In a sense he was out of step with his time. Although a rebel, he was more of a classicist than a romantic or modernist, which his opponents often were.

When he was accused of throwing out everything old and putting back nothing new, he answered, "When Hercules cleaned the Augean stables, he did a good day's work."

"Actually when Cohen pleads guilty to the charge of being 'merely critical, negative, or destructive,' he is doing his philosophy an injustice," said a former pupil, Daniel J. Bronstein, in a review of *A Dreamer's Journey* in *City College Alumnus* (October 1949). He quoted Cohen to prove his point:

The main function of teaching philosophy should be the opening of the human mind to new possibilities, rather than the inculcation of any new set of doctrines. To me, this did not mean the old-fashioned liberation of the mind from all traditional beliefs, but rather the supplying of students with new points of view that would enrich their outlook and thus help them to attain genuine intellectual

426

independence. This in practice meant attempting to teach future scientists, lawyers, economists, and citizens to think philosophically about the problems of science, law, economics, and citizenship.

"We still have a great deal to learn," Bronstein concluded, "about the process of teaching citizens to think philosophically about the problems of human concern, but whatever can be said of its difficulties it is not a 'merely critical' or 'negative' attitude."[1]

"Builder of bridges," Cohen was once called by his old friend and fellow philosopher Cornelius Krusé. Cohen spanned gaps between destructive and positive thinking. For him criticism and creation represented complementary poles. He could not have been so constructive without his criticalness, which gave him practicality and balance.

His relevance to the problems of today can best be comprehended in view of the bridge that he sought to erect between what C. P. Snow calls the two cultures, scientific and humanistic. The scientific method, which Cohen applied to both domains, served as his bridge. In our age of ultra-specialization and ever-increasing fragmentation of knowledge, his message is that philosophy, in its ancient broad sense, must build the multitudinous links of a unified approach.

Other chapters of this book indicate how Cohen joined philosophy to intellectual disciplines such as science, social science, history, religion, literature, and, most effectively, law. Felix Cohen, in his Foreword to *American Thought,* points out some of the chasms that his father was instrumental in bridging: he related logic, which since the days of Aristotle had been treated as a subject by itself, to the natural and the social sciences, as well as to mathematics and philosophy. The gap between classical and scientific studies, so ingrained in academic life, was spanned when the Cohen-Drabkin *Source Book in Greek Science* demonstrated that far from being a product of Baconian empiricism, science has origins in ancient Greece. He combined the scholarly and the practical life most notably, as we have seen, in Jewish affairs. His internationalism was evinced in scholarly and humanitarian ways, as he sought to bring foreign cultures and our own into closer rapport. Two years after the outbreak of World War I, he wrote this message to Xavier Léon, editor of France's leading philosophical journal.

March 7, 1916

M. Xavier Léon
Secretaire de la Rédaction de la Revue
  de Métaphysique et de Morale

My dear M. Léon:

No philosophical review is so highly prized on this side of the Atlantic as the one which you so ably direct; and I want to express to you my profound appreciation and delight that in these dark and trying days you are still able to continue that splendid intellectual tradition which has made France the intellectual leader of humanity.

I am moved to this expression of my sentiments by the receipt of the unusually excellent number devoted to Malebranche. With best wishes,

Respectfully yours,

MORRIS R. COHEN

When World War I disrupted the international congresses of the philosophers, at Cohen's suggestion the American Philosophical Association organized a Committee on International Cooperation after the War. In 1922 the association authorized the committee to help German and Austrian philosophical libraries bring their collections up to date through gifts of recent American philosophical publications. Cohen collected books, current periodicals, and money from the association's membership and forwarded them to the *Notgemeinschaften* of Germany and Austria.

Meanwhile, there was catastrophe in Japan; fires resulting from severe earthquakes had damaged the library of the Imperial University of Tokyo. In 1923 the American Philosophical Association voted library aid to Japan. Again, Cohen collected the materials. At the invitation of Lucius C. Porter, the executive secretary of the Harvard-Yenching Institute in Peiping, China, he contributed to that country in 1924 and again in 1936 a bibliography of references in the philosophy of science.

Cohen was among the philosophers active in arranging for the first international congress of philosophy ever convened in the United States. For the 6th International Congress of Philosophy, held at Harvard in September 1926, Cohen as a member of the Executive Committee was in charge of arranging a session on legal philosophy. It was a beginning; legal philosophy in this country had come of age internationally.

The Northern and Southern Hemispheres had maintained little contact with each other philosophically when Cohen proposed to Cornelius Krusé, secretary-treasurer of the American Philosophical Association, that it arrange a Congress of Latin and North American philosophers. The association's national board of officers voted unanimously that Cohen's Carus Lectures be read at the First Interamerican Congress of Philosophy. That was in 1942, but wartime travel restrictions forced them to be read instead at The City College. Since then, the Interamerican Congresses of Philosophy have provided fruitful opportunity for philosophical exchange.

Cohen carried his philosophic vision and method to people beyond the ivory tower. He appeared in a variety of semipopular periodicals, and at times in newspapers as the author of letters to the editor. The full story of his close association with *The New Republic,* for example, has never been told. As part of its inner circle, from its inception in 1914 through 1936, he was a regular contributor of articles, reviews, and editorials, sometimes unsigned, more often under the nom de plume Philonous. They undoubtedly helped *The New Republic* in those early years to attain its special position in American letters. Until 1926 much of his writing—in jurisprudence, social problems, education, literature, and religion, as well as philosophy, logic, and ethics—was channeled through its pages. He was a demon book reviewer, also. Of his forty review articles for *The New Republic,* many were later inserted into his books. At sixteen he had longed to try his hand at newspaper work. Now he was having a fling as Socratic journalist. His initiative in spreading knowledge of Peirce and Santayana, which we have elsewhere traced, was characteristic of his contribution to culture.

Institutions of learning and individuals in philosophy, law, and other fields sought Cohen's guidance. Brigadier General Douglas MacArthur, superintendent of the United States Military Academy, sent him West Point's annual report for 1920, with its proposed reorganization of the curriculum and course of training. "I would deeply appreciate any comment or suggestion," he wrote. William Kilpatrick, professor of education at Teachers College, asked Cohen to suggest a man to teach the general theory of education. "We three now here," he specified, "belong in general to the John Dewey school of thought. We should be glad to bring in a variant point of view (not, however, we think the Hegelian). . . . We . . . would be much interested to find someone who has studied with you or has your general point of view." Harry A. Wolfson of Harvard thanked Cohen for his advice on organizing Ph.D. research there in medieval Jewish philosophy. The University of Virginia's Corcoran School of Philosophy asked him for a bibliography of legal philosophy. The Johns Hopkins University, organizing an Institute for the Study of Law, asked his help. Lehigh consulted him when launching a seminar in philosophy of history. Wagner College, organizing a department of philosophy, turned to him for advice. Charles W. Morris, organizing the International Congresses for the Philosophy of Science, asked Cohen in 1934 for suggestions in writing the history of scientific philosophy in America. Krusé, of the American Philosophical Association, which adopted Cohen's suggested topic for its 1937 plenary session, "The Nature of the Causal Relation in the Light of Recent Physics," called it "really your symposium." On behalf of the American Historical Association, Merle Curti invited him to preside over a 1940 session on causality. A psychologist wanted references to thinking machines. Others asked for information about St. Thomas, G. H. Mead, Babbitt, Einstein, Hogben, Voltaire's deism, Ingersoll and atheism, ultramodern education. They seemed to consider Cohen an institution in himself, a one-man "Information Please."

Not even prison walls proved a bar to his influence. Nathan Leopold, under life sentence for the Leopold-Loeb murder, wished to embark on a learned translation, and welcomed Cohen's suggestion that he translate Kepler; he sought advice as to how to procure the necessary documents.

Authors of manuscripts in many fields turned to him for aid. His impact on the economist John R. Commons of the University of Wisconsin is a story in itself. Professor Commons submitted to Cohen drafts of his writings for criticism of the way he, Commons, applied Cohen's principle of polarity to economic reasoning. On April 14, 1937, he wrote Cohen:

> I am trying to make use of your principle of Polarity in comparing the theories of Justice Roberts and Justice Stone in the AAA case, enclosed, with the idea that it is applicable generally to methods of reasoning in Economics. A preceding use I made a couple of years ago is now being printed in the Centennial Book of the N.Y. University Law School. . . .

On May 28, 1937, Commons wrote again.

> Recently I sent you a copy of the enclosed paper. . . . This paper is a chapter in proposed elementary book to be named Investigational Economics. . . .
>
> I have been so greatly helped by your book *Reason and Nature* that I want to send the whole thing to you after revision, before sending to publisher. Do not be alarmed.
>
> In one of the articles "Value in Law and Economics," (Law Quarterly) I make use of your discussion of polarity, and again in this article.
>
> Sincerely
> JOHN R. COMMONS
>
> I ought to add, this article was written to lay foundations for redrafting AAA legislation to make it constitutional if Justice Roberts would change his mind. Have had help from Agriculture Dept. at Washington and have sent to them suggestions for redrafting.

In his multitudinous extracurricular activities, Cohen combined diligence with imagination. He sought neither personal power nor self-promotion. He did not care whether his patent rights to ideas were respected so long as the ideas themselves were spread. He gave his time, his knowledge and judgment selflessly to others. Although he neither joined nor founded a school of philosophy, he reached a wider segment of the population than do most technical philosophers. Perhaps he was not always consistent, but he scored.

Cohen himself was painfully aware of the discrepancy between his aspirations and the incompleteness of their realization. The vision that dominated his intellectual life was to help build an Encyclopedia of Philosophy that would do for the twentieth century what Diderot and D'Alembert did for the eighteenth. He didn't live to complete all the books he planned, still his former student, Milton Konvitz, now professor of law and industrial relations at Cornell, has called him "the most encyclopedic philosopher our century has thus far known, a twentieth-century Aristotle."[2]

Cohen faced, if he did not solve, many of the intellectual dilemmas that beset us, and some people feel an intellectual companionship thereby. Kenneth Olson, of Smith College's government department, told his student Marianne J. Rosenfield, Cohen's granddaughter, that such was his bond to Cohen. Huntington Cairns said that "Cohen shares with John Dewey the distinction of being the most popularly influential of contemporary thinkers.

"It has become the habit now-a-days," adds Cairns, "to observe that there is a dearth of original ideas in his works. . . ."[3] Cohen has been called merely negativistic—even by some who profit from his ideas—a high priest of the contemplative life who, like Rodin's Thinker, had nothing to do but sit and meditate.

The obvious, Cohen's role as *animateur,* has escaped general recognition. The slight figure with the unsquelchable spirit was above all a sower of ideas. Only time can measure the harvest to be reaped. We can see now, however, how positive was his most comprehensive contribution, that of intellectual animator of America.

The Portrait in Retrospect

In the twilight of Cohen's years, the tragic mood of his adolescence would sometimes steal upon him, and he would brood: he had spread himself too thin, his absolutes were never pursued to their ultimate limits. His lifework was incomplete, he would never live to "actualize his potentiality."

Yet in the end Morris' youthful dreams came true. "My principal characteristic," he had written in his early diary, "is a love for books." He amassed a fabulous library that, bequeathed to his alma mater, is now housed in a special room of the Morris Raphael Cohen Library.

"The next principal characteristic is my great desire to be good," he had continued on that New Year's Day so long ago. In the sixty-odd years of his life he gave ample demonstration of social conscience and moral stature. He lived in the heroic tradition exemplified by Davidson. In the end he spent himself for the Jewish cause. The man whom Holmes called a holy man had lived the good life.

"What shall be the purpose of my life?" he asked. "The paying of my debt towards my parents." Even when he had not enough dollars to go around, he saw to it that some went to his father and mother.

"I am not only a reformer but a revolutionist." His youthful words became in a sense prophetic. At least, whenever he found anything to disapprove of—and the occasions were multitudinous, in philosophy, in education, and in society—his voice would be lifted up in protest that often proved effective. Intellectually, his inclinations remained iconoclastic.

"I would try to bring socialism to the real American," he had stated, "through the newspaper and platform. I would not follow as 'disciple' of the Socialistic leaders but would have ideas of my own." In that sense, he fulfilled his dream to become "a socialist agitator."

"The ambition I now possess to the greatest degree is for journalism," confessed the youth growing up in the Age of Reform, when the progressive mind was a journalistic mind. Again, his wish became a reality.

"Thinking of Scott pouring out book after book," the lad in 1897 was "fairly struck with a feeling of awe and admiration." Morris in time turned into a prolific writer.

He had thought of becoming "perhaps a lawyer." That was about as close to it as he ever came, but he more than made up for his lack of a law degree by his influence on our jurisprudence.

The author of "The Journal of a Boy Philosopher . . . Trying to Learn How to be Wise" lived to write philosophy that is considered wise. He who had resolved: "To improve my Knowledge of Everything and Something," was later called a twentieth-century Aristotle.

At eighteen he expressed the hope "of obtaining a position at C.C.N.Y. in philosophy." Fourteen years later, the goal was won. He who longed to be some day a teacher, as a teacher won fame.

"To become isolated from mankind is not to be happy," he had written. "It is not enough to look on, I must join in." And join in he did.

Sam Cohen said of his brother after his death:

I know he became a little more mellow in his later years, but not much. The Morris I remember was the great teacher who threw old traditions out of the window and made the students think for themselves. He was the philosopher who put philosophy into the law and made thousands of people in all fields admire him. He was the man who in his armchair debates made lawyers and statesmen, philosophers and scientists, look like school boys when he got through with them. . . .

"He came up the hard way," said Morris' old aunt. Sometimes his students and even his friends must have felt as if he were forgetting to pull his punches. He played the game hard, but he never became a hard man.

His story is part of the epic of America; he loved and served the country that had given him opportunity.

Its national philosophy [he once said in a speech] has been that the greatest wealth of a nation consists in the energy of its individual men and women and that such energies are most advantageously liberated by free education and the abolition of hereditary class distinctions. I speak with feeling on the subject because as an immigrant boy, like so many million others, I have been accorded these benefits to an extent that no other country in the world would have offered.

In 1940 Morris Cohen's name was inscribed on the Wall of Fame at the American Common of the World's Fair, which commemorated outstanding Americans of foreign birth, Negroes, and Indians. Cohen was cited for his "outstanding contribution to the field of philosophy."

He was a naturalistic philosopher, Socratic teacher, encyclopedic savant, champion of liberalism, dedicated Jew, intellectual *animateur,* author for his day and for posterity. Some of the projects and ideas for which he furnished the wellsprings flow on, others may emerge with time.

Emily Dickinson once said of a contemporary, "He has the facts but not the phosphorescence of learning." Cohen had both.

Mary's faith in her husband proved justified in the eyes of the world. The intellectual scene in America would never be quite the same after Morris had his hour upon the stage. The truth of his words in *Reason and Nature* echoes still: "Our reason may be a pitiful candle light in the dark and boundless seas of being. But we have nothing better and woe to those who wilfully try to put it out." Despite the polarity of his approach and of his effort to combine action with reflection, unity lay in his reliance throughout on the light of reason.

Like the Spanish knight of the windmills, he sallied forth to do battle against odds. He acknowledged at seventeen, "I never give in even when I am hopelessly beaten." From our age of increasing conformism, it is well to look back on his example. His life may be pictured as a crusade for reason. The banner to which he rallied his fellow men was far less romantic than Don Quixote's. On it were inscribed cool words—logic and scientific method. What made the quest even harder was his view of history as the cemetery of doomed hopes. Without illusions, in a world of power politics and materialistic goals, he nonetheless kept his armour untarnished, his vision pure, his faith triumphant. He accepted the vassalage of the body, yet proclaimed the sovereignty of the spirit. As he once noted: "Not in victory is heroism, but in the continued painful struggle."

NOTES

CHAPTER III: *Davidson, Cohen, and the Heroic Tradition*

1. *The Letters of George Santayana,* edited by Daniel Cory, Scribner, 1955, p. 15.
2. Thomas Davidson, *The Education of the Wage-Earners,* edited by Charles M. Bakewell, Ginn & Co., Boston, 1904, p. 95. Hereinafter referred to as Bakewell. Davidson's letters to his class are quoted from Chapter 5.
3. This and the preceding quotation from Bakewell, *op. cit.,* p. 101.
4. A. J. Kovar, *Thomas Davidson, A Modern Socrates,* p. 9, the closing lecture of the Thomas Davidson Memorial Series (The Cooper Union Forum, New York City, March 29, 1955).
5. William Knight, *Memorials of Thomas Davidson,* Ginn & Co., Boston, 1907, p. 139. Hereinafter referred to as Knight. Fortunately, extracts of letters from Davidson to Cohen were printed therein. The originals were lost during Cohen's lifetime.
6. Ralph Barton Perry, *The Thought and Character of William James,* Little, Brown, Boston, 1935, Harvard Univ. Press, Cambridge, Mass., 1948, Vol. I, p. 760.
7. Louis I. Dublin, "Thomas Davidson: Educator for Democracy," *The American Scholar,* Spring 1948, p. 205.
8. Perry, *loc. cit.*
9. Cohen, *The Meaning of Human History,* Open Court Pub. Co., La Salle, Ill., 1947, The Carus Lectures, p. 276 (second edition, paperback, 1961).
10. Bakewell, *op. cit.,* pp. 92–93.
11. William James, "A Knight-Errant of the Intellectual Life," *McLure's Magazine,* Vol. 25 (May 1905), p. 9.
12. Written by Cohen, I suspect, or at least adapted from his annual report for the Thomas Davidson Society to be incorporated into the Alliance's published Annual Report for 1903, pp. 67–68.
13. Knight, *op. cit.,* pp. 147, 151.
14. Bakewell, *op. cit.,* p. 49.
15. *Ibid.,* p. 183.
16. *The American Hebrew,* Vol. 82, p. 561.
17. Knight, *op. cit.,* pp. 83, 85–86.
18. Cohen, *A Dreamer's Journey,* Beacon Press, Boston, 1949, p. 117.
19. *Ibid.,* p. 111.
20. Knight, *op. cit.,* p. 83.
21. *A Dreamer's Journey,* p. 116.

CHAPTER IV: *The Citadel of Harvard*

1. *The Development of Harvard University,* edited by Samuel Eliot Morison, Harvard Univ. Press, 1930, p. lxii.
2. William James, *Memories and Studies,* Longmans, Green & Co., 1911, p. 355.
3. See Cohen, "Kant's Doctrine of the *Summum Bonum,*" read at the meeting of the American Philosophical Association, 1908, and published in the *Phil-*

osophical Review, Vol. 18 (1909), pp. 179–80. At the association's meeting in 1923, "Prof. Cohen's paper on 'The Romantic Element in Kant's Philosophy' was intended to save the Eastern Division from the reproach of ignoring entirely the general celebration of the anniversary of Kant's birth. . . . there was much that was original and suggestive in the exposition. . . ." (H. Schneider, *Journal of Philosophy,* 1924, p. 47.) See also Cohen, "A Critique of Kant's Philosophy of Law" in *The Heritage of Kant,* edited by George T. Whitney and David F. Bowers, Princeton Univ. Press, 1939.

4. The first quotation is from Felix Frankfurter, *Of Law and Men,* edited by Philip Elman, Harcourt, Brace & World, 1956, pp. 265–66; the rest are from Harlan B. Phillips, *Felix Frankfurter Reminisces,* Reynal & Co., copyright © 1960 by Harlan B. Phillips, pp. 20, 22, 19.

5. *A Tribute to Professor Morris Raphael Cohen, Teacher and Philosopher,* privately published by "The Youth Who Sat at His Feet," New York, 1928, p. 41.

6. Cohen had helped Charles Bakewell to edit Thomas Davidson's *The Education of the Wage-Earners,* Ginn & Co., Boston, 1904.

7. The Scottish philosopher Edward Caird published an American edition of his *A Critical Account of the Philosophy of Kant* in 1889. The book was a classic. Cohen wrote to Mary to send him his Caird from home. Friedrich Paulsen, German neo-Kantian, was the author of *Introduction to Philosophy,* used as a text by James.

8. Lloyd Morgan, a Harvard biologist, who worked in animal psychology.

9. Arthur L. Mayer, brother of Leo Mayer. Cohen continued his friendship with the Mayers. Arthur distinguished himself in the cinema industry, Leo as a doctor in orthopedics.

10. "The Gospel of Relaxation for the East Side," *Alliance Review,* Vol. 2 (1902), pp. 354–60, 449–56. Republished, *The American Hebrew,* Vol. 71 (May 23, 1902), pp. 13–14.

11. Ralph Barton Perry, *op. cit.,* Vol. II, p. 447.

12. Cohen, *American Thought,* The Free Press, Glencoe, Ill., 1954, p. 286.

13. *A Dreamer's Journey,* p. 132.

14. *American Thought,* p. 288.

15. Rollo Walter Brown recounts what happened when Mrs. Royce tried to give a tea, perhaps for the same ladies. Outside the front door, someone (?) had affixed mourning crepe. Respectfully, the guests tiptoed away. *Harvard Yard in the Golden Age,* Current Books, 1948, p. 47.

16. This quotation and the three preceding are from *American Thought,* pp. 278–80.

17. Thomas W. Higginson was a heroic character—author, Unitarian clergyman, ardent abolitionist, soldier, reformer, and advocate of women's suffrage. A close friend of John Brown, he led the first regiment of Negro soldiers in the Civil War and wrote an interesting account of it in *Army Life in a Black Regiment* (Houghton, 1870). From personal recollection he wrote biographies of Longfellow, Whittier, and Margaret Fuller. He was also coeditor of Emily Dickinson's poems.

18. This and the Royce letter are reproduced in *A Tribute to Professor Morris Raphael Cohen, op. cit.,* pp. 104–06.

19. *Ibid.,* p. 103.

20. Thanks are due Roderick Chisholm and Victor Lowe for showing me their notes.

21. Additional readings recommended for the philosophy of science course included: in *Reason and Nature,* chapters or sections on "Mechanism and Causality in Physics," "Mechanism and Vitalism," "History vs. Value"; in Santayana's

Reason in Science the chapters on dialectics, psychology, postrational morality, and ethics; Carl Snyder's *The World-Machine;* Campbell's "Philosophical Foundations of the Quantum Theory" in the *Journal of the Franklin Institute;* the discussion of probability in Poincaré's *Science and Hypothesis,* in Cohen and Nagel's *Introduction to Logic and Scientific Method,* and in their papers for the *Journal of the American Statistical Association,* Vol. 31 (1936).

22. Daniel J. Bronstein, "The Principle of Polarity in Cohen's Philosophy," *Freedom and Reason, Studies in Philosophy and Jewish Culture in Memory of Morris Raphael Cohen,* edited by Salo W. Baron, Ernest Nagel, and Koppel S. Pinson, The Free Press, Glencoe, Ill., 1951, pp. 44–58. See also the answer of Robert E. Larsen, "Morris Cohen's Principle of Polarity," *Journal of the History of Ideas,* Vol. XX (Oct. 1959), pp. 587–95.

23. Philosophers who studied under Cohen at Harvard included, besides those already mentioned, Henry Aiken, Harvard; John Mothershead, Stanford; David Savan, University of Toronto; Arthur Szathmary, Princeton; and Charles Stevenson of the University of Michigan, who, like Lowe, was an assistant in the department at the time.

CHAPTER V: *City College*

1. See the Shepard Papers, June 29, 1908, Benno Lewinson to Edward M. Shepard. Shepard, class of 1869, was chairman of the board of trustees. Cited in S. Willis Rudy, *The College of the City of New York: A History, 1847–1947;* The City College Press, 1949, p. 288.

2. The 1916–17 College catalogue describes the philosophy of civilization course thus: "A study of the philosophical and ethical principles which underlie the social institutions of civilized people and which form the basis of judgment as to the ethical values of social action." The second-term course, according to the catalogue for 1920–21 was: "A study of the meaning and basis of art, religion, literature and science as social institutions and as giving value to human endeavor." Cohen's metaphysics course is described in the catalogue for 1933–34: "A survey of the classical problems of the nature of existence, time and space, causality and teleology, cognition and value."

3. Later, Smullyan was recommended by Cohen for a Harvard graduate-school fellowship. Now professor of philosophy at the University of Washington, he has written with penetration on "The Philosophical Method of Morris R. Cohen," in *Freedom and Reason, op. cit.,* pp. 59–67.

4. *The Campus,* Vol. 48 (March 20, 1931), p. 4.

5. *A Dreamer's Journey,* pp. 150–51.

6. *Ibid.,* pp. 155–56.

7. *A Tribute to Professor Morris Raphael Cohen, op. cit.,* pp. 72–74.

8. *The Journal of the History of Ideas* would not have been possible without initial donations from The City College Research and Publication Fund (gift of the class of 1912), from Mark Eisner, '05, and from Dr. Joseph J. Klein, '06. Out of twelve members of the original board of directors, seven were connected with the College—four members of the Board of Higher Education (Professor Harry Carman, Messrs. Eisner, Klein, and Ordway Tead), Donald A. Roberts, '19, longtime secretary of the Associate Alumni, and Professors Overstreet and Cohen. Professor J. Salwyn Shapiro, who served with Cohen on the original board of editors, has remained on it along with, today, Professor Hans Kohn of the College.

9. *The Story of the Bertrand Russell Case,* Amer. Civil Liberties Union, 1941.

10. *A Dreamer's Journey,* p. 144.
11. Cohen, *The Faith of a Liberal,* Henry Holt & Co., 1946, pp. 273–74.
12. Felix S. Cohen, "Urbs Coronata: The College and the City," in *A Fighter for Justice,* edited by Theodore H. Haas for the Washington, D.C., Chapter of the Alumni of The City College of New York, 1956, p. 33.
13. Felix Frankfurter, "As I Remember Morris Cohen," *The City College Alumnus,* Vol. 54 (Nov. 1958), pp. 3–6.

CHAPTER VI: *Chicago*

1. With his collaborator, I. E. Drabkin, Cohen had already prepared a draft of their *Source Book in Greek Science* (McGraw-Hill, 1948). Cohen was trying to persuade McKeon to bring out a companion volume, a *Source Book in Medieval Science,* in the same series, sponsored by the American Philosophical Association. While at Harvard in 1938, Cohen read in medieval science, I gather from a fat sheaf of Harvard Library order slips among his notes. At Chicago in 1938 he worked on his *Prolegomena to Logic,* later entitled *A Preface to Logic.* In 1939 he concentrated on his *American Thought.* His major preoccupation in the summer of 1939 and the spring of 1940 was with his projected textbook on *Naturalistic Metaphysics,* which he did not live to finish. In the fall of 1940 he started working on *The Meaning of Human History,* which continued as his main effort throughout 1941.
2. Among Cohen's students in 1923 were Charles W. Morris, who later served as the chairman of the philosophy department at Chicago; Julius Seelye Bixler, who after being professor of religion at Smith College became president of Colby College; Agustin S. Alonzo of the University of the Philippines; and William H. Roberts of the philosophy department, University of Redlands, California.
3. "Recent Trends in Logic" included (1) logic and psychology—normative vs. descriptive science; (2) logic and linguistics—the nature of symbols and meaning; (3) logic and physical science—the nature of scientific methods and results; (4) logic, statistics, and probability; (5) logic, history, and critical judgments of value (axiology); (6) logic and the world order—cosmologic theories and syntheses.
4. Recollection by Carl G. Hempel, then research associate in philosophy at Chicago, now professor at Princeton.
5. In a letter to me in 1959, Max Rheinstein of the University of Chicago Law School calls professional participation in seminars "one of the most remarkable and most enjoyable particularities of our University. We are conducting not only a considerable number of seminars as joint enterprises of professors of the same department, but we have also a considerable number of interdepartmental seminars, and we have frequently made it a practice for professors to attend seminars of prominent colleagues, and quite particularly of famous guests. Professor Cohen's name was, of course, a special attraction."
6. Quotations from Dr. and Mrs. Sidney Kramer. He was completing his doctorate at Chicago at the time.

CHAPTER VII: *The Teacher*

1. Knight, *op. cit.,* pp. 146–47.
2. *A Dreamer's Journey,* p. 117.

3. *Ibid.*, p. 271.
4. *Ibid.*, p. 117.

CHAPTER VIII: *The Author*

1. Max Lerner, *The Harvard Law Review*, Vol. 47 (Dec. 1933), p. 380.
2. Granville Hicks, *The American Mercury*, May 1946, p. 624.
3. New York *Herald Tribune*, Jan. 31, 1947.
4. Perry Miller, *The Nation*, Vol. 168 (April 16, 1949), p. 447.

CHAPTER IX: *Journey in Philosophy*

1. *Studies in Philosophy and Science*, Henry Holt & Co., 1949, p. 4.
2. *Ibid.*, p. 3.
3. "The Place of Science in Modern Philosophy," speech reported in *The Campus*, Vol. 65 (Oct. 20, 1939), p. 4.
4. *Law and the Social Order*, Harcourt, Brace & World, 1933, p. 222.
5. *The Meaning of Human History*, p. 7.
6. H. A. Larrabee, *Journal of Philosophy*, Vol. 27 (Jan. 30, 1930), p. 78.
7. "The Faith of a Logician," *Studies in Philosophy and Science*, p. 7.
8. *Law and the Social Order*, p. 219.
9. *Reason and Law*, The Free Press, Glencoe, Ill., 1950, p. 133.
10. *The Meaning of Human History*, p. 139.
11. Cohen's "Legal Thought and Clear Distinctions" tells us "the failure to discriminate clearly between *distinguishing* and *separating* is one of the great obstacles to the advancement of real understanding. To separate two phases of a subject is to ignore their interconnections, while to distinguish the two is to clarify them and their function in the totality which includes them." *Reason and Law*, p. 160.
12. *Studies in Philosophy and Science*, p. 39.
13. *Preface to Logic*, Henry Holt & Co., 1944, p. 133.
14. References to scientific method are widespread in Cohen's writings. The principal sources, however, are *An Introduction to Logic and Scientific Method* (Harcourt, Brace, 1934), "Reason and Scientific Method" in *Reason and Nature* (Harcourt, Brace, 1931), "Philosophy and Scientific Methods" in *Studies in Philosophy and Science*, and "Method, Scientific" in the *Encyclopedia of the Social Sciences*, Vol. X (1934).
15. *Reason and Nature*, p. 99.
16. *An Introduction to Logic and Scientific Method*, p. 394.
17. *The Faith of a Liberal*, p. 146.
18. *Reason and Nature*, p. 83.
19. *Ibid.*, p. 108.
20. "The Holmes-Cohen Correspondence," see Chapter XVI.
21. "Method, Scientific," *op. cit.*, p. 395.
22. See Chapter XVII.
23. *A Dreamer's Journey*, p. 186.
24. *Studies in Philosophy and Science*, p. 47.
25. From *Jewish Social Studies*, 1939, reprinted in *Reflections of a Wondering Jew*, The Free Press, Glencoe, Ill., 1950.
26. *The Meaning of Human History*, p. 52.
27. *Reason and Nature*, "History vs. Value," especially p. 381.
28. *The Meaning of Human History*, pp. 294–95.

29. *Reason and Nature*, p. 410.
30. *The Meaning of Human History*, p. 33.
31. *Reason and Law*, p. 73.
32. *Ibid.*, p. 138, p. 74.
33. *Law and the Social Order*, p. 173.
34. *Ibid.*, p. 195.
35. *Reason and Law*, p. 80.
36. *Law and the Social Order*, p. 246.
37. *Reason and Law*, p. 82.
38. *Law and the Social Order*, p. 245.
39. "Communal Ghosts and Other Perils in Social Philosophy," *Journal of Philosophy, Psychology and Scientific Methods*, Vol. XVI, No. 25 (Dec. 4, 1919), p. 675.
40. *Studies in Philosophy and Science*, p. 83.
41. Nathan R. Margold, "Morris R. Cohen as a Teacher of Lawyers and Jurists," *Freedom and Reason, op. cit.*, p. 35.
42. From a letter of Esther Willard Bates to me, March 10, 1958.
43. *Holmes-Laski Letters*, edited by Mark DeWolfe Howe, Harvard Univ. Press, 1953, p. 1045.
44. *The Faith of a Liberal*, p. 395.
45. Huntington Cairns, "The Legal Philosophy of Morris R. Cohen," *The Vanderbilt Law Review*, Vol. XIV (Dec. 1960), p. 262.
46. *The Faith of a Liberal*, p. 396.

CHAPTER X: *Cohen on Dewey and Liberalism*

1. *Studies in Philosophy and Science*, p. 139. The essay, "Some Difficulties in John Dewey's Anthropocentric Naturalism," first appeared in *The Philosophical Review* for 1940. It was the text of Cohen's remarks at the Dewey meeting in 1939.
2. *The Faith of a Liberal*, p. 317 and *A Preface to Logic*, p. 202.
3. *Studies in Philosophy and Science*, p. 165.
4. From a copyrighted article in *U.S. News*, Vol. VI (April 11, 1938), p. 10.
5. *The Meaning of Human History*, p. 271.
6. Cohen's "Communal Ghosts and Other Perils in Social Philosophy," *op. cit.*, p. 675.
7. Joseph L. Blau, *Men and Movements in American Philosophy*, Prentice-Hall, 1952, pp. 343–44.
8. *A Tribute to Professor Morris Raphael Cohen, op. cit.*, pp. 20, 19.
9. "The Philosopher-in-the-Making," *Contemporary American Philosophy*, Vol. 2, edited by G. P. Adams and William P. Montague, Macmillan, 1930. The piece was reprinted in the John Dewey issue of the *Saturday Review*, Oct. 22, 1949. See pp. 10, 39.

CHAPTER XI: *Cohen and the Law*

1. *Law and the Social Order*, p. 173.
2. Pierre de Tourtoulon, *Philosophy in the Development of Law*, edited by Morris R. Cohen, Macmillan, 1922, Editorial Preface, p. xxiv.
3. *Law and the Social Order*, p. 197.
4. Margold, *op. cit.*, p. 43.
5. *A Tribute to Professor Morris Raphael Cohen, op. cit.*, p. 78.

6. *Law and the Social Order,* p. 209.
7. *Ibid.,* p. 159.
8. *Ibid.,* p. 214.
9. Quotation from Holmes in Introduction to Learned Hand, *The Spirit of Liberty,* edited by Irving Dilliard, Knopf, 1952, p. v.
10. *Law and the Social Order,* p. 34.
11. *Reason and Law,* pp. 75–76.
12. See Samuel Cohen (Morris' brother), "Recreational Entreprise on the Bowery," *Commentary,* Vol. XIV, No. 5 (Nov. 1952), pp. 479–84.
13. *Reason and Law,* p. 142.
14. The last three quotations are from *ibid.,* pp. 16, 18, 28.
15. *Law and the Social Order,* p. 102.
16. *Ibid.,* p. 109.
17. *Ibid.,* p. 63.
18. *Ibid.,* p. 60.
19. Louis P. Goldberg and Eleanore Levenson, *Lawless Judges,* Rand, 1935, Introduction by Morris R. Cohen, p. iii.
20. *American Thought,* p. 164.
21. *Law and the Social Order,* pp. 380–81. "The Process of Judicial Legislation," n. 86.
22. *Ibid.,* p. 201.
23. *Ibid.,* p. 150.
24. *Ibid.,* pp. 155–56.
25. *Reason and Law,* pp. 184–85.
26. *Law and the Social Order,* p. 197.
27. *Ibid.,* pp. 196–97.
28. *Ibid.,* p. 284.
29. *Preface to Logic,* see "Concepts and Twilight Zones," especially pp. 72–80.
30. See Cohen's "Communal Ghosts and Other Perils in Social Philosophy," *loc. cit.* The version in *Reason and Nature* is cut.
31. Harold Laski, "Morris Cohen's Approach to Legal Philosophy," *The University of Chicago Law Review,* Vol. 15 (Spring 1948), p. 587.
32. *Reason and Nature,* p. 408.
33. *Reason and Law,* p. 190.
34. *Reason and Nature,* p. 413.
35. *Law and the Social Order,* p. 213.
36. *Reason and Law,* p. 27.
37. *Reason and Nature,* p. 426.
38. *Law and the Social Order,* p. 182.
39. *Reason and Law,* p. 104.
40. *Law and the Social Order,* p. 285.
41. *Ibid.*
42. *A Tribute to Professor Morris Raphael Cohen, op. cit.,* p. 32.
43. *Ibid.,* pp. 37–40.
44. *Ibid.,* p. 32.
45. *Readings in Jurisprudence and Legal Philosophy,* Preface by Felix S. Cohen, p. v.

CHAPTER XII: *Mysticism and Rationalism*

1. See L. C. Rosenfield, "The Philosopher and the Poet, Morris Raphael Cohen and Edwin Arlington Robinson at the MacDowell Colony," *Palinurus,* Vol. 1 (April 1959), p. 35.

2. *The Nation*, Vol. 132 (1931), p. 412.
3. *American Thought*, p. 168.
4. *Studies in Philosophy and Science*, p. 32.
5. *Ibid.*, p. 31. "The Faith of a Logician" appeared in George P. Adams and William P. Montague, *Contemporary American Philosophy, op. cit.*, Vol. 1, pp. 220–47.
6. *The Faith of a Liberal*, p. 437.
7. *A Tribute to Professor Morris Raphael Cohen, op. cit.*, p. 80.
8. *Ibid.*, pp. 81–82.

CHAPTER XIII: *The Jew*

1. *A Dreamer's Journey*, p. 230. The passage continues: "In later years a considerable part of my reading and lecturing was directed to Jewish problems. The literature of the Old Testament which I studied as a child has never ceased to grip me, and in days of depression when I have had little energy for writing or study I have found the books of the Bible and Old Testament criticism most absorbing reading."
2. *Ibid.*, p. 215.
3. *Studies in Philosophy and Science*, p. 32.
4. *A Dreamer's Journey*, p. 231.
5. In 1924, Cohen lectured at the Menorah Association at the University of Pennsylvania, and in 1931 at Cornell's Hillel Chapter. He was devoted to the Yiddish Scientific Institute, first in Vilna and then in New York. He read one of his major papers for them. He delivered a notable address for the National Council of Jewish Social Work in 1934 and participated in a symposium held by the National Council of Jewish Women in 1936. On January 6, 1938, he spoke before a rally of a thousand students in the Great Hall of The City College to protest against the segregation of Jewish students in Poland. His talk, "Ghetto Benches in Poland," he then broadcast over the radio. He lectured in 1938 before the Association of Reform Rabbis of New York City and vicinity. The same year he spoke in New Haven on "A Jew Looks at the Modern World." The Young Men's Hebrew Association awarded him a citation of honor in 1939 for outstanding public service to the community.
6. *King Saul's Daughter: A Biblical Dialogue*, The Free Press, Glencoe, Ill., 1952.
7. See the Testimonial of Professor Salo W. Baron at the Memorial Services for Cohen, The New School for Social Research, February 2, 1947.
8. *The Faith of a Liberal*, p. 361. The essay was originally a contribution to *Religion Today*, edited in 1933 by Arthur L. Swift (McGraw-Hill). It is included in Walter Kaufmann's *Religion from Tolstoy to Camus*, Harper, 1961.
9. *A Dreamer's Journey*, p. 227.
10. *Ibid.*, p. 226.
11. *The Faith of a Liberal*, p. 333.
12. *A Tribute to Professor Morris Raphael Cohen, op. cit.*, p. 25.
13. *A Dreamer's Journey*, p. 226.
14. There were many devoted souls who served the Conference, among others Jerome Michael of Columbia Law School, William Gresser, Samuel Klaus, and Mr. and Mrs. Samuel Rosensohn. Marvin Lowenthal, now professor at Brandeis University, served as secretary to the Conference in 1935. Mark Hirsch, now a professor, then a student, served as Cohen's secretary in his home from September 1935 to March 1936. Not until 1937 did the Conference have Melvin M. Fagen as executive secretary.

15. See Salo W. Baron's *President's Report, 1940–43*, published by the Conference on Jewish Relations. His scholarly undertaking to co-ordinate research in Jewish sociology, *A Bibliography of Jewish Social Studies, 1938–1939*, was published by the Conference in 1941. Baron and Cohen wrote an Introduction to Abraham G. Duker's "The Situation of the Jews in Poland," a newsletter published in 1936 by the Conference. John Dewey, Franz Boas, Isidore Lubin, and many others lectured for the Conference.

16. Cohen contributed his "Philosophies of Jewish History" and a Foreword to the first issue of *Jewish Social Studies*, while for 1940 and 1941 he did eleven reviews.

17. *The Jewish Center*, Sept. 1941, pp. 5–8. Speech delivered May 24, 1941.

18. *Reflections of a Wondering Jew*, pp. 26–27.

19. See *A Dreamer's Journey*, pp. 219–20; *Emanu-El*, Vol. 72 (April 22, 1932), pp. 1, 16; *Jewish Standard* (Toronto), Vol. 5 (April 22, 1932), p. 138; and *Reflections of a Wondering Jew*, pp. 30–33.

20. *A Dreamer's Journey*, p. 218.

21. *Ibid.*, p. 214.

22. *Ibid.*, p. 224.

23. *American Jewish Archives*, Jan. 1953, p. 37.

CHAPTER XV: *Letters on Law*

1. The letters from Benjamin N. Cardozo are reprinted with the permission of the Trustees of Columbia University in the City of New York.

CHAPTER XVI: *The Holmes-Cohen Correspondence*

1. Letters and footnotes (the latter abridged and supplemented) are reprinted from "The Holmes-Cohen Correspondence," edited by Felix S. Cohen, *The Journal of the History of Ideas*, Vol. 9 (Jan. 1948).

2. In 1934 Cohen called on Holmes at the request of the American Jewish Congress to ask him for a statement on Hitler. The Justice, ninety-three, answered: "Why should I condemn anything in this world when I am no longer in it? But don't you think that the whole thing is rather insane? By the way, they say that my ancestors, the Wendells, were Dutch Jews." A month after Holmes's death, Cohen recounted the conversation to The City College *Campus*. He used the same words in a letter to Beryl H. Levy, adding Holmes's statement that the Wendells "were originally Vondells, who came from Holland." See *The Campus*, Vol. 5 (April 14, 1935), p. 1, and *Commentary*, Vol. 22 (Dec. 1956), p. 557.

CHAPTER XVII: *Friendship, Issues, and Ideas*

1. Except for Einstein's last letter, all the Einstein letters were in German and have been translated, thanks to Professors Herbert Schaumann and Cristoph Hering, Ann Demaître, Gene Cohen Tweraser, and Kurt Tweraser.

2. Einstein, *Ideas and Opinions*, Crown, 1954, pp. 79–80.

3. See "What I Believe" by Cohen (1931), reprinted in *The Faith of a Liberal*.

Conclusion

1. From a review of *A Dreamer's Journey*, The City College *Alumnus*, Vol. 45 (Oct. 1949), p. 8. Cohen is quoted from *The Faith of a Liberal*, p. 295.

2. "The Life and Mind of Morris R. Cohen," *Freedom and Reason*, *op. cit.*, p. 20.

3. *Vanderbilt Law Review*, Vol. XIV (Dec. 1960), p. 239. See also the first book on Cohen, Arturo Deregibus, *Il Razionalismo di Morris R. Cohen nella Filosofia Americana d'Oggi*, G. Giappichelli, Torino, 1960.

INDEX